HISTORY

a reference handbook

'Some histories are to be read, some are to be studied, and some may be neglected entirely, not only without detriment, but with advantage. Some are the proper objects of one man's curiosity, some of another's, and some of all men's; but all history is not an object of curiosity for any man. He who improperly, wantonly, and absurdly makes it so, indulges a sort of canine appetite; the curiosity of the one, like the hunger of the other devours ravenously and without distinction, whatever falls in its way.' *Letters on the study and use of history* by Lord Bolingbroke (1735).

'More than in any other countries there is a public in England and America which, without possessing an exact knowledge of history, heartily enjoys it and desires to be set in the way of understanding its critical processes.' Prefatory note, *English historical review* 1 (1) 1886.

HISTORY

a reference handbook

Alan Edwin Day

BA MPhil Dip Lib FLA

CLIVE BINGLEY
LONDON

LINNET BOOKS
HAMDEN · CONN

For Alexis, Cerin, Charmion and Rowan

FIRST PUBLISHED 1977 BY CLIVE BINGLEY LTD
16 PEMBRIDGE ROAD LONDON W11
SIMULTANEOUSLY PUBLISHED IN THE USA BY LINNET BOOKS
AN IMPRINT OF THE SHOE STRING PRESS INC
995 SHERMAN AVENUE HAMDEN CONNECTICUT 06514
SET IN 10 ON 12 POINT TIMES AND PRINTED IN THE UK
BY BILLING & SONS LTD GUILDFORD AND LONDON
COPYRIGHT © ALAN EDWIN DAY 1977
ALL RIGHTS RESERVED
BINGLEY ISBN: 0-85157-225-1
LINNET ISBN: 0-208-01536-1

Library of Congress Cataloging in Publication Data
Day, Alan Edwin.
  History: a reference handbook.

  Includes index.
  1. Great Britain—History —Bibliography. 2. United
States—History—Bibliography. 3. Canada—History—
Bibliography. 4. Australia—History—Bibliography.
5. Commonwealth of Nations—Bibliography. I. Title.
Z2016.D38 1977 (DA30) 016.909'04'2 76-28410
ISBN 0-208-01536-1

Foreword

The bibliographical apparatus serving historical studies is vast. Dictionaries, encyclopaedias, abstracts, bibliographies and book-lists, atlases and biographical works, guides to record offices and libraries, calendars and chronologies, all stand together on the shelves offering their various services to the librarian, the teacher, and the historian. The intention of this present handbook is to provide a guide to these reference aids and, at the same time, to indicate the main purposes and features of the equally varied forms of historical publications, definitive and standard textbooks, monographs and large scale cooperative histories, collections of texts and primary source material, learned and popular historical journals, which together occupy a significant sector of the book publishing industry. Notice is also taken of historiography and the methodology of history, the activities of the learned and publishing societies, and eminent annalists, chroniclers and historians. To the best of my knowledge no similar work exists; if one does it has successfully eluded my attention over a considerable period.

For the purposes of this book 'history' effectively signifies the political and constitutional history of the English people from the earliest times of which we have a true historical record. This decision was taken in the full knowledge that a Welshman ascended the English throne in 1485 and that the two ancient kingdoms of England and Scotland were formally united in 1707. The story of Great Britain and its expansion overseas is then covered and continued in the history of Australia, Canada and the United States and to a lesser degree in the history of New Zealand, India, and British Africa. I was encouraged to reflect that this followed the old and the new pattern of historical studies in schools and colleges, what we might call old-fashioned mainline

7

history, and the newer concept of area studies. In addition, to round off in tidy fashion, some significant universal histories are also considered.

Finally, it is my pleasant task to record my appreciation for the hospitality accorded me by the libraries of The Historical Association and the Institute of Historical Research. The staff of Leeds Reference Library who fetched and carried more books than they or I will care to dwell on deserve a special word of gratitude.

Leeds, April 1976   A E DAY

1 Acton, Lord (1834-1902) was appointed to the chair of modern history in the university of Cambridge in 1895 more for his stature and reputation as a formidable man of learning than for an established *canon* of historical writing in book form, although his journal publication had been prodigious. He had done much to entrench the reputation of the *English historical review* with his article on the 'German schools of history' in that journal's first issue. Even today his name carries an aura of scholarship which seems out of all proportion to his main published work, *Lectures on modern history* (which includes his famous inaugural lecture on the study of history), and *Lectures on the French revolution*. But he was the first English historian to acknowledge the historical revolution brought about by the opening of the archives of the European chancelleries and exemplified by the work of Ranke. 'History to be above suspicion or dispute,' he declared, 'must stand on documents, not opinions.' Whatever authority the *Cambridge modern history* gathered to itself owed a lot to Acton's planning and direction. For an authoritative summary of Acton's significance in English historiography recourse should be made to Professor Butterfield's *Man on his past* published in 1955.

2 Adam of Usk: his *Chronicon* continued Higden's *Polychronicon* from Richard II's reign to 1421. It is a little thin at first but full of interest for the period 1397-1421. In form it is reminiscent of a modern volume of memoirs and it was not written all at once, some events were recorded as they happened, others were noted down from memory.

3 Adams, Henry (1838-1918) wrote a monumental nine volume *History of the United States from 1801-1817* (1889-1891) highly regarded for its presentation of the home and foreign policies of the Jefferson and Madison administrations. Based on meticulous research, and notable for its strict impartiality, the *History* has been 'mined' by subsequent historians on numerous occasions.

4 'Africa; history of a continent' by Basil Davidson (Weidenfeld, 1966) is 'an attempt to trace a broad outline of African growth and change over some twenty centuries, to present a general and yet reasonably chronological survey of those years, as well as to suggest the long-range historical explanation of Africans and their development.' The essential theme of the work is the unity of Africa despite its formidable geographical barriers. The book is more than generously illustrated in black and white and colour but its scholarly intent is obvious by the citations in the brief guide to further reading which includes references to articles in learned journals and to material in other languages.

5 'Africa and the victorians; the official mind of imperialism' by Ronald Robinson and John Gallagher (Macmillan, 1961) is an enquiry into the motives behind victorian expansion as evidenced in Britain's involvement in Africa in the nineteenth century.

6 The African Association *for promoting the discovery of the interior parts of Africa* was formed out of one of the numerous dining clubs of the times, the Saturday Club, in 1788. It owed much of its influence to the prestige of Sir Joseph Banks, president of the Royal Society. During its forty three years of existence before it was merged into the Royal Geographical Society it played a great part in African exploration. Its history, activities, and publications are all discussed in *Records of the African Association 1788-1831* edited by Robin Hallett and published by Nelson in 1964.

7 'African history' by Philip D Curtis (AHA Service Center Series No 56) published in 1964 is a masterly and indispensable account of the post war burgeoning of African studies and the corrective new perspective African history transmitted to the study of world history. The scope of the pamphlet is best ascertained from its headings and subheadings. Part I 'The emergence of African history' includes 'The discovery of historical Africa' (the post-war interest and establishment of courses); and 'Teaching material' (texts, readings and *lacunae*). Part II 'pre-Colonial Africa' covers 'New techniques and new sources' (archaeology, linguistic studies, oral traditions, ancient writings); 'African civilization and world civilization' (agriculture and technology); 'The problem of Bantu migration'; 'Communication and isolated development'; 'Some myths and mythmakers'; and 'Tribes, cultures and states'. Part III 'Africa and the European' deals with 'The slave trade'; 'New interpretations of the pre-colonial period 1780-1880'; 'The "scramble" and its causes'; and 'The impact of European rule'. It is a pity that space did not allow the author to append a consolidated list of all the books mentioned in the text.

8 'The African past; chronicles from antiquity to modern times' by Basil Davidson (Longmans, 1964) is devised as a continuous narrative constructed from chronicles and records of travellers, merchants, soldiers, and scholars. There is an introduction, 'Africa in history,' including an interesting section on African and Asian records, and this is followed by extracts from over one hundred different sources many of them unobtainable in English. Unfortunately the extracts are not long enough either to be of much value to the student or of much interest to the general reader.

9 'The age of Arthur; a history of the British Isles from 350 to 650' by John Morris (Weidenfeld, 1973) is based firmly on the conviction that Arthur was as real a figure as any of the later kings of England. Consequently, this long survey of the history of the British Isles in the 'dark ages' met with a mixed reception on publication. The author claims to have collated all the texts of what exiguous original sources exist for this remote period. His interpretation of them rests on the convincing thesis that near contemporary authorities must reasonably be assessed as approximating to an accurate record of events. The book is divided into two clearly defined parts: the first is a straightforward chronological narrative whilst the second comprises an analysis of the church, education and the arts, and urban and rural English society. There is a table of dates arranged under appropriate headings; a summary of events; a bibliography divided into sources, modern works, and periodicals; and extremely detailed chapter notes. A profuse selection of maps completes a remarkable work.

10 'The age of discovery' by Wilcomb E Washburn (AHA Service Center Series No 63) published in 1966 is a breathless and excited scamper through the Norse discovery of Vinland, the quest for 'Asia', the invention of America; England, France and Spain in the New World; Maps and mapmakers; Europeans in Asia; and Exploration of the Pacific. A thorough bibliography limited to sources available in English slows the author down to a more scholarly pace.

11 'The age of Drake' by James A Williamson (1938) is one of A and C Black's *Pioneer histories* and relates the explosion of English seamen and traders into all parts of the navigable world in the tudor period. The exploits of Hawkins and Drake are narrated in full but the lesser names are not forgotten.

12 'The age of expansion; Europe and the World 1559-1660' edited by Hugh Trevor-Roper (Thames and Hudson, 1968) is the seventh volume of *The great civilizations* series. Its aim is 'to present ... an intelligible picture of a century in which Europe was itself radically transformed and by its expansion, began to transform the rest of the world too.' Individual chapters contributed by a succession of experts in the field discuss Spain, the Netherlands, Central Europe and the Thirty Years War; France, Britain, Eastern Europe, and end with a glance at the Near and Far East. The work is beautifully illustrated and in this respect fully measures up to the high standards we have come to expect from this publishing house.

13 'The age of Grey and Peel; being the Ford Lectures for 1926' by H W C Davis is still in print although first published by OUP in 1929. It is primarily concerned with the ideas and character of the Whig and Tory parties and with the intellectual, social and political movements that influenced opinion.

14 'The age of improvement 1783-1867' by Asa Briggs (1959) belongs to Longmans' *History of England*. Professor Briggs regards the period primarily as one of 'formative changes in the structure of the English economy, the shape of English society and the framework of government.' These three factors, economics, society and politics, are closely related in his text. There is a 'Note on books' to show the student the way to further study.

15 'The age of Peel' edited by Norman Gash was published in Arnold's *Documents of modern history* series in 1968. The extracts selected represent the three themes the author perceives as the predominant factors of the twenty year period 1828-1848: the

12

repudiation of the classic eighteenth century constitutional settlement; the conflict of institutions and interests between the established church and dissent, agriculture and industry; and the social and administrative problems caused by the urban proletariat.

16 **'The age of reform 1815-1870'** by E L Woodward, first published in the *Oxford history of England* in 1938 and revised in 1962, is acknowledged to be the standard one volume work on the period. The bibliography charts a steady course through the ever deepening shoals of nineteenth century historical records and must be regarded as the launching point for any advanced study.

17 **'The age of the renaissance'** edited by Denys Hay (Thames and Hudson, 1967) belongs to *The great civilizations* series. Humanism is the theme of most topics treated by various hands in this luxurious volume. Its growth from Florentine beginnings, its spread across Europe, and the search for new geographical horizons, achieve a remarkable coherence. The advantages of modern colour reproduction techniques are nowhere better in evidence than in this volume which above all others in the series surely justifies their use, costly though it may be. There is a select bibliography and a chronological chart.

18 **'The age of the Vikings'** by P H Sawyer (Edward Arnold, 2nd ed 1971) contributes a valuable reappraisal of the Danish colonisation of Britain although of course it ranges much wider. The author is convinced that historians of this early period must of necessity consider the evidence provided by the auxiliary sciences, archaeology, numismatics, and the study of place names, in order to supplement the meagre resources of the sagas and chronicles. In fact both types of evidence, archaeological and written sources, each have a chapter devoted to them. The story unfolded is an exciting one but the notes and bibliography make it clear that the general reader can hardly proceed further.

19 **'Albion's England'** or *Historical map of the same Island: prosecuted from the Lives and Acts and Labors of Saturne, Jupiter, Hercules, and Aeneas; Originalles of the Bruton, and the Englishman, and occasion of the Brutons their first aryvall in Albion. Containing the same Historie unto the Tribute to the*

13

Romaines, Entrie of the Saxones, Invasion by the Danes, and Conquest by the Normaines by William Warner (1558-1609) was first published in 1586 and went through five more editions by 1606 when it had expanded into sixteen books. It was a rhymed history written in fourteen syllable lines treating various legendary and imaginary incidents in British history, first to 1066, then in later editions to 1603, and owed its immense popularity to its patriotic sentiments.

20 'Album of American history' (OUP, 5 vols, 1944-1961) is an ambitious and entertaining collection of pictures: 'In this work the pictures themselves are the history, and the text assumes the subordinate role which pictures have had in the past.' The *Album* is a companion work to the *Atlas of American history*, the *Dictionary of American history* and the *Dictionary of American biography* and completes the grand survey of American life planned and executed by James Truslow Adams. Volumes: 1) *Colonial period*; 2) *1783-1853*; 3) *1853-1893*; 4) *1893-1917*; 5) *1917-1953*; 6) *Index.*

21 The Alexander Prize is awarded annually by the Royal Historical Society for an essay not exceeding 6000 words in length which must be a genuine piece of original research. It was established by L C Alexander in 1897. A full list of prizewinners who include a number of very well known historians is printed every year in the *Transactions.*

22 'America: history and life' (1964-) is published by the American Bibliographical Center-Clio Press as a special North American companion journal to *Historical abstracts.* Articles on United States and Canadian history appearing in over five hundred periodicals, society transactions and proceedings, and *festschrift* volumes are abstracted and arranged in broad geographical and chronological divisions: North America; Canada; United States to 1945; United States 1945 onwards; United States regional, state or local history; and historiography and methodology. Libraries outside North America should contact the European Bibliographical Center, Woodside House, Hinksey Hill, Oxford, OX1 5BE, for details of subscription rates, etc.

23 American Bibliographical Center Santa Barbara, California, established in 1955, has through a variety of publications, attempted to exercise bibliographic control over periodicals and book publication in the humanities, especially in history. Two notable ABC publications in this field are *America: history and life* and *Historical abstracts*. Its academic standing may be gauged by its research and publication services for the American Historical Association and the American Council of Learned Societies. The Clio Press, its book publishing imprint, concentrates on reference books and specialised bibliographies in history. In 1971 the European Bibliographical Center was set up in Oxford to expand its activities in the UK and Europe, and to provide marketing services to libraries outside North America.

24 'American civilization' edited by Daniel J Boorstin (Thames and Hudson, 1972), one of the *Great civilizations* series, is a 'kind of vivid critical inventory of the civilization of the United States, viewed from the late twentieth century.' In truth only the first chapter, 'Exploration's nation,' the role of discovery, is truly historical, most of the others are topical rather than a historical narrative.

25 'American colonial documents to 1776' edited by Merrill Jensen, was published by Eyre and Spottiswoode in the *English historical documents* series in 1955 and must be regarded as at least one of the most comprehensive and authoritative collection of documents compiled on either side of the Atlantic Ocean. The documents included were selected to illustrate the internal history of the original thirteen colonies on the American mainland, to indicate the essential factors in their relationship with London, and to mark the steps which led to the war for independence. This volume follows the normal pattern of arrangement of the series, ie a general section complete with a select bibliography providing a guide to source collections, periodicals, and modern works, precedes the documents grouped under appropriate subject headings: The foundation of the English colonies (Colonial charters, the promotion of colonisation, the founding of the first colonies); The evolution of colonial governments (political theory in the colonies, the constitutional bases of colonial governments, British policy and colonial governments, the evolution of colonial self government, and government within the colonies); and further sections on Economic development, Population and labour, Religion and education, Expansion and social discontent; British colonial policies and the Growth of colonial opposition 1763-1773 (The instruments of British policy, Colonial opposition and British retreat, The Pitt-Grafton ministry and the colonies, the colonies v the ministry, and the rise of revolutionary organisations); and The coming of the war for American independence 1773-1776 (the background of the first Continental congress, Warfare begins, King and parliament v The Continental congress, and the debate over independence). Many of these sections are equipped with a bibliography and there are three maps.

26 **'American explorers'** series consists of original narratives of early American exploration in seventeen volumes. They were first published under this general title by the Allerton Book Company of New York in 1922 although they had earlier been published as *The trail makers*, 1903-1905. Titles: *Narratives of the career of Hernando de Soto* (ed E G Bourne); *The wild northland* (Sir W F Butler); *Voyages and explorations of Samuel de Champlain* (ed E G Bourne); *History of the five Indian nations* (Cadwallader Colden); *The journeys of La Salle and his companions* (ed I J Cox); *A journal of voyages and travels in the interior of North America* (D W Harmon); *History of the expedition under Lewis and Clark* (ed J B McMaster); *Voyages through North America 1789, 1793* (Sir Alexander Mackenzie); *The journey of Cabeca de Vaca and his companions* (ed A F Badelier); and *The journey of Coronado 1540-1542* (ed G P Winship). The general editor was J B McMaster. A reprint of the complete series is available from AMS Press, New York.

27 **'American heritage; the magazine of history'** (1948-   ), sponsored by the American Association for State and Local History and the Society of American Historians, is a lavishly illustrated, fiercely patriotic, popular magazine published every two months by a McGraw Hill subsidiary, whose concern is 'anything that ever happened in America,' whose chief requirement is 'that the things we talk about must be interesting.' A ten year index 1954-1964 and another 1965-1970 are available.

28 'American heritage pictorial atlas of United States history' is one of the new style atlases including not only maps but also a lengthy narrative (60,000 words) together with an extensive range of historical pictures many of which are in colour. Over two hundred maps illustrate the American story from the last glacial epoch in North America to the United States entanglement in South East Asia. Other notable features include detailed illustrations of the American revolution and the civil war and an interesting collection of nineteenth century city views. A *de luxe* boxed edition in heavy buckram is available.

29 American Historical Association was founded in 1884 and chartered by Congress in 1899. Membership is open to all persons interested in historical studies and close relations with international, specialised, state, and local historical societies are maintained through conferences and correspondence. In an effort to offer constructive assistance in solving problems confronting teachers it operates the Service Center for Teachers of History which sponsors a series of pamphlets containing concise summaries of publications reflecting recent research. A comprehensive publication programme also includes *American historical review* (*qv*) the *AHA newsletter* and an *Annual report* addressed to Congress, in accordance with the act of incorporation, and to the secretary of the Smithsonian Institute. This comprises the proceedings of the association and in effect constitutes a report of the condition of historical studies in the United States. Its early history is surveyed in J Franklin Jameson's 'The American Historical Association 1884-1909' *American historical review* XV (1) October 1909: 1-20.

30 'The American Historical Association's guide to historical literature' published by The Macmillan Company of New York in 1961, replaces an earlier work *Guide to historical literature* (1931). 'The book should be a valuable aid to students, teachers, librarians and others who seek the most satisfactory works for historical studies. The *Guide* is in a sense a bibliographic panorama as well as an inventory of the best historical literature extant at the time of compilation. Its purpose is to furnish directions to the best means of gaining a broader knowledge of History. Although it is not designed for the specialist, it may serve to help him establish a good foundation for his later, more concentrated, research. It is an instrument of education and general reference' (*Introduction*).

Almost 20,000 annotated entries are divided into nine large sections arranged for the most part by geographical area and divided still further by form of literature organised on a standard pattern of bibliographies, encyclopaedias, gazetteers, collections of sources, general histories, histories of periods, areas, and topics, biographies, government publications, periodicals, and publications of universities and learned societies.

31 'American historical documents' is the series title of four volumes each presenting a collection of documents relating to significant events or statesmen, together with an introductory analysis of the historical background, suitable for sixth form, college or university students, published by the Cambridge University Press. Titles: *Slavery, race and civil war in America* by J R Pole (the general editor); *Westward expansion 1763-1890* by R A Burchell; *The USA in world affairs* by A E Campbell; and *The presidency* by M J C Vile.

32 'American historical review,' founded in 1895, is published five times a year by the American Historical Association. Each issue carries articles and reviews, obituaries, association notes, lists of the contents of *festschriften*, and a classified list of other books received. Up to the February 1976 issue another classified list of recently published periodical articles was also included three times a year but in the future these will be published separately. Back numbers from 1972 onwards are available from the association and earlier issues can be obtained from the Klaus Reprint Corporation. A *General index to volumes XLI-LX* (1935-1955) published by The Macmillan Company of New York (1962) is the fifth of a series of indexes: Vols, I-X (1895-1905); Vols, XI-XX (1905-1915); Vols, XXI-XXX (1916-1924); and, Vols, XXXI-XL (1925-1935).

33 'American History', a review of the current state and future trends in the bibliography of American history by Gerald D McDonald, chief of the American History and Genealogy Division of New York Public Library, appeared in *Library trends* 15(4) April 1967 : 718-729. In universities and colleges more people are

18

searching for the sources of history, more history is being published, and more historical societies are now active, than ever before. If librarians are to play their legitimate role, if all this mass of material and activity is to be controlled, a cordinating body of librarians, archivists and historians is needed to offer plans and guidance on preparing the necessary bibliographies. Mr McDonald comments on and evaluates over fifty existing bibliographies and ventures a forecast on the development of non traditional methods of compilation in the near future.

34 **'American history and historians', a review of recent contributions to the interpretation of the history of the United States'** (1952) by H H Bellot endeavours to give an account of the writing of American history 1890-1940 and to indicate the conclusions that have emerged. Each chapter is enhanced by the addition of an extensive bibliographical note.

35 **'American history atlas'** by Martin Gilbert (Weidenfeld, 1968) contains over 100 black and white maps ranging from the origins of settlement in America c 50,000 BC, to the cold war confrontations of the 1960s and must be regarded as indispensable for all higher secondary level and undergraduate courses in American history.

36 **'American history illustrated'** (April 1966-) is published monthly except during March and September by The National Historical Society. Its purpose, in its own words, is 'to make the intrinsically fascinating story of America come to life ... to accomplish this we intend to produce a magazine whose contents are based on solid research, yet that will be interesting, even exciting to read, while avoiding sensationalism.' Each issue presents four or five attractively illustrated articles 'about real persons or as clearly told accounts of specific events rather than as a succession of dull, abstract themes.'

37 **'American history told by contemporaries'** edited by Albert Bushnell Hart in five volumes (1897-1929) and published by Macmillan is an attempt to combine two purposes: 'to put within convenient reach of schools, libraries, and scholars authoritative texts of rare or quaint writings in American history, contemporary with the events which they describe; and ... to give, in a succession of scenes, a notion of the movement and connection of the history of America, so that from this work ... may be had an impression of the forces which have shaped our history, and the problems upon which they have worked.' Extracts deliberately include very little material from constitutional documents mainly on the grounds that these are available elsewhere and they do not possess 'the persuasive power of writings addressed by men to men.' In all cases the compiler prefers those materials which reflect the personality of the writer—journals, letters, reports, discussions, reminiscences—rather than more formal documents like charters, resolutions, statutes and treaties. Each volume commences either with one or two chapters of what is described as a practical introduction for teachers, libraries and students on sources of the relevant period and how to use them. Titles: *Era of colonization 1492-1689* (1897); *Building of the republic 1689-1783* (1898); *National expansion 1783-1845* (1901); *Welding of the nation 1845-1900* (1901); and *Twentieth century United States 1900-1929* (1929). There have been constant reprintings.

38 **'The American nation'** series, edited by Albert Bushnell Hart, originally consisted of twenty six volumes issued by Harper's of New York 1904-1907. It was an extremely reliable and reputable standard history of the United States, each volume being the work of an acknowledged authority and containing a bibliography of source and secondary material. Titles: *European backgrounds of American history 1300-1600* (E P Cheyney); *Basis of American history 1500-1900* (L Farrand); *Spain in America 1450-1580* (E G Bourne); *England in America 1580-1652* (L G Tyler); *Colonial self-government 1652-1689* (C M Andrews); *Provincial America 1690-1740* (E B Greene); *France in America 1497-1763* (R G Thwaites); *Preliminaries of the revolution 1763-1775* (G E Howard); *The American revolution 1776-1783* (C H Van Tyne); *The confederation and the constitution 1783-1789* (A C McLaughlin); *The federalist system 1789-1801* (J S Bassett); *The Jeffersonian system 1801-1811* (E Channing); *The rise of American nationality 1811-1819* (K C Babcock); *Rise of the new west 1819-1829* (F J Turner); *Jacksonian democracy 1829-1837* (W MacDonald); *Slavery and abolition 1831-1841* (A B Hart); *Westward extension 1841-1850* (G P Garrison); *Parties and slavery 1850-1859* (T C

Smith); *Causes of the civil war 1859-1861* (F E Chadwick); *The appeal to arms 1861-1863* (J K Hosmer); *Outcome of the civil war 1863-1865* (J K Hosmer); *Reconstruction, political and economic 1865-1877* (W A Dunning); *National development 1877-1885* (E E Sparks); *National problems 1885-1897* (D R Dewey); *America as a world power 1897-1907* (J H Latane); *National ideals historically traced 1607-1907* (A B Hart). An additional volume, *National progress 1907-1918* (F A Ogg), appeared in 1918 and an *Analytic index* to the original set of volumes, compiled by D M Mattheson, was published in 1908. To general regret the series was gradually phased out and from 1954 onwards it has been replaced by the same publisher's *New American nation series*.

39 **'An American primer'** edited by Daniel J Boorstin (University of Chicago Press, 2 vols, 1966) is a collection of laws and letters, speeches, declarations and documents of all kinds illustrating the American way of life. There are the usual standard items like the *Declaration of independence* and the *Gettysburg address* but also less familiar ones. Each document, with few exceptions, is printed in full and is preceded by a brief introduction explaining when, how and by whom the document was written, and is followed in similar fashion by an interpretation of its significance to modern America. Among the items included are *The Mayflower compact*, the *United States constitution* (Vol 1) and *Frederick Jackson Turner's address to the State Historical Society of Wisconsin* in 1893 on 'The Significance of the frontier in American history' (Vol 2). There is an index of authors, titles and editors, and of words and phrases.

40 **'The American revolution; a review of changing interpretations'** by Edmund S Morgan, No 6 in the AHA Service Center Series published in 1958, discusses the work of George Bancroft, Sir George Otto Trevelyan, George Louis Beer, C M Andrews, Lawrence Henry Gipson, Carl Becker, Sir Lewis Namier, Arthur Schlesinger Snr, and a number of other historians, in an attempt to decide what was old and what was new in the American revolution. There is a consolidated list of books referred in the text. It should be consulted in conjunction with *The reappraisal of* *the American revolution in recent historical literature* (*qv*), a pamphlet in the same series.

41 Andrews, Charles McLean (1863-1943) belonged to the 'imperial' school of American colonial history which opposed the traditional view of the American revolution as a struggle for political liberty by the colonists against an oppressive tyranny. In *The Colonial period of American history* (*qv*) he considered the colonists as part of the total British expansion overseas with London and not Boston or Jamestown as the nodal point of affairs. This *magnum opus* was based on a secure knowledge of the primary sources of the period, among his own extensive writings are two pioneering bibliographical works: *Guide to the manuscript materials for the history of the United States to 1783 in the British Museum* (1908) and *Guide to the materials for American history to 1783 in the Public Record Office of Great Britain*, 2 vols (1912-1914).

42 Anglo-American Conference of Historians consisting of representatives of British, American, and Commonwealth universities and learned societies and invited individuals, has met annually in July at the Institute of Historical Research since 1921 with the exception only of the war years. There are two types of meetings: the interim annual assembly, latterly consisting of two general and up to eight sectional meetings over two days; and quinquennial plenary conferences of five general sessions extending over four days. The proceedings are listed in the *Bulletin* of the Institute but there is no regular publication of papers read. During each interim meeting there is a display of historical works published in England during the previous year, and before each quinquennial conference a *Bibliography of historical works issued in the United Kingdom* (*qv*) is published. J F Jameson's 'The Anglo-American Conference of Professors of History' (*American history review* XXVII (1) October 1921: 58-63) describes the first meeting and Waldo G Leland's 'The Anglo-American Conference of Historians' (*Bulletin of the International Committee of Historical Sciences* 1 (1) October 1926: 99-103) summarises events of the first five years.

43 'Anglo-Norman England 1066-1154' by Michael Altschul (CUP, 1960) is a bibliographical handbook compiled for the Conference on British Studies. It lists and briefly comments on the most important books, articles, and texts, arranged first under Bibliographies, Catalogues, guides, and handbooks, and General surveys, then under all conceivable topics except Literature *per se*. There is an index of authors, editors and translators.

44 'The Anglo-Saxon age c400-1042' by D J V Fisher (1973), the third volume of Longman's *History of England*, is primarily a political and ecclesiastical history although the central social topics are not overlooked altogether. There is an excellent account of the literary and archaeological evidence in the first chapter besides a note on books which briefly reviews the general histories, the standard secondary works, and more modern studies.

45 'An Anglo-Saxon and Celtic bibliography (450-1087)' by Wilfrid Bonser (Blackwell, 1957) is a comprehensive uncritical bibliography of textbooks, monographs, general works and learned journal articles relating to this particular period of English history from the Anglo-Saxon invasions to the compilation of the *Domesday book* at which point Stenton's *Anglo-Saxon England* in the *Oxford history of England* also stops. Almost 12,000 entries are arranged according to a specially contrived enumerative classification scheme with General topics and historical source material, Political, Local, Constitutional, Social and economic, and Ecclesiastical history, Geography and place names, General culture, Archaeology, Numismatics and seals, Epigraphy, and Art as the main headings. Each item records author and title, an indication of its scope, and a citation if it is a periodical article. There is a list of periodicals and collective works including *festschrift* volumes abstracted. A separate *Indices* volume provides an author and a subject and topographical index.

46 'Anglo-Saxon charters; an annotated list and bibliography' by P H Sawyer (No 8, Royal Historical Society Guides and Handbooks) published in 1968, lists the charters granting land or secular rights over land, purporting to have been issued in preconquest England. It is in two parts: charters of which reasonably full texts survive; and defective and mutilated charters of which only parts are still extant. A bibliography and concordance precede a list of manuscripts and printed sources. The main body of the work, the charters, are arranged under royal charters, grants by the laity, by bishops and other ecclesiastics, miscellaneous texts, wills and bequests, and bounds. For each text a brief description with date, names of grantor and grantee and place comes first, a list of manuscripts together with notes of facsimiles or other reproductions follow, then a list of printed versions and translations, with a bibliography of discussions or citations of the various charters with special attention to comments on authenticity.

47 'Anglo-Saxon chronicle' was first compiled in the reign of Alfred, possibly at the instigation of the king himself in the year 893. It remains unique in that it is the only substantial record of events written in the vernacular and not in Latin in the whole of western Europe in the early medieval period. Some early annals of Wessex, a few from the north, parts of Bede's history, lists of kings and bishops, and a number of oral traditional stories were incorporated in the text. On completion copies were despatched to monasteries the length and breadth of England for further copying as were its continuations. Seven manuscripts are still extant: the earliest, now in the library of Corpus Christi College, Cambridge, written in the same hand of about 900, covers the period from the creation down to the year 891 with the history of Wessex not unnaturally looming large. It was continued intermittently until 1070. From the 10th century onwards the manuscripts begin to show discrepancies partly because of local influences and partly because some instalments were never received. Surprisingly the *Chronicle* continued after the conquest but it gradually declined, English was now the language of a conquered people, the governing class conversed in Norman-French and employed Latin for official documents. Not every period receives full coverage but generally speaking the *Chronicle* is an invaluable, near contemporary record of events spanning over 500 years (one manuscript does not end until 1154), accurate in outline although it can be misleading in detail. Without it our knowledge of much of Anglo-Saxon history would be sketchy indeed. *The Anglo-Saxon chronicle*, edited by Dorothy Whitelocke (1951) gives all versions together with a modern translation. There is also a convenient Everyman edition.

48 **'Anglo-Saxon England,'** founded in 1972, is an annual publication from the Cambridge University Press. It reflects the contemporary sense of identity and common purpose now pervading the various academic disciplines with an interest in this period and is intended to encourage their further cooperation, to stimulate a closer investigation of less familiar forms of evidence, and thus to promote fresh areas of knowledge. Each issue contains up to sixteen articles and a classified bibliography of all books, articles, and significant reviews published in any branch of Anglo-Saxon studies during the previous year.

49 **'Anglo-Saxon England'** by F M Stenton (3rd ed, 1971), the second volume of the *Oxford history of England*, is destined to remain for a very long time to come the definitive study of this obscure period ranging from the emergence of the earliest English kingdom c550 to the establishment of the Anglo-Norman monarchy 1087; every possible aspect of Anglo-Saxon society is covered in this broad survey. The bibliography is of the utmost significance in this particular volume, the original authorities need more care than usual, but they are arranged here in admirable fashion: annals; history and biography; letters, charters, and laws; records; and incidental sources (ie, coins, archaeology and architecture, and place-names).

50 **'The annals of America,'** a year by year record of the ideas and issues that influenced United States history, is published in nineteen volumes by the Encyclopaedia Britannica Educational Corporation. Almost three thousand extracts from speeches, court decisions, laws, newspaper editorials, periodical articles, pamphlets, book reviews etc, chronologically arranged, and each prefaced by a description of its historical context and significance, form the most comprehensive collection of American historical source material ever assembled. Each volume contains a chronology providing a condensed historical outline of the period covered, an introduction sketching the highlights of the time, an author index for biographical information, and a map section. Titles: *Discovering a new world 1493-1754; Resistance and revolution 1755-1783;*

Organising the new nation 1784-1796; Domestic expansion and foreign entanglements 1797-1820; Steps towards equalitarianism 1821-1832; The challenge of a continent 1833-1840; Manifest destiny 1841-1849; A house dividing 1850-1857; The crisis of the Union 1858-1865; Reconstruction and industrialisation 1866-1883; Agrarianism and urbanisation 1884-1894; Populism, imperialism, and reform 1895-1904; The progressive era 1905-1915; World war and prosperity 1916-1928; The great depression 1929-1939; The Second world war and after 1940-1949; Cold war in the nuclear age 1950-1960; The burdens of world power 1961-1968; and *Detente and domestic crisis 1969-1973.* In addition there are three complementary volumes, an *Index* volume, a chronological listing of the extracts, together with a proper name index and an author and source index; and a two-volume *Conspectus,* a subject index of the complete work. *The annals* is intended for use in the United States and is not distributed overseas.

51 'Annual bulletin of historical literature' (1911-   ), published by the Historical Association, is a comprehensive survey and assessment of all literature pertaining to history written during the year in book and periodical form. Each issue contains sections by different hands beginning with the method and philosophy of history and historiography and continues on a chronological pattern. At the moment the *Bulletin* appears approximately three years after the year listed.

52 'The annual register,' the oldest surviving periodical publication in Britain, first made its appearance in 1758, edited by Edmund Burke. The first issue was not content with a review of the year but included an account of what is now known as the Seven Years War from its beginning. An ordered presentation of facts has remained editorial policy down the years and, as each volume succeeds another, the files have become an invaluable source of information providing an uninterrupted record of events that historians have not been slow to plunder. Considering the span of time involved the contents and arrangement of the *Register* have not significantly altered over the years. Today each volume begins with the history of the United Kingdom over the past year followed by a similar review for other regions of the world. Then come various topical sections ending with a series of important documents. An advisory board comprising representatives of the Royal Institute of International Affairs, the Arts Council, the British Association for the Advancement of Science, the Royal Historical Society, and the English Association, came into existence in 1947 although responsibility for the *Register* remains very much in the hands of the present publisher, Longman. 'The Annual Register 1758-1958' by Asa Briggs was included in the preliminary matter of the 1958 volume.

53 'Antecedents of the Rolls Series; issues in historical editing' is the title of an article by Lester J Cappon which appeared in the jubilee issue of the *Journal of the Society of Archivists* 4 (5) April 1972: 358-369. 'The preservation and use of the public records of Great Britain are marked in the nineteenth century by two closely related, yet quite separate, developments: the formation and expansion of a centralised administration of the national records through the Public Record Office, established in 1838; and the publication of documentary history on a national scale. Both stemmed from the Record Commission beginning in 1801 and both became the responsibility of the Master of the Rolls.' Dr Cappon skilfully follows the anfractuous history of these developments, adjudges the contributions of the personalities involved, investigates the different interpretations of the editor's role in the elucidation and presentation of scholarly texts, and frequently refers to his authorities.

54 Anvil Books is a paperback series published by Van Nostrand Reinhold of New York and consists of original analyses of major problem areas of history and the social sciences, incorporating the most recent research, and contributed by distinguished scholars. Each book includes a selection of pertinent documents. Titles of particular interest include *Documents in American history* by Richard Morris; *Defeat of the confederacy* and *Fifty basic civil war documents* both by H S Commager; *Short history of Canada* by J J Talman; and *British constitutional history since 1832* and *Cardinal documents in British history* both by R L Schuyler and C C Weston.

55 'Archives' the journal of the British Records Association (1949-   ) is published every Spring and Autumn. Contents include articles, papers read at the BRA annual conference, reviews, obituaries, and news items. An author-title index is published every two years. Back issues are available from William Dawson and Sons Ltd, Cannon House, Folkestone, Kent.

56 '**The art of history; a study of four great historians of the eighteenth century**' by J B Black (1926) examines sympathetically and critically the *credenda* of Voltaire, Hume, Robertson and Gibbon of the theory and practice of history, contrasting them with those of twentieth century historians. 'The motive lying behind the entire essay, is that the intimate union between literature, philosophy, and history, so amply demonstrated in the writings of Voltaire and his "school," is not merely an ideal of the eighteenth century but one which bears a validity for all time.'

57 **Asser** (d 929) is noted for his *De Rebus Gestis Aelfredi* (Life of King Alfred) which describes his reign in detail down to the year 887, ie, thirteen years before Alfred's death. It relies heavily on the *Anglo-Saxon chronicle* and there are many scholars who denounce it as an 11th century forgery.

58 '**An atlas of African history**' by J D Fage was first published in 1958 and reprinted many times since then. It is compiled in the firm intention of treating the continent and its inhabitants 'as the central point around which influences and actions coming from outside can be seen in perspective.' The earliest map is 'Roman Africa', the latest shows the pattern of alien rule in the 1960s, and the atlas concludes with a series of economic studies. All maps are clearly drawn in black and white and the historical notes attached to many of them add a delightful touch of scholarship.

59 '**Atlas of American history**' editor-in-chief, J T Adams, was planned when the lack of a concise, easy to use, carefully plotted and authoritative historical atlas became apparent whilst research on the *Dictionary of American history* was in progress. The most urgent need was for a collection of maps that would provide a sound geographical basis to American history by locating places as they actually existed, and precisely where they existed, at a specified time. The present atlas, noteworthy for its maps on the colonial period, the revolutionary, 1812 and civil wars, and the expansion westwards, was designed to be of immediate use to professional scholars as well as in schools and colleges and at home. Historians familiar with the appropriate area and period supervised the compilation of the maps which are in black and white and arranged on a chronological pattern. All told there are 147 maps and an index which directs the user to a precise map or enables him to follow the development of a particular area. The descriptive annotation accompanying each map is not always legible in later reprintings. The publishers are Charles Scribners of New York.

60 'The atlas of world history' by Colin and Sarah McEvedy is published by Hart-Davis and consists of eight separate volumes presenting the history of man in the form of historical maps accompanied by a comprehensive narrative text. All maps are coloured and each volume is fully illustrated with line drawings and photographs. When completed the atlas will be a useful addition to any library. Vols: *From the beginning to Alexander the Great* (1970); *The classical world* (1973); *Dark ages* (1972); *Medieval world; European expansion; Revolution; Colonial empires; Modern age.*

61 'Australia' a social and political history edited by Gordon Greenwood (Angus and Robertson, 1955) is a cooperative history by a small number of historians on the staff of several Australian universities sponsored by the Commonwealth of Australia jubilee celebrations committee. The broad aim was to produce a history which would display the manifold nature of Australian development at any given point. The balance of emphasis has been tilted towards post 1890 developments in order to offset the lack of authoritative secondary works for this period. There is a selective classified general bibliography confined to published material which has appeared after 1928, the closing date of the material cited in the Australian volume of the *Cambridge history of the British Empire.* The chapter bibliographies have no such limitation.

62 'Australian dictionary of biography' is based on the Australian National University of Canberra and published by the Melbourne University Press. It is 'an all-Australian, Commonwealth-wide venture' and is the product of close cooperation between the history departments in all Australian universities, history and genealogical societies, and individual scholars. The actual writing of the entries, selected after provisional lists had been widely circulated and amended, has been shared by university historians and members of learned societies, and by members of the editorial staff. Some names omitted because of lack of material are placed on a biographical register, at the editorial offices, which is circulated regularly to Australian libraries. Volumes published so far: *1788-1850 A-H* and *I-Z; 1851-1890 A-C, D-J, K-Q.* A fourth *R-Z* will complete this section and six volumes are planned for the period 1891-1939. Douglas Pike has acted as general editor 1966-1973.

63 Australian Historical Association was formed in 1973 on the initiative of university history departments. Its objectives are to encourage historical study, teaching and research; to formulate archive and library policies and to express opinions on such issues of public policy as concern historical study; to circulate general information relating to the profession such as developments in teaching, research, and the accumulation of resources; to organize general and local meetings and symposia; and to make secretarial and administrative arrangements to carry out the objectives of the association. Membership is open to 'all individuals and organizations who subscribe to the objects of the association and who pay the annual subscription'.

64 Bale, John (1495-1563), fiercely partisan protestant Bishop of Ossory, was the compiler of *Illustrium Majoris Britanniae Scriptorum hoc est, Angliae, Cambriae, ac Scotiae, Summarium,* first published in 1549 and enlarged in the 1559 edition to 900 entries. It purports to be a biographical dictionary of British authors although many are admitted on very slight grounds, and takes the form of an alphabetical list of authors together with details of their writings. At times extreme religious opinions detract from its value. A printed version edited by R L Poole and Mary Bateson was published in 1902.

65 Bancroft, George (1800-1891) was once hailed by Americans as their national historian. Not only was his *History of the United*

States (10 vols 1834-1874) the first detailed account of the original colonies, their quarrel with the crown and their struggle for independence, it also served at a time of internal strife to remind them of their essential unity. Later historians may deplore his transparent partisanship; his heroes (American) and villains (English) are perhaps too vividly contrasted, but they confirmed and expressed the delusions traditionally nurtured by most nineteenth-century Americans. His research and industry were commendable but his conclusions, based on a preconceived philosophy that the advance of mankind had reached its apogee at the American Revolution, remain detached from reality.

66 'Barnwell chronicle' (1227) includes annals from the Incarnation to the year 1225 and is especially valuable for its analysis of political events and for its use of contemporary documents (many of which are now lost) for the period 1202-1225. Only one manuscript which belonged to Barnwell Priory in Cambridgeshire has survived. The text was included in Stubbs edition of *Memoriale Fratris Walteri de Coventria* (*Rolls series* 1872-1873).

67 'Basic documents in American history' by Richard B Morris, an Anvil Original first published by Van Nostrand in 1956 but subsequently enlarged, contains almost fifty documents ranging from *The Mayflower compact* to J F Kennedy's presidential proclamation declaring a quarantine of offensive weapons to Cuba.

68 'Basic documents in Canadian history' by James J Talman (Anvil Original, Van Nostrand, 1959) begin with a description of Cartier sailing up the St Lawrence in 1535 and end very neatly with the government's announcement of its decision to go ahead with the St Lawrence Seaway and Power Project in 1954. A number of the extracts are concerned with Canadian relations with the United States.

69 'Basic documents on the confederation and constitution' by Richard B Morris was published as an Anvil Original by Van Nostrand Reinhold in 1970 and illuminates the political and constitutional problems facing the newly independent United

States of America in 1783. A number of the documents were published for the first time in this collection.

70 The Bayeux tapestry is a roll of linen twenty three feet long and almost twenty inches wide probably commissioned by Odo, Bishop of Bayeux, upon which was embroidered in eight different colours the sequence of events from Harold's visit to Normandy in 1064 to his defeat at the Battle of Hastings two years later. It is now generally accepted that it was executed within living memory of the conquest (possibly at Canterbury) and may safely be regarded as an authoritative primary historical source for the Norman invasion ranking alongside William of Poitier's *Gesta Willelmi* (*qv*).

71 Beaglehole, John Cawte (1901-1971) became fascinated by the story of Captain Cook when writing *The exploration of the Pacific* for A and C Black's *Pioneer histories* in the 1930s. From then onwards this most internationally known of all New Zealand historians devoted his professional career to the writing of an adequate biography of Cook. First however he decided it was necessary to arrive at a definitive text of Cook's journals. Together these tasks occupied him thirty years until at length they were published in volumes 34-37 in the Hakluyt Society's *Extra series* 1955-1974. Alan Moorehead in his Note to *The fatal impact* (1966) described his masterly editing and annotation of Cook's original journals as illuminating Pacific travels as nothing had done before and continued 'it is not too much to say that any account of Cook's discoveries can hardly hope to be more than an appendage, if not a plagiarism of his work.'

72 Beard, Charles Austin (1874-1948) is chiefly remembered for his *An economic interpretation of the constitution of the United States* (1913) described as 'one of the half dozen most influential books written in American history' in which he cites convincing evidence that the members of the Constitutional Convention 1787 produced a constitution deliberately contrived to bolster their self interests at the expense of many of the ideals that had inspired the revolution, that the common man had in effect been sold down the river to benefit a few uncommon men. Later in his career in cooperation with his wife he produced a massive synthesis of

American history and life in *The rise of American civilization* in two volumes (1927), *America in midpassage* (1939), and *The American spirit* (1942). Towards the end of his life they again cooperated on *The Beard's basic history of the United States* a comparatively short and extremely readable history, published by Doubleday (Macmillan in England) in 1944 which was revised in 1960 by their son, William, as *The Beard's new basic history of the United States.*

73 'Bede' commonly called the Venerable (c673-735) has justly been named as the father of English history. As a Northumbrian monk working in the libraries of Jarrow and Wearmouth monasteries he had access to Irish and Roman scholarship. His numerous writings fall easily into three categories: Scientific, historical, and theological, but it is his *Historia ecclesiastica gentis Anglorum* which is regarded as his masterpiece. It is divided into five books: a geographical survey of Britain based on the writings of earlier chronicles and including some well known episodes like the mission of St Augustine in 597; the second book relates events from the death of Gregory to the death of King Edwin of Northumbria 603-632; book three takes the story up to 664 which covers the confrontation and subsequent harmony of the Celtic and Roman churches at the Synod of Whitby; book four concerns the work of the early churchmen like Theodore of Tarsus who became Archbishop of Canterbury in 669; and the last book is the source of much of our knowledge of Colomba and concludes with a not inconsiderable list of his own writings. As a historian Bede is scrupulously impartial and anxious to record only well attested fact. Whenever possible he cites important documents in full in the sure knowledge that verbatim documentary evidence is worth far more than even the most extensive summaries or quotations, and he is always very careful to distinguish incontrovertible facts from mere rumour or tradition. The lasting popularity of Bede's history of the English church and people is evidenced by the comparatively large number of surviving manuscripts and the constant listing of his work in the catalogues of medieval monastic libraries. Of his scientific writings that of most interest here is his mathematical method of calculating the date of Easter, a particular bone of contention between the Celtic and Roman churchmen. He was also the first to use the BC-AD system of dating events, a practice which gained general acceptance as his history was copied in continental *scriptoria*.

74 'The Bedford historical series' published by Jonathan Cape has no essential unity of theme or purpose. It consists of well established, standard books, many of them biographical studies, notable for their soundness of scholarship and for their readability, qualities not always found in harness. Outstanding titles: *Queen Elizabeth* by J E Neale, *Thomas More* by R W Chambers, *Mr Secretary Cecil and Queen Elizabeth* by Conyers Read.

75 'The beginnings of English society' by Dorothy Whitelocke, first published in 1952, is the second volume of the *Pelican history of England*. It is a compelling synthesis of the varied sources of the period still extant and slowly builds a cumulative picture of a remarkable outpost of culture and civilisation. Intended for the intelligent general reader, there is a select bibliography for those who wish to pursue their studies further.

76 'Best books on the British Empire; a bibliographical guide for students' by Evans Lewin (Royal Empire Society, 2nd ed, 1945) includes the best works on the general description, administration, economics, history and native races of the dominions, colonies and India published 1910-1944. There is no attempt to evaluate the items listed. It is arranged in twenty two sections on a geographical basis supplemented by an index of authors. John Flint's *Books on the British Empire and Commonwealth* (1968) has updated Lewin's guide.

77 'Bibliographical guide to the study of the literature of the United States of America' by Clarence Gohdes (Duke Univ Press 2nd ed, 1963) undertakes to provide lists of books to aid the professional student in the acquiring of information and in the techniques of research and is specifically intended for teachers, reference librarians and more especially for postgraduate students preparing theses for higher degrees. Arrangement is by form and subject. The first seven sections list books offering help on the methodology of literary and historical study, historical research techniques, definitions of terms, the preparation of manuscripts for publication, and miscellaneous bibliographical information.

34

Chapters 9 and 10 American History: General tools and special studies provide annotated lists of some titles of importance.

78 'Bibliography and the historian' edited by Dagmar Horna Perman (Clio Press 1968) consists of studies prepared for the Conference of the Joint Committee on Bibliographical Services to History held at Belmont, Maryland, in May 1967. The committee, consisting of representatives of professional organisations, editors of major historical journals, bibliographers and librarians, devoted most of their time to developments in technology. Other papers deal with bibliographical developments in the Library of Congress, new systems of bibliographical service with regard to periodical literature and research in progress, and a comparison of bibliography in history and the new bibliographical services in sciences and the social sciences. Then follows a survey of traditional bibliographies available to historians and a discussion of what new forms of bibliographical control are needed in history. Conclusions on this latter topic argue that if historians want to ensure that their professional needs are considered in the development of new bibliographical systems they must be aware of these, and in devising their own projects they must heed the experiences of other disciplines.

79 'Bibliography of British history' issued under the direction of the American Historical Association and the Royal Historical Society of Great Britain, traces its origins at least back to 1909 when the two societies named committees to discuss the question of cooperating in publishing continuations of Gross's *Sources and literature of English history from the earliest times to about 1485* (*qv*). The first world war hindered progress and a fresh start was made when the decision was taken to go ahead with separate British and American volumes. Although each volume is complete in itself, they all more or less correspond in pattern and arrangement. They are intended for the serious student and are, in fact, the starting point for all advanced work in their period, being much more concerned with source material than secondary authorities. Each volume provides a selective survey of the material, many items are furnished with brief descriptive or critical comment, and short introductory paragraphs, generally indicating the more significant books, preface most main subdivisions in turn. Political, constitutional, legal, ecclesiastical, military and naval, economic, social and cultural, and local history are all accommodated and are preceded by a general reference works category which includes bibliographies and catalogues, library resources, periodical and society publications, pamphlet collections, and manuscripts. Four volumes have been published so far by OUP, *viz: Tudor period 1485-1603* (Conyers Read 1933, second edition 1959); *Stuart period 1603-1714* (Godfrey Davies 1928, second edition by Mary Frear Keeler 1970); *The eighteenth century 1714-1789* (Stanley Pargellis and D J Medley 1951). A supplement is in preparation; 1789-1851 in preparation; *1851-1914* (H J Hanham 1975).

The early hopes and plans for this project are closely outlined in Henry Tedder's 'The forthcoming Bibliography of Modern British History,' *Transactions Royal Historical Society* 3rd series, VIII, 1914: 41-54.

80 'A bibliography of British history (1700-1715); with special reference to the reign of Queen Anne' by William Thomas Morgan (Bloomington, Indiana, 5 vols 1934-1942) was planned principally as a work of reference for research students and scholars in the fields of English history and literature. Educationally of course the connection between the two disciplines is especially justified in this period. As Professor Morgan remarked, it was the age when literary men were statesmen and statesmen were men of letters. The main sources for both the literary student and the historian are therefore identical. Entries are arranged in an interesting fashion: a general chapter on bibliographical aids is followed by eighteen sections listing contemporary pamphlets and memoirs in chronological order. Then come source materials; correspondence and autobiography; periodical materials; plays; secondary works; and unpublished manuscripts. There is a comprehensive author and title index. For the most part entries are without annotation but a page or so of explanatory notes precedes every chapter. Despite its title the work is concerned mainly with English history.

81 'A bibliography of English history to 1485; Based on the sources and literature of English history from the earliest times to about 1485 by Charles Gross' edited by Edgar B Graves and issued under the sponsorship of The Royal Historical Society, The

American Historical Association and The Medieval Academy of America (OUP 1975) is basically a revision of Charles Gross' work which has through many vicissitudes finally emerged forty years after a third edition of that work was first mooted in 1935. Over 7000 entries are encompassed in five parts and Volume 2. Pt I General works and auxiliary sciences includes Bibliographical guides, journals, and auxiliaries of historical studies; Pt II Archives, source collections and modern narratives; Pts III-V are chronological sections: From prehistory to Anglo-Saxon conquest; The Anglo-Saxon period; and From Normans to Tudors. Then follows Volume 2 (the first volume presumably comprises the foregoing) which is a classified sequence: modern political narratives, military and naval history, land tenure, agrarian society, urban society, the church 1066-1485, modern studies of the medieval church, and intellectual interests. To comment on this superb bibliography verges on acute and gratuitous presumption, it is enough to say that the information contained within it goes far beyond a mere listing of authors and titles; its detailed informative annotation, its references to other sources, the tight editing so unobtrusive yet so obvious when noticed, all contribute to an extremely valuable addition to the world of historical scholarship.

82 'Bibliography of historical atlases, and hand-maps for use in schools' by R F Treharne published by the Historical Association in 1939, is now of use only for its evaluation of some school atlases of yesteryear.

83 'Bibliography of historical works issued in the United Kingdom 1946-1956' compiled for the sixth Anglo-American Conference of Historians by Joan C Lancaster (1957), is a broadly based completely unannotated list concerned only with works originally issued in the UK. Similar volumes compiled by William Kellaway have followed and coverage is now complete to 1970 *viz: 1957-1960* (1962); *1961-1965* (1967) and *1966-1970* (1972).

84 'Bibliography of historical writings published in Great Britain and the Empire 1940-1945' by L B Frewer (1947) was edited for the British National Committee of the International Committee of Historical Sciences using the material prepared for the *Inter-*

national Bibliography of Historical Sciences (qv) but not published because of the war. It is a selective list covering all aspects and all periods of history, arranged in the same manner, under the same headings as the *International bibliography.*

85 'A bibliography of modern history' (1968) is the response to the criticism voiced when the *New Cambridge modern history (qv)* appeared devoid of bibliographies. It is designed to stand alone as a useful guide to schoolteachers and undergraduates and as a companion volume to the *New modern.* The lists are arranged in three sections each relating to four volumes of the history: A 1493-1648 (Vols I-IV); B 1648-1793 (Vols V-VIII); and, C 1793-1945 (Vols IX-XII). Entries are mostly supplied by the contributors to the *History* and within these sections the arrangement varies: some find a broad alphabetical basis suits their purposes, others prefer a subject arrangement. The emphasis is on material reasonably accessible rather than manuscript or similar esoteric sources.

86 'A bibliography of the historical works of Dr Creighton ... Dr Stubbs ... Dr S R Gardiner and the late Lord Acton' edited for the Royal Historical Society by W A Shaw (1903) consists of check-lists arranged in form divisions: Works, Introductions and prefaces, Lectures, Articles, Letters and reviews, Edited matter, Charges and sermons, which all underline the amazing wide ranging energy and stupendous prolificity of these victorian scholars. A number of unsigned periodical articles are recorded.

87 'Bibliotheca Australiana' is the collective title of an extensive series of facsimile editions of significant journals and histories recording Pacific exploration from the sixteenth to the nineteenth centuries. In all, seventy eight volumes are available, mostly in the English language, in one of two standard sizes. A brochure is available either from Nico Israel, Keizersgracht 526, Amsterdam, or the Da Capo Press, 227 West 17th Street, New York.

88 'Biography as history; men and movements in Europe since 1500' (1963) is No 49 in the AHA Center Series. The nature of biography and its relation to history is expanded on the theme that 'Without people history is inconceivable; the history of a country, an idea, a policy means the men who built it, or thought it, or carried it through.'

89 'Bohn's antiquarian library' (1847-1893), later taken over by G Bell, was for many years the standard edition of medieval texts. They have largely been superseded by the authoritative *Oxford medieval texts* series (*qv*).

90 'Books on the British Empire and Commonwealth; a guide for students' by John Flint, published by OUP, in 1968 on behalf of the Royal Commonwealth Society, replaced an earlier work, *Best books on the British Empire* edited by Evans Lewin published by the Royal Empire Society in a second edition twenty years earlier. The aim here was to select important books published since 1940 of help in understanding the Commonwealth and the role of its member nations. After a general section 'The British Empire and Commonwealth' entries are arranged under geographical headings subdivided by appropriate descriptive subject headings with a bias towards history and politics. It is a straightforward list, there are no annotations.

91 'Books to build an empire; a bibliographical history of English overseas interests to 1620' by John Parker was published in Amsterdam by N Israel in 1965. It consists of a dozen extensive bibliographical essays recording and describing the early printed books which illustrate the growth of English interest in those territories which subsequently formed part of the British Empire. The author's intention was to include all English books published in the period 1481-1620 of geographic interest and all which indicate attitudes for and against the concepts of establishing an English empire abroad, promoting overseas commerce, or missionary work among heathen peoples. In all some 267 titles are mentioned. For the benefit of librarians, collectors, and anti-quarian booksellers, each receives a standard bibliographical description in a chronologically arranged bibliography. There is also a list of secondary sources.

92 'The bookseller' is the organ of the British book trade. In February and August the normal weekly issue is replaced by the Spring or Autumn Export Number devoted to the books due to appear in the forthcoming publishing season. Publishers' announcements of their books are preceded by not very critical editorial comments on the books arranged under broad subject headings of which History and archaeology is one. Although it would be an exaggeration to suggest either section is exhaustive, together they provide a most useful advance indication of what is to be published, and therefore constitute a valuable book selection guide.

93 '**Britain after the glorious revolution 1689-1714**' edited by Geoffrey Holmes was published in 1969 as the first of Macmillan's *Problems in focus* series. A long introduction, 'Post-revolution Britain and the historian' by the editor is followed by another ten chapters each on a separate topic and each contributed by a different writer. Unlike other volumes in the series there is no general bibliography but each chapter concludes with a bibliographical note as a guide to further reading.

94 '**Britain between the wars 1918-1940**' by C L Mowat (Methuen, 1955) is indispensable for the student of the modern period. It is a detailed, expertly documented survey of political and economic events, always proceeding at a scholarly pace and in well-argued fashion, taking care to guide the reader through the tangled thickets of opinion, and selecting with an authoritative discrimination from the copious wealth of authorities at the contemporary historian's disposal. Now available as a mammoth sized University Paperback, it must be regarded as the standard and definitive history of the period.

95 '**Britain Commonwealth and Empire 1901-1955**' by Paul Knaplund (Hamilton, 1956) regards the history of Britain's overseas empire in the period covered not as 'the decline and fall of a mighty imperial structure, but the rise and fulfilment of an historic mission by the peoples of the British Isles.' The book is divided into two chronological parts, 1901-1931 and 1931-1955, and the same pattern is followed in each: a dependable analysis of the role and power of Britain and then a scrutiny of the politics and economics of the constituent parts of the Empire-Commonwealth. The purpose of the geographically classified bibliography is to present titles to aid students who are interested in particular topics treated in the text. There are sixteen maps of various degrees of clarity.

96 'Britain in modern times' is a multi volume textbook in nine individual parts, each of which is separate in itself, covering one aspect of British history 1815-1914 for secondary level students. Published by Collins Educational Books the series provides a complete overall picture of the period. In these days of financial stringency Collins regard the flexible approach of this set of books (which may be acquired piecemeal over an estimated span of time) as being especially attractive to hard hit education authorities.

97 'Britain in the Pacific Islands' by W P Morrell (OUP, 1960) is confined mainly to the nineteenth century although it commences with the first contacts between the European invaders and the island peoples and ends with an Epilogue devoted to the twentieth century. Hawaii and New Zealand are excluded. Professor Morrell has drawn heavily on the reports and journals of the various missionary societies.

98 'Britain in the twentieth century 1900-1964' by E E Reynolds and N H Brasher is a concise factual account published by the Cambridge University Press in 1966 and is obviously intended for sixth form use. A paperback edition is available.

99 'Britannia; a history of Roman Britain' by Sheppard Frere was published in 1967 as the first of Routledge's ambitious *History of the provinces of the Roman Empire* series. First it presents a study of the background of pre-Roman iron age peoples and this is followed by chapters on all aspects of the life and administration of the province. All the results of recent archaeological discovery are considered but no attempt is made to discuss the archaeology of Roman Britain as such, although the most important archaeological literature is included in the bibliography which is arranged by chapter. There are thirty two plates collected at the end of the work which is also adequately endowed with maps.

100 'Britannia' *sive Florentissimorum Regnorum Angliae, Scotiae, Hiberniae, et Insularum adjacentium ex intima antiquate Choro-*

graphica Descriptio by William Camden (1551-1623), the first comprehensive topographical survey of the three kingdoms, was first published in 1586. It was originally planned to delineate the topography of Roman Britain and to stress British involvement in the ancient world and in contemporary European scholarship; it was written in Latin, the *lingua franca* of scholars, and it did not appear in English translation until the sixth (folio) edition in 1610. The framework of the book was the Celtic tribal areas of Britain as recorded in the pages of the classical geographers with the English shires superimposed. It was a well researched work, Camden himself reported 'I have diligently perus'd our own Writers; as well as the Greek and Latin ones, that mention the least tittle of Britain. I have examin'd the publick records of this Kingdom, Ecclesiastical Registers, and Libraries, Acts, Monuments, and Memorials of Churches and Cities; I have search'd the ancient Rolls, and cited them upon occasion in their own stile.' At the end of the seventeenth century, when an enlarged edition was called for, it is significant that the basic Celtic framework was retained, sure confirmation of the respect the *Britannia* continued to command. A team of scholars including Thomas Tanner, John Aubrey, John Evelyn, Samuel Pepys and White Kennet, under the editorship of Edmund Gibson, contributed extra material to bring the work into line with contemporary antiquarianism. The new edition was published in 1695, again in folio, and although there was a later revision under the supervision of Richard Gough it is this 1695 edition that is regarded as definitive. It includes a life of Camden, 'a catalogue of some books and treatises relating to the antiquities of England,' and Antoninus's itinerary through Britain. The arrangement is by county sections, each of which is accompanied by a map. A facsimile edition with an introduction by Stuart Piggott was published by David and Charles in 1971. Another notable work of Camden's was *Annales rerum Anglicarum et Hibernicarum regnante Elizabetha* the first volume of which to the year 1589 was published in 1615; the second volume completed in 1607 was not published until 1625.

101 The British Academy came into being as a consequence of the first meeting of the International Association of Academies held in Paris in 1900. Whereas the Royal Society was preeminent in the scientific field no comparable institution could claim to represent United Kingdom historical or philosophical societies. The Royal Society invited a number of eminent academics and scholars to discuss the formation of a new umbrella institution for the Humanities. At first it was thought that the Royal Society might enlarge its scope but that view failed to find favour by the fellows. Certain of those persons who had received the society's invitation decided to go ahead independently and a meeting was held at the British Museum late in June 1901. A provisional general committee was constituted and in December the new body, with the support of the Royal Society, petitioned the king for the grant of a royal charter. The British Academy for the Promotion of Historical, Philosophical, and Philological Studies was duly incorporated in August 1902. When the International Association of Academies met for the second time in 1904 the British Academy took its place along with the Royal Society. A factual summary of its progress may be read in Sir Frederic Kenyon's *The British Academy: the first fifty years* (1952) and a more lively account of its rejuvenation in Sir Mortimer Wheeler's *The British Academy 1949-1968* (OUP 1970). Its current activities, research, lectures, publications, are outlined in the annual report printed in the annual *Proceedings* which commenced publication in 1903. Most of the papers presented there are issued in pamphlet form including the annual Raleigh Lecture on History (*qv*). Informative if eulogistic obituaries of deceased fellows are also to be found in the *Proceedings*. An *Index to volumes I-XX (1901-1934)* consisting of author-title plus a few subject headings, with lists of lectures and publications, was published in 1937. *A cumulative index to the proceedings of the British Academy vol 1 (1903) to vol 54 (1968)* compiled by K Balasundara Gupta was issued by The Scarecrow Press in 1971.

102 'British antiquity' by T D Kendrick (Methuen, 1950) 'is in the main concerned with sixteenth century England and the transition from medieval to modern antiquarian thought' especially with regard to the traditional notions of the founding of Britain. There are also chapters on British history in the middle ages and appreciations of John Rous and William of Worcester, two antiquarians of the previous century. John Leland and William Camden are treated at length in this fascinating book on the struggle between long cherished legendary tales and the incipient demands of historical scholarship in the hearts and minds of contemporary patriotic Englishmen.

103 British Association for American Studies was founded in 1955 by a group of university lecturers following the last of four conferences sponsored by the Fulbright Commission which took place at Oxford and Cambridge 1952-1955. Although most of its members are historians, other disciplines such as geography, politics, etc, are all included within its scope. Its aim is to foster the serious study of the United States within the United Kingdom especially by collecting and disseminating information and by improving British library resources. A bulletin was innovated in 1956 which was issued in a new series in 1960. *The journal of American studies* began publication in 1967.

104 'British book news' is a monthly journal published by The British Council which includes a number of bibliographical articles in addition to about 250 book reviews arranged under broad headings of which History and geography is one. The prompt appearance of these reviews is welcome to librarians anxious to allocate their limited book funds most effectively.

105 'British colonial developments 1774-1834; select documents' by Vincent Harlow and Frederick Madden (OUP, 1953) includes original and hitherto little used material intended to give a balanced view on overseas events and their subsequent influence on British colonial policy. The extracts are arranged under six main headings: British penetration into the Indian and Pacific Oceans; Constitutional developments, the problems of representative government; Commercial affairs especially the old colonial system and the principle of reciprocity in North America and the West Indies; the modification of this system in Cape Colony; Emigration and settlement in Australasia, Canada and Africa; Frontier problems; and, lastly, Humanitarian principles and colonial policy, ie, the slave trade and the treatment of indigenous populations.

106 'British colonial policy in the age of Peel and Russell' by W P Morrell (OUP, 1930) examines the revolution which transformed London's colonial policy throughout the 1840s. It is based on a study of parliamentary debates, of the most influential newspapers and journals, the private papers of some of the main participants in official affairs, and also of the correspondence of the secretary of state with the various colonial governors. The bibliography lists manuscript and printed source material in addition to the books, pamphlets, and articles consulted. Almost forty years later Professor Morrell continued the story in his *British colonial policy in the mid-victorian age* (OUP, 1969). Together the two volumes provide a distinguished introduction to the many studies which start with the British Empire at the zenith of its majesty and power before what now seems the inevitable decline and fall. The second volume concentrates on the development of self government in South Africa, New Zealand, and the West Indies and is as expertly researched as the first.

107 'The British Commonwealth of Nations' by Sir Ivor Jennings was first published in Hutchinson's University Library in 1948. The current fourth edition (1961) has been largely rewritten to take into account the drastically altered political and constitutional structure of the Commonwealth. Contents include a brief history of each area and a discussion of the laws, government and free association of Commonwealth members.

108 'The British Empire; its structure and spirit' by E A Walker (OUP, 1943) traces the history of the empire from its beginnings, but concentrates on the period since 1833, and in even more detail from 1914 onwards. It was issued under the auspices of the Royal Institute of International Affairs.

109 'The British Empire and Commonwealth in recent historiography' by Philip D Curtin was the first of a series of bibliographical articles surveying historical works published during the period 1927-1957 sponsored by The Conference on British Studies. It appeared in the *American historical review* LXV (1) October 1959: 72-89 and traces the trend in imperial history studies which reflect the change in structure of Empire and Commonwealth as evidenced in its related bibliography. It was subsequently included in *Changing views on British History* (qv).

110 'The British Empire before the American revolution' (Knopf, 15 vols, 1936-1970) by Lawrence Henry Gipson has been aptly described as 'the most distinguished multi volume work by any living American historian.' It is beyond question history on the grand scale and has occupied Professor Gipson's attention for close on fifty years. Vol XIV *A bibliographical guide to the history of the British Empire 1748-1776* (1969) does not claim to be exhaustive but it is almost impossible to conceive a more comprehensive bibliography of this relative short span of less than thirty years. After a general chapter, seven others are arranged chronologically with that on the North American colonies by far the most lengthy. Within each chapter entries are listed under four headings; bibliographical aids, printed source material, secondary works, and maps and cartographical aids, and are interspersed with brief notes and comments. Vol XV *A guide to manuscripts relating to the history of the British Empire 1748-1776* (1970) is equally monumental. Relevant archives in the London depositories are cited followed in turn by other British record offices, those of France and Spain, Canada, the West Indies and the American colonies. The meticulous research and effective use of primary material, the detail of this vast history, the assiduous recording of the manuscript and printed source material described above, are truly impressive; American historical scholarship at its formidable best. Arthur Lower's 'Lawrence H Gipson and the first British Empire: an evaluation,' *Journal of British studies* 3 (1) 1963: 57-58 is a masterly analysis of the whole work.

111 'The British Empire 1815-1939' by Paul Knaplund (Harper, 1941) follows the imperial achievement in plain narrative form. Four chronological sections combine general chapters with others devoted to the principal events in each important region. A working bibliography provides references to more exhaustive guides to the literature.

112 'British historians' by E L Woodward was published by Collins in their *Britain in pictures* series (1943) which are now fetching stiff prices in the bookshops. A pleasant saunter through historiography, it is packed with illuminating and entertaining anecdotes and comments. It is incorporated in *Impressions of English literature* edited by W J Turner (Collins, 1944).

113 '**British historical facts 1830-1900**' by Chris Cook and Brendan Keith (Macmillan Press, 1975) is a source book of facts and figures. Extensive lists of 'top people,' those who achieved high political, military or administrative office during the victorian period, form the kernel of the work. The difficulties encountered in compiling it, mentioned in the bibliographical note at the end, serve to underline its usefulness.

114 '**British history atlas**' by Martin Gilbert (Weidenfeld, 1968) has for its central theme the story of the British Isles but within that theme wars and alliances, expansion and empire overseas, industry and trade, all find a place. The earliest of its 118 black and white maps is 'The Celts in Britain,' the latest 'The British Commonwealth 1967.'

115 '**British history 1815-1939**' by J R Edwards (1970) is the final volume in the *Bell modern histories*. It is a balanced and comprehensive survey of a momentous period in our national history, concentrating mainly on political matters, but at the same time clarifying the complex social and economic issues and problems that from time to time threatened the social order.

116 '**British history 1870-1914 reconsidered; recent trends in the historiography of the period**' by John Clive is included in the series of bibliographical articles sponsored by the Conference on British Studies. It reviews all the important literature on the period published since the second world war. The author reminds us that 'more and more historians of the recent period have come to see their work as part of an endeavour to understand the structure and articulation of the various parts of modern British society as a whole.' It appeared in *The American historical review* LXVIII (4) July 1963: 987-1009, and was reprinted in *Changing views on British history* (*qv*)

117 '**British history in the nineteenth century and after 1782-1919**' by G M Trevelyan (1937) retains its value as a general narrative of political and social developments at home, in the colonies, and in India. More detailed studies are indicated.

118 'British history since 1926' by C L Mowat (Historical Association, 1960) is a short, highly selective bibliography excluding the military and diplomatic history of the second world war. Otherwise all aspects of modern British history are covered in a chronological and classified sequence.

119 'British history since 1760; a select bibliography' by Ian R Christie, no. 81 in the Historical Association's *Helps for students of history* series, was published in 1970. First comes a short introductory bibliography section followed by the main listing of the standard works and most important monographs, accompanied by brief comments, in a general and three chronological sections, each of which is further subdivided under subject headings. There is an author index.

120 'British monarchy series' published by Batsford provides the general reader with lively and authoritative period histories arranged round successive royal houses. They are copiously illustrated and those who wish to pursue their studies further are well catered for in the annotated bibliographies. Titles: *The Saxon and Norman Kings* by Christopher Brooke; *The Plantagenets* by John Harvey; *The Tudors* by Christopher Morris; *The Stuarts* by J P Kenyon; *The first four Georges* by J H Plumb; and *Hanover to Windsor* by Roger Fulford. They are all available as Fontana paperbacks.

121 'British national archives; government publications sectional List' no 24, revised 1 January 1975, lists all publications issued by the Public Records Offices in London and Belfast, the Scottish Record Office and the House of Lords Record Office.

122 'British overseas expansion and the history of the Commonwealth' by W P Morrell (Historical Association, 1970) deals with a longer period of time and a larger geographical area than most of the association's bibliographies. Yet within its comparatively modest limits it succeeds in listing sections on the first British Empire, the older Commonwealth (Canada, Australia, New Zealand and South Africa), the Commonwealth in Asia (India, Pakistan, Sri Lanka and Malaya), Tropical Africa, the Commonwealth in the Seven Seas, and other topics like Imperial policy and

Commonwealth government and Oceanic enterprise and sea power. Collections of documents and atlases are cited in addition to general treatises and textbooks.

123 'The British political tradition' series published by A and C Black reflects the empirical nature of the discussion of political issues which has been continuing in Britain without stop since the sixteenth century. It was formulated to meet the needs of readers interested in political ideas but who had neither the time, patience, or opportunity, to track down crucial speeches or fugitive pamphlets even if these could be found. Each volume contains an introductory essay by the editor and sufficient explanation to render each extract intelligible. In some instances volumes are concerned with a particular crisis, in others the development of a particular view has been traced over a period of years, and sometimes a recurrent problem has been singled out for attention. Whatever the method the essence of British political thought and discussion in the last two centuries has been well documented with selections of original material from speeches, books, pamphlets, letters, and newspapers. Titles (with editors' names): *The debate of the American revolution 1761-1783* (Max Beloff); *The debate on the French revolution 1789-1800* (Alfred Cobban); *Britain and Europe: Pitt to Churchill 1793-1940* (James Joll); *The conservative tradition* (R J White); *The English radical tradition 1763-1914* (S Maccoby); *The concept of empire: Burke to Attlee 1774-1947* (George Bennett); *The challenge of socialism* (H M Pelling); and, *The liberal tradition: from Fox to Keynes* (Alan Bullock and Maurice Shock). The general editors are Alan Bullock and F W Deakin.

124 'British politics in the nineteenth century' edited by Eugene C Black, published in 1970, is included in Macmillan's *Documentary history of western civilisation* series. The documents selected range from the last years of George III to the last years of Edward VII and touch upon men, events, institutions, and constitutional theory. Political philosophy, imperial and foreign policy are deliberately excluded. The documents are arranged in four chronological sections; each document is prefaced by a short, explanatory introduction setting it in its context and is supported by recommended reading. There is a highly selective general bibliography and an imaginative year by year chronology in vertical columns headed Governments, Domestic events, Cultural highlights, and Imperial and foreign affairs.

125 British Records Association emerged from the British Records Society in 1932 as a national organisation to coordinate and encourage the work of individuals, authorities, societies and institutions interested in the conservation and use of records. Its aims are threefold: to serve as a link between all concerned in the custody, preservation, study and publication of documents; to promote an informed body of opinion on the necessity for preserving records and to advise on the disposal of papers through its Records Preservation Series and to make technical information available in collaboration with the Society of Archivists; and to further the use of records as historical material especially through publication. Its journal is *Archives* (*qv*). Since 1959 it has received a grant in aid for the work of the Record Preservation Section, a centre for the reception and distribution of unwanted documents.

126 'Brut; or the chronicles of England' originally written in French, closing in the year 1333, was a history of England from mythical times. At the end of the 14th century it was translated into English with a continuation down to 1377. Further continuations took it first to 1419 and then to 1461 at which stage it was selected by Caxton to form the basis of his *Chronicles* and thus became the first printed English history. Vergil, Hall, Stow, and Holinshed were all indebted to it. The large number of surviving manuscripts, the frequent use made of it by other writers, and the numerous printed editions in the period 1480-1530, testify that it was probably the most popular history of the 15th and 16th centuries but it was strangely overlooked and it was not until 1906 when it was included in the Early English Text Society series that it began to receive the attention it deserves. The Tudor discussion on the authenticity of the earlier parts of *The Brut* and other British histories is well summarised in T D Kendrick's *British antiquity* (1950).

127 Bryant, Sir Arthur (1899-   ) is the author of a number of extremely popular and readable histories which are eagerly sought after by the book clubs. Historians of the calibre of G M Trevelyan and C V Wedgwood have bestowed lavish praise on his work; other 'academic' historians preserve a reticent silence. He belongs to the J R Green, Winston S Curchill mould, indeed several reviewers have likened his florid prose to Churchill's and have compared their common love of king and country. His works fall naturally into well defined groups. *The story of England* planned to stretch to four volumes, so far encompasses two, *Makers of the realm* (1953) which carries the story to Edward I's reign, and *The age of chivalry* (1963) which covers the fourteenth and fifteenth centuries. In these he confesses to be writing 'for both young and old, for those who know a little of England's past and for those who know scarcely anything at all ... My *Story of England* makes no claim to originality; it merely tells a familiar tale in a new way. It is not a work of scholarship, but only a collation of the scholarship of others ... My history contains fewer names, battles, political events and acts of parliament, but dwells longer on certain deeds and words that stirred the hearts of Englishmen and awoke their imagination.' These words may fairly be taken as representative of the whole Bryant canon but then his sort of eminently readable books, shorn of scholarly paraphernalia distracting to the general reader, has always been accorded an honourable place in the art of writing history. His trilogy on the Napoleonic wars, *The years of endurance 1793-1802, Years of victory 1802-1812,* and *The age of elegance 1812-1822* (1942-1950) concentrates in the first two volumes on the military, naval and diplomatic history of the period with stress on the domestic scene arriving in the third volume. Latterly Sir Arthur has turned to social history, *The medieval foundation* (1966) and *Protestant island* (1967). An earlier biographical trilogy of Samuel Pepys, *The man in the making, The years of peril,* and *The saviour of the navy* (1933-1938) attracted much favourable comment.

128 'Bulletin of the Institute of Historical Research' began publication in 1923 and was issued thrice yearly although it now appears only twice, in May and November. It was intended as a means of communicating the activities of the institute to those engaged in historical research and of ensuring that the knowledge accumulated there was made more widely available. Primarily therefore its function is to provide a record of the work done at the institute thus avoiding competition with other historical journals. And just as the institute itself existed for the promotion of historical research so it was envisaged that the *Bulletin* would add to historical knowledge by publishing addenda and corrigenda to works like the *Dictionary of national biography* and the *New English dictionary* or the collections of historical manuscripts such as *Rymer's foedera*, the *Rotuli parliamentarum*, and the journals of the two houses of parliament, works edited up to 200 years previously and which were not likely to be re-edited in the foreseeable future. The *Bulletin* would also record newly discovered manuscripts. In the matter of current research the *Bulletin* in its earlier years published summaries of theses compiled by research students at the institute and as research activity gradually increased, starting with volume 7, (1929-1930), it carried a feature 'Historical research for university degrees' previously recorded in the Historical Association's journal *History*. Eventually it was decided that *Historical research for university degrees in the United Kingdom* (*qv*) should appear as annual supplements to the *Bulletin* published separately. Today a typical issue carries half a dozen articles, Notes and documents, Historical news (including details of conferences), and the accession and migration of manuscripts. Back numbers of the past two years may be obtained from the Institute and earlier issues from William Dawson and Son Ltd, Back Issue Department, Cannon House, Folkestone, either as original or reproduced copies.

129 Burnet, Gilbert (1643-1715) played a not inconspicuous part in the events leading up to the 1688 revolution and consequently his *History of my own times* remains not only a literary classic but also an indispensable work in understanding those turbulent times despite some omissions and inaccuracies. The most valuable part of the text is obviously that relating events of which he had first hand knowledge but he was not always as fully informed as he supposed. The text itself has a confused history and does not always follow a manuscript surviving in the Bodleian Library. H C Foxcroft's *A supplement to Burnet's History of my own times* (1902) unravels the tangle and includes fragments of Burnet's memoirs upon which much of the history was based.

130 Butterfield, Sir Herbert (1900-   ): Apart from his work in modern European diplomatic history, Professor Butterfield has provided a lengthy corrective to the Namier school, *George III, Lord North, and the people 1779-80* (1949), in which he challenges Namier's methods and conclusions. An early work, *The whig interpretation of history* (1931), comprehensively exposed the fallacies of that particular school of historians. *Man on his past: the study of the history of historical scholarship* (1955) is also essential reading for all those with an interest in historiography. An appreciation of Butterfield as an historian by Sir Dennis Brogan appears in *The diversity of history* (1970), a *festschrift* volume in honour of Sir Herbert which also contains a bibliography of his writings to 1968.

131 '**Calendar of charter rolls**' in six volumes covering the period 1226-1516 were issued by the Public Record Office (1903-1927). Royal charters were the means in the middle ages whereby grants of land and other privileges were confirmed.

132 '**Calendar of close rolls**': almost sixty calendars of this sort, covering the period 1227-1509, have been issued by the Public Record Office. All writs and orders emanating from the crown and addressed to individuals were folded, or closed, hence the name.

133 '**Calendar of fine rolls**': the Public Record Office has published twenty two calendars of this sort covering the period 1272-1509. Fines refer to payments made to the crown for writs, licences, grants and pardons, etc.

134 '**Calendar of letters and papers, foreign and domestic, of the reign of Henry VIII**' edited by J S Brewer, J Gairdner, and R H Brodie, in twenty two volumes, was issued by the Public Record Office 1864-1920. Abstracts of the patent rolls and many other documents not classed as state papers are included.

135 '**Calendar of patent rolls**' for the reigns of Henry III (6 vols), Edward I (4 vols), Edward II (5 vols), Edward III (16 vols), Richard II (7 vols), Henry IV (4 vols), Henry V (2 vols), Henry VI (6 vols), Edward IV, Edward V and Richard III (3 vols), Henry VII (2 vols), Edward VI (6 vols), Philip and Mary (4 vols), and Elizabeth I (6 vols), are published by the Public Record Office. Patent rolls announced royal acts, granting and leasing land, appointments to various offices and presentations to ecclesiastical benefices. So called because they were issued 'open.'

136 'Calendar of state papers and manuscripts relating to English Affairs, existing in the archives and collections of Venice' available from the Public Record Office in thirty eight volumes are of especial interest for the tudor and stuart periods. The reports of the Venetian ambassador in London throw valuable light on contemporary events.

137 'Calendar of state papers, colonial': The Public Record Office has steadily published almost fifty volumes mostly relating to America and the West Indies 1574-1738 over the last 100 years.

138 'Calendar of state papers, domestic': over 100 volumes in this particular category covering the tudor and stuart period 1547-1704 have been issued in the Public Record Office's massive publication programme in the last 120 years.

139 'Calendar of state papers, foreign': these cover the reigns of Edward VI, Mary, and Elizabeth I and were published by the Public Record Office 1861-1950. A list and analysis of those for Elizabeth I was edited by R B Wernham in 2 vols 1964-1969.

140 'Cambridge ancient history,' designed as the first part of a continuous history of the peoples of Europe, was published in twelve volumes 1923-1939. No apology was offered for beginning with the early civilisations of Egypt and Babylon, stated as being of far more importance than the barbarous life of nomadic tribes in Europe itself. In the same fashion as its two predecessors, the *Medieval* and *Modern* histories, each chapter was contributed by a different historian under the guidance of a central group of editors who, having studied the criticism levied against these great cooperative histories, made a virtue out of necessity by declaring that occasionally different writers might express or imply different opinions thereby disturbing the reader's peace of mind. However, this should be regarded as characteristic of the ground being covered. They also voiced the hope that the *History* would be comprehensible to the general reader yet scholarly enough for the professional student. Extremely detailed bibliographies arranged by form and subject for each chapter are to be found at the end of each volume. Five volumes of plates intended primarily to present evidence in pictorial form were issued during the same period. Volumes: I *Egypt and Babylonia to 1500 BC*; II *The Egyptian and Hittite empires to c1000 BC*; III *The Assyrian empire*; IV *The Persian empire and the west*; V *Athens 478-401 BC*; VI *Macedon 401-301 BC*; VII *The Hellenistic monarchies and the rise of Rome*; VIII *Rome and the Mediterranean 218-133 BC*; IX *The Roman republic 133-44 BC*; X *The Augustan empire 44 BC-AD 70*; XI *The imperial peace AD 70-192*; XII *The imperial crisis and recovery AD 193-324*. In the 1950s it was obvious that the first two volumes would need to be completely rewritten in the light of the substantial accumulation of knowledge since the early 1920s. For the same reason each volume would of necessity be divided into two parts. And, instead of waiting until each volume was ready, chapters would be issued as fascicles so that they would be available to readers at the earliest opportunity. Both volumes have now appeared: I (Part One) *Prolegomena and prehistory* (1970); I (Part Two) *Early history of the Middle East* (1971); II (Part One) *History of the Middle East and The Aegean region c1800-1300 BC* (1973); and II (Part Two) *1380-1000 BC* (1975). A new edition of the first volume of plates is in preparation.

141 'Cambridge history of Africa' was first conceived in the 1950s but plans were shelved because serious study of African history had only just been established in the new African universities. In 1966, however, J D Fage and Roland Oliver were commissioned as general editors of the new project. They were immediately confronted with the familiar problems that beset large cooperative histories and in this case these were compounded by the fact that scholars of many nations were still in the throes of exploring many periods of the continent's history. At first the editors were most concerned with the volumes covering the earliest and latest periods: in the former case the results of archaeological discovery threatened to revise opinions almost hourly; in the latter, the ending of colonial rule was swiftly changing traditional historical perspectives. Five volumes, ending in 1875, were planned initially, of which the earliest, *Africa before 500 BC*, would be the last to appear, but in the event eight volumes are now envisaged. The direction of the first five volumes was entrusted to a volume editor who was in close touch with the general editors and who had himself made an outstanding contribution to African history. Contributors to each volume were to be kept to a minimum and each was asked to survey a particular area for the whole of the period covered by that volume, considering not only research completed but also that still in progress, and, if possible, to fill in any *lacunae*. It seems likely that the last three volumes may assume a slightly different pattern with a larger number of shorter chapters each reflecting the contributors' own work and interest. By far the greatest problem for editors and contributors is the incessant publication in the field and the constant substantial revision of draft copy this demands. It transpired that *Vol 4 From c1600 to c1790* was the first volume to be published in 1975. Eight chapters are contributed by scholars in English, Israeli, Tanzanian, and American universities; each chapter concludes with bibliographical essays and discursive comments on source materials. A general bibliography of reference books arranged by chapter is conventionally placed at the end of the volume. *Vol 5 From c1790 to c1870* (1976) mirrors the increasing European activity in trade, exploration, missionary work, and political annexation. The arrangement is regional. The remaining volumes are promised to appear 'at more or less regular intervals.'

142 'Cambridge history of British foreign policy 1738-1919' edited by A W Ward and G P Gooch (3 vols, 1922-1923) discusses the relations of the British Empire, 'the conditions at home and abroad which governed the conduct of those relations, the principals more or less consistently followed in the conduct of them, and the personal influence of the principal British agents responsible.' It admits to a national point of view and openly states it seeks to vindicate British foreign policy against its detractors. Each chapter is contributed by a British scholar and is subdivided into sections on particular aspects or episodes and the work ends with a substantial chapter on the administrative system of the foreign office. Extracts from a number of documents previously unpublished or inaccessible are included in appendices and each volume has a short bibliography designed to complement those to be found in the *Cambridge modern history*.

143 'Cambridge history of India' (1922-1953) follows the familiar Cambridge format although this is perhaps the least satisfactory of all the massive histories. The second volume has never been published, the third attracted a measure of criticism, and a seeming attempt at revision in the 1950's met with an abortive end. Volumes: 1 *Ancient India*; 3 *Turks and Afghans*; 4 *Mughal period*; 5 *British India 1497-1858*; 6 *The Indian Empire 1859-1918* (A 1964 reprint provided an opportunity to add a further ten chapters 1919-1947). Vols 5-6 form Vols 4-5 of the *Cambridge history of the British Empire*. A supplementary volume: the *Indus civilization* first published in 1953, was in fact a revised chapter from Vol 1.

144 'The Cambridge history of the British Empire' (1929-1963) presents the long story of colonization and imperial planning from the tudors to the 1920s. It follows the *Cambridge modern* pattern in that eminent scholars from England and the dominions were invited to cooperate in writing a comprehensive history of the British Empire, a task quite obviously beyond any one man. The aim in the earlier volumes is to show the outlook of the mother country on imperial problems, in the later volumes it is the outlook of each dominion. The hope was to 'exhibit the present stage of knowledge of the subject and lay a foundation on which future generations ... may build.' This hope was fully realised, these volumes are frequently quarried by later historians. As in other Cambridge histories the bibliographies, selected lists of the most important sources both documentary and published, are especially useful, the coverage of official records and parliamentary reports being exceptionally valuable. At one time a companion atlas was envisaged but in the event this did not materialize. Volumes: 1 *The old empire, from the beginnings to 1783*; 2 *Growth of the new empire 1783-1870*; 3 *The Empire—Commonwealth 1870-1919*; 4 *British India 1497-1858*; 5 *Indian Empire 1858-1918*; 6 *Canada and Newfoundland*; 7 pt 1 *Australia*; 7 pt 2 *New Zealand*; 8 *South Africa, Rhodesia and the protectorates*. Vols 4 and 5 form Vols 5 and 6 of the *Cambridge history of India* (*qv*).

145 'Cambridge medieval history' (8 vols, 1911-1936) was planned by J B Bury to cover the entire field of European medieval history and devised along the same lines as the *Cambridge modern*. It was intended to serve the general reader as a clear and interesting narrative, and the student as a summary of ascertained facts with indications (not discussions it was at pains to make clear) of disputed points. In addition, of course, it acts as a standard work of reference. It was a truly international effort, contributors being drawn from over a dozen different countries. A slight innovation from the *Cambridge modern* is an introduction, in the form of a general historical sketch designed to give an overall view of the period in relation to those which follow it, being added to volumes three to seven. A portfolio of illustrative maps was issued in conjunction with each volume as it appeared. Volume VI is largely given over to general chapters on trade, warfare, architecture, religion and learning, and similar topics, which transcend the chronological limits of the various volumes. Long delays occurred in publication, the 1914-1918 war prevented volume III from appearing until 1922, and the whole project seemed overburdened by the natural deaths of both editors and contributors, and eventually the eight volumes took a quarter of a century to complete. Volumes: I *The christian Roman Empire and the foundation of the teutonic kingdoms*; II *The rise of the Saracens and the foundation of the Western Empire*; III *Germany and the western empire*; IV *The eastern Roman Empire*; V *Contest of empire and papacy*; VI *Victory of the papacy*; and VIII *The close of the middle ages*. Over forty years after it was first published in 1923 volume IV was entirely replanned and rewritten to take account of the results of the immense amount of research completed during that time. The original volume was jettisoned with regret 'but each generation must write its own histories: hence the complete abandonment of the old volume IV.' In this new two part volume, *The Byzantine Empire Part I Byzantium and its neighbours* (1966) and *Part II Government, church and civilization* (1967), more emphasis was placed on administration, the arts, social life, literature and science, and much more space devoted to the political history of the empire. In 1939 C W Previte-Orton, one of the editors of the full set of volumes, was asked to write a concise version intended as a continuous history suitable for students requiring an overall view of medieval Europe without losing the essential value of the original work as a source of reference. He was afforded complete discretion regarding the use of words and phrases employed in the parent volumes. *The shorter Cambridge medieval history* was eventually published in two volumes in 1952: Vol I *The later Roman Empire to the twelfth century* and Vol II *The twelfth century to the renaissance*. A bow was made in the direction of the general reader, who it was considered would be unlikely to have reference works close to hand, by the inclusion of illustrations and genealogical tables as well as maps. But the omission of any guide to further reading seems a misguided economy.

146 'The Cambridge modern history' (12 vols, 1902-1910). When, in 1896, the syndics of the Cambridge University Press decided to publish a general English universal history they immediately turned to Lord Acton, then Regius Professor of Modern History. In October he presented a detailed report: 'I propose to divide the history of the last 400 years into short chapters, averaging thirty pages, each complete in itself, and dealing with one topic, or a single group of events, accurately defined. And I would distribute them among the largest number of available writers, inviting every English historian who is competent, to contribute at least a chapter. It would be history not as it appears to the generality of instructed men, and is taught all the world over, but as each of the several parts is known to the man who knows it best. There would be a clean text, without footnotes, or foreign quotations, or references to particular authorities. The name of the author would be the reader's security for obtaining, without discussion or parade, the most perfect narrative that any English or American scholar can supply, in the appointed space ... It is a unique opportunity of recording in the way most useful to the greatest number, the fullness of the knowledge which the nineteenth century is about to bequeath. A mere reproduction of accepted facts would fall below the occasion, and behind the memorable date.' There existed, he continued, a situation in which the supply of documents from the recently opened archives of Europe exceeded the supply of histories. 'The honest student finds himself continually deserted, retarded, misled by the classics of historical literature, and has to hew his own way through multitudinous transactions, periodicals and official publications ... By the judicious division of labour we should be able ... to bring home to every man the last document, and the ripest conclusion of international research. Ultimate history we cannot have in this generation; but we can dispose of conventional history ... now that all information is within reach, and every problem has become capable of solution. If we treat history as a progressive science, and lean especially on that side of it, the question will arise how we justify our departure from ancient ways, and how we satisfy the world that there is reason and method in our innovations ... To meet this difficulty we must provide a copious, accurate catalogue of well digested authorities ... Our principle would be to supply help to students, not material to historians. But in critical places we must indicate minutely the sources we follow, and must refer not only to the important books, but to articles in periodical works, and even to original documents, and to transcripts in libraries ... Therefore the essential elements of the plan I propose for consideration are these: Division of subjects among many specially qualified writers; Highest pitch of knowledge without the display; Distinction between the organic unity of general history and the sum of national histories, as the principle for selecting the distributing matter; Proportion between historic thought and historic fact; and Chart and compass for the coming century.' Tragically, Lord Acton himself never contributed a chapter before his death in 1902 although the plan was entirely his. A particular historical event of single importance was chosen as the theme for each volume, a method which would free the work 'from the necessity of adhering rigorously to the precise limits of chronology or geography.' Throughout the successive periods strict adherence was insisted upon to the conception of modern history as a single entity and restricted to political events, economics, and social life. In accordance with Acton's report, footnotes and quotations were severely discouraged but each chapter was equipped with a full bibliography, sometimes of quite staggering proportions. Professional reaction at the time of publication and subsequently, has been mixed. A genuine admiration for the scholarship displayed was coupled with criticism of cooperative history in practice. Charges of duplication, overlapping, and repetition were all levied with some justification. In the 1960s the work was replaced by the *New Cambridge modern (qv)* but it remains doubtful whether the new work will ever attain the same degree of authority the original series achieved when first published. The full story of its beginnings may be read in *The*

Cambridge modern history. An account of its origin, authorship and production (1907). 'Acton and the CMH Republication and reassessment,' published in the *TLS* 19th February 1971 to mark its reissue in a library edition, is a fine critique. Volumes: *The renaissance; The reformation; The wars of religion; The thirty years war; The age of Louis XIV; The eighteenth century; The United States; The French revolution; Napoleon; The restoration; The growth of nationalism; The latest age.* Vol XIII *Genealogical tables and lists and general index* appeared in 1911. *The Cambridge modern history atlas* (1912) is arranged according to the order of narrative followed in the main work and includes all the place names mentioned. At the same time it stands as a complete atlas of modern history in its own right, illustrating the progress of European history from the fifteenth century and the history of colonial expansion. A substantial introduction (118 pages) complete with its own index of local names is followed by 141 coloured maps and a general index.

147 'Cambridge studies in medieval life and thought,' a series of learned monographs inaugurated by G G Coulton in 1920, eventually proceeded to fourteen volumes before the war. Perhaps the most notable of these were Coulton's own *Five centuries of religion* and Eileen Power's *English nunneries.* In the 1950s the series was revived under the general editorship of David Knowles and then in 1969 a third series with Walter Ullman as editor commenced which, it is hoped, 'will offer in a single collection some of the best work now being done by the younger medievalists.' If anything the volumes so far published tend to be even more esoteric than the two preceding series.

148 Camden Society for the publication of early historical and literary remains was formed in 1838 with the general object of perpetuating and rendering accessible 'whatever is valuable but at present little known amongst the materials for the civil, ecclesiastical, or literary history of the United Kingdom' to be achieved by the publication of historical documents, letters and ancient poems, which no ordinary trade publisher in his right mind would risk handling. At first there was no scarcity of members either private or institutional, the society had been formed at a time when antiquarian curiosity had achieved respectability, joining hands with university scholarship in a sustained effort to rescue old texts and records from obscurity. But in time resources dwindled, an unfortunate project to publish a general index to the society's publications foundered disastrously, the membership declined, and when a suggestion was floated in 1896 that the society should merge with the Royal Historical Society on the realistic proposition that their combined membership could support both societies' publications without undue strain there were few voices raised in opposition. In 1897 the Camden Society accordingly forsook its separate identity. A short history appears in *The Royal Society 1868-1968* by R A Humphreys (1969). *Publications*: a large number of volumes of texts together with substantial introductions and editorial notes were published in the 60 years of the society's separate existence. The Old Series 1-115 appeared 1838-1872; The New Series 1-62 from 1871 to the society's demise in 1897, the last three being published by the Royal Historical Society. The Camden 3rd Series 1-104 were published 1900-1963, and the 4th Series continues from 1964. *A descriptive catalogue of the works of the Camden Society: stating the nature of their principal contents, the period of time to which they relate, the dates of their composition, their manuscript sources, authors, and editors* by John Gough Nichols was published in 1862 and updated in 1872 and 1881 for the first series only. A full list of publications 1838-1868 is printed in *A centenary guide to the publications of the Royal Historical Society 1868-1968 and of the former Camden Society 1838-1897* published in 1968.

149 'Canada; a short history' by Gerald S Graham published in Hutchinson's *University library* in 1950, is an interpretative survey of Canadian history 'from outside rather than within North America' and designed 'to give as much weight to European as to continental or indigenous influences'. It ranges in scholarly and succinct fashion from the political and economic foundations of French Canada to the emergence of the dominion as an influential voice in world affairs in the post war period. There is a brief reference list of books for further reading.

150 'Canada; a story of challenge' by J M S Careless (CUP/ Macmillan, 1959) presents the major facts of the dominion's history with special reference to the influence of France, Britain and the United States and the interrelationship of the English and French speaking communities. Incredibly, there is no bibliography.

151 'The Canadian centenary series' (Toronto: McClelland and Stewart, London OUP) is a history of Canada in eighteen volumes devised to mark the Centenary of the confederation, and is intended as a balanced, interpretative, varied, and comprehensive political, economic, and social history to satisfy the needs of both general readers and scholars. It is a cooperative work, each volume being written by a leading Canadian historian. Impressive bibliographies to each volume add distinction to what is destined to become a standard authoritative series. Volumes: *Early voyages and Northern approaches* by Tryggvi J Oleson; *The beginnings of New France 1524-1663* by Marcel Trudel; *Canada under Louis XIV 1663-1701* by W J Eccles; *New France 1702-1743* by Jean Blain; *New France 1744-1760* by G F S Stanley; *Quebec 1760-1791* by Hilda Neatby; *Upper Canada 1784-1841* by Gerald M Craig; *Lower Canada 1792-1841* by Fernand Oullet; *The Atlantic provinces 1712-1857* by W S MacNutt; *The Union of the Canadas 1841-1857* by J M S Careless; *The fur trade and the northwest to 1857* by E E Rich; *The critical years 1857-1873* by W L Morton; *Canada 1874-1896* by P B Waite; *Canada 1891-1921* by R Craig Brown and G R Cook; *Canada 1922-1939* by Roger Graham; *The opening of the Canadian North 1870-1914* by Morris I Zaslow; *The north 1914-1967* by Morris I Zaslow; *Canada 1939-1967* by D G Creighton. Publication in paperback has commenced.

152 Canadian Historical Association has as its objectives the encouragement of historical research and public interest in history; the preservation of historical sites and buildings, documents, relics, and other significant heirlooms of the past; and the publication of historical studies as circumstances permit. It already publishes the papers read at annual meetings and the Canadian Historical Association Booklets, of which thirty or so have so far been published, designed to provide concise accounts of specific historical problems for general readers, for teachers, and for specialist historians.

153 'Canadian historical review' (1920-   ), published quarterly by the University of Toronto Press, continues *The review of historical publications relating to Canada* which flourished 1896-1919, and serves two major purposes: as an outlet for scholarly articles, and to provide information necessary to keep historians abreast of developments across the country. In addition to the usual contents, each issue contains a feature, 'Recent publications relating to Canada' in which all new publications in this field are listed in broad categories, eg, 'Canada's commonwealth and international relations,' 'History of Canada,' 'Provincial and local history' and then by other subjects. Five cumulated index volumes, including two for the older journal, spanning the years 1896-1949, have been published, providing a guide to articles and reviews, and also author and subject references to the titles recorded in the 'Recent publications' feature.

154 'Canadian journal of history/Annales canadiennes d'histoire' (1966-   ) publishes contributions in all fields of history other than Canadian three times a year. Contents include articles, reviews and notes of events. Published by Journal of History Ltd with subsidies from University of Saskatchewan and the Canada Council.

155 'Canadiana before 1867' is a reprint series of historically significant works issued under the auspices of La Maison des Sciences de l'Homme in Paris; the Humanities Research Council of Canada; The Social Science Research Council, Ottawa; and Toronto Public Library. All the sixty odd titles are listed in *A bibliography of canadiana* (1934) edited by F M Stanton and Marie Tremaine and reissued by Toronto Public Library in 1965. Orders and enquiries related to the series should be addressed either to S R Publishers Ltd, East Ardsley, Wakefield, Yorkshire, England, or The Johnson Reprint Corporation, 111 Fifth Avenue, New York, NY 10003.

156 Capgrave, John (1393-1464) an Augustinian friar of Lynn in Norfolk was a voluminous writer whose *Liber de illustribus Henricis* (1444) so called to honour the reigning monarch includes some Holy Roman Emperors besides the first six English kings bearing the name. He professes to maintain a strict impartiality but in fact tenders a sycophantic eulogy of the Lancastrian line. His *Chronicle of England* which comes to an abrupt end in the year 1417 was mainly derived from Thomas of Walsingham.

157 **'Cardinal documents in British history'** is a collection of source materials relating to political, constitutional, and legal aspects of British history compiled by R L Schuyler and C C Weston and published in paperback form as an Anvil Original by Van Nostrand in 1961. There are two parts: England and the United Kingdom includes extracts ranging from Bede's *Ecclesiastical history* concerning Augustine's mission in 597 tó *Let us face the future*, the Labour Party's manifesto in 1945; The British Empire-Commonwealth starts with a passage from Hakluyt's *Discourse* (unpublished until 1877) and closes with part of Harold Macmillan's famous Wind of change speech in 1960.

158 **Carlyle, Thomas** (1795-1881) was, in modern terminology, addicted to the cult of personality: history was the story of heroes, great men who shaped the world's destiny along with their own. Two works in particular, *Oliver Cromwell's letters and speeches* (1845) and *The history of Friedrich II of Prussia, called Frederick the Great* (6 vols, 1858-1865) epitomize his belief that history is nothing more than the biographies of great men. From there it is a fatally easy step to their glorification and to the doctrine that might is right. He retains his own special place in English historiography if only for his rescue of Cromwell from obloquy. His early masterpiece *The French revolution* (3 vols, 1837), at the same time a dramatic and colourful narrative yet riddled with his own dark torments, still ranks as one of the great works of English literature although its historical value is restricted by his inadequate understanding of the period.

159 **'The cartoon history of Britain,'** compiled by Michael Wynn Jones and published by Tom Stacey in 1971, presents British politics from 1720 (the year of the South Sea Bubble) up to date through the satirical and sometimes scurrilous eyes of the cartoonist. From Hogarth to Osbert Lancaster, Gillray to Giles, the Cruikshanks to Cummings, John Tenniel to Vicky, savage caricature and gentle irony illuminate national history over two hundred and fifty years.

160 Cass, Frank & Co Ltd, have over the past decade excelled in publishing in reprint form long out of print books of prime importance for new university courses in specific area studies. Standard and classic texts, especially travellers' journals, have steadily poured from the press and their back list now contains several hundred titles. Of particular interest are the *African travels and narratives* series designed to republish a select corpus of travel literature, and the *West Indies studies* series presenting a similar comprehensive selection of early accounts and narratives. It is fair to say that without this publishing programme many university courses now running could never have started. Other areas now covered are Russia, the Levant, Islam, Asia, Australasia and the Pacific, and Latin America. Informative catalogues may be obtained from 67 Great Russell Street, London WC1 3BT.

161 Central Africa Historical Association is an overseas branch of the Historical Association. Its publication programme includes pamphlets on African history and also an annual journal *Rhodesian history.*

162 'The century of revolution 1603-1714' by Christopher Hill (1961) is the fifth volume in Nelson's *History of England.* It is an attempt to comprehend what happened to the structure of England in that time, to communicate in outline the all embracing transformation of English life which unfolded so dramatically. 'The object of this book is to try to understand the changes which set England on the path of parliamentary government, economic advance and imperialist foreign policy, of religious toleration and scientific progress.'

163 'Chambers atlas of world history' comprises thirty one maps relating to the ancient world, twenty four to the medieval period, thirty eight to the modern era, and fifteen to the twentieth century. The maps are brightly coloured and are designed to illustrate the movement and progress of history. A full unabridged paperback edition was issued in 1975. Barnes and Noble are the United States agents.

164 The Champlain Society, named after Samuel de Champlain (1567-1635), explorer and first governor of French Canada, was founded in the early years of the century as a publishing society to make available a wide range of rare and inaccessible material related to the history of Canada. The publications of the Champlain Society were issued to members as follows:

First Series (1907-   )

1 *The history of New France* by Marc Lescarbot.

2 *The description and natural history of the coasts of North America (Acadia)* by Nicholas Denys.

3 *Documents relating to the seignorial tenure in Canada, 1598-1854.*

4 *The logs of the conquest of Canada.*

5 *New relation of Gaspesia; with the customs and religion of the Gaspesian Indians* by Chretien Le Clercq.

6 *A journey from Prince of Wales's Fort in Hudson's Bay to the Northern Ocean in the years 1769, 1770, 1771 and 1772* by Samuel Hearne.

7 *The history of New France Vol II* by Marc Lescarbot.

8-10 *An historical journal of the campaigns in North America for the years 1757, 1758, 1759, and 1760* by John Knox.

11 *The history of New France Vol III* by Marc Lescarbot.

12 *David Thompson's narrative of his explorations in Western America, 1784-1812.*

13-15 *Select British documents of the Canadian war of 1812.*

16 *Journals and letters of Pierre Gaultier de Varennes de la Verendrye and his sons, with correspondence between the governors of Canada and the French court, touching the search for the Western Sea.*

17 *Select British documents of the Canadian war of 1812 Vol III Pt 2.*

18 *Documents relating to the early history of Hudson Bay.*

19 *John McLean's notes of a twenty-five years' service in the Hudson's Bay territory.*

20 *Relation of the voyage to Port Royal in Acadia or New France* by Sieur de Diéreville.

21 *Journals of Samuel Hearne and Philip Turner.*

22 *Documents relating to the North West Company.*

23 *Travels in the interior inhabited parts of North America in the years 1791 and 1792* by Patrick Campbell.

24 *The Hargrave correspondence 1821-1843.*

25 *The long journey to the country of the Hurons* by Gabriel Sagard-Theodat.

26 *The journal of Captain James Colnett aboard the Argonaut from April 26, 1789 to November 3, 1791.*

27 *Loyalist narratives from Upper Canada.*

28 *The letters of Letitia Hargrave.*

29 *The diary of Simeon Perkins 1766-1780.*

30-31 *The history of Canada, or New France* by Francois Du Creux.

32 *The Walker expedition to Quebec 1711.*

33 *Dufferin-Carnarvon correspondence, 1874-1878.*

34 *Red River journal and other papers relative to the Red River resistance of 1869-1870.*

35 *Lord Selkirk's diary, 1803-1804; a journal of his travels in British North America and the North Eastern United States.*

36 *The diary of Simeon Perkins 1780-1789.*

37 *Records of the Nile voyageurs 1884-1885. The Canadian voyageur contingent in the Gordon relief expedition.*

38 *The Canadian journal of Lady Aberdeen 1893-1898.*

39 *The diary of Simeon Perkins 1790-1796.*

40 *David Thompson's narrative 1784-1812.*

41-42 *Diary and selected papers of Chief Justice William Smith 1784-1793.*

43 *The Diary of Simeon Perkins 1797-1803.*

44 *The papers of the Palliser expedition 1857-1860.*

45 *Journal of a voyage on the North West Coast of North America during the years 1811, 1812, 1813 and 1814* by Gabriel Franchere.

46 *The journal of Major John Norton 1816.*

47 *Telegrams of the North-West campaign 1885.*

48 *Customs of the American Indians compared with the customs of primitive times* by Father Joseph Francois Lafitan.

The Works of Samuel de Champlain in six volumes plus a boxed portfolio of plates and maps appeared as an unnumbered series 1922-1936.

Ontario Series: The provincial government of Ontario invited the society to prepare and publish a separate documentary series of volumes relating to the history of the province in the 1950s. The government undertook to defray publishing costs and editorial expenses; the first made its appearance in 1957.

1 *The valley of the Trent.*

2 *Royal Fort Frontenac.*

3 *Kingston before the war of 1812.*

4 *The Windsor border region. Canada's southernmost frontier.*

5 *The town of York 1793-1815 a collection of documents of early Toronto.*

6 *Muskoka and Haliburton 1615-1875 a collection of documents.*

7 *The valley of the Six Nations a collection of documents on the Indian lands of the Grand River.*

9 *Thunder Bay District 1821-1892 a collection of documents.*

In the 1930's the society agreed to publish an annual volume of documents in collaboration with the Hudson's Bay Record Society (*qv*). Twelve of these were published 1938-1949 after which publication continued independently by the Record Society.

1 *Journal of occurances in the Athabasca department by George Simpson, 1820 and 1821, and report.*

2 *Colin Robertson's correspondence book, September 1817 to September 1822.*

3 *Minutes of council Northern Department of Rupert Land 1821-31.*

4, 6-7 *The letters of John McLoughlin from Fort Vancouver to the governor and committee.*

5, 8-9 *Minutes of the Hudson's Bay Company 1671-1674, 1679-1682, 1682-1684.*

10 *Part of dispatch from George Simpson Esqr, Governor of Ruperts Land.*

11 *Copy-book of letters outward 29 May 1680—5 July 1687.*

12 *James Isham's observations on Hudson's Bay, 1743.*

Facsimile editions of the first thirty six volumes of the main series are available from the Greenwood Press, 51 Riverside Avenue, Westport, Connecticut 06880, USA, as is a microfiche edition of the thirty six volumes as a total entity. Enquiries from the United Kingdom and Europe should be directed to Westport Library Services, 3 Henrietta Street, London, WC2E 8LU.

165 'Changing views on British history; essays on historical writing since 1939' were edited for the Conference on British Studies (*qv*) by Elizabeth Chapin Furber and published by Harvard University Press in 1966. The essays were sponsored by the conference and first appeared in a number of learned journals.

A preface contributed by the editor presents a swift survey of the development of historiography over twenty five years and concludes, 'apart from obvious areas ... the impression gained is that the great bulk of work reflects a largely insular point of view ... In all periods there is room for more exploration of common problems awaiting solution by the comparative method.' Essays (all of which are treated separately) include: 'From Hengist and Horsa to Edward of Caernavon' by Bryce Lyon; 'High history or hack history: England in the later middle ages' by Margaret Hastings; 'The taste for Tudors since 1940' by Lacey Baldwin Smith; 'English history 1558-1640' by Perez Zagorin; 'Writings on Oliver Cromwell since 1929' by Paul H Hardacre; 'The later Stuarts (1660-1714)' by Robert Walcott; 'Early hanoverian England (1714-1716)' by William A Bultmann; 'The reign of George III in recent historiography' by Jean Hecht; 'England and Wales 1820-1870 in recent historiography' by Roger W Prouty; 'British history 1870-1914 reconsidered' by John Clive; 'Some recent writings on twentieth-century Britain' by Henry R Winkler; and 'The British Empire and Commonwealth in recent historiography' by Philip D Curtin. Oxford University Press are the UK publishers.

166 'Chronicles and annals a brief outline of their origins and growth' by R L Poole (1926) describes how chronicles were written in the middle ages. It is a slight work based on some long vacation lectures in Oxford.

167 'The chronicles of America series' edited by Allen Johnson and published by the university presses of Yale and Oxford 1918-1921 in fifty volumes provides an authoritative introduction to American history for the general reader and college student. Six additional titles were issued in 1950 edited by Allan Nevins. Each volume concludes with a descriptive bibliographical note. Titles: *The red man's continent* (Ellsworth Huntington); *The Spanish conquerors* (Irving Berdine Richman); *Elizabethan sea dogs* (William Woods); *Crusaders of New France* (William Bennett Munroe); *Pioneers of the old south* (Mary Johnston); *The fathers of New England* (Charles M Andrews); *Dutch and English on the Hudson* (Maud Wilder Goodwin); *The quaker colonies* (Sydney G Fisher); *Colonial folkways* (Charles M Andrews); *The conquest of*

New France (George M Wrong); The eve of the revolution (Carl Becker); Washington and his comrades in arms (George M Wrong); The fathers of the constitution (Max Farrand); Washington and his colleagues (Henry Jones Ford); Jefferson and his colleagues (Allen Johnson); John Marshall and the constitution (Edward S Corwin); The fight for a free sea (Ralph D Paine); Pioneers of the old southwest (Constance Lindsay Skinner); The old northwest and The reign of Andrew Jackson (both by Frederic Austin Ogg); The paths of inland commerce (Archer B Hulbert); Adventurers of Oregon (Constance Lindsay Skinner); The Spanish border lands (Herbert E Bolton); Texas and the Mexican war (Nathaniel W Stevenson); The forty-niners (Stewart Edward White); The passing of the frontier (Emerson Hough); The cotton kingdom (William E Dodd); The anti-slavery crusade (Jesse Macy); Abraham Lincoln and the union and The day of the confederacy (both by Nathaniel W Stephenson); Captains of the civil war (William Wood); The sequel of Appomattox (Walter Lynwood Fleming); The American spirit in education (Edwin E Slosson); The American spirit in literature (Bliss Perry); Our foreigners (Samuel P Orth); The old merchant marine (Ralph D Paine); The age of invention (Holland Thompson); The age of big business (Burton J Hendrick); The armies of labor (Samuel P Orth); The masters of capital (John Moody); The new south (Holland Thompson); The boss and the machine (Samuel P Orth); The Cleveland era (Henry Jones Ford); The agrarian crusade (Solon J Buck); The path of empire (Carl Russell Fish); Theodore Roosevelt and his times (Harold Howland); Woodrow Wilson and the world war (Charles Seymour); The Canadian dominion (Oscar D Skelton); The Hispanic nations of the New World (William R Shepherd); From Versailles to the new deal (Harold V Faulkner); The era of Franklin D Roosevelt (D W Brogan); The struggle for survival (Elliot Janeway); War for the world (Fletcher Pratt); The United States in a chaotic world and The new deal and world affairs (both by Allan Nevins).

168 'Chronicon ex Chronicis,' or the Worcester Chronicle is a history of England beginning with the creation and ending in 1140, originally commissioned by Bishop Wulfstan. It revived the Anglo-Saxon chronicle annalistic arrangement and at first it was merely a compilation from acknowledged authorities but after

1121 its value as an independent source in its own right increased as the writer recorded contemporary events, sometimes adding local detail. It was published in the same manner as the *Anglo-Saxon chronicle*, copies being sent to other monasteries where it was copied, edited, and amended to suit local needs.

169 'Chronology of African history' by G S P Freeman-Grenville (OUP 1973) displays in tabular fashion the principal events and dates in African history 1000 BC-1971. Six columns across the double page note the migration of peoples, the principal dynasties, wars and treaties, the emergence of modern states etc, in Egypt and North Africa, western, central, eastern, southern Africa, and events relating to Africa in the rest of the world.

170 'Chronology of the modern world; 1763 to the present time' (Barrie and Rockliff, 2nd ed, 1969) by Neville Williams was the first of a series of chronologies which not only serve as comprehensive dictionaries of dates from the year 800 AD onwards but also place events and achievements in the arts and sciences in their historical context. On each left hand page political events are listed under exact calendar dates, on the right hand page opposite sections list in turn achievements in politics, economics, law and education; science, technology and discovery; scholarship; philosophy and religion; art, sculpture and architecture; music; literature; the press; drama and entertainment; sport; statistics; and births and deaths. A very full index accommodates entries for persons, places and subjects. Other titles on exactly similar lines are *Chronology of the expanding world 1492-1762* (1969) also by Neville Williams and *Chronology of the medieval world 800-1491* (1972) by R L Storey.

171 Churchill, Sir Winston (1874-1965). What is so startling about Churchill's histories is not that they are so readable but, in such a busy active life, they were ever written at all. His stature as a historian relies on a comparatively few but highly successful works: two biographies, one of his father, *Lord Randolph Churchill*, 2 vols, (1906), the other, *Marlborough: His life and times*, 4 vols, (1913-1938) openly intended to rescue his illustrious ancestor from Macaulay's denigrations; his chronicles of the shattering world wars of the twentieth century, *The world crisis*, 4 vols

72

(1923-1927) and *The second world war*, 6 vols (1948-1954); and also *A history of the English-speaking peoples*, 4 vols (1956-1958) stressing the common heritage of the British and American people in the hope they would continue the close cooperation especially evidenced in the 1939-1945 war. His claim as a historian has encountered some doubts because he employed research workers and consulted academics before he started to write. Nobody, however could reasonably question the authentic Churchillian prose style nurtured on his reading of Gibbon and Macaulay whilst a cavalry subaltern in India. *The world crisis* and *The second world war* may indeed be autobiography masquerading as history but not since Julius Caesar has a man of action and affairs so masterly narrated events in which he himself played so predominant a part. *Churchill as historian* (1968) by Maurice Ashley, one of his research assistants in the thirties, analyses Churchill's methods of writing history and examines his work.

172 Clarendon, Edward Hyde, Earl of (1609-1674) played a prominent part in the affairs of the nation from the Long Parliament, through the civil wars and *interregnum* and on to the post-restoration era before he fell from grace in 1667 and went into exile. He then resumed a history originally embarked upon in 1646 and combined it with some chapters of autobiography, the final work, *History of the rebellion and civil wars in England begun in the year 1641*, being published posthumously 1702-1704. This is obviously of prime importance to later historians examining the period, but, despite his ambition to leave a strictly impartial account, the *History* is marred at times by his own political prejudices, and he sometimes indulges in that inescapable use of hindsight that afflicts statesmen when writing their memoirs. Nevertheless, his account makes splendid history and it is enriched with acute observations on the leading figures of the times based on a profound intuitive knowledge of human nature. Selected extracts from the *History* were published by OUP in their *World's classics* series in 1955.

173 'Classics of British historical literature' series published by the University of Chicago Press consist of abridged versions with modern introductions of famous histories long out of print. The latest titles are E A Freeman's *History of the Norman Conquest* and David Hume's *History of England*.

174 Collingwood, R G (1889-1943) is best known as a historian for his volume *Roman Britain* in the Oxford History of England and for *The idea of history*, published posthumously, 'an essay in the philosophy of history' or 'a philosophical inquiry into the nature of history regarded as a special type or form of knowledge ... leaving aside ... the further question how that inquiry will affect other departments of philosophical study.' The major part of *The idea of history* is concerned with an historical account of how the modern idea of history developed from Herodotus to the twentieth century, the second section consists of a philosophical reflection on the nature, matter and method of history. Published by OUP, it is also available as a paperback.

175 'The Colonial and Imperial Conferences 1887-1911; a study in imperial organisation' by John Edward Kendle (Longmans, 1967) is published for The Royal Commonwealth Society as one of their *Imperial studies* series. It provides a detailed account of the formation and development of the conference system concentrating on the post Boer war period. The respective influences of the colonial office staff, the political leaders of the dominions and the Round Table Movement are closely investigated. As is to be expected of a book which has emerged from a doctoral thesis, it is based largely on archival resources which are indicated in the extensive bibliography arranged in four sections under manuscript sources, printed primary sources, secondary sources, and unpublished theses.

176 'The colonial history series' published by Dawsons of Pall Mall comprises reprints of mainly nineteenth century works long out of print. Titles include *The colonization of Australia 1829-42 The Wakefield experiment in Empire Building* by R C Mills (1915); *History of the colonies of the British Empire* by R M Martin (1843); *Ashantee and the Gold Coast* by John Beecham (1841); and the *Proceedings of the Association for Promoting The Discovery of the Interior Parts of Africa*.

177 'The colonial period of American history' by C M Andrews (Yale University Press/OUP, 4 vols, 1934-1938) approaches events from the English point of view in the long held conviction that 'to place the colonies in their rightful historical setting and so to discover what colonial history is all about it would be necessary to reexamine the evidence from the natural course of historical development—disregarding all preoccupations based on later events,' thus according a new perspective to the period by emphasising the role of the mother country in shaping events and stressing that the colonies were not independent states. Previous historians had never 'seemed willing to believe that England's relations with the colonies were determined by nothing more sinister than an instinctive and self-protective effort to ensure her own national stability and security … '. It was a salutary reappraisal.

178 'Colonialism in Africa' (CUP 5 vols 1969-1975) edited by L H Gann and Peter Duignan, Senior Fellows, Hoover Institution, Stanford University, is intended to serve the specialist as well as the general reader by summing up the knowledge available of the impact of European imperialism on Africa south of the Sahara. It also presents hitherto unpublished material based on original research. Some contributors outline the state of knowledge in their particular subjects, others present new material, whilst still others rescrutinize conventional conclusions. Published when new generations of scholars are attempting to write African history from an African viewpoint, and at a time when enormous quantities of material are being released from European and African archives, this set of volumes attempts to synthesize research for those historians not terribly well acquainted with periods or topics outside their own specialities, or in unfamiliar languages. Vols 1 and 2 *History and politics of colonialism 1870-1914, 1914-1960,* strike a balance between a Eurocentric and an Afrocentric approach to imperialism, providing an analysis and summary of the major problems. Vol 3 *Profiles of change* offers additional information on the social aspects of colonial Africa; Vol 4 *The economics of colonialism* is self explanatory. Vol 5 *A bibliographical guide to colonialism in sub-Saharan Africa* is an excellent literature guide often acquired separately by libraries. Although it emphasises historical material it also cites works in other disciplines, notably anthropology. In the light of the heavy publishing programme in the production of African reference books now coping with scholarly demands, it is thought by the compilers that this will be the last single volume survey before more specialized bibliographies on particular colonial powers, regions, or topics are prepared. The guide is selective but it should prove sufficient to direct students and research workers through the daunting mass of colonial literature. Impressive outlines of archive and library resources, together with a review of periodi-´ cals, government documents, library catalogues, and lists of theses are provided, and much unfamiliar material in French, German, Italian, Portuguese and Afrikaans is presented. It is arranged in three sections: Guide to reference materials and the libraries and archives in western Europe and the United States; a subject guide to the literature; and an area guide arranged by colonial power, region, and country, each colonial section being divided into atlases, periodicals, bibliographies, and reference works. Critical comments on these items indicate their worth.

179 'The Commonwealth' by Nicholas Mansergh, published in Weidenfeld's *History of civilisation* series (1969), is concerned in general with the origins, development, pattern, and experiences of the commonwealth and, more specifically, with its contribution to political thought. 'The object is not detailed narrative but interpretation and analysis against a chronological background.' It is divided into three parts: 'The foundation members and the nature of their association,' the developing relations between Great Britain and the 'old' dominions; 'The British Commonwealth of Nations 1914-1947,' the creation of the Irish Free State, the problem of India, and economic affairs; and 'The commonwealth,' the break-up of empire, the end of the colonial period, and the constitutional position of the crown. It is equipped with the usual scholarly appendages: detailed chapter notes and an extensive bibliography, maps, and numerous illustrations.

180 'Commonwealth; a history of the British Commonwealth of Nations' by H Duncan Hall (Van Nostrand, 1971) is a massive quarto of over 1000 pages. The author has examined the minutes and proceedings of the various colonial and imperial conferences from 1887 onwards including many unpublished documents in an attempt to focus on the commonwealth as a political institution. Those matters regularly occupying the top of the agenda, political and constitutional relations, foreign affairs and defence, capture his closest attention. Seventy pages of notes and references, an appendix of the text of significant documents, and a bibliography which includes the reports and minutes of the conferences 1887-1937 form an impressive addition to the scholarly apparatus.

181 'Commonwealth history' is an annotated booklist prepared for the *Commonwealth in books* exhibition held at Australia House, London, in April 1968 and published jointly by the National Book League and the Commonwealth Institute. All the titles included were displayed at the exhibition and were in print at the time. Only books on the overseas commonwealth were exhibited. The arrangement follows a geographical pattern.

182 The Commonwealth Institute Library and Resource Centre, in consultation with the Librarian of the Royal Commonwealth Society, compiles a number of annotated and classified book lists variously known as 'Commonwealth bibliographies' or 'Selected reading lists for advanced study.' *The Commonwealth a basic annotated bibliography for students, librarians and general readers* compiled by Christiane Keane (Commonwealth bibliographies no 1, 1974) also gives details of items suitable for schools and colleges including Teachers' guides to study resources and other institute publications on sale in the institute shop. Copies of all Commonwealth bibliographies may be obtained gratis from the Librarian, Commonwealth Institute, Kensington High Street, London W8 6NQ.

183 'A complete history of England' *with the lives of all the kings and queens thereof from the earliest account of time to the death of his late majesty William III containing a faithful relation of all affairs of state ecclesiastical and civil,* published in three folio volumes in 1706, was the outcome of a suggestion made by Sir William Temple to a group of London booksellers in 1695 that a collection of the works of well known historical writers should be made to form a continuous history of England. Volume I contained A history of Britain to William the Conqueror by John Milton; From the conquest to the end of Edward III (Samuel

Daniel); The reigns of Richard II to Henry VI (newly writ in Mr Daniel's method); Edward IV (John Habington); Edward V and Richard III (Sir Thomas More); and Henry VII (Francis, Lord Bacon). At the end of every chapter a summary of 'eminent men and remarkable occurrences' from Holinshed was appended. Volume II included Henry VIII (Lord Herbert of Cherbury); Edward VI (John Hayward); Queen Mary (Francis Godwin, Bishop of Hereford); Elizabeth and Annals of James I (Camden); and History of James I (Arthur Wilson). Suitable histories for Charles I onwards did not exist and so White Kennett (1660-1728), Bishop of Peterborough, accepted an invitation to write the whole of the third volume. He hoped to present an impartial and severely chronological account of this controversial period .of recent history. His text included a literal transcription of nearly every document recorded unaccompanied by comment, and he was infinitely painstaking to consult the mass of contemporary pamphlet literature; he gave extensive quotations of parliamentary speeches, and incorporated a good deal of Clarendon's *History of the rebellion*. He published the volume anonymously; no prudent writer, he explained would set a name to a history of his own times 'for it is impossible to please, or to be thought impartial, till posterity find out his plain and honest dealing.' But inevitably his own opinions and prejudices forced their way into his writing which at times developed into a tirade against popery and the misuse of arbitrary power by Charles II and his brother James. Nor could his anonymity be preserved. G V Bennett's *White Kennett* published by SPCK, in 1957, includes a chapter on his historical writings.

184 'The concept of empire: Burke to Attlee 1774-1947' edited by George Bennett was published by Adam and Charles Black in *The British political tradition* series in 1953. Almost 130 extracts from speeches and debates, letters and minutes, parliamentary reports, essays and articles, mirror the changing views of the British official classes towards imperial policies. There is a short list of books for further reading.

185 'The concise encyclopaedia of world history' edited by John Bowle (Hutchinson, 1958) in twenty chapters each written by a different hand attempts to remedy European parochialism by presenting the landmarks in the history of non European peoples. There is a geographical emphasis throughout. Each chapter is provided with a map because 'only through a grasp of the structural features of the continents can military, economic and cultural movements become intelligible and memorable.' Obviously only an outline can be provided in the separate chapters but these are not mere popularisations, they are truly informative and assume a degree of interest and an ability to comprehend an authoritative text. A second revised edition in a more convenient format was published in 1971.

186 '**A concise history of Australia**' by Clive Turnbull (Thames and Hudson, 1965) is a popular, lavishly illustrated history in four parts: precolonial Australia, the early colonial era, the growth of the nation, and postwar expansion. The bibliography, which is arranged by topic, provides a list of works in print at the time of writing.

187 '**A concise history of Canada**' by Gerald S Graham (Thames and Hudson, 1968) is described by the author as 'a compressed piece of reconstruction.' After a geographical introduction, attention is focused in turn on the discoverers, pioneers, conquerors, reformers, builders, and the managers who have contributed to the emergence of Canada as an influential world power. There is a bibliography arranged by period and by subject.

188 '**A concise history of the British Empire**' by Gerald S Graham (Thames and Hudson, 1970) describes the origins and growth of the Empire from the end of the fifteenth century to the first world war with an epilogue summarising the transition from empire to commonwealth. It is a straightforward chronological account with each stage of the British expansion overseas, and the subsequent political and constitutional changes, placed in their context at appropriate points; it is intended as 'an individual synthesis that may conceivably serve as a bridge to more substantial and sophisticated studies.' Authoritative suggestions for further reading, arranged by chapter, signpost that bridge more than adequately.

189 **The Conference on British Studies** was founded in 1951 when it transpired that the meetings of the American Historical

Association were assuming mammoth proportions. Eastern, midwestern, and western sections were formed in order to bring about more intimate and manageable meetings. It is now recognised as the official organisation in the United States and Canada of scholars working in the field of British history and culture; its status as such is acknowledged by the American Historical Association of which it is an affiliated member. *Publications:* A number of historiographical articles sponsored by the conference in a variety of learned journals were collected in *Changing views on British history* edited by Elizabeth Chapin Furber (1966) (*qv*); *Current research in British studies by American and Canadian scholars* edited by Anthony H Forbes and Marion J Johnson published by the Northern Michigan University Press in 1964; and the *Journal of British studies* whose function it is to publish analytical, exegetical, interpretative, and synthetical articles, began publication in 1961. Also a number of bibliographical handbooks (published by Cambridge University Press for the Conference) which cover all aspects of British history except literature and are specifically intended for advanced students and mature scholars, emphasis being given to the most scholarly and advanced publications. As handbooks they are well named and are obviously designed to provide as comprehensive bibliographies as are possible in convenient portable form. Each includes 2,000-2,500 items classified into wide categories, with explanatory and subjective comments adding to their general utility. Titles so far published: *Anglo-Norman England 1066-1154* by Michael Altschul (1969); *Late medieval England 1377-1485* by Delloyd J Guth (1976); *Tudor England 1485-1603* by Mortimer Levine (1968); *Restoration England 1660-1689* by William L Sachse (1971); *Victorian England 1837-1901* by Josef L Altholz (1970); and *Modern England 1901-1970* by Alfred F Havighurst (1976).

190 'The constitution of England from Queen Victoria to George VI' by Arthur Berriedale Keith (Macmillan, 2 vols, 1940) remains the standard authority on the constitutional history of this particular period. It is a comprehensive magisterial survey of all aspects of the duties, privileges, and functions of the crown, cabinet, parliament, the party system, the executive departments of state, the civil service, and the judiciary.

191 'A constitutional and legal history of medieval England' by Bryce Lyon (New York, Harper, 1960) is so contrived that it offers a treatment of the subject 'more advanced than that found in the usual surveys by American scholars and less difficult than that written by the majority of English scholars.' The object is to summarise the most authoritative opinions on the complex issues raised by the study of English institutions in the middle ages. The text is closely related to Stephenson's and Marcham's *Sources of English constitutional history* (qv) and follows its general pattern of arrangement being divided into six parts: The Anglo-Saxon period; The Norman kings; Henry II and his sons; Henry III and Edward I; Edward II to Richard II; and the houses of Lancaster and York, each systematically arranged into chapters concerned with the various main themes of the period. Generally speaking each part is introduced by a chapter on the relevant sources followed by another on political history in order to provide the student with an understandable background to these confused times. There is a comparatively short general bibliography preceding the text, and, in addition, each of the six main divisions concludes with a more specialised and critical list of publications in book and journal form.

192 'The constitutional documents of the puritan revolution 1625-1660' by S R Gardiner, still in print from Oxford University Press although first published in 1869, was designed to serve either as a basis for the study of constitutional history of this particularly important period or as a companion to the political history of the time. Many of the documents included may be found elsewhere although not always easily accessible; the especial value of this work is its consolidation in one volume of essential source material.

193 'Constitutional documents of the reign of James I AD 1603-1625' by J R Tanner (CUP, 1930) is a companion volume to the same author's *Tudor constitutional documents* and is arranged on the same pattern, *ie* an introductory section of the main historical themes of the period followed by a selection of relevant documents illustrating the various constitutional crises. It has largely been superseded by J P Kenyon's *The Stuart constitution* (1966).

194 'A constitutional history of England' in five volumes with R F Treharne as general editor was planned by Methuen in the late 1930s. It was to be 'a synthesis of recent work directly or indirectly concerned with English constitutional history' taking note of the study of administrative history which had occupied two generations of scholars and all relevant material which had come to light in economic, social, legal, political and ecclesiastical history. To this end the aim of the series was 'to define the present position of our knowledge in the field ... stating the matters of which there is general agreement, and reviewing, as impartially as possible, the points where opinions differ or where theories are still too new to have been subjected to decisive discussion.' In the event only one volume appeared *A constitutional history of England 1642 to 1801* by Mark A Thomson (1938) which proceeded steadily through the constitutional turmoils of the seventeenth century and on to the act of union of 1801. A bibliographical appendix contains a note on sources and a list of later work in book and journal form. The other projected volumes must be considered war casualties.

195 'Constitutional history of England in the fifteenth century (1399-1485); with illustrative documents' by B Wilkinson (Longmans, 1964) follows roughly the same pattern as the three volumes of the same author's *Constitutional history of England* (qv). The documents are arranged in chapters preceded by an introduction and details of relevant recent work in books and journals.

196 'The constitutional history of England 1216-1399' by B Wilkinson, published in three volumes by Longmans Green (1948-1958), pays tribute to Stubb's pioneer work but offers a wider interpretation of the evolution of the medieval constitution with more emphasis being placed on the social and economic conditions and on the political traditions without which constitutional history cannot be truly understood. The selection of documents is intended to indicate the problems pinpointed by modern research. Each volume opens with a substantial introduction to provide a proper background to the chapters which follow. A list of recent work in books and articles and an introduction to specific documents precede the selected extracts chapter by chapter. Volumes: *Politics* and the constitution 1216-1307; Politics and the constitution 1307-1399; and The development of the constitution 1216-1399.

197 'The constitutional history of medieval England; from the English settlement to 1485' by J E A Jolliffe (Black, 4th ed, 1961) met with a mixed reception when first published in 1937 on the grounds that it would be required reading for other scholars but that for students, perhaps unfamiliar with the period, it was dangerously unorthodox although based on a wide reading of the original authorities. Gaillard Lapsley's 'Mr Joliffe's construction of early constitutional history' (History XXIII (89) June 1938: 1-11) makes interesting reading.

198 'The constitutional history of modern Britain since 1485' by D L Keir (Black, 9th ed, 1969) describes the working of the main organs of government whilst at the same time analysing the political and social events which exercised an influence on their development. The emphasis is 'to show how government has been conducted by living and changing communities of men sharing a common political tradition.' The tudor foundations, the stuart controversies, the beginnings of parliamentary monarchy, and democratic reforms, are unfolded in solid and reliable fashion.

199 'Constitutional relations between Britain and India' edited by Nicholas Mansergh (HMSO, 1970—in progress) derives from a government decision to publish documents illustrating the transfer of power from Great Britain to India and Pakistan in 1947, and the events leading up to it, which was announced by the prime minister in the commons, 30 June 1967. The scheme of publication closely follows the Foreign Office series Documents on British foreign policy and, just as in that series, the editors are given unrestricted access to the official archives of the India Office and India Office Library. The documents are arranged by topic and each of the hefty quarto volumes includes a summary of documents by chapter, a list of the holders of principal offices of government in Britain and India, a brief chronology, a glossary of Indian terms, an index of persons named with biographical notes, and a subject index. Volumes published to date:

1 The Cripps mission January-April 1942.
2 'Quit India' 30 April—21 September 1942.

3 *Reassertion of authority, Gandhi's fast, and the succession to the viceroyalty 21 September 1942—12 June 1943.*

4 *The Bengal famine and the new viceroyalty 15 June 1943—31 August 1944.*

5 *The Simla Conference: background and proceedings 1 September 1944—28 July 1945.*

200 '**Contemporary England 1914-1964**' by W N Medlicott (1967) is the last volume in Longmans' *History of England*. The never ending series of domestic and world crises are all examined with dextrous skill. In particular it is the democratization of English politics, the achievement of the welfare state, and its consequent social revolution, the industrial and commercial transformation, the tremendous growth of mass communications, which provide the background to home affairs; and the two world wars, the emergence of a commonwealth of nations from the empire, the establishment of international organisations, the special relationship with the United States, and the maintenance of Britain's role as a central banker, that silhouette Professor Medlicott's account of these tumultuous years.

201 '**Contemporary sources and opinions in modern British history**' edited by Lloyd Evans and Philip J Pledger (Warne, 2 vols, 1967) was designed to act as a companion volume to the authors' political and social history *Triumph and tribulation* and the readings are so organised as to follow that work's text, but as the development of each topic is provided with a general outline, and as there are also explanatory comments linking the extracts, these two volumes may be used independently. The readings are intended to provide teachers and students with a readily accessible set of contemporary opinions, official statements and documents, in order to facilitate the problem-solving approach to history. Rather more social than political topics are considered. A general introduction discusses the historian's methodology and also includes a guide to the evaluation and use of primary sources.

202 '**Crisis of empire; Great Britain and the American colonies 1754-1783**' by Ian R Christie, published in Edward Arnold's *Foundation of modern history* series in 1966, presents a chronological narrative of events based on modern research. A select bibliography describes the standard guides to the literature, the general outlines of the period, the more important monographs on special aspects, and the selections of documents now increasingly finding publication.

203 **'The crisis of imperialism 1865-1915'** by Richard Shannon was the first volume of Hart-Davis, MacGibbon's *Paladin history of England* to appear when published in 1974. The author describes his period as a time when 'British society became urbanised and suburbanised, democratised; general assumptions about social relationships and politically legitimate behaviour shifted from the basis of vertical hierarchic community groupings to stratified classes: in a word, it became modern.' The attempts of successive administrations to grapple with increasingly complex social forces are examined in detail. There is a chronology, and an extremely useful section of biographical notes on the outstanding public figures of the times, and a list of suggested books for further reading.

204 **'The crisis of parliaments; English history 1509-1660'** by Conrad Russell (1971) is included in the *Short Oxford history of the modern world* and has lodged for itself a secure future as a standard textbook for this particular period which still retains its attraction for college and university examiners. It integrates political, social, and economic factors in its two main themes, the political and constitutional effects of a rapid inflation and the difficulties emanating from the conscious attempts to achieve a religious uniformity. There is a select bibliography, the precise intention of which is a little hard to ascertain: it is apparently neither a list of works consulted in the author's research nor is it a guide to further reading.

205 **'The critical historian'** by G Kitson Clark (Heinemann, 1967) is dedicated 'to all those who, whether in school or college, have the great responsibility of teaching history' and is a study of how historical evidence is built up, and sometimes distorted. The method of establishing historical proof is compared to that of other disciplines. An examination of notable forgeries and deceptions, an account of some inept editing of documents, and a description of how a British prime minister deliberately destroyed embarrassing evidence, provide tangible examples of the danger of uncritical history.

206 'Dark age Britain; some sources of history' by Henry Marsh (David and Charles, 1970) examines the most important British and English historians who shed light on the history of Britain from the first English descents to the reign of Alfred the Great. These include Gildas, Nennius, the *Annales Cambriae*, the *Brut y Tywysogion* (*Chronicle of the Princes of Wales*), the *Anglo-Saxon chronicle*, Bede, Asser, William of Malmesbury, and Geoffrey of Monmouth. Although essentially a 'popular' book there is a useful note on the history of the texts and their translations. Many sample pages of early manuscripts are reproduced and translated.

207 'The dark ages; the making of European civilization' edited by David Talbot Rice (Thames and Hudson, 1965) is the 4th volume of the *Great civilizations* series. There are four main sections: The east, with chapters on the lands beyond the eastern frontiers of the Roman Empire, Islam and the Arab conquests, and a history of Armenia; Byzantium; Migration and settlement, covering the nomadic tribes who wandered across Europe from the north and east; and the new Europe, Charlemagne, the empire, and the establishment of feudal Christendom. Each chapter is written by a different authority and is accompanied by a select bibliography. The full range of byzantine and carolingian art is well served by the publisher's customary sumptuous provision of illustrations, and an eye catching chronological chart completes an impressive volume.

208 Dawson, William and Sons are specialist publishers of learned journal reprints both in conventional form and on microfiche. Several learned societies have also handed over files of back numbers of their journals to take advantage of the firm's expertise in marketing this type of material. A special *History* folder is obtainable from Cannon House, Folkestone, Kent, CT19 5EE.

209 'Degree course guide: History' is published every two years by CRAC in a completely revised edition and aims to provide comparative information about first degree courses at British universities. In addition to the list of courses available, information is also given on the different approaches to the subject, teaching methods, seminars and tutorials, examinations, drop out rates, continuous assessment, and dissertations. Other topics discussed are course contents, language requirements, entrance and selection procedures, and grants.

210 'Descriptive catalogue of materials relating to the history of Great Britain and Ireland to the end of the reign of Henry VII' by Thomas Duffus Hardy (Rolls Series 3 vols in 4, 1862-1871) is a sterling work of scholarship laboriously but triumphantly recording and describing the sources of early British history both printed and in manuscript. It was the author's proud boast that for the first time all the known sources were presented in one continuous sequence. Strictly confined to the history of Britain, the material is arranged chronologically under the year in which the latest event is recorded and not under the period in which the author flourished. Similarly, all biographies are enumerated under the year in which the person commemorated died, a method which allows the material for any one year to be seen at a glance, and, provided the reader has a fair idea of when the author was writing, enables him to reliably estimate the value of the narrative. A brief analysis of each major text further enhances the value of this immense work. If even major libraries understandably jib at the cost of a full reprint edition of *The rolls series* they would be well advised to consider the purchase of these particular volumes.

211 'The development of dominion status 1900-1936' edited by Robert MacGregor Dawson (OUP, 1937) provides a concise account of what dominion status implied as well as the story of its development. This is followed by a very much larger section consisting of contemporary documents: official reports, blue books, newspaper and journal articles exemplifying these two themes. The two parts are linked together by the use of appropriate cross references. The work was reprinted by Frank Cass in 1965 which in itself suggests it retains some permanent value.

212 'The development of the study of seventeenty-century history,' a paper read to the Royal Historical Society by C H Firth and printed in its *Transactions* 3rd series, VII 1913: 25-48, is a rare example of an acknowledged authority discussing the source materials of his chosen period. He outlines the earliest available writings and weighs their value, he records the inaccessibility of official documents and the attempts to harvest their contents, and scrupulously examines the various methods and conclusions of seventeenth century biographers and successive generations of historians.

213 'Dictionarum Saxonico-Latino-Anglicum' (1659) compiled by William Somner, the first Anglo-Saxon dictionary, was instrumental in the resurgence of Anglo-Saxon studies at Oxford and Cambridge at the end of the stuart and in the early years of the hanoverian period.

214 'Dictionary of American biography' (OUP and Scribners, 20 vols 1928-1936) was published under the auspices of the American Council of Learned Societies with generous financial support from the *New York times*. It includes all noteworthy people who made a significant contribution to American life and culture, a conscious effort being made to move away from the traditional pattern of soldiers, statesmen and clergymen. A classification of occupations, trades and professions was devised and various authoritative opinions were canvassed on recommended lists of subjects to be treated. Contributors were asked to base their articles on original sources which were to be appended as bibliographies to each article. They were strictly enjoined to appraise the circumstances and influences that shaped their subjects' careers. To ensure accuracy editorial staff were maintained at the Library of Congress. The resources of the American Antiquarian Society were also at the disposal of the editor and contributors. The length of the articles was in the main determined by the material available: five articles are over 10,000 words, Benjamin Franklin, Thomas Jefferson, Abraham Lincoln, George Washington and Woodrow Wilson, whilst seventy others are over the 5,000 mark. A separate *Index to volumes I-XX* appeared in 1937 on the initiative of the publishers. At appropriate intervals the council issues supplemental volumes and to that end maintains an editorial body to receive corrections, additions and new material. So far three such volumes have been published: *Vol XXI supplement one (to December 31st 1935)* (1944), *Supplement two (to December 31st 1940)* (1958), and *Supplement three 1941-1945*

(1973). A *Concise dictionary of American biography*, a one volume edition condensed from the original work and the first two supplements appeared in 1964 and is manifestly a more attractive purchase to most British libraries. A 'Brief Account of the Enterprise' was published in Volume XX.

215 'Dictionary of American history' (OUP and Scribners, 5 vols and an index volume, 1940) was a conscious attempt to meet the demand for a quick reference work to satisfy enquiries on specific historical facts and events. Over 6000 articles, the work of more than a thousand historians who took part in the venture, cover all aspects of American history. Each article is brief, deals with a separate and distinct topic, and concludes with references to further reading. Subject headings 'to which the average user of the work would most naturally turn,' extensive cross references, and a commendable analytical index, complete its scholarly appearance. *Supplement I 1940-1960*, updating the original five volumes, was added to the series in 1961. The *Concise dictionary of American history* (1963) was the end product of an attempt to scrutinize each entry of the main work in order to decide whether it should remain intact, be abbreviated, or be omitted altogether. At the end of the day any information which the general reader could reasonably hope to find in the *Dictionary* was retained and the new abridgment reflects the breadth and depth of the original work to a surprising degree.

216 'A dictionary of British history' edited by J A Brendon (1937) was in its day a useful compendium of institutions, incidents, and individuals most frequently referred to by historians. 'Thousands of such references, touching upon all aspects—political, constitutional, social, economic and military—of the history of the British commonwealth and dependent empire are here concisely amplified.' A number of appendices list English, Scottish and British sovereigns, (English) Princes of Wales, the chief ministers of the Crown from the Norman Conquest, Archbishops of Canterbury and York, the Governors-General and Viceroys of India, and the national revenue and expenditure and National Debt from 1688.

217 'Dictionary of Canadian biography' was called into existence through the generosity of a private benefactor who bequeathed a considerable sum of money to the University of Toronto 'for the purpose of undertaking, and so far as possible carrying on from time to time as occasion may require, a work similar in principle and scope to the *Dictionary of national biography* published in England, but devoted to the biographies of persons who were either born in Canada or subsequently resided therein.' Work started in earnest in 1959 when a general editor was appointed and the task of publishing it was allocated to the University of Toronto Press which was vastly experienced in handling substantial volumes. The entries are intended to be 'fresh and scholarly in treatment based on reliable (where possible first hand) sources, precise and accurate in statements of fact, concise, but presented in attractive literary form. Though adequate factual material is of prime importance, biographies should not be mere catalogues of events. They should appraise circumstances which shaped careers, and should indicate ... ancestry, parentage, education, physical and social environment, and the other formative influences ... they should leave the reader with a definite impression of the personality and achievements of the subject in relation to the period in which he lived and the events in which he participated.' In length they vary between short notes of 200 words and 8,000-10,000 words articles perhaps constituting about one percent of the total number of entries. Most fall between 300-1,000 words. The whole work is arranged on a chronological basis, each volume covering a specific number of years and being self contained with its contents listed alphabetically in conventional fashion. The periods are arranged so as to produce volumes of approximately equal size and will therefore be shortened as they approach the present day. This system enables a more logical presentation in that persons closely associated are to be found within the same volume. They comprise in fact separate histories and can be bought and studied separately and when the time comes the method adopted will readily lend itself to the task of revision. Eventually cumulative indexes and epitome volumes are envisaged which will cater for the reader who cannot remember the precise dates of the person he is looking up. At the time of writing four volumes have appeared: Volume I *1000 to 1700* (1966); II *1701-1740* (1969); III *1741-1770* (1974); and X *1871-1880* (1972).

The usual features, introduction, editorial notes, abbreviations, the biographies, and a general bibliography, are common to all four volumes but some include introductory essays of relevance to that particular period. 'The Indians of northeastern North America' by Jacques Rousseau and George W Brown, 'Glossary of Indian tribal names' (also in Vols II and III), 'The northern approaches to Canada' by T J Oleson and W L Morton, 'The Atlantic region' by George MacBeath, and 'New France 1524-1713' by Marcel Trudel appear in Vol I; 'The administration of New France' by Andre Vachon in Vol II; and 'The French forces in North America during the seven years' war' by W J Eccles and 'The British forces in North America during the seven years' war' by C P Stacey in Vol III. A French language edition, *Dictionnaire biographique du Canada*, is published by *Les Presses de l'Universite Laval* in Quebec. Libraries in the United Kingdom should address their enquiries to the Oxford University Press, London.

218 'The dictionary of English history' originally compiled by Sir Sidney Low and F S Pulling revised and enlarged by F J C Hearnshaw, Helena M Chew and A C F Beales (1928) was intended when first published in 1884 to serve as a convenient handbook to the whole field of English history. Although it was recognised that it was scarcely possible to cover such a vast and ill defined subject an attempt was nevertheless made to produce a book which would provide all the biographical, bibliographical, chronological, and constitutional information of the kind the general reader as well as the student would be likely to require. A number of young scholars who subsequently made their mark as historians, notably T F Tout, compiled the entries. After four partial revisions in the period 1896-1910 it was decided in the 1920s that the accumulation of new topics and fresh names thrown up by the passage of years warranted a completely new edition. At the same time the opportunity was taken to revise many of the original entries in the light of the advance of knowledge since the first edition appeared forty years previously. It was reprinted by the Gale Research Company in 1971.

219 'Dictionary of historical allusions' by Thomas Benfield Harbottle (1903) is a useful source for identifying sobriquets and careless off hand references to all manner of places and events. It was reprinted by the Gale Research Company in 1968.

220 'A dictionary of modern history 1789-1945' by A W Palmer (1962) is a modest 'guide to the states of the modern world in action'. Sixth formers requiring concentrated information on places, events, persons, battles etc will find it attractive but the author emphasises it is intended as an aid to study, not a substitute for it. A Penguin edition was published in 1964.

221 'The dictionary of national biography'. Work began on this gargantuan reference work in 1882. The prime criterion for inclusion was entry in a previously published collection of names and so over 200 biographical and historical works were scanned (the complete *Gentlemans magazine* being counted as one!) including all British biographical dictionaries, and obituaries from *The times*. Research workers were recruited from young Oxford graduates and trained in the *Dictionary* by the *Dictionary* for the *Dictionary*. The first volume of lives appeared at Christmas 1884 and thereafter a new volume in alphabetical progression was published every quarter day until the project's completion, Midsummer 1900. It was first intended that the closing date for inclusion would be 31 December 1900 but it was decided that the death of Queen Victoria, 22 January 1901, offered a 'better historical landmark'. Several worthies of course died whilst the work was in progress and others had been accidentally omitted. These were included in the *First supplement* completed in three volumes in 1901. The editorial organisation was then dismantled but the editor continued work on an *Epitome* and *Index*. Each of the lives was condensed and the *Concise dictionary* appeared in 1903. By using thinner paper the main work is now published in twenty one volumes instead of the original sixty three with the *Supplement* in one volume. Decennial supplements with an accumulated index since 1901 have also been published, the full series now comprises Vols I-XXI (A-Z) and Vol XXII *Supplement*, and *Twentieth century DNB* in 6 volumes to 1960. *The concise dictionary* has also been updated, now appearing in two volumes: Part I from the beginnings to 1900 and Part II 1901-1950. In 1921 A F Pollard (*qv*), one of the *Dictionary's* outstanding researchers, founded the Institute of Historical

Research (*qv*) which began to collect corrections and these have appeared in the institute's *Bulletin* since it began publication in 1923. In 1966 the reprint firm, G K Hall & Co, published *Corrections and additions to DNB cumulated from the Bulletin of the Institute of Historical Research covering the years 1923-1963*. Some dissatisfaction has been voiced in recent years about *DNB*'s deficiencies: since 1901 there has been no way of admitting people whose claims have been overlooked. But it seems most unlikely that the main work will ever be revised, the cost would literally be prohibitive. As it is, doubts continue whether *DNB* is living up to its proud boast of including 'every name about which information is likely to be sought in the future by the serious student'. Entries take the form of signed articles often written by specialists who claim personal knowledge of their subjects. J L Kirby's 'The Dictionary of national biography', *Library Association record* June 1958 is a valuable summary of *DNB*'s history, especially for the part played by George Smith, Leslie Stephen and Sidney Lee, and also includes many useful references.

222 **'Dictionary of world history'** (1973). General editor G M D Howat, advisory editor A J P Taylor. A record of events, movements and ideas from the first records of western and eastern civilizations to 1970. Emphasis is placed on politics but social, economic, military and, to a lesser extent, scientific matters all receive attention. Entries rarely exceed 500 words in length and the average length is nearer 100. Longer entries are initialled.

223 **'The discovery of Australia'** by Andrew Sharp (OUP, 1963) presents a survey of the progressive discovery of the coasts of Australia as evidenced by the original records of the discoverers. The journals of Captain James Cook loom large but there is a representative collection of Portuguese, Dutch and French sources. Of especial interest are the extracts from primary charts covering segments of coast where the discoveries occurred. A list of publications cited in the text is appended.

224 **'The discovery of New Zealand'** by J C Beaglehole (OUP, 2nd ed, 1961) was first published by the Department of Internal Affairs, Wellington, in the New Zealand Centennial Surveys in 1939. Its object was to provide as clear an account as could be devised in compact form of the European discovery of the New Zealand islands. There is a preliminary chapter on the Maori voyagers. Notes on the sources are divided by chapter.

225 'Dissertations in history; an index to dissertations completed in history departments of United States and Canadian universities 1873-1960' by Warren F Kuehl (University of Kentucky Press, 1965) is an extremely valuable compilation in so far as other sources of information are not easily accessible. Strictly limited to dissertations written under formally organised departments of history for which a doctorate degree was awarded on the grounds that any extension of this principle would have rendered the whole project impracticable, it was compiled from Library of Congress volumes, H W Wilson and University Microfilms lists and library catalogues, and claims to be as accurate as uncertain university records allow. It was completed just before the publication of the *Directory of American scholars: history* edited by Jacques Cattell (1964) and after a comparison an extra 100 entries were inserted. In avoiding duplication of research and heavily overworked areas it confers an obvious and indispensable boon to the active American research industry. It makes no effort to indicate which dissertations have been published because of the difficulty in ascertaining exactly what constitutes 'publication.' It is arranged alphabetically by author with a subject and title index along the lines of the American Historical Association's *Guide to historical literature*. A second volume *1961—June 1970* was published in 1972.

226 'Dissertations on British history 1815-1914; an index to British and American theses' (Scarecrow Press, 1974) lists 2300 theses accepted for higher degrees in British and American universities 1914-1972. Authors, titles, degrees, institutions and dates of award are given and there are author, person and places, and a general subject index.

227 'The divided society; party conflict in England 1694-1716' edited by Geoffrey Holmes and W A Speck and published in Edward Arnold's *Documents of modern history* series in 1967 is a bibliographical oddity in that the dust wrapper and the title page both bear the subtitle *Parties and politics in England 1694-1716* a tipped in label giving a corrected title. Why this correction should have been deemed necessary is not apparent especially as the documents included concentrate on the struggle between Tory and Whig 'as it developed in Parliament and in parliamentary elections, in government, and not least in society at large.' The authors deliberately selected material not readily accessible to students rather than include familiar items to be found easily elsewhere. The documents are arranged in four groups each prefaced by explanatory text: The course of conflict (to 1715); The conflict of party in society; The substance of conflict; and The arenas of conflict.

228 'A documentary history of England' *1 1066-1540* by J J Bagley and P B Rowley and *2 1559-1931* by E N Williams (Penguin Books) presents the essential passages of the most important religious, political, constitutional and social documents 'which played a major part in forming our national institutions' and thus in the development of our society. Each document is introduced and placed in its historical context for the convenience of the general reader.

229 'Documentary history of the United States,' edited by Richard B Morris, published by Harper and Row of New York, presents volumes of extracts from contemporary documents annotated sufficiently to place them in their historical context. A general introduction and an extensive bibliography complete the scholarly apparatus. There are two series: chronological and topical. Titles of chronological series (with editors): *The discovery of America* (D B Quinn); *The puritan tradition in America* (Alden T Vaughan); *The Spanish tradition in America* (Charles Gibson); *The French tradition in America* (Y F Zoltvany); *The Dutch and quaker traditions in America* (Milton M Klein); *Bases of plantation society* (Aubrey Land); *Great Britain and the American colonies 1606-1763* (Jack P Greene); *The American revolution* (Richard B Morris); *Confederation and constitution* (Forrest MacDonald); *The early republic 1789-1828* (Noble E Cunningham); *The opening of the west* (Jack M Sosin); *The west 1830-1890* (Gilbert C Fite); *The age of Jackson* (Robert V Remini); *Documents in the history of slavery* (Stanley Elkins and Gerald Mullin); *The reform impulse 1828-1847* (Walter Hugins);

The civil war (James P Shenton); *Reconstruction, the new south, and the negro* (La Wanda and John Cox); *The transformation of American society 1870-1890* (John A Garraty); *The issues of the populist and progressive eras 1892-1912* (Richard M Abrams); *The far west in the twentieth century* (Earl Pomeroy); *World war, reform, and reaction* (Stanley Coben); *The new deal* (William E Leuchtenburg); *United States and world war II* (Louis Morton); and *Domestic issues since 1945* (Robert E Burke).

230 **'The documentary history of western civilization',** published by Macmillan, comprises upwards of fifty books subdivided into large groups *ie* 'Ancient and medieval history of the west'; 'Early modern history'; 'Revolutionary Europe 1789-1848'; 'Nationalism, liberalism and socialism'; and 'The twentieth century'. Each book prints (usually) the full text of various important documents of the period covered, all set in their historical context, thus providing in convenient form for the student and research worker the raw material of history which might otherwise be difficult to locate.

231 **'Documents and speeches on British commonwealth affairs 1931-1952'** edited by Nicholas Mansergh (OUP, 2 vols 1953) was issued under the auspices of the Royal Institute of International Affairs. The work consists almost entirely of official reports, ministerial speeches, and extracts from government acts illustrating the constitutional developments which took place in the twenty years following the Statute of Westminster. The first volume proceeds from the results of that statute, to economic policies, foreign policy and defence, Indian constitutional reforms, the complex Irish problem, the abdication and the outbreak of war. The second volume opens with the partition of India, and continues with the secession of Ireland, inter-commonwealth tensions, financial and economic matters, the changing commonwealth membership, and the novel consideration of republics acknowledging the Queen as head of the commonwealth. The two volumes serve an invaluable purpose in assembling together source materials which otherwise would be scattered in many different and sometimes inaccessible volumes. They were followed by the same editor's *Documents and speeches on commonwealth affairs 1952-1962* (1963) concerned firstly with constitutional developments successfully reconciling national aspirations with a supranational organisation and, secondly, with the external policies of member states, including the Suez crisis which in the view of one Canadian minister almost dissolved the commonwealth.

232 '**Documents of American history**' by H S Commager (New York, Appleton-Century-Crofts, 2 vols) was first published in 1934 and has been frequently updated since. They present in convenient fashion the fundamental sources of American history from the age of discovery onwards. For the most part they are limited to official and quasi-official documents. Each is preceded by a short note and a bibliography indicating respectively information necessary to comprehend its import and where additional information may most conveniently be found. *Speeches and documents in American history* by Robert Birley (OUP *The world's classics* series, 4 vols, 1944) may be more easily obtained by British libraries and in any case they rely heavily on Commager.

233 '**Documents of medieval history**' is a new series announced by Edward Arnold to be published clothbound and in paperback which is intended to be similar in scope and style to the popular *Documents of modern history* series except that the volumes will be shorter. The general editor is G W S Barrow.

234 '**Documents of modern history**', a low priced series published by Edward Arnold intended in the first instance for universities and colleges. The plan is to illustrate major topics in British, European and world history, with no particular bias towards politics or constitutional matters, in the firm conviction that all fields of human activity may be studied with profit. In fact most volumes are concerned with prominent historical themes rather than a routine chronological coverage of specific historical periods. At the moment ten or so volumes have been published and many more are in preparation. The general editors are A G Dickens, Professor of Modern History University of London and director of the Institute of Historical Research, and Alun Davies, Professor of Modern History, University College Swansea.

235 '**Documents on British foreign policy 1919-1939**' (HMSO, 1946-   ): The Secretary of State for Foreign Affairs announced in the House of Commons, 29 March 1944, the government's decision to publish such a series: 'The documents will be published in a series of volumes which will be issued one by one as and when they are ready. The volumes will form a continuous chronological series, but in order to make available as soon as possible documents dealing with events most relevant to the outbreak of the present war, it is proposed, for purposes of publication, to divide the work into two parts: the first part to begin with the year 1919, and the second part to begin with the year 1930. The preparation of each part will be undertaken simultaneously.' Each volume includes documents relating to a given period of time divided into subject chapters as a compromise between a strictly chronological or topical arrangement. In selecting the documents for inclusion priority was given to instructions sent to British missions abroad, reports from these missions of business transacted with foreign governments, records of negotiations conducted in London, and verbatim reports of conferences attended by ministers of state. At the time of writing, the first series comprises nineteen volumes (1947-1974) covering the years 1919-1922; Series 1A introduced in 1963 to accelerate publication has reached its sixth volume covering the period immediately after the Locarno agreement 1925 down to 1928-1929; the second series volumes 1-13 (1946-1973) covers the period 1930-1936; and the third series, introduced in 1947 to publish at an early date the volumes relating to the period from the March 1938 plebiscite in Austria to the outbreak of war in 1939 is complete in nine volumes (1949-1955). The eminent historians responsible for editing the documents requested they should be allowed unreserved access to the foreign office archives and for complete freedom in selection. They report that these conditions have been fulfilled to their entire satisfaction.

236 Dugdale, Sir William (1605-1686) is justly renowned for his *The antiquities of Warwickshire* (1656), a milestone in English local history, and a little unjustly for the *Monasticon Anglicanum* (3 vols 1655-1673) which was largely the work of his fellow scholar Roger Dodsworth. This latter work, based on exhaustive research, added a new dimension to the study of English feudalism, emphasising for the first time the true importance of medieval monastic charters, although there are some comparatively minor blemishes in that some were copies of inferior versions and that a few forged documents were accepted at their face value. Nevertheless this documentary record of the English monasteries marked the opening of a new stage in English antiquarian research into the medieval period. A sympathetic portrait of Dugdale can be found in David Douglas' *The English scholars* which also provides a convincing demolishing of the inflated reputation of the 1817-1830 edition of the *Monasticon* under the editorship of John Caley, Henry Ellis and Bulkeley Bandinel.

237   Eadmer (1064-1144): a Canterbury monk, chaplain to Archbishop Anselm, is one of the chief authorities for English history during the reigns of William II and Henry I by virtue of his *Historia Novorum in Anglia* (*History of modern times in England*) in six books which although fashioned as the second part of a biography of Anselm, placing him in his historical context, is in effect a contemporary narrative of political and ecclesiastical events at a time when the two were closely intertwined. He first sets the scene for Anselm's primacy by relating the political history of England from the end of the tenth century down to the Norman conquest before continuing with a reasoned account of the reforms of Anselm's illustrious predecessor, Lanfranc. From the time Anselm ascended to the archiepiscopal throne he is rarely offstage and after his death, when criticism of his alleged neglect began to be voiced, Eadmer was impelled to add a further book justifying his actions. As the archbishop's chaplain, Eadmer was close to the centre of affairs and consequently was able to write with first hand knowledge and also to furnish the *Historia* with extensive documentation, quoting verbatim from Anselm's correspondence like the 'Life and letter' volumes of nineteenth century biographers. His merit as a historian thus rested on a calm and sober appraisal of events he had watched from close range. He is less pretentions than William of Malmesbury but is capable of vivid and dramatic passages. But he suffered from the biographer's occupational hazard of narrating events entirely from his subject's point of view and he was not above incorporating false evidence if it suited him although these attempts at falsification are so blatantly transparent that they do not seriously detract from the *Historia's* worth as a reliable authority. For an English text refer to R W Southern's edition in the *Oxford medieval texts* series.

238 'The earlier Tudors 1485-1558' by J D Mackie (1952), a volume of the *Oxford history of England*, marks the transition from the middle ages to the renaissance and the reformation. On this last topic Professor Mackie was writing before the publication of G R Elton's *England under the Tudors* (*vide infra*) which suggests that the two accounts need to be read in conjunction. The bibliography is especially valuable for its appreciations of the contemporary chronicles and narratives still extant and the collections of documents and sources made available in published form in the last century and a half.

239 **Early English Text Society** was founded in 1864 by F J Furnivall primarily to make the mass of unprinted texts of early English literature available to students. These publications are known as the *Original series*. From 1867-1920 an *Extra series* was published consisting of texts already published but which were either difficult to obtain or which were regarded as unsatisfactory editions. From 1921 onwards all regular publications were listed and numbered as part of the *Original series*. A new *Supplementary series* of occasional publications to be issued only when funds allow was started in 1970. All are in print either in conventional editions or in reprint form. Many titles are of immediate interest to historians. *A list of publications 1864-1975* including terms of membership etc, may be obtained from Dr Anne Hudson, Executive Secretary, Lady Margaret Hall, Oxford, England.

240 'Early hanoverian England (1714-1760); some recent writings' by William A Bultmann was first published in the *Journal of modern history* XXXV March 1963: 46-61 and then reprinted in *Changing views on British history* (*qv*). During the past thirty years this period has benefited from meticulous research and the new approach, pioneered by Sir Lewis Namier, has uncovered 'a wealth of information about elections, party structure, the sovereign's role in politics, and the power and tactics of ministers of the crown.' Still more needs to be accomplished, as yet 'any general account must necessarily be based upon a difficult and often irreconcilable combination of still to be superseded older, orthodox works on the one hand and an incomplete patchwork of revisionist literature on the other.'

241 'Early modern British history 1485-1760' by Helen Miller and Aubrey Newman (Historical Association, 1970) is a select bibliography concentrating on books published during the last thirty years intended to introduce students to the best secondary literature available. In this particular pamphlet, unlike some others published in the same *Helps for students of history* series, there is very little annotation of the thematic and chronologically arranged entries.

242 'The early Stuarts 1603-1660' by Godfrey Davies (2nd ed 1959) the ninth volume in the *Oxford history of England* is a detailed narrative of political, constitutional, religious, and diplomatic history leavened with chapters on social and economic matters, colonial policy, education and science, literature, and the arts.

243 'Early tudor government' by Kenneth Pickthorn was published in two volumes, *Henry VII* and *Henry VIII*, by the Cambridge University Press in 1934 and is still recognised as the most authoritative study on the subject along with G R Elton's more specialised *Tudor revolution in government* (1953). Pickthorn's two volumes vary slightly in treatment, the first leans towards an analytical survey whilst the second follows a more chronological pattern.

244 Educational Publications publish a series of slide sets produced in collaboration with the Historical Association intended to fill the gaps in visual aids for history teaching. Details of these and a wide variety of other media resources from EP, Bradford Road, East Ardsley, Wakefield, West Yorkshire, WF3 2JN.

245 'Edward the Confessor' by Frank Barlow (Eyre and Spottiswoode, 1970) in the *English monarchs* series is a major definitive study based upon a close rescrutiny of the sparse, reliable, primary sources that survive. 'The basic task of the modern historian,' the author declares, 'is to try to reconstruct Edward in his contemporary setting' and especially to uncover the Edward who existed before the Norman conquest took place.

246 'Edward IV' by Charles Ross (Eyre Methuen, 1974), a volume in the *English monarchs* series, 'is essentially a study in the power-politics of late medieval England' and in his examination of the struggle between crown and nobility the author discerns a paradox in Edward's final triumph over the rebellious feudal lords and his sad failure to secure a peaceful and undisputed succession to the throne for his son. A note on narrative sources (appendix 1) is a useful contribution towards an understanding of the period.

247 Edwardes, Michael (1923-   ) must now be acknowledged as the authoritative historian of the rise and fall of the British empire in India. A succession of books over the last ten years has won acclaim from academic and general reader alike. *Last years of British India* (1963) is 'an attempt to display and examine the many and diverse ingredients of an historical event and to disentangle them from the web of propaganda and special pleading;' *High noon of Empire: India under Curzon* (1965) reexamines the nature of British rule in India and the ideas and beliefs that lay behind it at an earlier stage. *Glorious sahibs: the romantic as empire-builder 1799-1838* (1968) scrutinises the careers of four East India Company officers whose 'sense of the past made them want to preserve the best of India, instead of forcing on India even the best of Europe.' *Plassey: the founding of an empire* (1969), *Red year: the Indian rebellion of 1857* (1973) and *A season in hell: the defence of the Lucknow residency* (1973) retell well known episodes in Anglo-Indian history with much new material unearthed from unpublished manuscript sources. *British India: a survey of the nature and effects of alien rule* (1967) is not an orthodox history, taking as its theme the meeting of two civilisations and its consequences.

248 'The eighteenth century; Europe in the age of enlightenment' edited by Alfred Cobban (Thames and Hudson, 1969) belongs to the *Great civilizations* series. The pattern of royal government, the rococo and baroque architecture, the beginnings of technological advance, economics, overseas settlement, war, the world of ideas, the social condition of the people, and the end of the *ancien* *regime* are all covered by the various contributors. A profuse and lavish use of illustrations enlivens the text. There is also a map and a select bibliography.

249 'The eighteenth-century constitution 1688-1815; documents and commentary' by E Neville Williams (CUP, 1960) is divided into sections on the revolution of 1688, the central government, parliament, local government, the church, and the liberties of the subject. The author is able to draw on a more varied range of sources than either Elton or Kenyon in the tudor and stuart volumes of this Cambridge series: diaries, letters, cabinet minutes, pamphlets, sermons, newspapers, local records, state trials, and parliamentary debates, all yield first-hand information. There is an extensive and classified bibliography which in this case is not limited to works cited in the editor's commentaries on the documents.

250 'Eighteenth century England' by Dorothy Marshall (2nd ed 1974), the eighth volume of *Longman's history of England*, intended for the general reader or student approaching the period for the first time, synthesizes the increasing results of the research of the last forty years. A narrative treatment is supported by two introductory chapters, 'The economic and social background of the age' and 'The background of political life on the accession of George I.' It is now available as a paperback.

251 'The elizabethan age' is the general title of a trilogy by A L Rowse and comprises *The England of Elizabeth* (1950); *The expansion of elizabethan England* (1955); and *The elizabethan renaissance* in two volumes, *The life of the society* (1971) and *The cultural achievement* (1972). In the first volume, subtitled *The structure of society*, the author is concerned 'to expose and portray the small society—touch, vigorous, pulsating with energy—that accomplished those extraordinary achievements and made the age the most remarkable in history.' First the surviving visible and intangible elements of elizabethan England are reviewed and followed by a study of the tudor topographers. Then come the constituent parts of the elizabethan fabric: agriculture and industry, economics, law and government. The theme of the second volume is the excursions into Scotland, Wales and Ireland

and then the explosion of maritime adventure in search of the Indies. The author is characteristically emphatic that it is his intention to contribute to historical knowledge to which end he has included a good deal of unpublished primary source material. The two volumes of the last work in the trilogy were originally planned as one but their length demanded they be divided: the first depicts the social life of the age, the court, the gentry *etc.*, whilst the second investigates the cultural background. It is an impressive achievement by an outspoken and sometimes controversial historian.

252 'The elizabethans' America; a collection of early reports by Englishmen on the new world' edited by Louis B Wright (1965) is number two of *The Stratford Upon Avon library* published by Edward Arnold. After an introduction dealing with the economic, social, and diplomatic background of the process of colonisation there follow extracts from the narrative and descriptive reports of the wonders and mysteries of the new world. All extracts are prefaced by notes on their sources.

253 Elmham, Thomas, a Nottinghamshire prior and for a long time chaplain to Henry V was the author of *Gesta Henrici Quinti Angliae Regis* of most value for the two periods when he accompanied the King to France. He provides an eye witness account of the siege of Harfleur and the Battle of Agincourt. But even relating events of which he had no first hand knowledge it is obvious he is relying on accurate information. He owed little to his contemporaries.

254 Elton, G R (1921-   ), our foremost historian of the tudor period, broke new ground with *The tudor revolution in government: administrative changes in the reign of Henry VIII* (1953) in which he first nominated Thomas Cromwell as a candidate for urgent reassessment as a central figure in the history of his times, in practice the effective ruler of the state, the chief of police, and the instigator of far-reaching reforms. *Policy and police: the enforcement of the reformation in the age of Thomas Cromwell (CUP,* 1972) offers an example of how the newly reconstructed cromwellian machinery of state actually operated. Professor Elton's papers and reviews from learned journals are collected in

104

Studies in tudor and stuart politics and government (CUP, 2 vols, 1974) which opens with his first ever printed article in the *Journal of roman studies*! He has also been active in debating the principles and practice of writing history not to mention his editing of source documents. These facets of his writings are considered elsewhere in the present work. In addition he edited the second volume of the *New Cambridge modern history*.

255 **'Empire in the Antipodes; the British in Australasia 1840-1860'** by John M Ward was published by Edward Arnold in the *Foundations of modern history series* in 1966. It is a brief study of the specifically British factors of fundamental importance in the growth and expansion of the Australasian colonies in the mid-nineteenth century. The effects of successive changes in British imperial and commercial policies on this new empire in the South West Pacific are also assessed. Of especial interest is a chapter on the reluctance of the Australian colonies to proceed to self-governing status and how it was left to the colonial office to ensure that Australia kept pace with Canada in this respect. There is an extensive annotated bibliography arranged by chapter.

256 **'Empire into commonwealth'** by Sir Percival Griffiths (Benn, 1969) aspires to be an objective account of British imperialism and a fresh reappraisal of British imperial history. The gradual march of events is faithfully recorded from the early voyages of the fifteenth century to the stage when each country enjoying commonwealth membership achieves its national independence. Twelve maps and a bibliography divided by chapters enhance this book intended for the interested layman.

257 **'Empire to welfare state; English history 1906-1967'** by T O Lloyd was published in 1970 as one of the first volumes in the *Shorter Oxford history of the modern world*. The story of England's at times painful transition from a proud position at the centre of empire to an off-shore European island is recounted in a straightforward manner. The political and economic implications of this severe change in status are analysed as is the emergence of two super-powers. There is an extensive critical general bibliography and also further annotated bibliographies for each chapter.

258 'The encyclopaedia of American history' (New York, Harper, 4th ed 1970) condenses into one volume all the essential historical facts about American life and institutions. A continuous narrative, in which dates, events, achievements and persons stand out, is arranged in four sections: Part I, Basic chronology tells the story of the major political and military events in exploration, settlement and revolution and proceeds to recount the main political and constitutional developments at national and federal levels. Part II deals with nonpolitical matters such as population and immigration, science and invention, thought and culture. Part III is a thirty two page updated supplement of the two previous sections up to the 1969 moonlandings, and Part IV gives the biographies in rather fuller detail than is usual in such works of 400 notable Americans.

259 'An encyclopaedia of the modern world; a concise reference history from 1760 to the present' edited by Richard B Morris and Graham W Irwin (NY Harper, London: Weidenfeld, 1970). The statistics of this monster book are impressive: 1068 pages of text, 203 of index, and over fifty maps. There are two parts, Basic chronology, a year by year record of events in the diplomatic, military, and political sphere, arranged under the following headings: Democratic revolution in the western world 1760-1825; Asian and African world 1760-1870; Age of western nationalism 1789-1914; Age of imperial rivalry 1870-1914; Era of world war 1914-1945; and the post-war world 1945-1968. Topical chronology covers social, economic, and constitutional history on a world-wide basis together with a history of scientific thought and culture.

260 'An encyclopedia of world history: Ancient, medieval and modern' (5th ed, 1972) compiled and edited by William L Langer was first published in 1940 and ultimately derives from Karl Ploetz's *Auszug aus den alten, mittleren und neueren Geschichte.* A factual handbook for students and the general reader, it is now truly universal in coverage and designed so that the dates stand out prominently in a continuous narrative. Maps and genealogical tables are amply provided together with lists of potentates, universities, etc. The publisher is Houghton Miflin.

261 'England and the discovery of America 1481-1620' *from the Bristol voyages of the fifteenth century to the pilgrim settlement at Plymouth: the exploration, exploitation, and trial-and-error colonization of North America by the English* by David Beers Quinn (Allen and Unwin, 1974) is described by the author as not 'a detailed connected narrative and analysis but rather an exposure of successive points of interest, information, or synthesis which exemplify some of the problems of documenting and understanding a process which we know even today very imperfectly.' It is divided into five parts: Searches in the Atlantic; Discovery in the west; Sailors and colonies; Economic and religious discontents; and Preludes to permanent settlement; and an important 'Bibliography of books and articles on American exploration and colonization,' arranged chronologically by historical period. There is a generous provision of maps and illustrations.

262 'England and Wales 1820-1870 in recent historiography; a selective bibliography' by Roger W Prouty, reprinted in *Changing views on British history*, first appeared in *The historian* 24, May 1962: 270-307, and concentrates to a large extent on economic, industrial and sociological aspects of historical studies for this period.

263 'England before Elizabeth' by Helen Cam published in Hutchinson's *University library* (1950) is oriented towards political history and traces the evolution of England into a unified kingdom 'under the stress of competition for power, the disciplinary influence of christianity, the stimulus of invasion, the compression of conquest, the centralisation of government, the standardisation of institutions.'

264 'England before the Norman conquest; being a history of the Celtic, Roman and Anglo-Saxon periods down to the year AD 1066' by Sir Charles Oman, the first volume of Methuen's *History of England*, has passed through many editions to take advantage of new evidence forthcoming from advances and discoveries in archaeology since it was first published in 1910. The author was a man of forcible opinions and did not shed them easily but when at length he was persuaded that new evidence really demanded new interpretations he was generous in acknowledging his sources.

There is no separate bibliography but there is a long disquisition on the authorities for the Anglo-Saxon period.

265 **'England 1870-1914'** by R C K Ensor (1936) the next to last volume of the *Oxford history of England* is divided chronologically into three sections, the first up to the resignation of Gladstone's third cabinet in 1886, the second to the death of Queen Victoria, and the edwardian period down to the outbreak of the first world war. The social and political themes running through the volume are the conversion of English government into a democracy; the transformation of the English people into at least a partially educated and literate society; the collapse of English agriculture; the serious competition for overseas markets; and the formation of the British Empire. The bibliography tackles the truly immense embarrassment of sources and authorities with remarkable aplomb and efficiency.

266 **'England in the age of the American revolution'** by L B Namier was intended by the author to be the first volume of a larger work when it was first published by Macmillan in 1930 but even then he was uncertain whether circumstances would allow him to complete it. Widely recognised as Namier's greatest work it prompted the remark on publication that hitherto there had been three ways of writing history, Gibbon's, Carlyle's, and Macaulay's, but now there was a fourth, Namier's. A long introductory section, 'The social foundation,' precedes the main body of the text which is headed 'Book I. Government and parliament under the Duke of Newcastle' and consists of a close examination of parliamentary politics of the period. The concluding sentence reads 'My next book, if ever written, will be on "The rise of party," ' but this particular book never in fact reached the light of day and when, twenty five years later, he resumed the work, Namier delegated a number of young protégés to write further volumes under his original title now employed as the general title of the series. His own early work, rewritten and renamed *Newcastle and Bute,* took its place in the appointed series. The first of the new volumes was John Brooke's *The Chatham administration 1766-1768* (1956) a study of the origin of parties dealing in the main with the coteries and cliques who formed the opposing factions which during this period hardened into the alignments they assumed during the

American revolution. It follows the attempts of the elder Pitt to establish a stable government that would command the confidence and trust of both crown and parliament. *The end of North's ministry 1780-1782* (1958) by Ian Christie traces the failure of Lord North's attempts to hold on to office in the face of defeat in the American war of independence. Bernard Donoughue's *British politics and the American revolution: The path to war, 1773-75* (1964) examines the desperate English attempts in the intervening period between the Boston tea party, December 1773, and the descent into war at Lexington and Concord in April 1775 to preserve their transatlantic empire. At the same time, like all the volumes in this very much Namier inspired series, it takes a close look at the parliamentary groups battling for control of the administration.

267 'England in the eighteenth century' by J H Plumb, published in the *Pelican history of England* in 1950, is divided into three convenient chronological sections: the ages of Walpole, Chatham, and Pitt. Within each the interrelationships of social, agrarian and industrial factors and the complex nature of politics are investigated and summarised. Imperial and foreign affairs, the loss of the American colonies, the beginnings of empire in India, and the almost incessant French wars receive due attention.

268 'England in the late middle ages' by A R Myers (1952) forms the fourth volume in the *Pelican history of England*. Covering the years 1307-1536 the author perhaps stresses political history rather more than his predecessors in the series but how otherwise could a true picture of this turbulent and significant period in the national development be sketched? The book list, a few suggestions for introductory reading, is confined to secondary works although one or two periodical articles are mentioned which 'can be read with great pleasure and equal profit by any educated person.' To such a reader this modest volume itself offers a vast erudition worn very lightly.

269 'England in the late middle ages' by K H Vickers (1913), the third volume of Methuen's *History of England*, covering the period from the accession of Edward I in 1272 to the end of the wars of the roses in 1485, is a straightforward political, diplomatic and military narrative with almost no concession to social or economic affairs apart from a perfunctory glance at the agrarian discontents of the mid-fourteenth century. There is no bibliography as such but a most valuable list of authorities is appended.

270 'England in the late middle ages; a political history' by M H Keen (1973) replaces the volume by K H Vickers of the same title in Methuen's *History of England*. Its theme is the heavy burden which eventually proved unendurable placed on the state by the incessant civil and foreign wars in which no fewer than five kings forfeited their thrones. The insufficient financial resources of the crown and its inability to match the power of the feudal aristocracy are well outlined in this new study which is neatly arranged so as to present narrative and discursive thematic chapters alternatively. A refreshing number of recent journal articles are cited in the bibliography.

271 'England in the nineteenth century 1815-1914' by David Thomson (1950), the eighth title in the *Pelican history of England*, discusses the major social changes which distinguish this particular period. 'The aim has been to paint the main outlines with a broad brush and to introduce as much factual detail ... as is necessary to demonstrate the nature, inter-connexions, and significance of the social changes described.' A list of suggested books for further reading is appended.

272 'England in the reign of Charles II' by David Ogg (OUP, 2 vols, 2nd ed, 1956) contains interspersed analytical chapters on the fighting services, land and people, revenue and taxation, etc, and narrative chapters on political and constitutional events. The same author's *England in the reigns of James II and William II* continues the story in similar fashion.

273 'England in the seventeenth century' by Maurice Ashley was described by C V Wedgwood, herself a no mean historian of the period, as 'a closely packed portmanteau of varied knowledge and mature thought' when first published in the *Pelican history of England* in 1952. Certainly it is a masterly commentary on the numerous and varied political and constitutional changes which punctuate the stuart experience. Cultural affairs are not forgotten and receive their due attention. In a somewhat rueful introduction to the 1966 reprint the author remarks that at least one new book on seventeenth century England is published every week either in England or in the United States but undeterred by this sobering thought he presents an extensive bibliography.

274 **'England in the twentieth century 1914-1963'** by David Thomson, which completed the *Pelican history of England* when published in 1965, is arranged in three chronological sections: from great war to great depression 1914-1929, from world crisis to world war 1930-1945, and from welfare state to affluent society 1946-1963. The prominent role played in world affairs is well to the fore but, as the author unequivocally states, the bedrock of any history of England for this period 'must be an unravelling of the events and their consequences which accumulatively turned the England of Asquith into the England of Macmillan.' Here they are unravelled uncommonly well.

275 **'England since Waterloo'** by Sir J A R Marriott (1913), the seventh volume of Methuen's *History of England*, covers the period up to the close of the victorian era. In a note to the thirteenth edition published in 1945 the author admits that its tone is hopelessly victorian but adds that it is not certain that the social, economic and political suppositions of that particular period 'will not in the long run prove less unsound than it is today fashionable to assume.'

276 **'England 1200-1640'** by G R Elton (Hodder, 1969) in the *Sources of history* series consists of what Americans call long bibliographical essays. Narratives, *ie*, chronicles, annals, and histories; official records of the royal administration, the great courts and parliament; church records; those of the lesser courts; private estate and business archives; legal records; and books and writings during the periods before and after the invention of the printing press, are all surveyed in precise but comprehensive fashion. There is a characteristically trenchant final two chapters on non-documentary sources and a summary on the duties and materials of present day historians of the period.

277 'England under Queen Anne' by G M Trevelyan, published in three volumes 1930-1934, is a splendid unfolding of events from a masterly historian who still cherished the belief that there should be no distinction between history written for the student or the general reader. War and politics, the two inextricably bound together in the shape of Marlborough, form the theme of the work as is clearly indicated in the choice of titles: *Blenheim, Ramillies and the union with Scotland*, and *The peace and the protestant succession*.

278 'England under the hanoverians' by Sir Charles Grant Robertson was first published in the *Methuen history of England* in 1911 but went through many reprintings in the next fifty years. It was designed 'to trace the ordered development of an imperial, constitutional and industrial state,' linking the evolution of the constitution, and the underlying economic forces, with the central issues of political history. No fewer than twenty three appendices augmenting the text; a generous provision of maps; and a bibliography, arranged under form, chronological and subject headings, intended to provide students with a reliable guide to advanced study, all remind us that the Methuen series was long regarded as the most authoritative history of England on the market.

279 'England under the Normans and Angevins 1066-1272' by H W C Davis, the second volume of Methuen's *History of England*, has been reprinted several times since it was first published in 1904. Although it is the political and constitutional events that provide the main body of the narrative, there is some assessment of the art, literature, and social life of the period.

280 'England under the stuarts' by G M Trevelyan first published in 1904 and reprinted many times since, is the fifth volume of Methuen's *History of England*. It simultaneously traces the evolution of a peculiarly national and idiosyncratic system of government whilst engaging upon an examination of the social life of the period. There is a fussily arranged bibliography which was compiled 'with the double purpose of assisting the general reader to books which he will care to read and of pointing out to the student some works where his studies can profitably commence' but which is in fact more likely to cause him to miss at least half

112

the references. Nevertheless, J H Plumb in his study, *G M Trevelyan*, first published as a pamphlet in the *Writers and their work* series for the British Council by Longmans, and later reprinted in *Men and places* (1963), describes it as 'far and away the most impressive volume in this series ... when the others have been forgotten, it will still be read.'

281 **'England under the tudors'** by G R Elton (1955) replaces A D Innes' volume of the same title in Methuen's *History of England*, emphasising the contribution the author has made in the period he has made his own. When his book first appeared it occasioned no little stir, his abrupt treatment of long held theories and interpretations reverberated in college common rooms. 'In some parts of the story I have gone farther in being up to date than may be generally liked,' he proclaimed. 'I have come to some conclusions, especially about the place of Thomas Cromwell, the importance of the 1530s, and the nature of the tudor polity, which—though by no means necessarily original—go counter to some accepted notions.' 'Confronted,' he continued, 'with a choice between writing what I think to be true and repeating what I believe to be doubtful, I could not but choose the former.' Particular attention in the bibliography is paid to recent publications which are not included on earlier lists.

282 **'England under the yorkists and tudors 1471-1603'** by P J Helm (1968) is one of Bell's *Modern histories*. Besides political and constitutional factors there is ample treatment of social, economic and cultural matters. The author takes full advantage of recent research and also provides a most imaginative method of breathing life into what constitutes for many general readers a difficult and complicated period by including extracts from contemporary works at the end of many of the chapters. In addition each chapter is furnished with a short list of books and articles whilst suggestions for further reading oddly appear at the front, before the text.

283 **'England's quest of eastern trade'** by Sir William Foster was one of A and C Black's original volumes in their *Pioneer history* series when first published in 1933. The author recounts the adventures of the explorers and traders with verve and enthusiasm.

The period of time covered ranges from Willoughby and Chancellors' search for a route to Cathay and ends aptly with the establishment of a regular trade with China in the 1670s. There are bibliographical notes for each chapter describing original source materials and no fewer than thirteen maps to chart the more significant journeys and expeditions.

284 'English colonisation of North America,' edited by Louis B Wright and Elaine W Fowler, published in 1968, belongs to Edward Arnold's *Documents of modern history* series. The documents included are designed to provide provocative suggestions of the main lines of development in the thirteen British colonies in North America that became the United States. They are topically arranged in chapters: Competing claims for the new world; Motives and propaganda for colonisation; Charters, compacts and laws; Religion and education; Economic development; Relations with the Indians; People and conditions of life; and, Plans of union-grievances against England. Each document is furnished with a concise explanatory introduction.

285 'English constitutional conflicts of the seventeenth century 1603-1689' by J R Tanner (CUP, 1928) is the printed version of a series of lectures delivered in the University of Cambridge. A list of parliaments 1603-1689 and an extensive bibliography complement the text.

286 'English constitutional history' by S B Chrimes originally published in the *Home university library* (1948) is now available in a fourth edition (1967) as number sixteen of the *Oxford paperbacks university series*. It summarises in scholarly and convenient fashion the development of the English constitution from the later middle ages to the twentieth century. There is a useful bibliography.

287 'English constitutional history' by S B Chrimes and I A Roots (1958) is one of the Historical Association's *Helps for students of history* series. It is a short but all embracing bibliography arranged chronologically in the first instance and then under classified headings and is obviously intended for undergraduate use if only

114

because it includes material published in learned journals presupposing easy access to a good academic library.

288 'The english experience; a survey of English history from early to modern times' by John Bowle (Weidenfeld, 1971) is written in the conviction 'that the undoubted historical success of England, so remarkable in relation to its size, has been a triumph not of any commitment to abstract political principles but rather to the absence of it; to a tradition of pragmatism both in the theory and conduct of affairs.' Although this is no textbook, a thread of political history sets social and cultural history firmly in context. Twenty pages of notes provide the key to further reading.

289 'English historians' edited by A J Grant (1906) was originally issued in the *Warwick library of English literature* a decade earlier, and it is limited to historians writing in English to the consequent exclusion of medieval historians and chroniclers writing in Latin. Practically a quarter of the book is taken up by a survey of English historiography ending with a discussion of the contemporary state of history and its likely development. This is followed by two sections: extracts to illustrate the view taken by historians at different periods of the objects and methods of history; and, secondly, passages illustrating the method and style adopted by historians at different periods. The emphasis throughout is on the nineteenth century.

290 'English historical documents' (Eyre and Spottiswoode, 12 vols 1953-   ) attempt to provide on a large scale a wide selection of the fundamental sources of English history and so facilitate the consultation of original authorities. Within each period a comprehensive body of primary evidence has been gathered with the aim of presenting material with scholarly accuracy and without bias in accordance with the strictest demands of modern scholarship. Each volume begins with a general introduction and a critical bibliography to assist further research. Editorial comments are restricted to elucidating the texts and readers are left to make their own judgements. A detailed contents list in each volume affords a good guide to the classified extracts which are arranged chronologically. The cost of each volume ranges between £8.00 and £22.00 which suggests that only large libraries can buy the complete set, but schools and colleges offering advanced level English history courses might well invest in the appropriate volume(s) of this authoritative work which must be ranked with the massive achievements of nineteenth century scholarship. Titles (with their editors):

1 c500-1042 (Dorothy Whitelock) 1955
2 1042-1189 (David Douglas and George Greenaway) 1953
3 1189-1327 (Harry Rothwell) 1975
4 1327-1485 (A R Myers) 1969
5 1485-1558 (C H Williams) 1967
6 1558-1603 (Douglas Price) in preparation
7 1603-1664 (Mary Coate) in preparation
8 1660-1714 (Andrew Browning) 1953
9 American Colonial Documents to 1776 (Merrill Jensen) 1955
10 1714-1783 (D B Horn and Mary Ransome) 1957
11 1783-1832 (A Aspinall and E Anthony Smith) 1959
12 1) 1833-1874 (G M Young and W D Handcock) 1956
12 2) 1874-1914 (W D Handcock) in preparation

The general editor is David Douglas.

291 'English historical documents 1906-1939' edited by J H Bettey (Routledge, 1967) presents central extracts from a number of important and significant documents enabling students to read for themselves items which are frequently referred to but which are not always easily accessible. Topics covered include the beginning of the welfare state; the constitutional crisis leading up to the Parliament act of 1911; South Africa: the payment of salaries to MPs; The first world war; industrial troubles; India; Ireland; the formation of the national government in 1931; the statute of Westminster; and the various international disputes and agreements prior to the second world war. Each document is prefaced by an introductory note outlining its historical context and significance.

292 'English historical literature in the fifteenth century' by C L Kingsford (1913) traces the literary development of English historiography during a crucial period in the course of which it changed from a purely monastic occupation to the beginning of a new epoch when historians, encouraged by a growing national consciousness and the new learning, began to assume modern

116

dress. Contents include a study of the works of Thomas Walsingham representing the old order; the biographers of Henry V by which successive stages in historical method can be discerned; the *London chronicle* and *Brut* to illustrate the beginnings of historical writing in English; Sir Thomas More's *History of King Richard III*, the first historical work of outstanding literary merit in the English language; with a concluding chapter on sixteenth century historians as the heirs to the period under discussion. There is an appendix of chronicles and historical pieces previously unprinted and the bibliography consists of printed editions of original authorities and a list of the manuscripts described or noticed in the text.

293 'English historical review' can claim to be the oldest quarterly journal of historical scholarship in the English speaking world, its first issue arriving in the bookshops in January 1886. It was greeted by a fourth leader in *The times* (16 January) which opened a little unpropitiously: 'The heart sinks when a new magazine or review is announced,' although a little further on it admitted, somewhat reluctantly one feels, that the new arrival 'has an aim which saves it from the reproach of a mere addition to the general turmoil,' and concluded that it had 'a satisfactory prospect of success.' In the early years of this century the *Review* was described as being 'obviously addressed to the scholar of ripe erudition' and Denys Hay in his article 'The historical periodical: some problems' (*qv*) pithily summarises the *EHR*'s unique position: 'The solid, highly particularised and annotated articles in the *EHR* are the hard, gritty bricks from which the Great Wall of history is steadily, if slowly built.' Half its space is devoted to articles and notes and documents on all aspects of medieval and modern history, the other half to reviews and short notices of books, and a section reviewing periodical articles is an annual feature. From time to time *EHR supplements* are published, 'devoted to work scholarly in character and similar in presentation to matter published in the review, but too long for inclusion as an article and too short for publication as a book.' Unusually, the *Review* is owned by Longmans, a major publishing firm, and not by a learned society. The reason for this and other details of the founding of the *EHR* may be read in 'The beginnings of the English historical review' *EHR* XXXVI (CXLI) January 1921:

1-4, and further in chapter eleven, *The life and letters of Mandell Creighton* by his wife (2 vols 1904).

294 '**English historical scholarship in the sixteenth and seventeenth centuries'** *a record of the papers delivered at a conference arranged by the Dugdale Society to commemorate the tercentenary of the publication of Dugdale's Antiquities of Warwickshire* edited by Levi Fox was published by OUP for the society in 1956. Contents include 'The public records in the sixteenth and seventeenth centuries' (R B Wernham); 'Politics and historical research in the early seventeenth century' (Philip Styles); 'The study and use of charters by English scholars in the seventeenth century' (H A Cronne); 'Antiquarian thought in the sixteenth and seventeenth centuries' (Stuart Piggott); and 'The value of sixteenth and seventeenth century scholarship to modern historical research' (Sir Maurice Powicke, V H Galbraith, M D Knowles, and E F Jacob).

295 English Historical Society printed accurate, uniform and elegant editions of the most valuable English chronicles from the earliest period down to the accession of Henry VIII during the years 1838-1856. This task was undertaken because so many texts were available only in costly and unsatisfactory editions carelessly transcribed or injudiciously edited. In the volumes issued much material such as the tedious general world history from the creation, deluge, or the Nativity which introduced many chronicles was expunged as were the annals lifted verbatim from earlier chroniclers. The text employed was collated from the most reliable manuscripts in an effort to restore it to its original purity. A preface consisting of a personal history of the particular author, the importance and credibility of the narrative, its sources, and a discussion of the extant manuscripts, especially the one used, accompanied each work.
List of titles with editors:

Opera historica (Bede) Joseph Stevenson, 2 vols 1838-1841.

Chronicon Ricardi Divisiensis de rebus gestis Richardi Primi regis Angliae/Historia Brittonum (Nennius)/*De excidio Brittaniae* (Gildas). Joseph Stevenson, 1838.

Gesta regum Anglorum (William of Malmesbury) Thomas Duffus Hardy, 1840.

Chronica sive flores historiarum (Roger of Wendover). Henry Cox, 4 vols 1841-1842. Appendix (Matthew of Paris) 1844.

Annales (Nicholas Trevet) Thomas Hog, 1845.

Codex diplomaticus aevi Saxonici John Kemble 6 vols 1839-1848.

Chronica sui temporis (Adam Murimuth) Thomas Hog/*Gesta Stephani* Richard Sewell, 1846.

Chronicque de la traison et mort de Richart Deux Benjamin Williams, 1846.

Chronicon ex chronicis (Florence of Worcester) Benjamin Thorpe 2 vols 1848-1849.

De gestis regum Angliae (Walter of Heminburgh) Hans Claude Hamilton 2 vols 1848-1849.

Henrici Quinti Angliae regis gesta Benjamin Williams 1850.

Historia rerum Anglicarum (William Petit) Hans Claude Hamilton, 1856.

296 'English history; a survey' by Sir George Clark, general editor of the *Oxford history of England*, published in 1971 by OUP, is in no way a shortened version of that history but a single volume work depicting 'how the English people came to form a community; what kind of community it has been in its successive stages of development; and what have been its relations with the other communities to which English people have belonged, or with which they have had dealings.' In the course of 500 pages it is obviously impossible to give equal treatment to all possible topics but the significant events are recorded at an appropriate length in a scholarly and urbane manner. A delightful christmas gift for anyone who has the slightest interest in English history.

297 'English history 1558-1640; a bibliographical survey' by Perez Zagorin which takes a selective view of the writings on elizabethan and early stuart political, constitutional, military, religious, social and economic, and cultural history published in the last twenty years. It forms one of the Conference on British Studies sponsored articles and appeared in the *American historical review* LXVIII (2) January 1963: 364-384. Subsequently it was included in *Changing views on British History* (*qv*).

298 '**English history 1914-1945**' by A J P Taylor (1965) completed the *Oxford history of England*. 'For ten of the thirty one years this volume covers,' the author exclaims, 'the English were involved in great wars; for nineteen they lived in the shadow of mass unemployment.' These two themes, together with their political and diplomatic history, preoccupy Professor Taylor who freely confesses that after they had received adequate treatment there was little room left for other matters but few would quibble at this. The bibliography is outstanding not only for its wide coverage but also for its outspoken comments on many of the books and important personages cited. It begins with a typically trenchant condemnation of the 'fifty year rule' on the use of official documents (subsequently, of course, relaxed into a thirty year rule) which Taylor regards as an inexplicable and quite unjustifiable rigmarole. The work experienced a mixed reception: Henry Pelling's review in the April 1966 issue of *Past and present* was particularly severe in listing errors. A Penguin edition was published in 1970.

299 '**English monarchs**' (1964-   ) a series of studies edited by David C Douglas and published by Eyre Methuen are substantial histories revolving round the life of a particular monarch. Some are more avowedly biographical in intention, others are 'life and times' histories, all are scrupulously based on contemporary sources and are obviously designed as definitive histories of their several periods. Titles: *William the Conqueror* by David C Douglas; *James I* by David Mathew; *Henry VIII* by J J Scarisbrook; *Edward the Confessor* by Frank Barlow; *Henry VII* by S B Chrimes; *Henry II* by W L Warren; and *Edward IV* by Charles Ross. Other titles are in active preparation.

300 '**The English revolution; an introduction to English history 1603-1714**' by I Deane Jones first published by Heinemann in 1931 but subsequently reprinted is avowedly a work 'not of research in the strict and august sense, but of introduction and interpretation' and one which is based on the material the sixth form or undergraduate student is expected to read, namely standard histories, specialised monographs, and those documents easily accessible. It is intended to encourage the wide reading of seventeenth century historical literature. The central theme is the 'triumph of the idea of parliamentary supremacy based on the political rule of the propertied classes.' There is a list of books for general reference and each chapter concludes with suggestions for further reading.

301 'English scholars 1660-1730' by David C Douglas (2nd ed, 1951) is concerned with that remarkable body of late seventeenth and early eighteenth century historians who transformed medieval studies by their assiduous research into early texts and their enthusiasm for antiquarian pursuits. The work of men like William Dugdale, Coke, Selden, Rymer, and John Aubrey, is carefully examined and the religious and patriotic zeal which inspired their studies is accurately traced and recorded.

302 'English society in the early middle ages' by Doris Mary Stenton (1951) is the third volume of the *Pelican history of England* and covers the period 1066-1307. Although concentrating largely on social history the political, constitutional and administrative developments are not forgotten. There is a select list of essential dates and a list of suggested further reading.

303 Ethelweard (died 998?) a member of the royal house of Wessex compiled the *Monumenta Historica Britannica* towards the end of the tenth century. Unfortunately it relies largely on the *Anglo-Saxon chronicle* although it is valuable for disentangling the genealogy of the West Saxon kings. An English translation by A Campbell is included in the *Oxford medieval texts* series.

304 'Europe and the world in the age of expansion' is the general title of a series of ten volumes edited by Boyd C Shafer for the University of Minnesota Press which investigates the nature and impact of European culture and civilisation on the rest of the world. Emphasis is given to the discoveries and explorations and territorial expansions, the complex relationships between the colonized and colonizers, and the gradual progress to independence of the former colonial territories. The English publisher is the Oxford University Press.

305 'The European discovery of America; the northern voyages AD 500-1600' (1971) and *The Southern Voyages A.D. 1492-1616* (1974) by S E Morison is a major definitive work beginning with

121

the semi-legendary Irish voyages and ending with the early Western plantations. In Admiral Morison the American people are fortunate to possess an historian who brings a practical sailor's experience in chronicling the voyages. He looks with a sceptical eye on some of the wilder theories, is zealous in his research in European archives, and is indefatigable in retracing the early discoverers' routes both in the air and afloat. Each chapter concludes with extensive notes examining the bibliographical record. It is to be hoped that Admiral Morison's plan to return to the northern voyages of the early seventeenth century, announced in his preface to the first volume, comes to fruition.

306 **'European manuscript sources of the American revolution'** by W J Koenig and S L Mayer (Bowker, 1974) is a selective guide to resources in European archives, libraries, and museums, and also in private collections for the years 1763-1785.

307 **'The European nations in the West Indies 1493-1688'** by Arthur Percival Newton was published in 1933 as one of the original volumes of A and C Black's *Pioneer histories*. It offers a study of the broad lines of development of national policies in the Caribbean, English, French, Dutch, and Spanish, as a whole, with the history of individual islands examined only when it played a prominent part in general affairs. There are four rather cluttered maps.

308 **'Everyman's dictionary of dates'** was first published in 1911 and has triumphantly passed through many revisions since then. As the title implies it is aimed at the general reader. In selection prominence was given to countries, institutions and dynasties of universal influence with a slight bias towards Britain; other countries etc, of lesser influence were accorded less space. The arts, sciences, philosophy, religion, invention and miscellaneous facts of general interest or notoriety are all recorded. In the main there are three types of heading: short entries on specific matters; narratives (of countries); and longer classified entries. A helpful list of this last category is included at the beginning.

309 **'Everyman Library'** possibly the best known and most successful of all the inexpensive reprint series, was the brainchild of J M Dent and was introduced in 1906 with the simultaneous publication of fifty titles. By the end of the first year it had reached 155, the 500 mark was achieved in 1910, and a thousand by 1956. From the beginning, history took its place as one of the originally planned sections of the library and many famous historians appeared in the Everyman list: Carlyle, Froude, Gibbon, J R Green, Hallam, Macaulay, Mommsen, Parkman, Prescott etc, etc. The classics section and travel also contain titles of considerable interest. Indispensable for the library with limited funds Everyman volumes still appear in conventional publisher's cloth bindings although many titles are now also published as paperbacks. A complete catalogue of available titles may be obtained from J M Dent and Sons Ltd, Aldine House, Bedford Street, London WC2. The American publishers are E P Dutton of New York.

310 'The evolution of British historiography from Bacon to Namier' (1967) edited by J R Hale, examines the British contribution to the development of the historian's technique. Passages from twenty one distinguished historians, with one exception all of whom are described as pioneers, illustrate the evolution of modern British historical writing. The long introduction sets each historian in his own times.

311 'The exploration of New Zealand' by W G McClymount (OUP, 2nd ed, 1959) was first published by the Department of Internal Affairs in Wellington in 1940 as one of the volumes included in the New Zealand Centennial Surveys. It relates the exploration of the hinterland haphazardly conducted by shepherds, gold miners and missionaries etc. The references in the notes on the sources are also divided according to the occupation or profession of the various explorers.

312 'The exploration of the Pacific' by J C Beaglehole was first published by A and C Black as one of their *Pioneer histories* in 1934 but was revised and rewritten for the third edition of 1966 to take account of the work completed in the intervening period. It is a purely straightforward chronological narrative of European exploration of the Pacific from Magellan to Cook, *ie*, it is concerned mostly with the long search for the southern continent

123

and, incidentally, of the discovery of the main island groups. There is a bibliography consisting of primary authorities, collections of voyages, and modern works. Four, rather fussy maps, are also included.

313 'The explorers of North America 1492-1806' by John Bartlet Brebner (Black, 1933) belongs to the *Pioneer history* series. It is a detailed account intended for the general reader and was conceived on a continental basis including Spanish, French, Dutch, English, American, Canadian and Russian explorations. The aim throughout was to explain 'why men explored, where and when they went, and who promoted and supported the expeditions.' In the belief that the explorers' own words catch and hold the interest and attention of the reader the author allows himself liberal quotation. Each chapter then ends with a note as to where the complete narrative may be found. There are four maps.

314 'Fabric of British history' series, published by B T Batsford, includes both chronological and thematic volumes. Written and produced to a high standard they are particularly suitable for students on advanced college and university first degree courses. Titles: D P Kirby: *Making of early England*; Donald Mathew: *The Norman conquest*; Ivan Roots: *The great rebellion 1642-1660*; Sydney Pollard: *The wealth of Britain 1085-1966*; John Gough: *The rise of the entrepreneur*; and W R Ward: *Religion and society in England*.

315 Fabyan, Robert (d 1513) was the author of *The Newe Chronicles of Englande and of Fraunce* (1516) which extends from the arrival of Brutus in 1106 BC down to 1485. It has slight importance although he made some endeavour to reconcile various contradictions of different historians. A number of alterations to the text in later editions reflect the difficulties of writing history in disturbed times.

316 'The fall of the British Empire 1918-1968' by Colin Cross (Hodder, 1968) relates the sequence of events which marked the empire's virtual disappearance within fifty years of its hour of greatest triumph at the conclusion of the first world war. The internal history of each member country and the wider story of world events are mentioned only if they directly impinged upon imperial history. There are many illustrations.

317 'The far west in American history' by Harvey L Carter (AHA Service Center Series no 26) published in 1960 is especially useful to non American students in that it dilates on the hypothesis of Frederick Jackson Turner that it was the advance of American settlement westwards that encouraged American civilization to diverge from that of the old world. Whereas most nineteenth century historians generally stressed the obvious similarities between American and European civilizations by tracing the old world beginnings of American institutions, Turner attributed the equally obvious differences to the constant need for American society to begin again and again at each new frontier reached. In general, however, the conclusion is that the history of the Far West has been factual rather than interpretative. Themes considered in this bibliographical essay include the popular and romantic view of far western history, the factual viewpoint, the textbooks dealing with the history of the American frontier and various topics such as the great explorations, early settlements, cattlemen and homesteaders, and the Indians. Unfortunately much of the material mentioned will be of little help to British students because it is to be found only in state historical journals not immediately available in this country.

318 'The fate of a nation; the American Revolution through contemporary eyes' by William P Cumming and Hugh F Rankin (Phaidon, 1975) presents the American revolution as it appeared to the various participants. It is not simply a narrative history nor a selection of original documents but a combination of the two: a continuous narrative frequently interspersed with extracts from diaries, letters and reports written at the time. There are many aptly chosen maps and illustrations each accompanied by explanatory captions. An editorial decision to exclude all illustrations later than the year 1800 ensures this remains at least a very near contemporary record throughout. There are scholarly notes, a bibliography, and a chronological table. The American publisher is Praeger Publishers Inc, of New York.

319 'The federal age 1789-1829; America in the process of becoming' by Keith Berwick (AHA Service Center Series no 40) published in 1961 is an attempt to rescue this period from the surprising neglect it suffered until recent historians returned to it. The main themes of the period provide the section headings: Establishing the federal government; Origins of the party system; The foundations of American foreign policy; The Fruits of isolation; The old order passes; and Toward national self-discovery. There is an author-title list of books mentioned in the text.

320 Feiling, Keith (1884-) although not so prolific in his writings as many of his contemporaries nevertheless contributed a number of important works. *A history of England* (1950), a straightforward narrative, which stresses the period when Britain became a great power, has recently enjoyed a new lease of life with members of one of the larger book clubs. But his reputation depends mainly on '*A History of the Tory Party 1640-1714* (1924) and *The second Tory Party 1714-1832* (1938). *England under the tudors and stuarts* (1927) in the Home University Library and his political biography, *Life of Neville Chamberlain* (1946) also attracted favourable notice. A *festschrift* volume, *Essays in British history* edited by H R Trevor-Roper (1964), marked his retirement.

321 Festschriften is the name given to volumes of separate articles by friends, colleagues, and former pupils dedicated and presented to eminent scholars to mark their retirement or some other memorable occasion. Usually they include a bibliography of the writings (varying in quality) of the scholar in question. Articles in these volumes are by no means easy to trace, there is no regular analytical list although *Historical abstracts* manages to pick up most of them. Useful retrospective lists may be found in *Bibliographie internationale des travaux historiques publiés dans les volumes de mélanges 1880-1939* (Paris, Armand Colin, 1955). A second volume 1940-1950 was published in 1965. This work received financial assistance from Unesco and was published under the auspices of the International Council for Philosophy and Humanistic Sciences. It is in two parts: a list of *festschrift* volumes by country; and an analytical list classified first under

Auxiliary sciences and historiography including the theory of history, and then by topic, period, or area.

322 'Feudal Britain; the completion of the medieval kingdoms 1066-1314' by G W S Barrow (Edward Arnold, 1956) is intended as a general survey, emphasising the most important themes of the medieval ancestry of modern Britain, based closely on original sources and most recent research. Lists of contemporary rulers, archbishops and popes, genealogical tables, maps, and a classified bibliography, augment the text.

323 'Feudal England; historical studies on the eleventh and twelfth centuries' by J H Round. Although first published in 1895 it still retains magisterial authority, unusual for what is after all not a monograph but a collection of papers originally published in professional journals. Arranged in two sections, Territorial studies and Historical studies, the first is concerned with his seminal work on the system of land assessment as the necessarily preliminary to the introduction of the feudal system in England. 'Mr Freeman and the Battle of Hastings,' which forms the major part of the second section, earned a wide notoriety for its merciless demolition of Freeman's lack of research, casting grave doubts as to the scholarship of that author's *History of the Norman conquest*. A new impression of *Feudal England* with a foreword by Sir Frank Stenton was issued by Allen and Unwin in 1964.

324 'The feudal kingdom of England 1042-1216' by Frank Barlow (2nd ed, 1961), the fourth volume of Longman's *History of England*, considers that 'the only continuous thread which the sources give to the historian of this period is the fortunes of the great men—the bishops, the barons, and, above all, the kings—and it is not stupid to accept in the main this contemporary scale of values, for ... only a few men have the power, material or intellectual, to exert an appreciable influence on events.' In general, few would argue with this conclusion *for this particular period*.

325 'The fifteen decisive battles of the world' by Sir Edward Creasy (1851) remains the best known single work on this subject although largely superseded by Major-General J F C Fuller's *The* *decisive battles of the Western world and their influence upon history* 3 vols (1954-1956).

326 **'The fifteenth century 1399-1485'** by E F Jacob (1961) a volume in the *Oxford history of England*, concentrates on areas of study suggested by the most recent research: the acquisition of land and property by the great families of the realm; the social composition of parliament; the financial resources of the crown; and the total disregard for the *lex terrae* on the part of powerful individuals and groups. This is not usually a period which attracts the general reader but if a rare specimen did venture into the complexities of the age then he would be well served by the bibliography. University students would be well advised to study this *before* embarking upon their courses.

327 **'Films for historians'** (2nd ed, 1974) published by the British University Film Council, provides details of 360 films suitable for teaching political, social and military history to university level.

328 **'The first four Georges'** by J H Plumb was published by B T Batsford in their *British monarchy* series in 1956. It is an eminently readable account of the hanoverian kings providing an excellent introduction to the period which succeeds in incorporating and conveying the post-Namier viewpoint in easy fashion. The select bibliography is intended for the curious general reader and not for the scholar.

329 **'The flowering of the middle ages'** edited by Joan Evans (Thames and Hudson 1966) the fifth volume in *The great civilizations* series, is designed to bring alive to the general educated reader the social background of the later medieval period down to the renaissance. Chapters on the structure of medieval society, the monastic orders, architecture, the court, the universities, trade, and the invention of printing ushering in the new learning, are contributed by different hands. A breathtaking display of full colour illustrations, detailed chronological charts, and a select bibliography, add to the delight of this imposing work.

330 'Fontana library of English history' edited by G R Elton is intended to reinterpret familiar and unfamiliar aspects of English history. Each chronological period will be served by two volumes discussing it in relation to contrasting themes. The first volume published is *Politics and the nation 1450-1660* by D M Loades (1974). Further titles announced are *The growth of leisure* (Asa Briggs), *From universal church to multiple christianity 1450-1660* (Claire Cross), and *Agrarian boom and population pressure 1066-1272* (H E Hallam). Fontana is the paperback imprint of William Collins and there are no indications as yet that the series will be issued in hard covers.

331 'The Ford lectures'. Each year an eminent historian is invited to deliver a series of lectures in the University of Oxford. An invitation is regarded as one of the highest academic honours an English historian can receive. The lectures are frequently published by the Oxford University Press and subsequently achieve standard textbook status although strictly speaking this is not their intention. Some outstanding examples are *Statesmen and sea power* by Admiral Sir Herbert Richmond, *The wool trade in English medieval history* by Eileen Power, and *King George III and the politicians* by Richard Pares. At times the author's regular publisher issues the printed version, *eg, The making of victorian England* by G Kitson Clark (Methuen, 1962).

332 'The formation of England 550-1042' by H R P Finberg, published in the Paladin History of England in 1974, differs from previous textbooks in its treatment of political and especially of social history. The framework remains largely political but includes two chapters on the social structure of the early and late English periods. The main authorities and sources are outlined in the select bibliography.

333 'Formulare Anglicanum; a collection of ancient charters and instruments of divers kinds, from the Norman conquest to the end of the reign of Henry VIII' by Thomas Madox (1702) established the study of English charters of the Middle Ages on a scientific basis. No fewer than 800 edited documents prefaced by a long introductory essay were included. The work has never been superseded.

334 'Foundations of modern history' is the title given to a series of short historical studies whose purpose it is 'to provide within a limited compass, and at a reasonable cost, scholarly surveys of some of the fundamental developments which have influenced the civilisation and conditioned the outlook of the modern world.' The series also aims to illustrate the general direction of recent historical enquiry, especially in its relations with other disciplines, in addition to presenting selected periods of British history against the contemporary background of European development. Titles include: *Empire in the Antipodes 1840-1860* by John M Ward; *Britain and Europe in the seventeenth century* by J R Jones; *Crisis of empire: Great Britain and the American colonies 1754-1783* by I R Christie; and *Liberalism and Indian politics 1872-1922* by R J Moore.

335 'The founding of the second British empire 1763-1793' by Vincent Harlow is published in two volumes by Longmans. Volume I *Discovery and revolution* (1952) refutes the hypothesis that American independence, formally recognised in 1783, marks the end of one stage of empire and that an interval of ten years elapsed before Britain consciously set about winning a different sort of empire in the French revolutionary and Napoleonic wars. To this end the first chapters are concerned with the Tudor background and the eighteenth century Pacific enterprises. The search for eastern trade also precedes the treatment of Britain's relations with the North American colonies, supporting the theme that the second British empire began some thirty years before the collapse of the old colonial system signalled that the first had disintegrated. Volume II *New continents and changing values* (1964) concentrates on Indian affairs and the increasingly important commerce in the far east with general chapters on state control and mercantilism. The work ends with a section on Canadian commercial and political affairs. Unfortunately Professor Harlow died before he could complete the sections planned on Australia and West Africa but the work is destined to remain a standard authority on the east and on the Americas for years to come. Remarkably there is no bibliography.

336 'The fourteenth century 1307-1399' by May McKisack (1959), the fifth volume of the *Oxford history of England*, reassesses the period in the light of modern research. Politics, murder, and constant warfare are all treated at length but social and economic topics if overshadowed are not entirely forgotten. Students will be grateful for the guide to medieval chronicles and records outlined in the bibliography.

337 Freeman, E A (1823-1892) although a prolific writer on many historical topics is chiefly remembered for his strictly political *History of the Norman conquest* (6 vols, 1867-1879), the first real study of that particular period. He saw his work as a corrective to those of Augustine Thierry and Sir Francis Palgrave who, he declared, had each fastened on to half the truth and who had each suffered from 'a certain lack of critical power' and had therefore failed to distinguish between contemporary documents such as chronicles or charters and careless compilations of three or four hundred years later. His thesis was that the conquest was a turning point in English history not its beginning and that it was necessary to study the early history of both England and Normandy, especially from the time they came in contact with each other, in order to fully comprehend this. And so his work commences at the beginning of the 11th century, reaches its central core with Edward the Confessor, Harold and William, and draws to its close with an examination of the character of Norman rule during the reigns of William's sons. Unfortunately Freeman showed the self-same faults for which he had lambasted Thierry and Palgrave: he was not at home with manuscripts, he had no great palaeographical expertise, and consequently he relied overmuch on printed sources. His intolerance and acerbity aroused controversy and he did not always come off best in disputes over detail. Yet despite these minor faults his *History* has lasted, modern scholarship finds little to cavil at his main conclusion that the continuity of English history was not destroyed at the conquest but just put off course a shade. H A Cronne's 'Edward Augustus Freeman', *History* XXVIII (107) March 1943: 78-92 is a fine critique.

338 Froissart, Jean (1337-1404) is best remembered for his *Chronicles*, the first twenty six chapters of which are solely concerned with the history of England although the whole work also narrates the history of France and Spain and adjoining countries for the period 1326-1400. From 1356 Froissart is writing contemporary history based on eye witness accounts and occasionally on original documents. His work is now mainly of literary interest but the *Chronicles* remain of value especially for the hundred years war between England and France.

339 **'From Alfred to Henry III 871-1272'** by Christopher Brooke (1961), the second volume in Nelson's *History of England*, has a most valuable introductory chapter outlining the literary histories and chronicles upon which most of our knowledge of the period relies. The rapid growth of official documentation in the twelfth and thirteenth centuries is also briefly sketched. The whole book provides a splendid example of scholarly writing for a wide general public.

340 **'From Castlereagh to Gladstone 1815-1885'** by Derek Beales (1969), is the seventh volume of Nelson's *History of England* and is divided into four chronological parts each of which consists of a narrative of events followed by a discussion of economic life, political developments, social change, and the arts.

341 **'From Domesday book to Magna carta 1087-1216'** by Austin Lane Poole (2nd ed, 1955), the third volume of the *Oxford history of England*, is mainly concerned with the attempt to establish a continental empire and to achieve a hegemony over Scotland, Ireland and Wales. But the important constitutional issues are not forgotten, the story of Henry II's legal reforms and the events leading up to the signing of *Magna carta* receive due attention. The somewhat daunting records of the period are annotated well enough to reassure the most timid undergraduate.

342 **'From Hengist and Horsa to Edward of Caernarvon; recent writings on English history'** by Bryce Lyon first appeared in *Tijdschrift voor Geschiedenis* 76 (4) 1963: 377-422 and was afterwards included in *Changing views on British history* (qv). The publication of auxiliary studies, guides, and records; broad general works; and books and articles on politics and war, constitutional history, the common law, social and economic institutions, religious life, intellectual and artistic history, all receive detailed comment. In his concluding impressions Professor Lyon pays tribute to the excellent handbooks, guides and published records that have made their appearance but deplores the lack of new general surveys relating political history to the social, economic and religious forces at work. 'To be meaningful in our shrinking world,' he asserts, 'writing on medieval English history must increasingly portray England ... as an integral member of a Western European community.'

343 Froude J A (1818-1894), a disciple of Carlyle, found his hero in Henry VIII whom he advanced as the saviour of his nation in *The history of England from the fall of Wolsey to the defeat of the Spanish armada* (1856-1870), a twelve volume detailed narrative of what Froude conceived as England's struggle for existence against the overweening power of catholic Spain in the sixteenth century. Seldom has the phrase 'the king can do no wrong' been so uncritically accepted. And if the first half of Froude's great work belonged to Henry, the second found another hero in Lord Burleigh who it now appeared was the true author of England's greatness in the elizabethan age. The *History* attained the same level of popularity as Macaulay's, its prejudices matched those of the history reading public and consolidated the popular conception of the tudor conflict with Spain. But he came under severe, almost savage, criticism from discerning pens for his incredibly inaccurate and careless quoting and translating of his sources. Froude's huge success marks the closing of the age of 'amateur' histories, henceforward a more 'scientific' attitude would replace the broad canvases and the wide sweeps of historical horizons. To latter day historians Froude's *History*, and his posthumous work *English seamen in the sixteenth century* (1895) should be relegated to the realm of literature rather than true history.

344 Gardiner S R (1829-1902) has good claims to be regarded as the first of our modern historians. Rejecting contemporary interpretations of the seventeenth century, always one of the most popular fields of study in English history, because of the blatant party bias displayed by partisan historians, he resolved to return to the abundant source material, to sift through it carefully, relying on primary sources rather than subjective memoirs or polemic pamphlets, and to write his history year by year in a bold effort to avoid marring objective truth by a distorted hindsight. There was a danger, of course, that his *History* would descend into a set of annals, and in truth his literary style lacked colour and excitement, but his compelling use of facts triumphantly averted all possibility of disaster. Slowly the great work took shape, *History of England from the accession of James I to the outbreak of the civil war, 1603-1682* (10 vols 1883-1884), *History of the great civil war 1642-1649* (3 vols 1886) and *History of the commonwealth and protectorate 1649-1660* (4 vols 1903), which even today is still acknowledged to be essential reading for students of the period. In between times he edited a dozen volumes for the Camden Society and became editor of the *English historical review*.

345 Geoffrey of Monmouth (d. 1155) enjoys a wide fame for his *Historia Regum Britanniae* written some time between 1136 and 1139, which quickly became one of the most popular books of the medieval period. It was based on Nennius' *Historia* (*qv*) and a 'certain ancient book written in the English language' alleged to have been presented to him by Walter, Archdeacon of Oxford. Geoffrey's purpose was to relate, in a fervour of patriotism, the history of the British people from the mythical Brutus, a descendant of Virgil's Aeneas who had given his name to Britain, down to Cadwallader the last British king, *ie*, from the twelfth century BC to the seventh century AD. Three kings in particular dominate his narrative; Brutus, Belinus who reputedly captured and sacked the city of Rome, and, above all others, Arthur. He was at pains throughout to glorify the British stock (he was himself of Welsh descent), he stressed the 'voluntary' nature of Britain's association with Rome, and glossed over their defeat at the hands of the Anglo-Saxons by devising the mysterious circumstances of Arthur's death, and by Merlin's prophecy that Arthur would come again once he had recovered from his wounds. He also hinted of a natural alliance between Britons and Normans in that they were both enemies of the Saxons, an astute political move designed to appeal to the Norman court. William of Newburgh (*qv*) writing later in the twelfth century was the first to denounce the *Historia* as nothing more than fiction but lately there have been one or two curious instances where archaeology has confirmed some of Geoffrey's incidental detail. But despite the strictures of orthodox

134

historians, his account of Arthur and Merlin fathered a whole literary genre in the Welsh, French, and German epic romances which together make up the Arthurian legend and it is in the sphere of literature rather than history that Geoffrey of Monmouth rightly belongs. Lewis Thorpe's translation in the *Penguin classics* series offers a convenient outline of Geoffrey's purpose, his sources, biographical detail, and a literary appreciation, plus a short bibliography indicating other scholarly texts and studies. What must surely be the last word was uttered by J S P Tatlock in *The Legendary history of Britain* published by the University of California Press in cooperation with the Medieval Academy of America in 1950.

346 Gervase (1145-1210?), a Canterbury monk, began writing his *Chronica*, a history of Christ Church from St Augustine to the close of the twelfth century set against the background of national history. This was partially incorporated into his *Gesta Regum*, a political history of England starting with the arrival of the mythical Brutus, which is of most value for its contemporary chronicle of the reign of King John. He was the first to define the difference between the art of history and the writing of chronicles: the historian tries to capture his readers' interest by an elegance of style, whereas the chronicler relies on a brief and simple record; both are endeavouring to present a truthful account. The text edited by Stubbs appeared in the *Rolls series* in 1879.

347 'Gesta Regis Henrici Secundi' erroneously associated with the name of Benedict of Peterborough, begins in 1170 and ends in 1192, and is a simple and uncomplicated near contemporary historical narrative betraying an intimate knowledge of government administration and constitutional matters. It is more abundantly documented than previous twelfth century chronicles: royal correspondence, administrative measures, treaties, and royal itineraries all being inserted. The chronicle was continued 1192-1202, carefully written and containing an even larger proportion of documents by Roger of Howden. Both these texts, edited by Stubbs, were printed in volumes 49 and 51 of the *Rolls series*.

348 'Gesta Stephani' is an interesting chronicle of Stephen's reign by an unknown author which bears all the hallmarks of a near contemporary record of events from 1135 onwards and which for the years 1142-1147 is almost the only surviving authority. Whoever the author was he certainly seems to have had access to reliable sources of information. It is chiefly noted for its vividly accurate topography, its expert knowledge of warfare, and for its laudatory treatment of the king. K R Potter's translation is available in the *Oxford medieval texts* series.

349 Gibbon, Edward (1737-1794) holds an unassailable position in the fields of English literature and English historiography for his *Decline and fall of the Roman Empire*, the first volume of which was immediately hailed as a lasting contribution to letters on its publication in February 1776, although there was much controversy over two chapters relating the rise of christianity. Another five volumes completed the work over the next twelve years. In a famous passage Gibbon has recorded how he first conceived the work: 'It was at Rome, on 15 October, 1764, as I sat musing amidst the ruins of the capitol, while the barefooted friars were singing vespers in the temple of Jupiter, that the idea of writing the decline and fall of the city first started to my mind.' In all, his work presents a continuous history from the second century AD, when 'the empire of Rome comprehended the fairest part of the earth, and the most civilized portion of mankind' down to the fall of Constantinople to the Turks in 1453. There are two sections: the first covering three centuries to the breakdown of the empire in the west in 480; and the second another 1000 years of the eastern empire so resplendently established by Constantine. This uneven balance in content undoubtedly reflects Gibbon's own interest, his knowledge of Latin sources far excelled his skill with later chronicles. Yet in his account of the Byzantine empire can be discovered much of his best work as he describes how the dark forces which finally destroyed the empire were assembled and unleashed on the embattled city which had assumed the mantle of Rome. But it was by no means entirely for its content that the *Decline and fall* remains unique in English historical writing, his controlled (some would say ponderous) style admirably suited the thunderous march of events, imposes its own rhythm on the reader, and ensures its near immortality even though modern research has inevitably uncovered new facts and ushered in new interpretations. The full text is available in the Everyman Library and in OUP's *World classics* series. An abridged version edited by D M Low was published in 1960. *Edward Gibbon* by C V Wedgwood, no 66 in the *Writers and their work* series published by Longmans for the British Council and The National Book League, offers an authoritative, readable, and concise study together with a select bibliography.

350 Gildas (d 570): his *Liber Querulus de Excidio et Conquestu Britanniae* (Ruin and conquest of Britain) is the earliest surviving history written by a native of Britain. It is in two parts: a history of the interval between the Roman occupation and the advent of the Anglo-Saxons; followed by a lamentation of the indolence and irreligion of five named British kings which permitted the invaders to settle. Unfortunately he indulges too often in moral indignation, if he had written more on what he had seen himself or heard from men of the preceding generation his history would be far more instructive. At times he is peculiarly vague and uneven, he omits much which could be expected to be included, yet at other times he seems remarkably well informed. He remains the only historian who was even remotely contemporary with this dim and misty period. His sources are exclusively continental.

351 'Goldentree bibliographies in American history' originally published by Appleton-Century-Crofts and now taken over by AHM Publishing Corporation of Northbrook, Illinois, are designed to provide students, teachers and librarians with manageable selective guides to the significant literature of American history. All major periods are covered whilst additional volumes are devoted to important subjects. At the moment sixteen of these convenient, inexpensive, soft cover bibliographies, are available and may be safely recommended for library and lecture room use.

352 Grafton, Richard (c1500-1572?) printer, publisher, MP, was the author of *Chronicle at large* published in two volumes in 1569. At the time the only histories available were 'annals' *ie*, year by year summaries of the main recorded historical events. The *Chronicle* was something different although it began, as was customary, with the creation but instead of the usual chronicle this was an outline of history, presenting the general development of mankind before proceeding to a history of Britain. The first volume brought the story down to immediately prior to the Norman conquest. In the next volume Grafton wrote what was in effect the first critical history of England down to his own times, selecting his material from a number of authorities but ready to rely on his own judgements.

353 Graham, Gerald (1903-) a native of Canada whose professional career as a historian culminated in appointment as Rhodes Professor of Imperial History, Kings College, University of London, wrote extensively in the learned journals on naval and imperial history. His most substantial work was *Great Britain in the Indian Ocean: a study of maritime enterprise 1810-1850* (OUP, 1967). His retirement in 1970 was commemorated by *Perspectives of empire* edited by John Flint and Glyndwr Williams (Longmans 1973) which includes 'The historical writings of Gerald Sandford Graham' compiled by George Metcalf.

354 'Great Britain: foreign policy and the span of empire 1689-1971; a documentary history' edited with commentaries by Joel H Wiener (Chelsea House Publishers in association with McGraw Hill, 4 vols 1972). It is designed for the advanced research worker, the undergraduate and the general reader (!) and makes available a large number of documents of significance to the course of British history since the 1688 revolution. They are culled from many sources and include treaties, judicial reports, newspaper accounts, memoirs and contemporary tracts; some are uniquely important, whilst others reflect the changing pattern of events, but all 'are intended to inform, to illuminate, to entertain, and, most important, to deepen the readers understanding of a central development in world history—the rise and subsequent decline of Great Britain as a great imperial power.' Arrangement is under three headings: Foreign policy, to provide a broad perspective; Ireland is treated separately; and the third covers overseas development and the creation of the commonwealth.

355 'Great Britain in the twentieth century' by Henry R Winkler (AHA Service Center Series no 28) was first published in 1960. It is a bibliographical essay assessing the main contributions to historical scholarship concerned with Britain's very recent past although the period covered stops at 1945 because post war events are judged to be too contemporary for adequate historical treatment. Most of the works mentioned concentrate on one of the following aspects: the transformation of the machinery of government and the development of the cabinet system; the emergence of the welfare state; the rise of the Labour Party and the corresponding decline of the Liberals; the impact of two world wars especially on the economic structure; and foreign policy and diplomacy.

356 'Great Britain public record office lists and indexes' a catalogue of available basic reference sources to British national archives arranged by courts and departments to facilitate use is issued by Kraus Reprints. There is a dual arrangement: in the first section the volumes of the lists and indexes and supplementary series are organised by courts and departments to provide a subject guide to the archives, whilst in the second section there are numerical listings to the two sets. The departments concerned are the Admiralty, Chancery, Colonial Office, common law records, Exchequer, Foreign Office, Home Office, Duchy of Lancaster, The Palatinates, Paymaster-General's Office, Court of Requests, Sheriffs, Signet Office, Court of Star Chamber, State Paper Office, Board of Trade, Treasury, Court of Wards, and the War Office. Publication of the supplementary series is an ongoing programme by arrangement with Her Majesty's Stationery Office.

357 'Great historical enterprises' by David Knowles (Nelson, 1963) consists of four essays originally delivered as presidential addresses to the Royal Historical Society (1958-1961) and printed in their *Transactions*. They record the history of four great cooperative histories: the Bollandists, Maurists, the *Rolls series* and the *Monumenta Germaniae Historica*. Bound in the same book are two essays containing the substance of the Birkbeck Lectures at Cambridge 1962 with the general title of *Problems in monastic history*.

358 'The great rebellion 1642-1660' by Ivan Roots, published in Batsford's *Fabric of British history* series in 1966, stresses political and constitutional matters. It is particularly valuable for its interpretation of the decade leading up to the restoration. Notes on sources and a detailed annotated bibliography listing both books and journal articles confined mostly to work published since the war emphasise the scholarly nature of this account.

359 'The great trek' by Eric Anderson Walker was published in A and C Black's *Pioneer histories* series in 1934 and narrates the Boer exodus from the Cape Colony 1835-1840 and then further onwards into the Transvaal 1843-1848. There is no bibliography.

360 Green, J R (1837-1883) is remembered for his *A short history of the English people* (1874) in which he deliberately turned away from what he called the drum and trumpet type of history. 'At the risk of sacrificing much that was interesting and attractive', he wrote, 'which the constant usage of our historians have made familiar to English readers, I have preferred to pass lightly and briefly over the details of foreign wars and diplomacies ... and to dwell at length on the incidents of that constitutional, intellectual, and social advance in which we read the history of the nation itself.' Frequent reprintings and expansion into a larger, illustrated work testify to his popular success.

361 'The growth of the British Commonwealth 1880-1932' by I M Cumpston was published by Edward Arnold in the *Documents of modern history* series in 1973. There are eighty two documents divided into two sections: the first is concerned with imperial conferences and policy, and the second deals with the various parts of the commonwealth. Good use is made of official British cabinet and parliamentary papers.

362 'Guide for research students working on historical subjects' by G Kitson Clark (CUP, 2nd ed, 1968) was specifically written for research students at Cambridge but despite it being closely linked to the supervisory system and the library of that university it was considered there would be sufficient matters of interest to postgraduate students working elsewhere to justify publication. Short but sound advice is offered on the objects of research, the choice of a subject, and the equipment needed. This is followed by notes on reviewing and presenting evidence and methodology. Then come some hints on research material and library guides to complete a practical and valuable little guide.

363 'A guide for students of New Zealand history' (Dunedin, University of Otago Press, 1973) by G A Wood is a concise guide to bibliographies and reference sources of use to the research worker in New Zealand history.

364 'Guide to atlases; world, regional, national thematic, an international listing of atlases published since 1950' by Gerard Alexander, Chief of the Map Division, The Research Libraries, of New York Public Library, and published by the Scarecrow Press in 1971, includes 434 historical atlases arranged by publisher. Only bare details are given—title, editor, place of publication, date, pages, and maps in colour, and size.

365 'Guide to illustrative material for use in teaching history' compiled by Gwyneth Williams for the Historical Association (1964) is arranged in six sections: Sources of material; Reference books; Types of material; and three indexing sections, Periods of history, Subjects, and Material relating to particular areas. 'It is by no means a comprehensive list of everything sold, hired or given away, but is a guide to what is known ... to be used by teachers of history, at one or more of many different levels.' Although there is no attempt to assess the quality of the items listed they were chosen either because they were in continual demand, typical of what was available, or simply because they were the sort of thing teachers required. Although the guide is obviously now ageing many schools still find it useful.

366 'Guide to periodicals and bibliographies dealing with geography, archaeology and history' compiled by E Jefferies Davis and E G R Taylor, under the direction of a committee representing the Royal Geographical Society, the Historical Association, Society of Antiquaries, the Institute of Historical Research, Royal Archaeological Institute, Royal Historical Society and other institutions, was issued by the Historical Association in their pamphlet series in 1938. Its purpose was to indicate sources of information regarding current work in the three disciplines.

367 'Guide to reference books' by Constance M Winchell (American Library Association, 8th ed, 1967) descends from Alice Kroeger's *Guide to the study and use of reference books* first published in 1902. Its purpose has changed little over the years: to list reference books basic to research and so to act as a reference manual for the library user and as a selection aid to the librarian. Serially lettered and numbered entries reflect those books likely to be found in a large general reference collection. History and area studies are grouped together in Section D and are sub-divided on a geographical basis. Within these divisions entries are listed under form headings: guides, bibliographies, historiographies, dictionaries, pictorial works, current surveys, and atlases. Each entry receives full critical and descriptive annotation and there is an author-subject index. A *First supplement 1965-1966* by Eugene P Sheehy was published in 1968.

368 'Guide to reference material' by A J Walford, intended for librarians in the building up and revision of reference library stock, for general and special library enquiry work, and as an initial step for research workers, is international in scope although with a slight British bias and aims 'to provide a signpost to reference books and bibliographies published mainly in recent years.' It is a three volume work arranged according to the Universal Decimal Classification with History taking its place in volume 2 *Social and historical sciences, philosophy and religion* (Library Association, 3rd ed, 1975). To some extent the coverage of history is fragmentary in arrangement: first there is a division by form of literature—bibliographies, manuals, encyclopaedias etc, which trails off into archives and records. Then the form division is repeated for archaeology, then by area, and then on to palaeography. Ancient history is next, first by form and then by area and so on to medieval and modern history by form subdivided by period and then by area again. Perhaps a simpler arrangement either by period or preferably by area might have been devised. Each item recorded is described and briefly annotated. It is a monumental and magisterial work, one of those which leads us to wonder how we ever managed without it and it has been of use in the compilation of this present book to check and corroborate points of fact. There is an author-title index.

369 'Guide to research facilities in history in the universities of Great Britain and Ireland' by G Kitson Clark and G R Elton (CUP, 2nd ed, 1965) was published to draw attention to the wide facilities and materials for historical research existing in British libraries with special reference to those outside London, Oxford, and Cambridge. University history departments were asked to indicate on a questionnaire in what aspects of history they regarded themselves as being particularly qualified to conduct research supervision, and what suitable libraries, manuscript collections, and microfilms of historical material were available in the neighbourhood. They were also asked to give details of postgraduate courses not leading to research degrees and to whom enquiries concerning admission should be addressed. The booklet is arranged alphabetically by name of university. A revised edition is obviously called for after ten years but much of the information, especially that on library holdings, retains its usefulness.

370 'Guide to resources for commonwealth studies in London, Oxford and Cambridge; with bibliographical and other information' by A R Hewitt was published by The Athlone Press for the Institute of Commonwealth Studies in 1957. Its purpose is to assist advanced research workers especially from overseas to locate material within the fields of history and the social sciences in libraries in the three main centres of research in the United Kingdom. It is arranged in three parts: Part I is a classified general survey of resources with sections on archive repositories and libraries, the public archives, private papers, the records of chartered and other companies, parliamentary papers and official publications, periodicals and newspapers, a concise survey of library resources by subjects, theses and research in progress, and bibliographies and reference works; Part II lists collections in London, Oxford, and Cambridge; and Part III lists universities in the United Kingdom offering facilities for commonwealth studies, research and advisory organisations, and an additional list of official and unofficial institutions and organisations concerned with various aspects of commonwealth affairs. There is a full index.

371 'Guide to sources of English history from 1603 to 1660 in reports of the Royal Commission on Historical Manuscripts' by Eleanor Stuart Upton (Scarecrow Press, 1952) is a subject index to materials on the early stuart period in collections represented in the first nine reports of the Historical Manuscripts Commission in both categories *ie*, those made by the commissioners at intervals to the crown, and the inspectors' reports on individual collections. Later reports on the same collections also fall within its scope.

372 'Guide to the contents of the Public Record Office' published in three volumes is largely a revision of M S Giuseppi's *A guide to the manuscripts preserved in the Public Record Office* (2 vols, 1923) and takes account of all material reaching the PRO up to the end of 1966. Vol I *Legal records* (1963) was published late enough to cover the enormous influx of records consequent to the Public Record Act of 1958. A general introduction to the records is followed in turn by full descriptive lists of the records of the various courts ranging from Chancery and Exchequer to lesser-known ones like the Court of the Honour of Peveril arranged according to administrative provenance, dictated partly by the date of the development of courts and offices concerned, and partly by their nature and mutual relation. Notes on the language and scripts of the records, the classification, and the card indexes in the search room, are contained in the introduction. Other useful editorial matter includes a key to regnal years with a chronological index to statutes cited in the text; a list of abbreviations; a glossary; and indexes of persons and places; and subjects. Vol II *State papers and departmental records* (1963) is a similar list arranged alphabetically by department. By dividing the records in this way, legal records and state papers, Vol I effectively comprises, together with legal and judicial records of all dates, all the national archives from *Domesday book* (1086) to the death of Henry VIII in 1509, with Volume II listing all documents subsequent to that date. Vol III *Documents transferred 1960-1966* (1968) describes the records added in that period and as most of them are of fairly recent origin this volume is virtually a supplement to the second.

373 'A guide to the historical and archaeological publications of societies in England and Wales, 1901-1933' compiled for the Institute of Historical Research by E L C Mullins (1968), complements *Writings on British history 1901-1933* (*qv*), and 'lists and indexes the titles and authors of books and articles upon the history and archaeology of England and Wales, the Isle of Man and the Channel Islands, issued to their members ... by more than four hundred local and national societies.'

374 'A guide to the papers of British cabinet ministers 1900-1951' compiled by Cameron Hazelhurst and Christine Woodland and published in 1974 is no 1 of the Royal Historical Society's guides and handbooks supplementary series. It complements Chris Cook's *Sources in British political history* for the same period and was in fact fashioned at the same 1967 Oxford conference that saw the conception of Dr Cook's work. The aim of the project was first to locate, then briefly describe, the private papers of every person of cabinet rank, including all holders of government offices which carried a seat in the cabinet at any time within the specified period. After much research the whereabouts of the papers of 325 cabinet ministers were traced and recorded here. Entries are arranged in alphabetical order of family name and include concise biographical details of each minister's political career, where his papers are filed, whether or not they are generally available, under what conditions, and whose permission should be sought in order to consult them. The contents of each collection are also indicated when this is feasible. It is hoped that the guide will be kept up to date by amendments and revisions published in a learned journal.

375 'Guide to the records of parliament' by Maurice Bond (HMSO, 1971) is a descriptive list of the complete range of records, both printed and manuscript, of both houses of parliament, dating from the fifteenth century to the 1969-1970 session, and also of other papers accumulated over the years in the House of Lords Record Office at Westminster, arranged according to the provenance of the documents. A concise history of the records, notes on the facilities for students in the record office, and a list of publications relating to the records, are included in a preliminary section. Then follow separate sections on the records of the lords, the commons, the Lord Great Chamberlain, the Clerk to the Crown, and others preserved at Westminster. The last section is concerned with three historical collections in the Lords' Record Office, in their library, and in the House of Commons library. Within each of these six parts informative introductions precede the lists of holdings, and useful bibliographies of works available for reference in the House of Lords Record Office Search Room are appended.

376 'A guide to the study of the United States of America' *Representative books reflecting the development of American life and thought* published by the General Reference and Bibliography Division of the Library of Congress in 1960, is divided into thirty two chapters of which General history is one, with others on Diplomatic history and foreign relations, Military history, and Local history, and is the response of the library to the increasing demand on its bibliographical services from university graduate and postgraduate courses at home and abroad. The guide is the result of a decision to bring together a series of bibliographic studies in one volume to prevent a wasteful duplication of effort in repeatedly satisfying the same enquiries. Each of the 450 books entered in the chapter on General history (divided under the following headings: historiography; general works; new world; thirteen colonies; American revolution; federal America 1783-1815; the middle period 1815-1860; slavery, civil war and reconstruction to 1877; Grant to McKinley 1869-1901; Theodore Roosevelt to Wilson 1901-1920; since 1920) contributes to an understanding of American life. On average the entries receive about 100 words of annotation intended not as reviews but primarily as aids to readers in eliminating material irrelevant to their immediate purpose. The chapters are prefaced with explanatory notes and the work is completed by an author, title, and subject index. For American and non-American libraries alike it serves as an extremely useful desk reference work.

377 'Guides to materials for West African history in European archives' is a series published by the University of London Athlone Press. *Materials for West African history in the archives of the United Kingdom* by Noel Matthews (1973) is arranged on a geographical basis: London first and then other towns and cities in alphabetical order. It lists all source material in record repositories, libraries and museums, and in the hands of business firms and private houses. By far the greater proportion of the documents noted belong to the official records at the Colonial Office or the Public Record Office. No attempt is made to include material relating to European diplomatic negotiations in the 'race for Africa' or the slave trade unless this is directly concerned with events in Africa. The collections of archives at the institutions included in the survey are briefly described, the times and terms of

146

reference are outlined, and the content of each document or collection is also indicated. Previous volumes in the series include *Materials for West African History in the archives of Belgium and Holland* by Patricia Green (1962); ... *in Portuguese archives* by A F C Ryder (1955); ... *in Italian archives* by Richard Gray and David Chambers (1965); and ... *in French archives* by Patricia Green (1968).

378 'The Hakluyt handbook' edited by D B Quinn (Hakluyt Society Publications Second Series vols 144-145, 1974) is intended to assist scholars and students to browse confidently amongst the writings of Richard Hakluyt and the extensive series of volumes issued by The Hakluyt Society. The first volume is arranged in three parts. Part one, 'A Hakluyt perspective,' is a conspectus of modern scholarship on various aspects of Hakluyt's work: 1 'Hakluyt's view of British history' (J H Parry); 2 'Richard Hakluyt, geographer' (G R Crone); 3 'Hakluyt and the economic thought of his time' (G V Scammell); 4 'Hakluyt's language' (N E Osselton); 5 'Hakluyt's nautical terms' (G P B Naish); 6 'Hakluyt as translator' (F M Rogers); 7 'Hakluyt's maps' (R A Skelton); 8 'From Hakluyt to Purchas' (C R Steele); 9 'Tudor travel literature: a brief history' (G B Parks); and 10 'Hakluyt's reputation' (D B Quinn). Part two, 'Hakluyt's use of the materials available to him,' consists of a series of studies which take the field of exploration covered in his work area by area and considers how successfully or otherwise he researched amongst the material actually or potentially available to him. These studies form extremely useful bibliographical essays. Part three, is a chronology of Hakluyt's life 1552-1616. Volume II contains Part four, 'Contents and sources of the three major works,' *ie*, *Divers voyages* (1582), *Principall navigations* (1589) and the second edition in three folio volumes (1598-1600); whilst Part five 'Hakluyt's books and sources' comprises 'The primary Hakluyt bibliography' by D B Quinn, C E Armstrong, and R A Skelton, 'Secondary works on Hakluyt and his circle' by L E Pennington, and, finally, a list of works published by the Hakluyt Society 1846-1973 arranged by E L C Mullins. The two volumes are well illustrated and conclude with an index of books and also a general index. An interesting account of the conception and birth of the handbook, 'Richard

Hakluyt and his followers' by D B Quinn, appears in the society's *Annual report* 1972.

379 The Hakluyt Society was formed at a meeting held at the London Library ten days before Christmas 1846. Its purpose was 'to print for distribution among the members the most rare and valuable voyages, travels, and geographical records, from an early period of exploratory enterprise to the circumnavigation of Dampier.' And although the restrictive *terminus ad quem* has long since disappeared the society's purpose of printing narratives of exploration and travel still continues. A high proportion of the society's publications are reprints of original English texts, the remainder are given in English translation, and cover every continent and ocean, comprising the writings of medieval travellers and cosmographers, the classic narratives of the age of great discoveries, and reports by later explorers. An appropriately qualified scholar is appointed as editor of each volume who provides whatever introductory material is deemed essential. All volumes are furnished with maps which whenever possible are reproduced in facsimile from the original works. Publications: a complete list of the first, second, and extra series of publications to date follows.

First Series:

1 *The observations of Sir Richard Hawkins* 1847. In his voyage into the South Seas in 1593.

2 *Select letters of Christopher Colombus* 1847. With other original documents relating to his four voyages to the new world.

3 *The discovery of Guiana* 1848. With a relation of the great and golden City of Manoa (which the Spaniards call El Dorado etc), performed in 1595 by Sir Walter Raleigh.

4 *Sir Francis Drake his voyage 1595* 1848. By Thomas Maynarde together with the Spanish Account of Drake's attack on Puerto Rico.

5 *Narratives of voyages towards the north-west* 1849. In search of a passage to Cathay and India, 1496 to 1631.

6 *The Historie of Travaile into Virginia Britannia* 1849. By William Strachey, first Secretary to the Colony.

7 *Divers voyages touching the discovery of America* 1850. Collected and published by Richard Hakluyt.

8 *Memorials of the empire of Japan* 1850. In the sixteenth and seventeenth centuries (includes the letters of William Adams).

9 *The discovery and conquest of Terra Florida* 1851. By Ferdinando de Soto. Translated by Richard Hakluyt.

10 and 12 *Notes upon Russia* 1851. Translated from *Rerum Moscoviticarum Commentarii* by Baron Sigismund von Herberstein.

11 *The geography of Hudson's Bay* 1852. Being the remarks of Captain W Coats, in many voyages to that locality 1727-1751. With extracts from the log of Captain Middleton on his voyage for the discovery of the North-West Passage in HMS Furnace 1741-1743.

13 *A true description of three voyages by the north-east* 1853. Towards Cathay undertaken by the Dutch 1594-1596 with their discovery of Spitzbergen and their residence of ten months in Novaya Zemlya.

14 and 15 *The history of the great and mighty kingdom of China* 1854.

16 *The world encompassed by Sir Francis Drake* 1855. By Sir Francis Drake, the Younger. Collated with an unpublished manuscript of Francis Fletcher, Chaplain to the Expedition.

17 *The history of the two Tartar conquerors of China* 1855. From the French of Pierre Joseph D'Orleans 1688.

18 *A collection of documents on Spitzbergen and Greenland* 1856.

19 *The voyage of Sir Henry Middleton to Bantam and the Maluco Islands* 1856. Being the second voyage set forth by the Company of Merchants of London trading into the East Indies. 1606 edition.

20 *Russia at the close of the sixteenth century* 1857. Comprising the treatise *The Russe commonwealth* by Giles Fletcher, and the travels of Sir Jerome Horsey.

21 *History of the new world, by Girolamo Benzoni, of Milan* 1857. Travels in America 1541-1546.

22 *India in the fifteenth century* 1858. Collection of narratives of voyages.

23 *Narrative of a voyage to the West Indies and Mexico* 1858. In the years 1599-1602. By Samuel Champlain.

24 *Expeditions into the valley of the Amazons 1539, 1540, 1639* 1859.

25 *Early voyages to Terra Australis* 1859. Collection of documents, and extracts from early manuscript maps from sixteenth century to Captain Cook.

26 *Narrative of the Embassy of Ruy Gonzalez de Clavijo to the Court of Timour* 1860. Samarkand 1403-1406.

27 *Henry Hudson the navigator 1607-1613* 1860. Original documents recording his career.

28 *The expedition of Pedro de Ursua and Lope de Aguirre* 1861. In search of El Dorado 1650-1661.

29 *The life and acts of Don Alonzo Enriquez de Guzman* 1862. 1518-1543.

30 *The discoveries of the world* To 1555. By Antonio Galvao.

31 *Mirabilia Descripta. The wonders of the east* 1863. By Friar Jordanus. c1330.

32 *The travels of Ludovico di Varthema* 1863. Egypt, Syria, Arabia, Persia, India, and Ethiopa 1503-1508.

33 *The travels of Pedro de Cieza de Leon 1532-1550* 1864. From Gulf of Darien to the City of La Plata.

34 *Narrative of the proceedings of Pedrarias Davila* 1865. In Tierra Firme or Castilla del Oro, and of the discovery of the South Sea and the Coasts of Peru and Nicaragua. By Pascual de Andagoya.

35 *A description of the coasts of East Africa and Malabar* 1865. Beginning of sixteenth century. By Duarte Barbosa.

36 and 37 *Cathay and the way thither* 1866. Collection of medieval notices of China.

38 *The three voyages of Sir Martin Frobisher* 1867. In search of North-West Passage 1576-1578.

39 *The Philippine Islands* 1868. By Antonio de Morga 1609.

40 *The fifth letter of Herman Cortes* 1868. To the Emperor Charles V containing an account of expedition to Honduras 1525-1526.

41 *The royal commentaries of the Yncas* 1869. By the Ynca Garcilasso de la Vega.

42 *The three voyages of Vasco da Gama* 1869.

43 *Select letters of Christopher Colombus* 1870. With other original documents relating to the four voyages to the new world.

44 *History of the Imams and Seyyids of Oman* 1870. By Salil-Ibn-Razik 661-1856.

45 *The royal commentaries of the Yncas Vol 2* 1871.

46 *The Canarian* 1871. Book of the conquest and conversion of the Canarians in the year 1402.

47 *Reports on the discovery of Peru* 1872.

48 *Narratives of the rites and laws of the Yncas* 1872.

49 *Travels to Tana and Persia* 1873. Narrative of Italian travels in Persia in the fifteenth and sixteenth centuries.

50 *The voyages of the Venetian brothers Nicolo and Antonio Zenio* 1873. To the northern seas in the fourteenth century.

51 *The captivity of Hans Stade of Hesse in 1547-55* 1874. Among the wild tribes of Eastern Brazil.

52 *The first voyage round the world by Magellan 1518-1521* 1874. Translated from accounts by Pigafetta and other contemporary writers.

53 and 55 *The commentaries of the great Afonso Dalboquerque* 1875. Second Viceroy of India.

54 *The three voyages of William Barents to the Arctic regions in 1594, 1595, and 1596* 1876.

56 *The voyages of Sir James Lancaster to the East Indies* 1877. With abstracts of journals of voyages to the East Indies during the seventeenth century, and the voyage of Captain John Knight 1606 to seek the North-West Passage.

57 *The Hawkins' voyages* 1877.

58 *The bondage and travels of Johann Schiltberger* 1878. From his capture at the battle of Nicopolis in 1396 to his escape and return to Europe in 1427.

59 *The voyages and works of John Davis the navigator* 1878.

60 and 61 *The natural and moral history of the Indies* 1879. By Father Joseph de Acosta.

62 *The commentaries of the great Afonso Dalboquerque Vol 3* 1880.

63 *The voyages of William Baffin 1612-1622* 1880.

64 *Narrative of the Portuguese Embassy to Abyssinia* 1881. During the years 1520-1527.

65 *The history of the Bermudas or Summer Islands* 1881.

66 and 67 *The diary of Richard Cocks* 1882. Cape merchant in the English factory in Japan 1615-1622.

68 *The second part of the chronicle of Peru 1532-1550* 1883. Vol 1—No 33.

69 *The commentaries of the great Afonso Dalboquerque Vol 4* 1883.

70 and 71 *The voyage of John Huyghen van Linschoten to the East Indies* 1884.

72 and 73 *Early voyages and travels to Russia and Persia* 1885. By Anthony Jenkinson and other Englishmen with some account of the first intercourse of the English with Russia and Central Asia by way of the Caspian Sea.

74 and 75 *The diary of William Hedges* 1886. During his agency in Bengal 1681-1687.

76 and 77 *The voyage of Francois Pyrard, of Laval* 1887. To the East Indies, the Maldives, the Moluccas, and Brazil.

78 *The diary of William Hedges Vol 3* 1888.

79 *Tractatus de Globis, et eorum Usu* 1888. A treatise descriptive of the globes constructed by Emery Molyneux published in 1592. To which is appended sailing directions for the circumnavigation of England from a fifteenth century manuscript.

80 *The voyage of Francois Pyrard, of Laval, Vol 2* 1889.

81 *The conquest of La Plata 1535-1555* 1889.

82 and 83 *The voyage of Francois Legouat, of Bresse 1690-1698* 1890. To Redriguez, Mauritius, Java, and the Cape of Good Hope.

84 and 85 *The travels of Pietro della Valle in India* 1891.

86 *The journal of Christopher Colombus* 1892. During his first voyage (1492-1493) and documents relating to the voyages of John Cabot and Gaspar Corte Real.

87 *Early voyages and travels in the Levant* 1892.

88 and 89 *The voyages of Captain Luke Foxe, of Hull, and Captain Thomas James, of Bristol* 1893. In search of a North-West Passage 1631-1632 with narratives of the earlier north-west voyages of Frobisher, Davis, Weymouth, Hall, Knight, Hudson, Button, Gibbons, Bylot, Baffin, Hawkridge.

90 *The letters of Amerigo Vespucci* 1894.

91 *Narratives of the voyages of Pedro Sarmiento de Gamboa to the Straits of Magellan 1579-1580* 1894.

92 to 94 *The history and description of Africa* 1895. By Al-Hassan Ibn-Mohammed Al-Wezaz Al Fasi, *ie*, Leo Africanus.

95 *The chronicle of the discovery and conquest of Guinea* 1896. By Gomes Eannes de Azurara.

96 and 97 *Danish Arctic expeditions 1605-1620* 1896. Includes Captain James Hall's voyage to Greenland in 1612.

98 *The topographia Christiana of Cosmos Indicopleustes* 1897.

99 *A journal of the first voyage of Vasco da Gama 1497-1499* 1898.

100 *The chronicle of the discovery and conquest of Guinea* Vol 2 1898.

Second Series: 1899-

1 and 2 *The embassy of Sir Thomas Roe to the court of the Great Mogul 1615-1619* 1899. From contemporary records.

3 *The voyage of Robert Dudley to the West Indies and Guiana in 1594* 1899.

4 *The Journeys of William de Rubruquis and John de Plano Carpino* 1900. To Tartary in the thirteenth century.

5 *The voyage of Captain John Saris to Japan in 1613* 1900.

6 *The strange adventures of Andrew Battell of Leigh in Essex* 1900.

7 and 8 *The voyage of Mendana to the Solomon Islands in 1568* 1901.

9 *The journey of Pedro Teixeira from India to Italy by land 1604-1605* 1901.

10 *The Portuguese expedition to Abyssinia in 1541* 1902.

11 *Early Dutch and English voyages to Spitzbergen in the seventeenth century* 1902.

12 *The countries around the Bay of Bengal* 1903. From an unpublished manuscript 1669-1679 by Thomas Bowrey.

13 *The voyage of Captain Don Felipe Gonzalez* 1903. To Easter Island 1770-1771.

14 and 15 *The voyages of Pedro Fernandez de Quiros 1595-1606* 1904.

16 *John Jourdain's journal of a voyage to the East Indies 1608-1617* 1905.

17 *The travels of Peter Mundy* 1905. In Europe and Asia 1608-1667.

18 *East and West Indian mirror* 1906. By Joris van Speilbergen. An account of his circumnavigation 1614-1617 including the Australian Navigations of Jacob le Maire.

19 and 20 *A new account of East India and Persia* 1909-1912. Travels of John Fryer 1672-1681.

21 *The guanches of Tenerife, the holy image of Our Lady of Candelaria* 1907. By Friar Alonso de Espinosa 1594.

22 *History of the Incas* 1907. By Pedro Sarmiento de Gamboa 1572.

23 to 25 *True history of the conquest of New Spain* 1908-1910. By Bernal Diaz del Castillo.

26 and 27 *Rise of British Guiana* 1911.

28 *Magellan's Strait* 1911. Early Spanish voyages.

29 *Book of the knowledge* 1912. Of all the kingdoms, lands ... in the world by a Spanish Franciscan in the middle of the fourteenth century.

30 *True history of the conquest of New Spain Vol 4* 1912.

31 *The war of Quito* 1913. By Cieza de Leon.

32 *The quest and occupation of Tahiti* 1913. By emissaries of Spain 1772-1776.

33 *Cathay and the way thither Vol. 2* 1913.

34 *New light on Drake* 1914. Spanish and Portuguese documents relating to the circumnavigation.

35 *The travels of Peter Mundy Vol 2* 1914.

36 *The quest and occupation of Tahiti Vol 2* 1915.

37 and 38 *Cathay and the way thither vols 3 & 1* 1914-1915.

39 *A new account of East India and Persia Vol. 3* 1915.

40 *True history of the conquest of New Spain Vol. 5* 1916.

41 *Cathay and the way thither vol 4* 1916.

42 *The war of Chupas* 1917. By Cieza de Leon.

43 and 49 *The book of Duarte Barbosa* 1918. An account of the countries bordering the Indian Ocean 1518.

44 to 46 *Travels of Peter Mundy Vol 3* 1919.

47 and 50 *The chronicle of Muntaner* 1920-1921.

48 *Memorias antiquas historiales del Peru* 1920. By Fernando Montesinos.

51 *Journal of Father Samuel Fritz* 1922. Travels in the River of the Amazons 1686-1723.

52 *Journal of William Lockerby in Fiji 1808* 1922.

53 *The life of the Icelander, Jon Olafsson* 1923.

54 *The war of Las Salinas* 1923. Civil war in Peru in sixteenth century by Cieza de Leon.

55 *Travels of Peter Mundy Vol 4* 1924.

56 *Colonising expeditions to the West Indies and Guiana 1623-1667* 1924.

57 *Francis Mortoft: his book* 1925. Travels through France and Italy 1658-1659.

58 *Papers of Thomas Bowrey 1669-1713* 1925.

59 and 61 *Travels of Sebastien Manrique 1629-1643* 1926-1927.

154

60 *Robert Harcourt's voyage to Guiana 1613* 1926.

62 *English voyages to the Caribbean* 1928. Spanish documents from the archives of the Indies at Seville.

63 *The desert route to India* 1928. Journals of four travellers by the great desert caravan route Aleppo-Basra 1745-1751.

64 *New light on the discovery of Australia* 1929. Journal of Captain Don Diego de Prado y Tovar.

65 *Voyages of Colombus* 1929. Select documents illustrating four voyages.

66 *Relations of Golconda in the early seventeenth century* 1930.

67 *Travels of John Sanderson in the Levant 1584-1602* 1930.

68 *The life of the Icelander, Jon Olafsson Vol 2* 1931.

69 *A Briefe Summe of Geographie, by Roger Barlow* 1931.

70 *Voyages of Colombus Vol 2* 1932.

71 *English voyages to the Spanish Main* 1932. English and Spanish documents 1569-1580.

72 *Bombay in the days of Queen Anne* 1933.

73 *A new voyage and description of the Isthmus of America* 1933. By Lionel Wafer and his secret report (1688) and Nathaniel Davis' expedition to the gold mines (1704).

74 *Peter Floris, his voyage to the East Indies* 1934. Journal 1611-1615.

75 *Voyage of Thomas Best to the East Indies 1612-1614* 1934.

76 and 77 *The original writings and correspondence of the two Richard Hakluyts* 1935. Introduction and notes by E G R Taylor.

78 *The travels of Peter Mundy Vol 5* 1936.

79 *Esmeraldo de Situ Orbis* 1936. By Duarte Pacheco Pereira.

80 *The voyages of Cadamosto* 1937. And other documents on West Africa in the second half of the fifteenth century.

81 *The voyage of Pedro Alvares Cabral to Brazil and India* 1937. Contemporary documents and narratives.

82 *The voyage of Nicholas Downton to the East Indies 1614-1615* 1938. Contemporary records and letters.

83 and 84 *The voyages and colonising enterprises of Sir Humphrey Gilbert* 1938-1939.

85 *The voyages of Sir James Lancaster to Brazil and the East Indies* new edition, 1940.

86 and 87 *Europeans in West Africa 1450-1560* 1941-1942.

Documents illustrating nature and scope of Portuguese enterprise and early English voyages to Barbary and Guinea.

88 *The voyage of Sir Henry Middleton to the Moluccas 1604-1606* 1943.

89 and 90 *The suma oriental of Tomé Pires* 1944. An account of the east from the Red Sea to Japan 1512-1515 and *The book of Francisco Rodrigues* Rutter of a voyage in the Red Sea, nautical rules, almanack and maps written and drawn in the east before 1515.

91 and 92 *The voyage of Captain Bellingshausen to the Antarctic Seas 1819-1921* 1945.

93 *Richard Hakluyt and his successors* 1946. A volume issued to commemorate the centenary of the Hakluyt Society edited by Edward Lynam.

94 *The pilgrimage of Arnold von Harff* 1946. From Cologne through Italy, Syria, Egypt, Arabia, Ethiopia, Nubia, Palestine, Turkey, France and Spain, 1496-1499.

95 to 97 *The travels of the Abbé Carre in India and the Near East 1672-1674* 1947-1948.

98 *The discovery of Tahiti* 1948. Journal of second voyage of HMS Dolphin round the world by George Robertson 1766-1768.

99 *Further English voyages to Spanish America 1583-1594* 1951. Documents from the archives of the Indies at Seville.

100 *The Red Sea and adjacent countries at the close of the seventeenth century* 1949.

101 and 102 *Mandeville's travels* 1953. Texts and translations.

103 *The historie of travell into Virginia Britania 1612* 1953. By William Strachey.

104 and 105 *Roanoke Voyages 1584-1590* 1955. Documents illustrating English voyages to North America under the patent granted to Walter Raleigh in 1584.

106 *South China in the sixteenth century* 1953. Narratives of Galeote Pereira, Gaspar da Cruz and Martin de Rada 1550-1575.

107 *Some records of Ethiopia 1593-1646* 1954. Extracts from the history of high Ethiopia by Manoel de Almeida together with Bahrey's history of the Galla.

108 *The travels of Leo of Rozmital through Germany, Flanders, England, France, Spain, Portugal and Italy 1465-1467* 1957.

109 *Ethiopian itineraries 1400-1524* 1955.

110 *The travels of Ibn Battuta AD 1325-1354* 1958.

111 *English privateering voyages to the West Indies 1588-1595* 1956.

112 *The tragic history of the sea* 1957. Narratives of the shipwrecks of the Portuguese East Indiamen *Sao Thome* (1589) *Santo Alberto* (1593) and *Sao Joao Baptista* (1622).

113 *The troublesome voyage of Captain Edward Fenton 1582-1583* 1957.

114 and 115 *The Prester John of the Indies* 1958. Narrative of Portuguese Embassy to Ethiopia 1520.

116 *History of the Taihitian mission 1799-1830* 1959. By John Davies.

117 *The travels of Ibn Battuta Vol 2* 1959.

118 and 119 *The travels and controversies of Friar Domingo Navarette 1618-1686* 1960.

120 *The Cabot voyages and Bristol discovery under Henry VII* 1961.

121 *A regiment for the sea and other writings on navigation by William Bourne of Gravesend, a gunner, 1535-1582* 1961.

122 *Commodore Byron's journal of his circumnavigation 1764-1766* 1962.

123 *Missions to the Niger* 1962. Friedrich Hornemann 1796-1798 and Gordon Laing 1824-1826.

124 and 125 *Captain Philip Carteret's voyage round the world 1766-1769* 1963.

126 and 127 *Austrialia del Esperitu Sancto* 1964. Documents on the voyage of Quiros to the South Seas 1605-1606.

128 to 130 *Missions to the Niger* 1965-1966. The Bornu mission.

131 *The journal and letters of Captain Charles Bishop on the north-west coast of America, in the Pacific, and in New South Wales 1794-1799* 1967.

132 *Further selections from the tragic history of the sea 1559-1565* 1968. Narratives of the shipwrecks of the Portuguese East Indiamen *Aguia* and *Garca* (1559), *Sao Paulo* (1561), and the misadventures of the Brazil ship *Santo Antonio* (1565).

133 to 135 *The Letters of F W Ludwig Leichhardt* 1968.

136 and 137 *The Jamestown voyages under the first charter 1606-1609* 1969. Documents relating to the foundation of Jamestown and the history of Jamestown colony up to the

departure of Captain John Smith, last President of the Council under the first charter, early in October 1609.

138 and 139 *Russian Embassies to the Georgian kings 1589-1605* 1970.

140 *Sucesos de las Islas Filipinas* 1971. (See First Series, No 39.)

141 *The travels of Ibn Battuta AD 1325-1354 Vol III* 1971.

142 *The last voyage of Drake and Hawkins* 1972. (Sequel to III above).

143 *George Peard's journal of the voyage of HMS Blossom to the Pacific 1823-1828* 1973.

144 and 145 *The Hakluyt handbook* 1974. Edited by D B Quinn.

146 *Yermack's campaign in Siberia* 1975.

Extra Series:

1 to 12 *The principal navigations, voyages, traffiques, and discoveries of the English nation* 1903-1905. By Richard Hakluyt.

13 *The texts and versions of John de Plano Carpino and William de Rubruquis* 1903. As printed by Richard Hakluyt 1598.

14 to 33 *Hakluytus posthumus or Purchas his pilgrims* 1905-1907.

34 to 37 *The journals of Captain James Cook on his voyages of Discovery Vol I, The voyage of the Endeavour 1768-1771* 2nd ed 1970. *Vol II, Voyage of the Resolution and Adventure 1772-1775* 2nd ed 1971. *Vol III, The voyage of the Resolution and the Discovery 1776-1780* 1967. *Vol IV, The life of Captain James Cook* by J C Beaglehole, 1974.

38 *The journal of Christopher Colombus* 1960.

39 *The principall navigations ... 1589* (photolithographic facsimile edition with an introduction by D B Quinn and R A Skelton), 1965.

40 *The diary of A J Mounteney Jephson* 19. Emin Pasha relief expedition 1887-1889.

41 *The journals and letters of Sir Alexander MacKenzie* 1970.

42 *Ying-yai sheng-Ian by Ma Huan 1433* (Triumphant visions of the ocean shores), 1970.

The first series was reprinted by Burt Franklin (subsequently absorbed into the Lenox Hill Corporation), New York, 1963; and the second series and the extra series by Klaus Reprint. There are individual entries for Richard Hakluyt and his successors (2nd Ser, No 93) and The Hakluyt handbook (2nd Ser, No 144-145) in the present work. Membership of the society is open to all who are interested in its work.

380 'Hakluyt's voyages' once described by J A Froude as 'the prose epic of the modern English nation,' was compiled by Richard Hakluyt (1552-1616), the elizabethan patriot, maritime historian, and propagandist. His first notable collection was *Divers voyages touching the discoverie of America and the Ilands adjacent unto the same, made first of all by our Englishmen, and afterward by the Frenchmen and Britons: And certaine notes of advertisements for observations, necessarie for such as shall heerafter make the like attempt* ... published in 1582 to encourage English colonial enterprises in America, but the culmination of his work, compiled 'to publish the maritime records of our own men, which are hitherto scattered and buried in dust,' was *The Principall Navigations, Voiages and Discoveries of the English nation, made by Sea or over Land, to the most remote and farthest distant Quarters of the earth at any time within the compasse of these 1500 yeeres* ... which first appeared as a quarto volume of over 800 pages in 1589. It was 'devided into three severall parts, according of the Regions whereunto they were directed': *The First, conteining the personall travels of the English unto Judaea, Syria, Arabia, the river Euphrates, Babylon, Balsara, the Persian Gulfe, Ormuz, Chaul, Goa, India, and many islands adioyning to the South parts of Asia; together with the like unto Egypt, the chiefest parts and places of Africa within and without the Streight of Gibraltar, and about the famous Promontorie of Buona Esperanza. The Second, comprehending the worthy discoveries of the English towards the North and Northeast by Sea, as of Lapland, Scrikfinia, Corelia, the Baie of S. Nicholas, the Isles of Colgoieve, Vaigats, and Nova Zembla toward the great river Ob, with the mightie Empire of Russia, the Caspian Sea, Georgia, Arminia, Media, Persia, Boghar in Bactria, and divers kingdoms of Tartaria. The Third and last, including the English valiant attempts in searching almost all the corners of the vaste and new world of America, from 73 degrees of Northerly latitude Southward, to Meta Incognita, Newfoundland, the maine of Virginia, the point of Florida, the Baie of Mexico, all the inland of Nova Hispania, the coast of Terra Firma, Brasill, the river of Plate, to the Streight of Magellan: and through it, and from it in* the South Sea to Chili, Peru, Xalisco, the Gulfe of California, Nova Albion upon the backside of Canada, further than ever any Christian hitherto hath pierced. Whereunto is added the last most renowmed English navigation, round about the whole Globe of the Earth. This tripartite framework was filled in with a chronologically arranged series of original narratives which, with the exception of a few accounts of journeys in the middle ages derived of necessity from the medieval chroniclers, were almost entirely those of eye witnesses. The narratives were supported and documented in modern fashion by extracts from the state archives, the records of the merchant companies, private letters and lengthy quotations from foreign tributes to English enterprise. But even this stupendous achievement was surpassed by the second edition published as The Principal Navigations, Voiages, Traffiques and Discoveries of the English Nation ... in three volumes a decade later, 1598-1600: each of the original parts was now a separate volume, the whole text increasing almost threefold. The medieval sections were greatly expanded by a quantity of chronicles and records on the advice of William Camden; Sir John Mandeville's fictitious travels peremptorily vanished but a whole range of new material was added; a new perspective was inserted by the inclusion of incidents illustrating the naval might of England, giving notice that England now regarded herself as an imperial power. Foreign voyages also found a place if they supplied detail not forthcoming from English sources so that the work, an incredible 1,700,000 words in length, now effectively comprised a history of travel and commerce, a maritime history of England, and a geographical description of all the new worlds now awaiting English merchants, and colonists. A facsimile reprint of the 1589 edition with a bibliographical introduction was published in the Hakluyt Society's Extra Series in 1965 and the full text of the second edition was last published in the same series in twelve volumes 1903-1905. There is an Everyman edition in eight volumes with an introduction by John Masefield. The principal voyages recorded by Hakluyt are listed in the National Maritime Museum catalogue of the library; Volume one Voyages and travel pp 5-7. The best studies of Hakluyt's works, are Richard Hakluyt and the English voyages by George Bruner Parks, Richard Hakluyt and his successors edited by Edward Lynam, and The Hakluyt handbook all of which are noticed separately in this present work.

381 Halévy, Élie (1870-1937) was an intensely anglophile French historian who approached English history with a determination to treat it in a spirit of critical sympathy and his knowledge of England has perhaps never been equalled by any other foreign student. His understanding and insight, especially of the genius of English nonconformity, was truly remarkable. The first three volumes of his *History of the English people in the nineteenth century* (1913-1923) dealing with the years 1815-1841 begins with a particularly brilliant survey of England on the eve of Waterloo. He then turned to his two volume Epilogue covering 1895-1914 perhaps because this was the period when England and France put aside their differences and drew closer together for their mutual advantage. He was still working to fill the gap 1842-1895 when he died, although his history was completed from his draft and notes. Published by Benn the work is also available in paperback arranged as follows: *England in 1815; The liberal awakening 1815-1830; Triumph of reform 1830-1841; Victorian years 1842-1895; Imperialism and the rise of labour 1895-1905;* and *The rule of democracy 1904-1914.*

382 Hall, Edward (c 1498-1547) was one of the new men who thrust themselves upwards in the tudor period and he fully supported Henry VIII's political and religious policies. His *Union of the two noble and illustre famelies of Lancastre and Yorke,* a history of events from the accession of Henry IV to the death of Henry VIII, was intended as a glorification of the House of Tudor. The opening chapters are of little value but for the early years of Henry VIII he remains an authority, especially for his account of the opposition to Wolsey's measures. Hall lifted much from Polydore Vergil but he wrote on a larger scale and carried his researches further afield. His narrative achieves a good literary style and later writers such as Holinshed and Stow, and, of course, Shakespeare, borrowed much of his material.

383 Hallam, Henry (1777-1859) first achieved fame as a historian for his *Sketch of Europe in the middle ages* (1818) but it is for *The constitutional history of England from the accession of Henry VII to the death of George II,* a polemic directed against tudor and stuart despotism and a panegyric in favour of the 1688 revolution and its consequences published in 1827, that his place in English historiography is assured. It was this work which may fairly be said to mark the beginnings of the 'whig' school of historians who dominated constitutional history for the next hundred years, those who were not writing in the whig tradition were busy denouncing it.

384 Hancock, Sir Keith (1898-   ) the Australian born imperial historian whose career culminated in the chairs of British Commonwealth Affairs in the University of London and of History in the Australian National University, is best known for his *Survey of British Commonwealth affairs* (OUP, 3 vols in 2, 1940-1942); his biography of Field Marshal Smuts, *The sanguine years 1870-1919* (CUP, 1962) and *The fields of force 1919-1950* (1968); and *Selections from the Smuts papers 1886-1919* (CUP, 4 vols, 1966). The October 1968 issue of *Historical studies* was arranged as a *festschrift* volume in honour of his seventieth birthday; items of particular interest included 'Hancock's Australia and Australian historiography' by C M H Clark, 'Hancock, Mansergh, and commonwealth surveys' by J D B Miller, and a select bibliography of Hancock's writings.

385 'Handbook for history teachers' the brainchild of the Standing Sub-committee in History of the Institute of Education in the University of London, was first published by Methuen in 1962, an entirely rewritten and revised edition appearing ten years later. It is intended to be a complete work of reference for teachers in primary and secondary schools and is divided into four sections. Part 1 consists of various articles on the teaching of history—methods, syllabuses, history's role vis-à-vis other studies, broadcasting and other audio-visual material, sixth form studies, and examinations. Part 2, 'School books' indicates in article form books available for specific geographical and chronological divisions of history classified according to their suitability for different age groups. Part 3 is a corresponding section on audio-visual materials including a useful list of the major producers and distributors. Part 4 is a select bibliography for advanced work again arranged in geographical and chronological chapters designed to act as a guide to teachers of advanced level courses.

386 'Handbook of British chronology' edited by F M Powicke and E B Fryde for the Royal Historical Society (2nd ed, 1961) includes a bibliographical guide to the lists of English office holders to 1800; lists of independent rulers of England, Scotland and Ireland; officers of state; bishops of England, Wales, Scotland and Ireland; and tables of councils and parliaments. It is published as 'a handy and useful contribution to the needs of historical students, not as a logical and rounded treatise.'

387 'Handbook of dates for students of English history' edited by C R Cheney for the Royal Historical Society (1961) is intended 'to provide a compact and convenient means of verifying dates, a work of ready reference which is required as much by the expert as the novice in the daily handling and checking of historical material.' Sections on the reckoning of time, the Julian and Gregorian calendars, blaze a trail through the by no means clear and straightforward thickets of chronology: The rulers of England; List of popes: Saints' days and festivals; Legal chronology; The Roman calendar; Calendars for all possible dates of Easter; and a Chronological table of Easter days AD 500-2000 all elucidate in succinct fashion possible pitfalls and quandaries.

388 'Handbook of record publications' by Robert Somerville published by the British Records Association as one of their pamphlet series (1951) was intended primarily for the editors of record publishing societies and provides a summary conspectus of the classes of records that have achieved publication and also indicates areas where publishing would be welcome. It has no pretensions to bibliography status.

389 'Hanover to Windsor' by Roger Fulford (1960) completes Batsford's *British monarchy* series. In this instance the author is less concerned with out-and-out biographical material in favour of an analysis of the position of the crown and the standing of the monarchy and its influence on political and social events. The result is an effective study of the transition of eighteenth century monarchy to the severely restricted monarchy of today. There is a select bibliography heavily weighted with political biographies and memoirs.

390 'Hanoverian England 1714-1737' by Leonard W Cowie (1967) is one of Bell's textbooks written primarily for sixth form students and describes in the opening chapters the general background of the period, land and people, the social scene, government and politics, religious movements, science and culture, the agrarian revolution, the industrial revolution, overseas commerce and colonization, before settling down to a detailed narrative of the political events of this much discussed century. Dr Cowie's practised hand successfully summarises recent research.

391 'The Hanoverians 1714-1815' by V H H Green (Edward Arnold, 1948) is a broad survey intended for the student and general reader of average intelligence needing an introduction to the period. The bibliography is limited to a list of recommended books for further reading together with a few articles from periodicals.

392 'Harvard guide to American history' (2 vols, 1974) derives from *Guide to the study and reading of American history* (1912) and is 'addressed to the intelligent general reader, to the student, to the scholar'. Its purpose is to select and indicate from the mass of material available that likely to be most useful to the searcher in political, social, constitutional and economic history. To this end the historical source material is arranged in large sections:—Research methods and materials (especially valuable); Biographies and personal records; Comprehensive and area histories; Histories of special subjects; America to 1789; the United States 1789-1860; Civil war and reconstruction; Rise of industry and empire; The twentieth century. These are further divided into chronological and thematic sub-sections some of which are critically assessed whilst others are simply lists. An index of names and a subject index complete an imposing work.

393 The Harvester Press is engaged upon an ambitious publication programme of research source material in recent British history. In particular ephemeral political sources such as *The liberal year book 1887-1939* and *The liberal and radical year book 1887-1889* in forty two volumes, *The Lloyd George liberal magazine* 1920-1923 (6 vols), and the *Labour year book 1895-1948* in thirty two volumes are once more seeing the light of day in reprint form. These volumes must be a positive boon to research workers and scholars who can now hope to find their primary sources more easily accessible without having to make special journeys to the copyright libraries. Other similar material is being published on silver halide microfiche, eg, *British general election campaign guides* issued by the Conservative Party between 1892 and 1950 and the *Fabian Society minute books*. A joint project with the Labour Party to publish substantial sections of the party's archives has commenced with the *National Executive Committee minutes 1900-1926*. A rolling programme ensures that the material available is carried forward year by year. The records of the Trades Union Congress are also being tapped, the *General Council minute books 1921-1932* are already on sale in microfiche form. Hitherto *Unpublished state papers of the English civil war and interregnum* are being issued on twenty five reels of 35 mm microfilm, a project undertaken in cooperation with the Public Record Office. Many of these documents are in uncalendared form and consequently have been overlooked by scholars in the past. Also issued on microfilm are the *Cabinet reports by prime ministers to the crown 1868-1916*, almost 1700 manuscript letters preserved in the royal archives of Windsor Castle, constituting the only record of cabinet meetings and decisions for the period 1868-1916. Catalogues and special brochures containing all essential details are available from 2 Stanford Terrace, Hassocks, Sussex.

394 Hearne, Thomas (1678-1835) was an industrious and prolific editor of medieval texts despite the most appalling difficulties, he was forced to rely on whatever texts he could borrow because all the great libraries were barred to him on account of his unrelenting and obdurate nonjuring politics. Largely due to the unremitting accuracy of his transcriptions and his reverential regard for original authorities his editions were in constant demand and were not superseded until the advent of the *Rolls series* in the latter half of the nineteenth century. A sympathetic and understanding study of his life and work may be found in David Douglas' *English scholars*.

395 'Heaven's command; an imperial progress' by James Morris (Faber, 1973) is the opening volume of a projected trilogy about the British Empire in the victorian period, relating the imperial story from the accession of Queen Victoria in 1837 to the diamond jubilee in 1897. It has no pretensions to be a standard, definitive history narrated in straightforward chronological fashion but is rather 'a pointillist portrait less of an age than of a conviction,' a series of vividly described episodes illustrative and emblematic of empire arranged in three parts: The sentiment of empire 1837-1850, The growing conviction 1850-1870, and The imperial obsession 1870-1897. The central volume of the trilogy *Pax Britannica the climax of empire* was in fact the first to be published in 1968. This portrays the empire at the height of its unsurpassed and unquestioned splendour in 1897 before its decline and fall after two world wars. The author regards it as 'a kind of historical travel book or reportage, limited in period ... but not in place.' A third volume tracing the imperial decline is planned and will include a bibliography covering the whole range of the trilogy.

396 Henry of Huntingdon (1080?-1155?) was commissioned by Alexander of Blois, Bishop of Lincoln, to write a history of the English peoples from the earliest times. The result, the *Historia Anglorum* (1129-1154) eventually extended into eight books, closing with the death of Stephen, but its value lies more in its confirmation of other sources rather than as an independent authority. His own sources for the earlier portion of the *History* at least until 1121 were Bede and the *Anglo-Saxon chronicle* and there is also a similarity with the works of William of Malmesbury and Orderic Vitalis. From time to time he indulged himself in embellishing the bare record with circumstantial detail he thought likely to be true; he was the first to note down the famous episode of Canute and the tides. His books enjoyed a wide contemporary currency. The text edited by Thomas Arnold appeared in the *Rolls series* in 1879.

397 'Henry VIII' by J J Scarisbrook (1968) of Eyre Methuen's *English monarchs* series is something between a private life of Henry and a comprehensive study of his life and times. It concentrates on diplomatic, political, and religious affairs to the exclusion of economic or social life and the history of government institutions during the reign. Intended as a replacement of A F Pollard's book first published in 1902 the author had access to source material Pollard did not use. A Penguin edition was published in 1971.

398 **'Henry II'** by W L Warren (Eyre Methuen, 1973) in the *English monarchs* series is a four part study of the familiar and less familiar aspects of Henry's reign. Politics, the government of England, the church, and the Angevin commonwealth are all treated at length based on a long narrative chapter entitled 'King, duke and count a chronological survey 1154-1182' which follows Henry's efforts to keep his kingdom intact and inviolate. In this way all the major themes receive an in depth examination without losing sight of the cardinal fact that Henry faced them all simultaneously. Like other volumes in the series it rests firmly on contemporary sources.

399 **'Henry VII'** by S B Chrimes (Eyre Methuen, 1972), a volume in the *English monarchs* series is 'a study of the impact of Henry Tudor upon the government of England.' Because of a mass of material still languishing unturned in the Public Record Office the author modestly describes this book as an interim report on the existing state of knowledge. The steps taken to establish the new dynasty securely on the throne and the personnel and machinery of government are two familiar themes treated at length along with a consideration of Henry's social, economic, legal reform, church and external policies.

400 **Hickes, George** (1642-1715) is remembered for a remarkable work, *Linguarum veterum septentrionalium thesaurus grammatico-criticus et archaeologicus* (1705) in which he enjoyed the assistance of many scholars notably Edward Thwaites, Humphrey Wanley and Sir Andrew Fountaine, and which contained a study of comparative philology to set Anglo-Saxon in its proper place in the family of languages, and a pioneering treatise on Anglo-Saxon history, reinforced by Wanley's catalogue of Anglo-Saxon manuscripts and Fountaine's comparable appendix on coins. This work, which won an immediate European reputation, may be regarded as the apogee of English research scholarship into the Anglo-Saxon period which flourished at the turn of the seventeenth and eighteenth centuries.

401 Higden, Ranulph (died 1364), a Chester monk, was the author of a universal history, the *Polychronicon*, written on the grand scale from the creation down to 1352 and intended to cover all known lands with special reference to England. Because of its claims to be comprehensive it became immensely popular with the growing lay reading public although, in truth, it is often episodic and derivative. Its popularity may be gauged by its translation into English by John of Trevisa who carried it down to 1360 and by its printing by Caxton who himself continued it further to 1482. *The universal chronicle of Ranulph Higden* by John Taylor (OUP, 1966) is a very useful study.

402 'High history or hack history; England in the later middle ages' by Margaret Hastings was first published in *Speculum* XXXVI April 1961: 225-253 and subsequently collected in *Changing views on British history* (*qv*). Political, constitutional and administrative history still revolves round the work of Stubbs and Tout, economic and social historians surface with contradictory answers to questions more appropriately asked of modern society, whilst cultural history has benefited from the greater respect accorded to the medieval mind and spirit. Sadly a trend away from English medieval studies in American universities is discerned, one possible reason being that the sources are still largely in manuscript despite the heavy publication of texts and calendars in the last thirty years.

403 Hill, Christopher (1912-   ) has been constantly preoccupied by the struggles of the English people to impose their own solution to the problems confronting them in the seventeenth century. *Puritanism and revolution* (1958) interprets the ideas which produced the revolution and their relation with the political and economic events of the times; *Society and puritanism in pre-revolutionary England* (1964) suggests there might have been non-theological reasons why the puritans enjoyed wide support; and *Intellectual origins of the English revolution* (1965) further investigates the prevailing political theories during the early stuart period. *The world turned upside down* (1972) studies the radical ideas of the dissident groups which mushroomed in the heat of events, the diggers, ranters, levellers, and quakers, who all looked forward to a revolution in society shaped in their own image.

404 'Historiae Anglicanae Scriptores Decem' a collection of English chronicles published in 1652, is an early example of a cooperative history, it being largely the work of Roger Twysden but with substantial contributions from John Selden and James Ussher. It was undoubtedly one of the best such editions and even today one stumbles across references to it.

405 'Historiae Anglicanae Scriptores Quinque' compiled by Thomas Gale and published in 1687 made many important English monastic chronicles available either for the first time or in superior texts, and provided a mass of material of which later scholars took full advantage.

406 'Historians against history; the frontier thesis and the national covenant in American historical writing since 1830' by David W Noble (University of Minnesota Press/OUP, 1965) defines the central tradition of American historians 1830 onwards. 'It is my thesis that the point of view of the modern American historian is directly related to the world view of the English puritans who came to Massachusetts. These Englishmen believed that the community they established in The New World was sustained by a covenant with God which delivered them and their children from the vicissitudes of history as long as they did not fail in their responsibility to keep their society pure and simple.' To support this thesis the author studies the works of George Bancroft, Frederick Jackson Turner, Charles A Beard, Carl Becker, Vernon Louis Parrington, and Daniel Boorstin.

407 'Historians books and libraries; a survey of historical scholarship in relation to library resources, organisation and services' by Jesse H Shera, published in Cleveland by The Press of Western Reserve University in 1953, is directed in the first instance at librarians in order that they might become 'more aware of the world of historical scholarship and the historian's demands upon the resources and services of a well-administered library.' Chapters on The scholar and history, History of historical writing, American historiography, Social and intellectual organisation of the work of the historian, The educator and history, and The general reader and history, summarise the major trends in changing historical concepts, explain how historical materials are arranged in libraries, and give an account of the various types of reference material indispensable for historical research.

408 'The Historians' contribution to Anglo-American misunderstanding; Report of a committee on national bias in Anglo-American history textbooks edited by Ray Allen Billington (Routledge, 1966) outlines the results of an investigation of history textbooks used in English and American schools by a team appointed by the Historical Association, the British Association of American Studies and the American Historical Association. In particular a study of the treatment of textbook coverage of the American war of independence, the 1812 war, and the first world war, revealed that the deliberate distortion of past years has been replaced by a more subtle bias. The book concludes with suggestions to authors and publishers on how this bias can be eliminated and how historical objectivity can be achieved.

409 'The historian's handbook; a descriptive guide to reference works' by Helen J Poulton (University of Oklahoma Press, 1972) offers brief but useful comments on the whole gamut of reference works likely to be of use to the college student in an attempt to guide him efficiently to the widely scattered and complex materials such as government documents, archives, newspapers, journals etc, confronting him. An opening chapter on library organisation sets the scene and then library catalogues, guides and bibliographies, encyclopedias and dictionaries, almanacs and year-books, serials, geographical aids, biographies, primary sources, and government publications are all considered in turn. There is a distinct American flavour and the work is particularly suited to American libraries.

410 'Historians in the middle ages' by Beryl Smalley (Thames and Hudson, 1974) was written 'with the aim of helping students and general readers to read medieval histories and chronicles with pleasure.' The period covered is from the ninth to the thirteenth century with backward glimpses of the Roman, jewish-christian and barbarian legacies. It is sumptuously illustrated.

411 'Historical Abstracts; bibliography of the world's periodical literature (1955-   )' is a complete abstracting service for the

170

modern period from 1450 onwards to the history profession, to librarians, and to research agencies and institutions, published by the American Bibliographical Center—Clio Press, Santa Barbara, California. It abstracts or cites relevant articles from 2200 journals, not all of which are exclusively historical, from eighty five countries; all entries are in English although the journals scanned are published in thirty different languages. Appropriate material to be found in *Festschriften*, proceedings, and other collections is also included. It accommodates articles relating to political, diplomatic, social and economic, cultural and intellectual history excepting American History which is covered by a sister publication, *America: history and life*. Originally only the period 1775-1945 was covered but since 1970, in a succession of changes, the period has stretched to 1450-1975 and there are now two parts: A *Modern history abstracts 1450-1914* which also caters for Historiography, the teaching of history and the history of libraries and B *Twentieth century abstracts 1914-1975*, each of which is bound and indexed separately. Two innovations commencing with the 1975 issue are short entry citations (*ie* complete bibliographical information plus brief annotation) used for articles from less central historical journals, and a subject profile index (SP index) now ensures that on average each entry attracts five index places. Each issue includes Table of contents, a Users' guide (consult this if in doubt as to coverage before or after 1970), the abstracts, and index; its classified arrangement is basically geographical. Three issues appear during the year with a fourth cumulated index issue appearing simultaneously with the third. Five year index volumes have also been published for Vols 1-5 (1955-1959), Vols 6-10 (1960-1964) and Vols 11-15 (1965-1969).

412 'Historical, archaeological and kindred societies in the British Isles' compiled by Sara E Harcup (2nd ed, 1968). The main alphabetical list giving date of foundation and address (or secretary's name and address) is indexed by topographical and subject lists.

413 The Historical Association. In the early years of this century the teaching of history in schools, colleges, and at university was exiguous at best and the time was ripe for concerted action to improve a very sorry state of affairs. At a meeting chaired by

Professor A F Pollard (*qv*) at University College London in May 1906 it was resolved to form an Historical Association. A committee was appointed to draw up a scheme and at a second meeting at the end of June a constitution was adopted and officers elected. The association's declared aims were to collect information on existing systems of history teaching at home and abroad by accumulating books, pamphlets, etc and by correspondence; to distribute information on methods of teaching and aids like maps, illustrations and textbooks; to encourage the establishment of local discussion centres; to represent the needs and interests of the study of history and the opinion of teachers to governing bodies, government departments, and other authorities having control over education; and to cooperate with the English, Geographical, Modern Languages, and Classical Associations in the pursuit of common objectives. All persons engaged or interested in the teaching of history were eligible for membership. Publications: Besides *History, Teaching history,* and the *Annual bulletin of historical literature* all of which may be found under separate heading, an impressive publishing programme continues to flourish. *A general series* of pamphlet essays, biographies of eminent historians and studies of important historical topics, is intended for students in sixth forms, colleges and universities. *Helps for students in history* pamphlet bibliographies on aspects of English, English local, and European history, were originally published by the SPCK 1918-1924 to provide help and guidance for the beginner in historical studies. In 1947 the association acquired the rights and reintroduced the series. The original fifty one SPCK issues have been reprinted by Wm Dawson and Sons. *Teaching of history* pamphlets are designed for school teachers and relate to work in the classroom *viz* suggestions for syllabuses in unfamiliar areas, articles on specialized materials, bibliographies, the problems of teaching particular groups, and educational psychology with special reference to the teaching of history. *Aids for teachers* pamphlets are now being absorbed into the series, *Appreciations in history* aimed at making available up-to-date assessments of historical problems and the most recent research. A separate *Publications* pamphlet may be obtained from the association. In recent years some questioning of the association's continuing role has arisen especially with regard to the needs of the university lecturers. The future of the library, founded when teachers had

172

difficulty in gaining access to scholarly books, now stocking some 6000 titles, is also under discussion. One school of thought holds that an imaginative move would be to offer it to a new university and replace it with a new film library, a collection of visual aids and an enlarged School Book Collection to display permanently text books available for use in schools, thus meeting more adequately the contemporary needs of the teaching profession. At the moment a book box scheme operates for corporate members allowing the borrowing of twenty five books for six months to supplement school and college libraries. A printed catalogue of the library, revised 1974, is available. A full record of the first fifty years of the Association *The Historical Association 1906-1956* (1957) was published to mark its jubilee.

414 'Historical association library catalogue' last revised in 1974 is a complete guide to the holdings of the association's library arranged alphabetically in sections listed according to the library's classification and there is an index of authors. All members of the association may borrow up to three books at any one time from this well stocked library of over 6000 volumes. Books may be retained for three months unless requested by other members. The library is open every weekday 10.00 am to 5.30 pm, and 10.00 am to 12.00 noon on Saturdays except for bank holidays.

415 'A historical atlas of Canada' edited by D G Kerr (Nelson 1960) ranges from the ice age to post war Canada in a sequence of 154 coloured maps, statistical diagrams and political charts, with accompanying text on the same page. It was prepared on the initiative and under the aegis of the Canadian Historical Association who were anxious to replace L J Burpee's *An historical atlas of Canada* published in 1927.

416 'Historical atlas of the United States' by Clifford and Elizabeth Lord (New York, Holt 1953) is intended for college students and designed to juxtapose basic social and economic maps against the background of political history. There are four sections: general maps; the colonial period; 1775-1865; and 1865-1950. The maps in black and white, and sepia, are adequate but hardly inspiring. A reprint in a library binding was issued by Johnson Reprints of New York in 1969.

417 'Historical atlas of the world' (W R Chambers/Barnes and Noble, 1970) is a handy, pocket sized volume suitable for school and university students which was first published in Oslo, 1962. It is divided into Ancient times, up to the Roman emperors (31 maps); Middle ages, the barbarian migrations to the voyages of discovery (23); Recent times, Charles V to Bismarck (27); and The twentieth century (14). The maps are drawn in six colours and combine with distinct legends to present a clear and uncluttered appearance.

418 'Historical bibliographies; a systematic and annotated guide' by Edith M Coulter and Melanie Gerstenfeld, published by the University of California Press (1935), was prepared to 'point the way to the printed materials required for minute research in almost any special field.' When it appeared the only other similar work was C V Langlois' long outdated *Manuel de bibliographie historique* (1896) which was of no practical use to those historians relentlessly pursuing the new type of academic history confined to explicitly limited topics instead of the old fashioned course covering broad historical themes and periods. Many bibliographies had been prepared to assist the historian in his new preoccupation, and the purpose of this work was to 'bring together in convenient form the important retrospective and current bibliographies of history, and those general bibliographical manuals deemed essential as a basis in bibliographical investigation.' The emphasis was heavily on the fields of history which were familiar in United States university history courses and the requirements of the American student were kept well in mind. The work is arranged by period, by country and by episode as follows: general; ancient world; Europe; voyages and colonial possessions; Asia; Africa; Oceania; and America. A brief description of each title is given and there is a detailed subject index.

419 'Historical geography of the British colonies' by C P Lucas (OUP, 1887-1920) aimed to provide 'a connected account of the Colonies, of the geographical and historical reasons of their belonging to England' and to explain 'the special place which each colony holds in the empire.' These volumes undoubtedly reflect the sentiments of the 'imperial' era but they comprised the first important and authoritative account of the origins of the entire

British Empire. Titles: C P Lucas: *Mediterranean and eastern colonies*, 1888 (2nd ed by R E Stubbs 1906); C P Lucas: *West Indies* 1890 (2nd ed by C Atchley 1905); C P Lucas: *West Africa* 1894 (3rd ed A B Keith 1913); C P Lucas: *South Africa I Historical—to the Boer war* 1897 (2nd ed 1913), II *Historical—Boer war to the Union* 1915, III *Geographical* 1897 (3rd ed by A B Keith 1913); C P Lucas: *Canada historical to 1763* 1901 (2nd ed 1916); H E Egerton: *Canada historical—since 1763*, 1908 (3rd ed 1923); J D Rogers: *Canada—geographical* 1911; J D Rogers: *Newfoundland* 1911 (2nd ed 1931); J D Rogers: *Australasia 1 historical and 2 geographical* 1907 (2nd ed R N Kershaw 1925); *India historical and geographical* 2 vols 1916-1920

420 **'Historical interpretations: I Sources of English medieval history 1066-1540 II 1540 to the present day'** by J J Bagley (David and Charles, 1972) 'describe and illustrate with examples the main types of written and printed records upon which is based our knowledge of the political, social, and economic history of England and Wales during the last four centuries, and ... include in the bibliographies the more obvious texts and collections of documents.'

421 **'The historical journal'** (1958-) is a continuation of *The Cambridge historical journal* (1923-1957) and is still edited from the university with the support of The Cambridge Historical Society. Containing research articles mainly restricted to the fifteenth century and onwards in period, review articles, communications and book reviews, it is now published quarterly. Back numbers of *The Cambridge historical journal* are available from Kraus-Thomson Reprint Ltd. An index to the *Journal* 1923-1974, containing alphabetical lists of articles and review articles by author, and book reviews by author and reviewer, was published in 1975.

422 **Historical Manuscripts Commission:** As early as 1857 a paper entitled 'The manuscript treasures of this country was read to the Birmingham meeting of the National Association for the Promotion of Social Science and two years later a memorandum to the prime minister asked for an enquiry into the manuscripts in private or corporate hands which 'are now lying useless and are in danger of decay, their contents never having been inspected, and their value being in many cases unknown even to the possessors of them.' But it took another ten years before there were further developments: on 2 April, 1869 the Royal Commission on Historical Manuscripts was constituted under the chairmanship of the Master of The Rolls and Records in Chancery and authorised 'to enquire what papers and manuscripts belonging to private families and institutions are extant which would be of utility in the illustration of history, constitutional law, science, and general literature, and to which possessors would be willing to give access.' To this end a circular was prepared and despatched with a copy of the commission to those in possession of manuscripts inviting their cooperation and assuring them that the object was solely the discovery of unknown manuscripts, and that in no circumstances would the manuscripts be removed from owners' custody without their request or consent. If, however, owners saw fit to entrust material to the commissioners it would be placed in the Public Record Office and be treated with the same care as if it formed part of the public muniments and would be immediately returned on request. There was a gratifying response, many hitherto unknown collections came to light and were examined by inspectors specially appointed. The Royal Commission, envisaged as a temporary investigating body, gradually translated itself into a permanent organisation. In 1945, as the result of a proposal made by the British Records Association to the Master of The Rolls, a National Register of Archives was established within the commission. And then in 1959 a new royal warrant further defined and extended the commission's sphere of activity. Records as well as manuscripts now fell within the commission's remit and their terms of reference now included the promotion and assistance of proper preservation and storage of archives, to assist those requiring to use these archives, to advise upon all general questions arising, and to coordinate the professional bodies concerned. Publications: These may be divided into reports, guides to the reports, and others of various kinds. *Reports:* 1) *Reports to the crown* by the commissioners of which there have been twenty five for the period 1870-1967 after which it was proposed to issue a report every five years. 2) *Annual report of the Secretary to the Commissioners* (1968-   ) including 'information hitherto published in the *Bulletin* of the National Register of

Archives and extended to cover the full range of the commission's activities and interests.' 3) Calendars of individual collections examined by the inspectors (these comprise the meat for historians to devour) whose size varies according to the accessibility and interest of individual collections, some extending into several substantial volumes. From 1870-1884 these were bound together with the *Reports to the crown* as appendices; 1875-1899 although still regarded as appendices they were bound separately and thenceforward they were independent publications. *Guides:* 1) *A guide to the reports on collections of manuscripts of private families, corporations and institutions in Great Britain and Ireland Part I—topographical* (1914) with a list and contents of reports, an index to short titles, and a topographical index. 2) This was continued by *Guide to the reports of the Royal Commission on Historical Manuscripts 1911-1957 Part I—index of places* edited by A J Hall (1973). 3) *Guide to the reports of the Royal Commission on Historical Manuscripts 1870-1911 Part II—index of persons* (2 vols, 1935-1938). 4) This was updated for the period 1911-1957 in 3 vols, by A C S Hall (1966). *Other publications:* an extensive joint publication series in conjunction with local record societies, formerly three volumes a year now restricted by government economy to two; lists and indexes of accessions to repositories reported to the National Register of Archives (*qv*); the Prime Minister's papers series; *Manuscripts and men*; and *Record repositories in Great Britain* (*qv.*) All the commission's publications are listed in *Publications of the Royal Commission on Historical Manuscripts* (*vide infra*). To mark the centenary of the commission four members of the staff were invited by the editor of the *Journal of the Society of Archivists* to give some account of the commission's activities from its inception and to indicate in what directions its vigour might lead it in its second hundred years. 'Origins and transformations' by Roger H Ellis, Secretary of the Commission; 'The National Register of Archives 1945-1969' by Felicity Ranger, Registrar; 'The use of the resources of the Historical Manuscripts Commission' by H M G Baillie, Assistant Secretary; and 'The prime ministers' papers' by John Brooke, Senior Editor, accordingly appeared in the April 1969 issue of the *Journal*. Until such time as a full scale history becomes possible these articles provide a most adequate interim report.

423 Historical novels. The insatiable demand for fiction of this sort at all levels remains a startling phenomenon of contemporary reading habits. From Walter Scott to Jean Plaidy, from Charles Reade to Georgette Heyer, deposed kings and reigning queens of the fiction libraries, historical romances continue to add substance to publishers' lists. A relaxed study of the *genre*, a rapid review of a number of selected titles, and a bibliography, appear in *Historical novels* by Helen Cam published in 1961 by The Historical Association. The problems facing the historical novelist are briefly assessed: 'The historical novelist with a proper respect for history has a very stiff task before him; not only must his facts and his concrete details be consistent with those established by research, but the atmosphere of belief, the attitudes and assumptions of society that he conveys, must be in accordance with what is known of the mental and emotional climate of the place and period.' 'History in fiction' by Mary Renault, herself one of the craft's most glittering practitioners, appeared in *TLS*, 23 March 1973. Author-Title lists of historical novels may be found under chronological divisions of names of continents and countries in *Cumulative fiction index 1970-1974*, compiled by R F Smith and A J Gordon, and published by the Association of Assistant Librarians (1975), a continuation of the previous volumes, 1945-1960 and 1960-1969. But the list to end all lists is *World historical fiction guide an annotated chronological, geographical and topical list of selected historical novels* compiled by Daniel D McGarry and Sarah Harriman White (Scarecrow Press, 2nd ed 1973) which endeavours to include only what are regarded as better works insofar as literary excellence, readability, and historical value can be measured. The author-title lists are arranged chronologically and then topographically. All told there are 6,455 books listed, those deemed suitable for junior high school students are marked YA *ie* young adult; the annotation consists of a one-line plot indication. There is an author-title index. For young people the National Book League's booklet *School library fiction 1 Historical fiction* (1966) provides an annotated list of 187 selected titles. Articles by Hester Burton, 'The writing of historical novels' and by Rosemary Sutcliff, 'History is people' to be found in *Children and literature* by Virginia Haviland (Scott, Foresman, 1973; Bodley Head, 1974) also throw shafts of light on this topic. The Youth Library Group of the Library Association have published in their *Storylines* series *The middle ages 1066-1485* (1972) and *Romans to Vikings* (1973). *Recent historical fiction for secondary school children* by Kenneth Charlton (Historical Association, 2nd ed, 1969) is a classified list of books written specifically for children since 1950 and *Historical novels for use in schools* (a daunting title) is a list of books in print at the time of compilation which 'have been found useful' published by the School Library Association. *Junior fiction index* (2nd ed, 1971) by Patricia Frend should also be consulted. In addition many public libraries distribute leaflets of recommended junior historical fiction.

424 Historical periodicals: guides. Still valuable is *World list of historical periodicals and bibliographies* edited by P Caron and M Jaryc for the *International bibliography of historical sciences* (1939) from material collected at the editorial offices from members and delegates of the National Historical Committees. Titles in or translated into English, French, German, Spanish or Italian are listed alphabetically together with details of initial date of publication, the names of directors and editors, frequency and place of publication, name of publisher, and the standard abbreviation for each title. Indexes of editors, abbreviations, and subjects are added. Supplemented by annual additions in the *International bibliography*. More up to date is *Historical periodicals an annotated world list of historical and related serial publications* edited by H Boehm and L Adolphus (Santa Barbara, Clio Press, 1961), 'an attempt to satisfy a need for an all-inclusive rather than an evaluative inventory.' Arranged in four sections: A History (all periods, and prehistory); B Auxiliary disciplines; C Local history; and D General publications provided they were judged to include at least twenty percent historical material. Full entries for the first two categories list title, frequency, and first year of publication, the most recent volume examined, the publisher or sponsoring institution, editor, and subscription rates. In preparation Boehm and Adolphus had full recourse to the files of *Historical abstracts* (they were editor and assistant editor respectively) and they also examined the two most recently completed volumes of each title. Perhaps the most useful guide for UK history students is the Historical Association's *A guide to historical periodicals in the English language* (1970) by J K Kirby in their *Helps for students* series which replaced an earlier *Guide to periodicals and bibliographies dealing with geography, archaeology and history* (1938). This excludes American local history journals and its coverage of other English speaking countries is very selective but it succeeds in comprehensively listing all the important British journals. Entries are grouped in six sections: Bibliographical guides and indexes; General historical periodicals; Periodicals devoted to a limited period; Periodicals with subject specialisation; Periodicals limited to a special area; and British local periodicals. In addition to the usual directory type information, comments and notes on any separately published indexes and also on variations from the normal make-up of learned journals are provided. A title index completes a very satisfactory bibliographical aid.

'The Historical Periodical: some problems' an article by Denys Hay who was at one time editor of *English historical review* appeared in the June 1969 issue of *History*. He distinguishes two great ages of historical periodicals: from the founding of *Historische Zeitschrift* in 1859 to the Historical Association's decision to assume responsibility for *History* in 1916, a period in which most of the more renowned journals began publication; and the second from 1916 onwards which is marked by a proliferation of journals increasingly devoted to precisely defined topics. Delays in publication, the type of article required, book reviews and finance, all come up for discussion.

425 'Historical problems studies and documents' edited by G R Elton for Allen and Unwin in London and Barnes and Noble in New York, comprise bibliographical essays and a selection of documents on specialised themes.

426 'The historical profession in the United States' by W Stull Holt (AHA Service Center Series no 52) published in 1963 expresses the author's concern that the wide gulf separating university professors and high-school teachers should not remain unbridged. He is attempting 'to reexamine fundamental purposes, to evaluate success or failure in achieving them, to plot a course or to correct idle drifting, and to remind all of their commitments and opportunities.' The obligations of the profession are twofold: to transmit by teaching and writing the existing body of knowledge and to increase that knowledge by research and writing. The part that the American Historical Association has played and should continue to play is examined. A discoursive list of references enhances this thoughtful and stimulating essay.

427 'Historical research for university degrees in the United Kingdom' started life as an annual supplement to the *Bulletin of the Institute of Historical Research* and up to 1954 was divided into two sections: Theses completed and Thesis in progress arranged alphabetically under university giving the degree awarded, title, author, and supervisor. From 1954 only *Theses completed* appeared in print, *Theses in progress* being duplicated from typescript and distributed to subscribers. In 1960 the method of arrangement changed so that theses appeared under broad chronological or topographical headings in an effort to display relevant information more efficiently. The two parts ceased to be issued as supplements to the *Bulletin* in 1967 and appeared as separate publications, both now being reproduced from a superior sort of typescript. At the time of writing the current issue is *List 36 Pt I Theses completed 1974* and *Pt II Theses in progress 1975*. These are prepared from information supplied by university registrars, secretaries of faculty boards, and heads of history departments. An accumulation *History research for university degrees in the United Kingdom: Theses completed 1901-1970* by Phyllis M Jacobs has now appeared listing over 7000 theses arranged in a classified order and indexed by author and subject.

428 'Historical societies in Great Britain' by George W Prothero (*Annual Report of the American Historical Association 1909*: 321-342) still has value in that it outlines the contemporary activity of societies many of which are still flourishing.

429 Historical studies (1940-   ) is published every April and October by the history department, University of Melbourne. Formerly titled *Historical studies Australia and New Zealand* it changed when the *New Zealand journal of history* began publication in 1967. Its articles, book reviews, notes and news are largely but not entirely Australian in content. 'Research work', theses completed and commenced, was an annual feature 1950-1975 but in future this information will be incorporated in a

181

newsletter of the recently formed Australian Historical Association (*qv*).

430 'Historical studies of the English parliament' by E B Fryde and Edward Miller (CUP, 2 vols, 1970) reprint important essays on English parliamentary history which first appeared in learned journals. In most instances these essays offer crucial reinterpretations of the evidence available relating to the development of parliament from its origins down to 1603. Long introductions to both volumes and the select bibliographies place these essays in their historiographical context.

431 'Historical study of the British empire' a bibliographical article by W F Craven published in *Journal of modern history* VI (1) March 1934: 40-69 notices the more significant trends in imperial historiography from the days of J R Seeley and J A Froude to those of J A Williamson, A P Newton, and the *Cambridge history of the British Empire*. The work of American scholars is also examined.

432 'Historical tables 58 BC-AD 1972' by S H Steinberg (Macmillan, 9th ed, 1973) enables 'teachers, students and the general reader to discover or recall what was going on in a given age in different parts of the world and in different fields of activity.' The history of the commonwealth and the United States is given a slight predominance. The work is arranged so that the left hand pages deal with international affairs whilst the right hand side is concerned with home affairs, constitutional or economic or ecclesiastical history, depending upon the period.

433 'Historical writing' a separate section of *The Times literary supplement* 6 January 1956, published to mark the jubilee of the Historical Association. Several eminent historians contributed articles: 'The larger view of history' by Geoffrey Barraclough; 'The French revolution' by Alfred Cobban; 'The American character' by Henry Steele Commager; 'Fifty years of tudor studies at London University' by G R Elton; 'Revisionism in Germany' by G P Gooch; 'Technology and science' by A R Hall; 'Official history' by W K Hancock; 'Renaissance origins' by E F Jacobs; 'The Historical Association' by W F Medlicott; 'The interaction of history and biography' by J H Plumb; 'Economic social history' by M Postan; 'Administrative history' by F M Powicke; 'The History of Parliament' by Frank M Stenton; 'Religion and economic life' by R H Tawney; 'The rise and fall of "pure" diplomatic history' by A J P Taylor; 'The limitation of historical knowledge' by Arnold Toynbee; and 'History and literature' by C V Wedgwood.

434 **'Historical writing in England c550-c1307'** by Antonia Gransden (Routledge, 1974) surveys all histories, chronicles, annals, biographies and local histories written in England up to the death of Edward I and all similar works written abroad which are of significant import for English history and historiography. The texts plus the important secondary authorities provide the basis of the survey in which the interests of students actually consulting this form of source material have been kept very much in mind throughout. Many of the most important writers, Gildas, Nennius, Bede, William of Malmesbury, Matthew Paris, are discussed in detail; others of lesser importance are grouped together in logical and chronological sequence. Considerable bibliographical information is included in the extensive footnotes and in part compensates for the lack of a systematic bibliography.

435 **'Historiography: a bibliography'** compiled by Lester D Stephens and published by The Scarecrow Press (1975) is an annotated reference guide to books and articles on the general theories of history, critical and speculative philosophies of history, the history of historical writing, studies of individual historians, and historical methodology.

436 **'The historiography of the British empire-commonwealth'** (Durham, North Carolina, Duke University Press, 1966) is a comprehensive, one-volume survey of the historical literature relating to the British Empire and Commonwealth, intended as a guide and bibliography for scholars, students, and librarians, written by twenty one acknowledged experts each of whom critically surveys at length the literature of a geographical area, with the emphasis on recent writing especially since world war two. An attempt is made to explain why the *corpus* of literature developed the way it did (a much harder task) and also to distinguish *lacunae* in research which graduate scholars might care to fill.

437 'History' edited by John Fines (1969) is one of Blond's teachers handbooks in which various contributors give specialised advice in a practical way on the most suitable books and visual aids, and consider the approach and content of history in the classroom. The use of archaeological material, fieldwork, museum visits, and the treatment of contemporary history are also discussed. John Fines' introduction states the vital importance of history teaching in schools today.

438 'History' the journal of the Historical Association, started life as a privately owned quarterly magazine in 1912 at a time when only the *English historical review* existed as a regular periodical exclusively devoted to history. The Historical Association immediately exercised a benevolent interest and most of its contributors were association members. In 1916 the magazine seemed likely to fold unless the association took it over. At their annual meeting in January it had been resolved that the association should possess an organ of its own to appeal not only to members but also to a larger public, and so the magazine was acquired and adopted as the association's official journal. Now published three times a year it has achieved considerable academic status, its contents no longer solely directed to practising teachers. A notable series of articles on libraries and archives has recently been well received. Wm Dawson and Sons have reprinted back issues including the original four volumes. An *Index* to the first fifty volumes of the new series 1916-1965 was published in 1970.

439 'History and historians in the nineteenth century' by G P Gooch (1913) summarises and assesses the achievements of historical research and portrays the master historians from Niebuhr and Ranke of the German school, Thierry and Guizot of the French, to Hallam, Macaulay, Carlyle, Froude, Stubbs, Freeman, Lecky, Seeley, Maitland, Acton, and other victorian 'giants'. Essential reading for all who would comprehend the effect of these celebrated historians on contemporary life and thought.

440 'History at the universities and the polytechnics' *A comparative and analytical guide to degree courses in history in the United Kingdom* (4th ed, 1975) edited for the Historical Association by R P Blows is now published with a spiral binding so that it may be easily amended whenever necessary. In addition to entry requirements, the curriculum and teaching methods of all university and first degree history courses are included.

441 The history book club when first announced in the 1960s offered a new book every month at a discount of twenty five percent with the opportunity of purchasing others at privilege prices with a free book on enrolment. At the time of writing it is owned by Purnell and operates on the pattern where members undertake to select at least four titles, all of which enjoy a discount of twenty percent or more, listed on a monthly news sheet, during their first year of membership. The introductory offer is three books at a fraction of their normal price. For details write to Purnell Book Services, PO Box 20, Abingdon, Oxon, OX14 4BR.

442 History guild is one of Book Club Associates group of book clubs owned by Doubleday and W H Smith's and is intended 'for everyone who delights in the clash of battle, the intrigue of politics, the pattern of social change.' In return for introductory bargain offers members undertake to buy at least three books in the first year of membership from over a hundred previewed in the free monthly magazine, *Chronicle,* and offered at a substantial discount on normal publishers' prices.

443 'History in depth' is a series published by Macmillan based on the belief that true historical perception requires a degree of immediacy and depth. Each volume examines a concrete problem relating to a particular event of outstanding importance and is arranged in an appropriate manner. Under the general editorship of G A Williams all volumes contain a major collection of original documentary material with an introduction, a full working bibliography and interpretive notes. Titles of special interest include *The peasants revolt of 1381* by R B Dobson; *The revolution in America 1754-1788* by J R Pole; *Puritanism in tudor England* by

H C Porter; and, *The early chartists* by Dorothy Thompson. Paperback editions are also published.

444 'A history of American life' a standard twelve volume series edited by Arthur M Schlesinger and Dixon Ryan Fox has been frequently reprinted by Macmillan since the volumes first appeared in the late 'twenties and through the 'thirties. Each volume provides a straightforward narrative and concludes with a long critical essay on authorities. Titles: *The coming of the white man 1492-1848* (Herbert Priestley); *The first Americans 1607-1690* (Thomas J Wertenbaker); *Provincial society 1690-1763* (James Truslow Adams); *The revolutionary generation 1763-1830* (Evarts B Greene); *The completion of independence 1790-1830* (John Allen Krout and Dixon Ryan Fox); *The rise of the common man 1830-1850* (Carl Russell Fish); *The irrepressible conflict 1850-1865* (Arthur Charles Cole); *The emergence of modern America 1865-1878* (Allan Nevins); *The nationalising of business 1878-1898* (Ida M Tarbell); *The rise of the city 1878-1898* (Arthur Meier Schlesinger); *The quest for social justice 1898-1914* (Harold U Faulkner); and, *The great crusade and after 1914-1928* (Preston W Slosson).

445 'History of American presidential elections 1789-1968' is a substantial four volume work edited by Arthur M Schlesinger Jnr, and published by Chelsea House in association with McGraw Hill in 1971. Each election receives a detailed analysis which is supported by a series of contemporary documents,, newspaper editorials and reports, excerpts from letters, party statements and campaign speeches.

446 'A history of Australia' by C M H Clark (CUP and Melbourne Univ Press) promises to develop into the definitive history of the commonwealth that has been lacking. Although only two volumes have so far been published their scholarly and well-researched approach combined with their inviting readability augur well for the completed work. Volumes: 1 *From the earliest times to the age of MacQuarie* (1962) and 2 *New South Wales and Van Diemen's Land 1822-1838* (1968).

447 'The history of Canada' by Kenneth McNaught (Heinemann Educational Books, 1970) recounts the dominion's history in fluent style. There is a bibliography arranged chronologically and seven useful maps. The Canadian publishers are Bellhaven House of Toronto.

448 'The history of civilization' a complete history of mankind from prehistoric times to the present day in numerous volumes designed to form a complete library of social evolution, edited by C K Ogden, was an ambitious project of the mid-thirties. Kegan Paul, now incorporated with Routledge, hoped to present the results of modern research throughout the whole range of the social sciences, 'to summarise in one comprehensive synthesis the most recent findings of historians, anthropologists, archaeologists, sociologists, and all conscientious students of civilization.' To this end a comparable and contemporary French series, *L'evolution de l'humanite*, was absorbed and used as a nucleus. An outline plan was drawn up of almost 100 titles arranged under three headings: Prehistory and antiquity, Christianity and the middle ages; and Modern history.

449 'History of East Africa' (2 vols, 1963-1965) is a cooperative history, *ie* each chapter written by a recognized authority, and purports to relate the history of the area from an African as well as a European point of view. Financed by the Colonial Science Research Council the project was directed jointly by the Oxford University Institute of Commonwealth Studies and Makerere University. The first two volumes carry the story from archaeological beginnings to 1950. A third volume is projected to cover the final stages to independence. Each volume is furnished with a select but substantial bibliography of published and unpublished sources.

450 'History of England from the conclusion of the great war in 1815' by Spencer Walpole, published in five volumes in 1886, provides a continuous narrative of British domestic and foreign policy for the period 1815-1858 with a description of 'the causes which have led to the moral and material development of the nation,' and also in brief outline form 'the events which have brought India under the sovereignty of England, and have led to the introduction of autonomous institutions into the larger British colonies.' It was followed in 1904 by *The history of twenty five years* in four volumes which carried the story forward to 1880. There are no bibliographies in either set of volumes but both are heavily armed with references to easily accessible authorities. Such histories are rarely written nowadays but they are still of immense value as general narratives.

451 **'A history of England'** published in ten volumes by Longmans and edited by W N Medlicott is a standard history intended to hold the interest of the general reader whilst at the same time appealing to the student. It incorporates the latest historical and archaeological research without forgetting that history takes an honoured place among the mental recreations of intelligent people. Each volume is of medium length; no set pattern of uniformity of style or treatment is imposed yet there is a unity of purpose. Authors of the various volumes are asked to avoid excessive detail but are requested to give particular attention to providing a synthesis of national life at any one time. Considerations of space inevitably prevent minute investigations into every topic but it is possible to deal comprehensively with essential themes. The short bibliographies do not supersede existing lists but call attention to recent publications and standard reference works. Titles published at the time of writing include *The anglo-saxon age* by D J V Fisher; *The feudal kingdom of England* by Frank Barlow; *The later middle ages in England* by B Wilkinson; *The tudor age* by James Williamson; *Eighteenth century England* by Dorothy Marshall; *The age of improvement* by Asa Briggs; and *Contemporary England* by W N Medlicott. The remaining volumes are in active preparation.

452 **'A history of England'** published by Thomas Nelson and Sons covers the entire period from the first Roman invasion up to 1955 in seven volumes. Although the scope of each book will inevitably vary according to the special circumstances of the period it deals with, it is claimed that they will all combine an analysis of the constitutional, social and economic, and cultural aspects with a clear chronological narrative which will not be submerged beneath a mass of detail. Each book is intended 'to be a stimulus to wider reading rather than a substitute for it; and yet to comprise a set of volumes, each, within its limits, complete in itself.' The general editors are Christopher Brooke and Dennis Mack Smith. Titles: *Roman Britain and early England* by Peter Hunter Blair, *From Alfred to Henry III* by Christopher Brooke, *The later middle ages* by George Holmes, *The century of revolution* by Christopher Hill, *The eighteenth century* by John B Owen, *From Castlereagh to Gladstone* by Derek Beales, and *Modern Britain* by Henry Pelling. A paperback edition entitled *The Sphere library history of England* is available.

453 'The history of England' a study in political evolution by A F Pollard was first published in the *Home university library* in 1912. Perhaps not all of its reasoning and conclusions would find ready acceptance by contemporary historians yet it still remains a first class condensed survey.

454 'A history of England 1815-1839' by Sir James Butler appeared in the *Home university library* in a second edition in 1960. Within its limited compass it presents a masterly survey of the political, economic, social and diplomatic history of the period.

455 'A history of historical writing' by Harry Elmer Barnes, originally published in 1937 and reissued by Dover Publications of New York in 1962, takes the form of a survey of historical writing beginning with the works of the Greek and Roman historians, proceeding to the early christian and medieval chronicles, humanistic writings, social and cultural history, to nineteenth and twentieth century historical scholarship. Concluding chapters on 'The rise of *Kulturgeschichte*,' 'History and the sciences of man,' and 'The new history and the future of historical writing' confirm the author's ability to analyse complex intellectual forces. It remains a superb evaluation of major schools of historical thought, the leading historians, and of their cultural background. For the new edition the bibliographies which are appended to each chapter are brought up to date.

456 'The history of historical writing in America' by J Franklin Jameson originally published in New York in 1891 considers the most important writers from the seventeenth century onwards beginning with Captain John Smith, 'the precursor, yet not the father of the American historical writers,' and ending with the *Narrative and critical history of America* edited by Justin Winsor. He concluded that American historiography had not reached 'anything like maturity but it is in a vigorous though raw adolescence.' It was reprinted by The Antiquarian Press in 1961.

457 **'The history of India; its study and interpretation'** by Robert I Crane (AHA service center series No 17) published in 1958 opens with a discussion of the problems of conceptualization and interpretation caused by the general inexperience of American teachers in this area. Sections on sources for Indian history and its treatment in textbooks are followed by a chronological procession through the consecutive stages of Indian history from the vedic period to post independence India. There is a select bibliography of the most useful titles mentioned in the text.

458 **History of mankind, cultural and scientific development** traces its beginnings to a conference of allied Ministers of Education held in London during the war at which a need for a global history emerged. In 1946 Julian Huxley revived the project in his report *Unesco: its purpose and its philosophy*. Five years later the International Commission for a History of the Scientific and Cultural Development of Mankind was established under the auspices of Unesco and work was started. The editorial plan was presented in the *Journal of world history*, a quarterly initiated and published by the commission in 1953. The final plan agreed to was that the history would be in six volumes, some in more than one part, and would be the first ever truly global history planned and written from an international standpoint by a number of scholars from different countries. None of the volumes would be concerned with national history, instead the emphasis would be four square on economic and social events, religious and cultural life, and artistic expression, not on the customary politics, constitutional or military affairs. In a word it was a deliberate attempt to synthesize mankind's heritage, strengthening the 'intellectual and moral solidarity of mankind'. Appropriately the history is published in many languages, the British publishers being George Allen and Unwin Ltd, the American Harper and Row of New York. At the time of writing one volume has still to appear. Titles: *Prehistory and the beginnings of civilization* by Jacquetta Hawkes and Sir

190

Leonard Woolley (1963); *The ancient world* in 3 vols by Luigi Pareti, Paolo Brezzi and Luciano Petech (1965); *The great medieval civilisations* in 3 vols by Gaston Wier, Vadime Elisseeff, Philippe Wolff and Jean Naudon (1975); *Foundations of the modern world 1300—1775* in two volumes by Louis Gottschalk, L C MacKinney and E H Pritchard (1969); *The nineteenth century* has not yet been published; and *The twentieth century* in two volumes by Caroline Ware, K M Panikkar and J M Romein (1966). Niels Steensgaard's article 'Universal history for our times' (*Journal of modern history* 45 (1) March 1973: 72-82) discusses the underlying assumptions of the project.

459 **'A history of New Zealand'** by Keith Sinclair (OUP, 1961) is an authoritative account in three parts: Maori and settler 1642-1870; colony into dominion 1870-1914; and New Zealand 1914-1956. There is an extremely useful critical bibliography. A revised edition was published as a Pelican Original in 1969.

460 **'History of parliament'** had its origins between the wars. In 1929 a committee was appointed by the First Lord of the Treasury (*ie* the prime minister) to report 'on the methods available for a record of the personnel and politics of past members of the House of Commons from 1264-1832, and on the cost and desirability of publication.' Three years later the committee reported favourably and on 19 July 1934 the government announced that it was prepared to authorise the publication of a history of the institution and personnel provided the cost of research could be secured from private sources. The object of the proposed history was to describe the people in parliament—their ideas, standing and politics—and to trace the gradual growth of parliamentary representation and government in Great Britain from the thirteenth century to the Representation of the People Act 1918. It was envisaged that the work would fall into seventeen or eighteen periods which when completed would be brought up to date. Each period would be served by three volumes: 1) The biographies of members arranged alphabetically together with an informed commentary on the facts disclosed; 2) The register, lists of all members of both houses in each parliament; 3) The conclusions which would summarise the development of parliament with documents, debates, and monographs on various aspects of parliamentary history. Further volumes on the parliaments of Scotland, Ireland, the Dominions, and India would follow. The first volume, *History of parliament, biographies of the members of the commons house 1439-1509* by Colonel Josiah Wedgwood, member for Newcastle-under-Lyme, was published by HMSO in 1936. Its companion volume *Register of the ministers and of the members of both houses 1439-1509* appeared in 1938 when it was reported that eight other volumes 1275-1918 were in preparation, the first being expected in 1939, and it was anticipated that in each case a register volume would follow about a year later. And there the project rested, in the event no more volumes were published, not even the third conclusion volume for 1439-1509, but its continuity was ensured by the appointment of a body of trustees drawn from both houses in 1940 to be responsible for its administration. It was revived in 1951 and the trustees placed the planning and preparation of the volumes and the recruitment of staff into the hands of an editorial board whose task it would be to divide the *History* into manageable proportions and to appoint suitable historians prepared to participate. The Institute of Historical Research provided accommodation. It was decided that Wedgwood's two volumes would not be incorporated into the new work. Publication began in 1964 with the appearance of three volumes by Sir Lewis Namier and John Brooke: *Vol I The House of Commons 1754-1790 Introduction survey, constituencies, appendices*, containing a survey of the politics of the period and their effect on the life and development of the house and a summary of electoral activities in each of the 314 constituencies giving the returns, notes and sources; *Vol II Members A-J* and *Vol III Members K-Y* providing succinct biographies of members, tracing how they came to be elected and the part they played in the proceedings of the house using whenever possible their own papers and reports of their contemporaries. Particular attention was paid to the more obscure figures. *The House of Commons 1715-1754* by R Sedgwick in two volumes *Introductory survey, appendices, constituencies, Members A-D* and *Members E-Y* followed in 1970. Acclaim for the project's learning and research from the professional establishment has been unstinted. Future plans announced so far include volumes for 1386-1422 (J S Roskell); 1509-1558 (S T Bindoff); 1558-1603 (Sir John Neale); 1660-1690 (B D Henning); and 1790-1820 (R G Thorne). Work has also started on the periods 1603-1660 and 1690-1714 and the editorial board are exploring the feasibility of revising the existing Wedgwood volumes and extending them back to 1422. If all this work in progress and planned materialises the whole work will be complete 1386-1820.

461 'A history of South Africa' by E A Walker was first published by Longmans in 1928 but has been reissued many times since. The author early recognised that the mutual relationships of western civilisation and tribal Africa would present one of the world's most intractable problems and it is this, and not the usual recounting of the colonies road to self government and eventual union, that constitutes his theme. The bibliography is confined to a list of books referred to in the text. A third edition 1957 was published under the title *A history of Southern Africa* to recognise the inclusion of much material relating to Rhodesia and Nyasaland.

462 'A history of the anglo-saxons' by R H Hodgkin (OUP 2 vols 3rd ed 1952) begins with a study of their original homeland on the Danish peninsula and ends with King Alfred's struggles against new waves of invaders. The two volumes are generously provided with maps and illustrations because of the dearth of written authorities but full use is made of those that have survived from Tacitus onwards. The contribution of recent archaeological research is also assessed.

463 'History of the British West Indies' (2nd ed, 1965), by Sir Alan Burns is a single volume history designed to give the general reader an outline history of all British colonies in or near the Caribbean. The title is slightly misleading in that the discoveries of Colombus are recorded as is the history of other nations' colonies in the area. An appendix, 'Books and other publications quoted or referred to', does not merit the description of bibliography.

464 'A history of the United States' by Edward Channing was published by Macmillan in six volumes 1905-1925. The author's treatment of the original colonies as parts of the British Empire which simply decided to follow a different constitutional pattern, and his conviction that the most important factor in the history of the nation was the victory of the Northern forces of union over the forces of secession in the South, are the individual features of this particular history. Volumes: *The planting of a nation in the new world 1000-1660; A century of colonial history 1660-1760; The American revolution 1761-1789; Federalists and republicans 1789-1815; The period of transition 1815-1848; The war for southern independence 1849-1865.* A *general index* supplementary volume compiled by Eva G Moore appeared in 1932.

465 'History of the western world' is the name given to a series of six books published by Weidenfeld and Nicolson, each written by a recognised authority, spanning the period from the end of the middle ages to the 1970s and attempting to interpret the major historical developments in such a way to provide new insights. The books are lavishly illustrated and may be regarded as general introductions for the serious reader. Three volumes were published in 1974: *The age of absolutism 1648-1777* (Maurice Ashley); *The age of revolution 1775-1848* (John Roberts); and *The age of expansion 1848-1917* (Marcus Cunliffe). Other titles in active preparation are *The end of the middle ages 1450-1550* (Helmut Divald); *The age of religious conflict 1550-1648* (Charles Wilson); and *The modern age 1917-1973* (Dietrich Bracher).

466 'A history of the world in the twentieth century' (Hodder, 1967) is written by three authors each of whom is responsible for a particular section of this hefty book: D C Watt (1899-1918), Frank Spencer (1918-1945), and Neville Brown (1945-1963). It concentrates on political events, although there are chapters on economic, scientific, technological matters etc, and focuses especially on international aspects on the premise that it is the relations between states that provide the stuff of world history.

467 'The history student's guide to the library' by John Fines (Phillimore, 1973) is a most practical booklet that was initially devised for a class of history students at a college of education to aid them in coping with the reference section of a good library. It is constructed in such a way that students are given an opportunity to work out their own salvation in tracing and making use of the literature available. 'In essence this work is designed as an introduction to the tools of the history student's trade.' Down to earth comments bespatter the entries which are arranged in four sections: Bibliography; records of record searching ie documents, guides to collections, and possible problems; Works of reference; and the nature and philosophy of history, historiography, and the writing of history. It is perhaps a little ambitious to expect college of education students to find their own feet in the manner indicated here and the sources listed imply that a fairly substantial academic library would be required to house them.

468 'History teaching atlas and notebook of British and world history from the earliest times to 1960 completely revised and redrawn' by C K Brampton (1968) is based on Wheaton's *History teaching atlas* of 1938 but with the addition of almost 20 new maps indicating the vast political changes resulting from the second world war and the emergence of former colonial territories to independent status. It is designed in such a way that material on each page is grouped under a single heading with opposite pages having some bearing on each other 'with each map saying not as much as can be said, but as little as is compatible with its being understood.' The maps are clearly defined in colour and at appropriate intervals a page of notes is inserted to elucidate events depicted by the maps.

469 'History today' commenced publication in 1951 and is an illustrated monthly magazine publishing short articles written by specialists intended for the intelligent general reader. Or, rather, as it was once described in its own pages, appealing to two types of reader: 'the general reader who is intrigued by history itself, and is willing to read it in unrelated bits and pieces; and the scholar who is interested in new work being done, and also in observing the errors and delusions of his colleagues.'

470 'History yesterday' by R W K Hinton is a sympathetic but realistic appreciation of the four great nineteenth century whig historians, Hallam, Macaulay, Stubbs, and Gardiner, and their 'fortunate' interpretation of constitutional history which asserted that the men who made the constitution knew what the proper constitution ought to be in their own time. It appeared in *History today* IX (11) November 1959: 720-728.

471 'Holinshed's chronicles' first appeared in 1577 in 3 volumes under the title: *The firste volume of the chronicles of England, Scotlande, and Irelande, conteyning the description and chronicles of England, from the first inhabiting unto the Conquest. The description and chronicles of Scotland, from the first originall of the Scottes nation, till the yeare 1571. The description and chronicles of Irelande, from the firste originall, untill the yeare 1547 (The laste volume ... conteyning the chronicles of Englande from William Conquerour untill this present tyme.* Raphael Holinshed was a translator employed by one Reginald Wolfe who was working on a universal history but when Wolfe died he abridged the history, persuaded William Harrison to write the Description of Scotland, Richard Stanyhurst and Edmund Campion the Description of Ireland, Richard Hooker to compile the history of Ireland, and issued the *Chronicles* under his own name (*faithfully gathered and set forth* by Raphaell Holinshed). In point of time the *Chronicles* were the first complete history of England written as a continuous narrative to appear in print. Although not an out and out plagiarist he did not disdain to lift material from Edward Hall and John Stow. His fame down the years has rested largely on the use Shakespeare made of the *Chronicles* in the history plays. A selection, *Holinshed's chronicles as used in Shakespeare's plays* edited by Allardyce and Josephine Nicholl, issued in Everyman's Library in 1927, presents passages arranged in chapters according to the plays. For a full discussion of Shakespeare's debt to Holinshed see volumes three and four of Geoffrey Bullough's *Narrative and dramatic sources of Shakespeare* (London: Routledge; New York: Columbia University Press, 8 vols 1957-1975).

472 Home university library of modern knowledge was founded in 1911 by the publishers Williams and Norgate, then passed to Thornton Butterworth, and finally was taken under the wing of the Oxford University Press in 1941. It was designed to make available to students authoritative texts in all branches of learning in convenient pocket sized volumes. History took a prominent place in the series whose editors have included H A L Fisher, Gilbert Murray, and Sir George Clark. Their names and the HUL's provenance testify to the high standard of scholarship offered. Titles of particular interest include *Medieval England 1066-1485* by F M Powicke; *England under the tudor and stuarts* by Keith

Feiling; *A history of England 1688-1815* by E M Wrong; *A history of England 1815-1918* by J R M Butler; *The English revolution 1688-89* by G M Trevelyan; *The history of England a study in political evolution 55 BC-AD 1911* by A F Pollard; *The British empire 1585-1928* by Basil Williams; *Canada 1754-1911* by A G Bradley; *South Africa 1652-1933* by A F Hattersley; and *The American civil war* by F L Paxson. Many titles previously published in this series are now reappearing in the *Oxford paperbacks university series.*

473 Horsley, John (1685-1732), a Northumberland schoolmaster and lecturer, is chiefly remembered for the *Britannica Romana or the Roman antiquities of Britain* published in 1732. This folio volume was described by Haverfield in his *Roman occupation of Britain* (1924) as 'till quite lately the best and most scholarly account of any Roman province that had been written anywhere in Europe' (p 75). It is arranged in three books: Book I *contains the history of all the Roman transactions in Britain, with an account of their legionary and auxiliary forces employed here ... also a large description of the Roman walls, with maps of the same laid down from a geometrical survey;* Book II *contains a compleat collection of the Roman inscriptions and sculptures which have hitherto been discovered in Britain ... ;* and Book III *contains the Roman geography of Britain, in which are given the originals of Ptolemy, Antonini Itinerarium, the Notitia, the anonymous Ravennas, and Peutinger's table, so far as they relate to this island, with particular essays on each of these ancient authors, and the several places in Britain mentioned by them.* The author claimed to have travelled several thousand miles 'to visit antient monuments, and reexamine them, where there was any doubt of difficulty' and his work is widely acknowledged as setting a standard for methodical and scientific investigation; his collection of inscriptions must be regarded as the foundation of all later work. Several pull out maps, over a hundred copper plate illustrations, a chronological table, an index to the inscriptions, geographical indexes of both the Latin and English names of the Roman places in Britain, and a general index, attest the scholarly nature of the work.

474 'How to find out in history' (1966) by Philip Hepworth is a survey of bibliographies and reference works and a selection of the more important secondary material in history and its related fields of biography, genealogy, and heraldry, designed to meet the needs of students.

475 Hudson's Bay record society owes its formation to the decision of the Hudson's Bay Company in the early 1930s to throw open its incomparable archives to *bona fide* scholars who were allowed access to all documents down to the year 1870. The Record Society was incorporated in April 1938 with the express purpose of publishing documents in full together with fair comment and criticism by way of introductions and notes. The first twelve volumes were in fact published in collaboration with the Champlain Society and are listed thereunder, and it was not until 1950 that they appeared independently under the sole imprint of the Record Society. Publications:

13 *Peter Skene Ogden's Snake Country journals 1824-25 and 1825-26.*

14-15 *Cumberland House journals and inland journal 1775-1779, 1779-1782.*

16 *John Rae's correspondence with the Hudson Bay Company on Arctic exploration 1844-1855.*

17 *Moose Fort journals 1783-85.*

18 *A journal of a voyage from Rocky Mountain Portage in Peace River to the sources of Finlays Branch and North West Ward in Summer 1824* by Samuel Black.

19 *London correspondence inward from Eden Colville 1849-1852.*

20 *Hudson's Bay copy booke of letters commissions instructions outward 1688-1696.*

21-22 *The history of the Hudson's Bay Company 1670-1870.* To alleviate the bulk of these two already substantial volumes notes were excluded but special copies including documents from the Public Record Office, the British Museum, Bibliotheque Nationale, and various private collections were offered to the British Museum Library, the University libraries of Oxford and Cambridge and to the Public Archives of Canada.

23 *Peter Skene Ogden's Snake Country journal 1826-27.*

24 *Northern Quebec and Labrador journals and correspondence 1819-35.*

25 *Letters from Hudson Bay 1703-40.*

26 *Saskatchewan journals and correspondence.*

27 *Andrew Graham's observations on Hudson's Bay 1767-91.*

28 *Peter Skene Ogden's Snake Country journals 1827-28 and 1828-29.*

29 *London correspondence inward from Sir George Simpson 1841-42.*

30 *Hudson's Bay miscellany 1670-1870.*

476 Hume, David (1711-1776) the Scottish philosopher, is best remembered as a historian for his *History of England from the invasion of Julius Caesar to the revolution in 1688* (6 vols 1754-1762). This work marks an important stage in the development of English historiography in that it included some small measure of social history for the first time. Beginning with two volumes on the stuarts it was at first a resounding failure; his tory principles upholding the royal prerogative making unpalatable reading in a whiggish age. Later, however, with its completion it met with a better reception, mainly because of his easy and graceful literary style. At times his bias and unsound and even unfair use of his authorities bring his interpretation under suspicion but his work is never dull and it was eventually recognised as a standard history. Its popularity may be gauged by its frequent reprintings and by the use made of his name first by Tobias Smollett (1721-1771) for his *History of England from the revolution to the death of George the second designed as a continuation of Mr Hume's history* which itself went through several editions, and then by Thomas Smart Hughes who carried the story to the accession of Queen Victoria. An illustrated edition of the three combined proved very popular but these later accretions may safely be discounted. *The Reign of James I and Charles I* extracted from the complete work, edited and with an incisive introduction by Duncan Forbes was published by Penguin Books in 1970.

477 'A hundred years of the British Empire' by A P Newton (1940) is a reliable summary of imperial events and policies from the accession of Queen Victoria down to the outbreak of the second world war. In the belief that a short book list on so vast a subject would be misleading and valueless the bibliographical note merely advises recourse to *The Cambridge history of the British Empire*. Sound advice if one is working in a well stocked library but equally valueless if not.

478 Hutchinson University Library intended for first year undergraduates, extends over a wide range of academic disciplines. Formerly at least three different series, History, British empire history, and American history, ensured many useful titles were kept in print over many years. In recent times the list has contracted but still includes some very interesting titles by authors of repute in both hard case and paperback form. A catalogue is available from the publisher.

479 'The imperial achievement the rise and transformation of the British empire' by John Bowle (Weidenfeld, 1974) forms a sequel to the same author's *The English experience* and is a conscious attempt to redress the contemporary doubts and denigration of the British Empire so prevalent among popular and even academic historians. It is a broad survey, chronological rather than geographical in arrangement, providing an interpretation of the empire set against modern world history intended for the intelligent general reader. A Penguin edition is available.

480 'Imperial commonwealth' by Lord Elton (Collins, 1945) is a chronological narrative intended for the ordinary reader 'of that greatest and most fruitful of recorded political achievements, the British Empire.' If its sentiments have dated just a little, the historical account retains its value. A few books for further reading are listed at the end of each of the eleven 'books' by which the work is arranged.

481 'Imperial sunset' by Max Beloff is a projected two volume work describing Britain's external relations during the period of imperial decline from the imperial conference of 1897 to the 1960s. Vol 1, *Britain's liberal empire* was published by Methuen in 1969 and takes the story down to 1921 when the empire had reached its maximum territorial extent. Largely based on unpublished private papers it examines the reactions of the English and dominion governing élites to the shattering world events that already threatened the empire's continuing stability. There is no bibliography but the work is heavily footnoted. The second volume has yet to appear.

482 '**An index of British treaties 1101-1968**' compiled and annotated under the auspices of the International Law Fund and the British Institute of International and Comparative Law by Clive Parry and Charity Hopkins (HMSO 3 vols, 1970) serves as a complete index to the *Treaty* series and includes all international engagements between the United Kingdom, the colonies, and the dominions, with foreign powers. All arrangements with African and Arab entities which were published and which were identifiable as having the nature of treaties are also included but not treaties between England and Scotland 'which no longer have international relevance.' Volume one contains an index of multilateral treaties by subject and an index of bilateral treaties by country and by subject. Volumes two and three are given over to the main chronological list of treaties 1108-1925, 1926-1968. Information provided includes title of the treaty, any subordinate instruments (*eg* secret articles, additional protocol, or exchange of notes), place and date of signature, date of ratification, when treaty came into force, duration, modification or renewal of terms, and an indication of where text may be examined. A valuable list of sources is appended.

483 India Office Library was founded as the library of the Honourable East India Company in 1801 at the East India House in London as a repository for the large number of oriental books and manuscripts acquired in India. In 1858 when the crown assumed the company's powers and responsibilities the library became administered by the India Office until that department was merged into the Commonwealth Office in 1947. By that time of course the collections had multiplied into vast proportions and it has long enjoyed special status as an official reference library and as a learned library for scholars. A detailed history of the library may be found in *The library of the India Office: a historical sketch* by A J Arberry (1938). Students and scholars intending to use the library should equip themselves with S C Sutton's *A guide to the India Office Library* (HMSO, 1967), an indispensable outline of its organisation, and of its collections of European and oriental manuscripts and printed books, drawings and prints, and publications.

484 'India Office Records:' strictly speaking these are not part of the India Office Library but are a separate entity; in practice however they have always been housed in the same building and nowadays operate under a unified staff, the librarian also acting as keeper of the records. They comprise the extant archives of the East India company and of the old India Office and fall into four main classes: original records; offical publications of the United Kingdom and pre-1947 Indian governments; a map collection; and a miscellaneous collection of oil paintings, water colours, drawings, prints and photographs. For further information refer to Joan C Lancaster's article 'India Office records' in *Archives* IX (43) April 1970: 130-141. Also very informative is the *India Office records report for the years 1947-1967* (HMSO, 1970).

485 Institute of Historical Research founded in 1921 largely at the instigation of A F Pollard, is a national and international centre for advanced work in history and also the centre for postgraduate studies in the University of London. It is now housed at the Senate House where it occupies thirty rooms and is conveniently positioned close to the British Library Reference Division (British Museum) and the Public Record Office. Recently it was described as 'an historical laboratory managed by the University of London with the support of and in consultation with teachers of history in other universities ... providing instruction in research by teachers of the London colleges, facilities for independent study in a specially designed library, a centralised pool of information on all matters of interest to historians, a centre where historical enterprises may find a home and pursue their objectives in varying forms of association with the institution,' (Guy Parsloe, *vide infra*). Among the enterprises domiciled at the institute are the *Victoria history of the counties of England* and the *History of parliament*. Publications: Besides the *Bulletin* and *Historical research for university degrees in the United Kingdom* (*qv*) there is a regular programme of *Special supplements*. Two articles specially written to mark the fiftieth anniversary of the institute provide a fascinating and intimate glimpse of it at work: Guy

Parsloe 'Recollections of the institute 1922-1943' and A T Milne 'Twenty five years at the institute 1946-1971,' *Bulletin of the Institute of Historical Research* XLIV (110) Nov 1971: 270-292.

486 'International bibliography of historical sciences' is edited from contributions received from national committees of the International Committee of Historical Sciences and published in Paris with the support of Unesco by Librairie Armand Colin. It traces its beginnings to a proposal from the American Historical Association to the 1923 International Congress of Historical Sciences held in Brussels and is a general bibliography comprehending the whole field of historical sciences but selective in the sense that only work of a high standard and which is of international application is included. Serially numbered entries are arranged under general historical bibliography; auxiliary sciences; the ancient east; Greek history; history of Rome, ancient Italy and the Roman empire; early history of the church to Gregory the great; Byzantine history; history of the middle ages; modern history general works; modern religious history; history of modern culture; modern economic and social history; modern legal and constitutional history; history of international relations; Asia; Africa (to colonisation); America (to colonisation); and Oceania (to colonisation). There is an index of names and also a geographical index. Volumes are complete 1926-1972 with the exception of volume 15 (1940-1946) which will be compiled should orders to the publisher warrant it. L B Frewer's *Bibliography of the historical writings published in Great Britain and the empire 1940-1945* (*qv*) fills the gap in part.

487 International Committee of Historical Sciences was called into existence to act as a central bureau of the International Congress of Historical Sciences (*qv*) and was formally constituted at Geneva in 1926. The objects of the committee were defined as the advancement of the historical sciences through cooperation. The committee was to organise meetings of the congress, prescribe its regulations, and publish their proceedings. There are a number of standing commissions of which one is responsible for the *International bibliography of historical sciences* (*qv*). An early outline written by J H Baxter appeared in *History* XV (57) April 1930: 27-33, and a definitive history, *The origin and beginning of* the International Committee of Historical Sciences, by Professor Halvdan Koht, was published in Lausanne in 1962.

488 International Congress of Historical Sciences was formed in order that scholars from different countries might meet, get to know each other personally, and benefit from the new material and new interpretations revealed in the papers presented and the discussions which followed. An organisation committee, the International Committee for Historical Sciences (*qv*) decides in advance the topics to be discussed. The first meeting, the outcome of suggestions by an eminent group of French historians, was appropriately held in Paris in 1898. Subsequent meetings have been arranged on a quinquennial basis: since the war congress has assembled in Paris (1950), Rome (1955), Stockholm (1960), Vienna (1965), Moscow (1970) and San Francisco (1975). There has been constant criticism at the way the congress is organised, particularly on the grounds that the meetings are too big, that chairmen have little knowledge of the topics of meetings they preside over, and seldom enforce the time limits theoretically in force on papers and participants in discussions, that some delegates appear to be determined to speak at all costs, that the number of languages employed leads to further confusion, and that in short the prime business of a conference is to confer which it is signally failing to do. In recent times the congress has comprised five sections: methodology, ancient, medieval, modern, and contemporary history. Before each congress some '*grand themes*' are designated with '*grand rapports*' and briefer '*rapports*' being prepared by a group of specialists and circulated beforehand. Each morning session is occupied by expert speakers on the '*grand themes*' whilst the afternoon is devoted to discussion. A resume of the congress' programme is published in a number of report volumes and extracts and reprints of papers appear in the *Bulletin of the international committee for historical sciences.*

489 'International history 1939-1970 a select bibliography' by Keith Sainsbury (Historical Association, 1973) presents texts chosen to illustrate a wide variety of opinions divided into four sections: wartime; the postwar period of Stalin and Truman; 1950s; and 1960s. After each section some pertinent comments enhance one of the most professional looking bibliographies published by the HA in their 'Helps to students' series.

490 **'International maps and atlases in print,'** published by R B Bowker in association with Edward Stanford in 1974, is designed for the dual purpose of acting as a practical user's guide to currently available world cartographical literature and of serving as a reliable bibliography in this specialised field. Entries, arranged according to the Universal Decimal Classification, indicate title, author, edition, place of publication, publisher, date, size, pagination, additional information, and price, in that order. General historical atlases are listed in the 100 world section on pages 29-31 with maps and wall maps on pages 13-15. Those relating to specific countries are entered under the appropriate country heading.

491 **'International medieval bibliography'** (1967-   ) is a half yearly list of all articles on medieval topics published in journals and *festschrift* volumes directed by P H Sawyer of the University of Leeds. The period covered ranges from 500-1500 and includes works on archaeology, art and architecture, literature and history, philosophy and theology, and is European in scope. Entries are arranged by topic and subdivided by area.

492 **'The interregnum the quest for settlement 1646-1660'** edited by G E Aylmer published in 1972 is one of Macmillan's *Problems in focus series*. A long introduction sets the scene and is followed by eight chapters examining the constitutional, political, social, economic, intellectual, religious and local aspects of these unprecedented years. Each chapter is supported by detailed notes and references and the annotated bibliography is also arranged in similar fashion.

493 **'An introduction to anglo-saxon England'** by Peter Hunter Blair (CUP 1960) gives a general introduction to the history of England from the latter part of Roman Britain until the advent of the Normans. The author is convinced that the study of this bewildering period is essentially a study of the sources. Two chronological chapters are followed by four others on the church, government, the economy, and letters. The bibliography has two additional sections on art and archaeology and original sources.

494 '**An introduction to contemporary history**' by Geoffrey Barraclough (Watts, 1964) postulates a clear distinction between modern and contemporary history. The former he regards as stretching back from 1890 (when Bismarck retired from the scene) through the familiar landmarks of The French revolution, the enlightenment, to the renaissance; the latter starts in 1961 when John F Kennedy was inaugurated as president of the United States. It is with the intervening period that Professor Barraclough is most concerned here. It is now available as a Pelican book.

495 '**An introduction to the administrative history of medieval England**' by S B Chrimes (3e, 1966) is No 7 in Blackwell's *Studies in medieval history series* intended to bridge the gap between textbooks and learned monographs. To this end the object is not to furnish bare outlines of fact but rather to offer university students a modern interpretation. In this present volume the author's purpose is 'to digest, put into perspective, and in some measure to interpret' the extensive literature published, mostly in learned journals, since T F Tout's monumental *Chapters in the administrative history of medieval England* (qv) beginning in 1920. His essential theme is the history of the central executive power administered by the King and his officials. The narrative is strictly chronological and each chapter is heavily footnoted. The third edition concludes with 'Recent contributions to the study of the administrative history of medieval England' a survey of literature first published in the *Annali* of the *Fondazione Italiana per la Storia Amministrativa* 1964.

496 '**An introduction to the history of central Africa**' (3rd ed, 1973) by A J Wills 'tries to give a balance to the story of the African peoples before the advent of the European and to each of the three Central African territories, whose historical association cannot be destroyed by the break-up of its present political form'.

497 '**An introduction to the history of West Africa**' by J D Fage (CUP, 3rd ed, 1962) reflects the switch in emphasis in the study of history in West Africa and is intended to meet the different needs of indigenous students and those of a wider public outside. Even so the external aspects of West African history inevitably predominate although a conscientious attempt is made to cover the pre-European period. A note on books for further reading indicates the range of books which should be available in a well equipped school or college library or which the enthusiastic teacher should be aware of.

498 'Introduction to the study of English history' by S R Gardiner and J B Mullinger (1881) was divided into two parts. The first, Introduction to English history is a straightforward narrative of cause and effect, of historical personages, tracing the life of the English nation from its ancient beginnings, for the purpose of orientating students so that they might have a clear fundamental knowledge of what preceded and what followed their chosen period. This part is of no special significance. But Part II, Authorities, is something else again being devoted to bibliographies, historical societies etc, in an introductory chapter, and then to the printed versions of contemporary and later writers for all periods of English history. Each writer receives enough comment 'as will enable the student to form a fairly accurate notion of each author's value as an authority.' General historians who have to all extent and purpose long been obsolete either through their own defects or from an 'imperfect acquaintance with the original manuscript sources' are omitted. Of course most of the non contemporary writers cited have themselves suffered from the ravages of time and have long since been forgotten, but even so, this section still retains its intrinsic historiographical interest.

499 'Introduction to the study of history' by C V Langlois and C Seignobos translated from the original French in 1898 remains almost indispensable preliminary reading for the student of history. It proposes 'to examine the conditions and the methods, to indicate the character and the limits, of historical knowledge. How do we ascertain, in respect of the past, what part of it is possible, what part of it is important to know? What is a document? How are documents to be treated with a view to historical work? What are historical facts? How are they to be grouped to make history?' The answering of these questions leads the reader into many strange and unsuspected byways: the auxiliary historical sciences, textual criticism; scepticism of documentary 'evidence;' history's relationship with the social sciences *etc, etc*. A reprint was issued by Frank Cass in 1966.

500 **'An introduction to the study of history'** by V H Galbraith, published by C A Watts in 1964, presents three parts: 'The historian at work,' originally written as a pamphlet for the BBC which surveys the materials available to the historian; 'Historical research and the preservation of the past' stresses the importance of printing original sources; and 'Research in action' is a case study of Asser's *Life of Alfred* which the author suggests is not all that it purports to be. A glossary, notes on the text, and a list of books for further reading complete a challenging and stimulating enquiry into the basics of historical study.

501 **'An introduction to the use of the public records'** by V H Galbraith (OUP 1934) remains the best concise description of the chief classes of records based at the Public Record Office. An introductory chapter outlines the history of archives in England, the historical origins of the different types of documents are examined, and there is a practical guide for the use of students about to visit the PRO for the first time.

502 **'James I'** by David Matthew (Eyre and Spottiswoode, 1967) considers in detail the successive and sometimes conflicting interpretations of James' life and times. It belongs to the *English monarchs* series.

503 **'Journal of African History'** was launched by the Cambridge University Press in 1960 following a conference on African history and archives sponsored by the School of Oriental and African Studies in 1957. It publishes articles, notes and comments, and book reviews and has consistently endeavoured to 'present the results of new research in the broader context of historical change whether on a regional or continental scale.' Now issued quarterly the *Journal* demonstrates the vast amount of work currently undertaken to establish the pattern of African history treated as an integrated whole rather than as the story of a series of incursions from outside.

504 Journal of contemporary history (1966-   ) is edited by the director of the Institute of Contemporary History and concentrates on the main issues confronting twentieth century Europe. Unusually containing articles only, no book reviews, it consciously attempts to bridge the gulf between the professional and the general student of history.

505 'Journal of imperial and commonwealth history' (1972-   ) focuses particular attention on British imperial policy, colonial rule, the rise of nationalism, decolonisation, the transfer of power, and the evolution of the imperial and commonwealth association. Three issues are published during the year, each containing six articles, book reviews and a short archival feature.

506 'Journal of medieval history' (1975-   ), published quarterly by the North-Holland Publishing Company of Amsterdam, is arranged in two parts. The first comprises four to six articles on European history (including Britain) of the period between the break-up of the Roman empire and the renaissance; and the second, 'new books: publishers' announcements,' hopes to record all important recently published works on medieval history.

507 'Journal of modern history' (1929-   ) was instituted after a committee of the American Historical Association invited the University of Chicago Press to undertake the publication of a historical review in the field of modern history. Its scope was determined as the history of Europe and its expansion from the renaissance to the close of the world war, and all aspects of the period, intellectual history and the history of the arts, came within its terms of reference equally as much as the more traditional political, religious, economic and social history. The type of material to be published included articles 'of the kind usually found in historical reviews; historical revisions, *ie*, short articles showing how traditional views have been modified by modern research; book reviews, and bibliographical surveys and notes of all kinds. Now published every March, June and September the *Journal* has changed very little, it still publishes only articles dealing with modern European history, although of course the 1918 *terminus ad quem* no longer applies, with the additional proviso that European imperial impingement upon other peoples falls within its scope. But starting with the March 1976 issue a new pattern of publishing articles will be introduced. Some will appear in the traditional form but others, more specialised in content and of interest therefore to only a fraction of the readership, will be listed in the table of contents together with a 150 word précis and will be available from University Microfilms either in microfilm or as a xerographic reproduction. This method has been devised to reconcile rising printing costs and the desire to publish professional work of a high standard but of limited interest. University Microfilms will advertise both title and precis in a quarterly periodical *Monograph Abstracts*.

508 **'The journal of Pacific history'** (OUP, 1966-) is now published twice yearly and 'serves historians, prehistorians ... and others interested in the study of man in the Pacific Islands ... and is concerned generally with political, economic, religious and cultural history'. The first issue contained J W Davidson's 'Problems of Pacific history'.

509 **'King George III and the politicians'** by Richard Pares (OUP, 1953) is the printed version of the Ford Lectures in the University of Oxford 1951-1952. The author, himself an eminent 'Namierite,' writes when the dust caused by Sir Lewis Namier's refutation of the nineteenth century 'whig' historians was beginning to settle. Topics discussed here are the reasons why so many amateurs turned to politics, the constitutional balance between king, lords, and commons, and the king's attempts to recover the political initiative and his subsequent failure.

510 **'King James and the revolution of 1688; some reflections on the historiography'** by Maurice Ashley appeared in *Historical essays 1600-1750 presented to David Ogg* edited by H E Bell and R L Ollard (A and C Black, 1963) and takes the form of a resumé of how this event was interpreted by contemporary and subsequent historians.

511 **'Kings and queens of England'** is the title of a series published by Weidenfeld and Nicolson in conjunction with Book Club Associates intended for the general reader. They are readable, well illustrated, written by reputable historians, and are not to be lightly dismissed. Titles: *King John* by Maurice Ashley; *Henry V* by Peter Earle; *Henry VIII* by Robert Lacey; *Elizabeth I* by Neville Williams; *Charles I* by David Watson; *Charles II* by Christopher Falkus; *James II* by Peter Earle; *George III* by John Clarke; *Victoria* by Dorothy Marshall; and, *Edward VII* by Keith Middlemas.

512 Knighton, Henry compiled a History of England from the time of King Edgar to the death of Richard II. It was admittedly based on Higden's *Polychronicon* but contains much else besides, being especially valuable for details of the Lollards and Wat Tyler's rebellion. The author was an admirer of John of Gaunt and appears to have had access to his letters etc.

513 Kraus-Thomson Organisation Ltd publish a vast number of archive lists and calendars, periodicals, reference works, books, and monographs as Kraus Reprints and issue a number of informative catalogues describing their ongoing publishing programmes which can be of the utmost value to librarians especially those in charge of recently formed collections likely to be lacking in older material such as extensive runs of learned journals or specialist books long out of print. Enquiries and requests for catalogues should be addressed to Kraus Reprint FL-9491 Nendeln, Liechtenstein or 16 East 46th Street, New York, NY 10017.

514 'Larousse encyclopaedia of ancient and medieval history' (Hamlyn, 1963), a translation from the *Histoire Universelle Larousse*, divides easily into two sections: the ancient world and the middle ages. In the first the empires of the fertile crescent take up a third with the remaining portion recounting the rise of the Alexandrian and Roman empires. The second, although mainly European centred, also explores the Arab invasions, the Mongols, and pre-Colomban America, thus going some way to meet the claims that the work makes 'valiant efforts to transcend the parochial western point of view', Arnold Toynbee's foreword is directed along the lines that the writing of universal history is a prerequisite step on the way to the unification of mankind. Ample black and white, and colour illustrations enhance the work.

515 'Larousse encyclopaedia of modern history from 1500 to the present day' (Hamlyn, 1972), an English translation from the original *Histoire Universelle Larousse*, is a straightforward account of the evolution of twentieth century civilization, arranged in six sections each of 2-5 chapters, and endeavours to answer the questions: How much does history affect our thinking and our everyday life? How do we differ from our ancestors? How much do we owe them? and, How much have we achieved? This lavishly illustrated volume (few pages are without at least one illustration) takes us over five centuries in which Europe dominated the world scene in a remarkably brief outline but it would be wrong to imagine that it is just another coffee-table book, it is truly informative and reads well.

516 'The later middle ages 1272-1485' by George Holmes (1962), the third volume of Nelson's *History of England*, is divided into two parts. The first half of the book describes English society at the end of the thirteenth century, whilst the second half is concerned with political events. An engaging discussion of medieval primary sources is sensibly placed in the introduction.

517 'The later middle ages in England 1216-1485' by B Wilkinson (1969), the fourth volume of Longman's *History of England*, emphasises the transitional nature of the period. Besides a straightforward narrative of the unfolding drama of events in the continuous dynastic and foreign wars there is also a constant examination 'of the interaction of these events with the machinery of government and with the social, economic, military, religious and cultural life of the country.'

518 'The later Plantagenets; a survey of English history between 1307 and 1485' by V H H Green (Edward Arnold, 1955) is a survey intended for the student who has only recently become acquainted with medieval history. It is strictly 'traditional' *ie*, it concentrates unashamedly on the political, diplomatic and military history of the period with a perfunctory glance at the medieval scene and religion in the first two chapters. Lists of contemporary rulers, archbishops of Canterbury, genealogical tables, maps, and a bibliography complete the scholarly apparatus.

519 'The later Stuarts 1660-1714' (2nd ed, 1956), the tenth volume of the *Oxford history of England*, was written by Sir George Clarke, the general editor of that work, and was appropriately the first volume to appear when it was first published in 1934. It set the pattern that subsequently has become so familiar: a broad survey of political events supplemented by chapters such as 'Intellectual and economic tendencies,' 'Literature and thought,' and 'Arts and social life' to present a balanced picture of England during the latter half of the seventeenth century.

520 'The later Stuarts 1660-1714; significant work of the last twenty years (1939-1959)' by Robert Walcott is a bibliographical article sponsored by the Confernce on British Studies. It is selective in scope, excluding new editions of source material and journal articles. All aspects of history are surveyed: political, religious, administrative, scientific, social and military. It appeared in *The American historical review* LXVII (2) January 1962: 352-370, and collected later in *Changing views on British history* (*qv*).

521 **Lecky, W E H** (1838-1903) won popular acclaim for his *History of England in the eighteenth century* (8 vols, 1878-1890) which is still eminently readable although it is uneven in content. He uncritically accepted the contemporary view of English eighteenth century history and was not above a tendency to partizanship. But his thoughtful analysis of the events leading up to the French revolution and his impartial account of the American rebellion have lasted well. He is particularly noted for his treatment of the religious and intellectual movements of his chosen period.

522 **Leland, John** (1506-1552) was appointed King's Antiquary in 1533, the only person ever to hold this office. Shortly afterwards he set out on a tour of England to search the surviving monastic libraries for ancient chronicles recording national history. At the same time his intention was to survey the material remains of the past, the monuments and the inscriptions, in an effort to link past and present by means of a grand topographical description. Of course he was before his time, the resources did not exist for such a work and he was doomed to failure. Leland never completed his manuscripts (his *Itinerary* did not find its way into print until long after his death) although subsequent antiquaries frequently consulted them.

523 Lingard, John (1771-1851) was an early forerunner of nineteenth century 'scientific' history, making it his first principle that history should be written from authentic sources and 'to admit no statement merely on trust, to weigh with care the value of the authorities ... Such vigilance is a matter of necessity to every writer of history.' As a catholic he was himself under close scrutiny: 'My only chance of being read by protestants depends on my having the reputation of a temperate writer.' His *History of England from the first invasion by the Romans to the revolution of 1688* (8 vols, 1819-1830) is closely argued and still a pleasure to read.

524 'List and index of the publications of the Royal Historical Society 1871-1924 and of the Camden Society 1840-1897' edited by Hubert Hall (R Hist Socy 1925) has largely been superseded by *A centenary guide to the publications of the Royal Historical Society 1868-1968 and of the former Camden Society 1838-1897* published in 1968.

525 The List and Index Society formed in 1965, publishes and distributes to members copies of lists and indexes from the Public Record Office and other British archives in the condition in which they are available to users at the date of publication. At the time of writing 120 had been published. In 1968 an additional special series of guides to archives specially prepared for publication was started. Eight of these have appeared to date.

526 'Little Arthur's history of England' by Maria, Lady Calcott (1785-1842) is still in print although it was first published as long ago as 1835 when it was an immediate success. In her foreword the author discloses 'This little HISTORY was written for a real little Arthur and I have endeavoured to *write* it nearly as I would *tell* it to an intelligent child.' If the next passage appears dangerously outmoded we must remember not to forfeit our own historical objectivity by judging her standards by those of today: 'I am indeed persuaded that the well grounded love of our own country is the best security for that enlightened philanthropy which is aimed at as the perfection of moral education. This is the feeling that has guided me in writing *Little Arthur's history*. If it should happily lay the foundation for patriotism in one single Englishman, my wishes will be answered, my best hopes fulfilled.'

527 'Lives of the queens of England from the Norman conquest' *now first published from official records and other authentic documents, private as well as public* by Agnes Strickland (12 vols. 1840-1848) was in fact the work of Agnes and her sister Elizabeth who flinched from public gaze. The work commences with an introductory chapter which contains all that the sisters could discover on the British and Saxon queens but the work proper begins with Matilda of Flanders, consort to William I, and ends with Queen Anne, the last of the stuart monarchs. In all thirty queen-consorts and four queen-regnants are commemorated. The *Lives* were diligently researched in the State Paper Office and in official French archive repositories and the authors were also allowed the use of the private papers of many old English families. A wide reading public delighted in the circumstantial topographical detail and the sympathetic treatment accorded to these mostly long forgotten ladies. After being out of print for some years Cedric Chivers Ltd, of Bath, published a facsimile reprint of the 1852 edition in eight volumes, with a new introduction by Antonia Fraser, at the request of the London and Home Counties Branch of The Library Association in 1972.

528 'The long white cloud' *ao tea roa* by William Pember Reeves was first published in 1898 but is now available in the New Zealand Classics series, with additional chapters, from Golden Press Pty Ltd, Auckland. Its republication is indicative of the book's reputation as a comprehensive political, social, economic and cultural history of New Zealand. Reeves served at various times in the New Zealand cabinet and as his country's agent-general in London. Part two by A J Harrop consists of six chapters comprising a brief commentary on the main political and economic events in New Zealand down to the 1970s with sketches of prominent personalities. There is a discursive appendix entitled 'New Zealand literature.'

529 'Longman atlas of modern British history' a visual guide to British society and politics 1700-1970 by C Cook and J Stevenson, is designed for advanced level students to be used in conjunction with a conventional textbook. Maps, graphs, and diagrams are linked with the text to outline British social, economic and political history.

530 Macaulay, Thomas Babington, Baron (1800-1859). The immediate phenomenal success of his *History of England from the accession of James II* describing the political experiences of the English people, or rather those classes who were politically influential during the years 1685-1700, owed much to Macaulay's own individual contributions to English historiography, *ie*, his attempts to insert comment on the social and economic aspects of his chosen period whenever a clear connection could be established between them and the unfolding political events, and also to his truly graceful literary style. His interest in the reasons why men took the decisions they did and his 'declamatory disquisition' method by which he enlivened his narrative by extravagant descriptions of opposing arguments in parliamentary debates and speeches induced the reader to imagine he was present when these stirring events took place. His use of printed ephemera, ballads, newspapers and polemic pamphlets, a novel practice for English historians, also contributed much to establish his authority. With the reaction against the 'whig' historians (Macaulay sat in a whig cabinet) his reputation declined and his conclusions challenged. *A commentary on Macaulay's history of England* by Sir Charles Firth was published by Macmillan in 1938 and reprinted by Frank Cass in 1964. This was originally planned to annotate an illustrated edition of the *History* published in six volumes 1913-1915 by indicating where subsequent research had modified Macaulay's conclusions. There are also interesting chapters on the genesis of the *History*, Macaulay's method, and his use of authorities.

531 'Magna carta' by J C Holt, published by Cambridge University Press in 1965 to mark the seven hundred and fiftieth anniversary of its signing, presents the charter in the context of twelfth and thirteenth century politics, administration, and political thought. Although Professor Holt's main concern is the political

216

situation in 1215 and immediately afterwards he finds space to consider the interpretation imposed on the charter by subsequent constitutional lawyers and historians down to the eighteenth century. The complex history of a number of various texts and previous similar documents is described in detail in a series of nine appendices which also include the full text of the charter itself. An impressive list of references complete a distinguished monograph.

532 Mahan, A T (1840-1914) was a serving officer in the US Navy whose *Influence of sea-power upon history 1660-1783* (1890), 'an examination of the general history of Europe and America with particular reference to the effect of sea power upon the course of that history', earned him recognition far beyond naval circles. Today his book is an acknowledged classic.

533 Maitland, F W (1850-1906), widely acknowledged as the *nonpareil* of the historical giants of the victorian period, was a prolific writer on English law and institutions in the middle ages. *Memoranda de parliamento* (1893), a seminal work which was an unconscionable long time a-sprouting; *The history of English law* (1895), almost entirely his although he shared the title page with Sir Frederick Pollock; and *Domesday book and after* (1897) which, despite recent changes in opinion, is still regarded as 'one of the great, fundamental books of English history' (H E Bell: *Maitland a critical examination and assessment* 1965); witness his powers and continuing influence on medievalists. He was instrumental in founding the Selden Society. Helen H Cam has chosen and introduced the *Selected historical essays of F W Maitland* (CUP, 1957), her introduction should be closely studied together with the monograph quoted above.

534 'The major international treaties 1914-1973; a history and guide with texts' by J A S Grenville (Methuen, 1974) is a collection of texts plus explanatory introductions of these essential primary sources of modern world history intended for students. A paperback edition is available.

535 Major issues in history is the name of a series published by John Wiley of New York which now extends to over thirty volumes dealing with various aspects, periods, and areas of world history. Each volume is solidly based on primary sources and secondary authorities. Titles of particular interest include *Humanism, reform and reformation in England* edited by A J Slavin (1969), *The partition of Africa* edited by R O Collins (1969), *Impact of the Norman conquest* edited by C W Hollister; and *Magna carta and the idea of liberty* edited by J C Holt (1972). English librarians should address their enquiries to John Wiley and Sons, Baffins Lane, Chichester, Sussex, PO19 1UD.

536 'Makers of history' published by Collins is a series of popular biographies of men and women who made history written by leading historians. Selected titles: *Queen Elizabeth* by Milton Waldman; *Sir Francis Drake* by J A Williamson; *Abraham Lincoln* by Herbert Agar; and *Chatham* by J H Plumb.

537 The making of America series published by Macmillan is designed to make the best of historical writing available to the general reader who is not a specialist in American history. Each volume presents a factual record, and an analysis of the political events, economic trends and social and cultural developments of its period, together with a bibliographical essay. Titles: *The formative years 1607-1763* by Clarence V Steeg; *Fabric of freedom 1763-1800* by Esmond Wright; *The new nation 1800-1845* by Charles M Wiltse; *The stakes of power 1845-1877* by Roy F Nichols; *The search for order 1877-1920* by Robert H Wiebe; and *The urban nation 1920-1960* by George E Mowry.

538 'The making of early England' by D P Kirby published by Batsford in their *Fabric of British history* series in 1967 covers the period between the end of Roman Britain to the coming of the Normans and is divided into two distinct sections. The first is a chronological narrative of the significant events of the period, whilst the second deals with Government and society, and Cultivation and commerce. The 'select' bibliography, stated by the author to concentrate in the main on books and articles of importance which are likely to be accessible to the general reader, is in fact extremely detailed and includes material that could be expected only on the shelves of an old established and well stocked, large public library. A map and some imaginatively chosen illustrations complete an impressive work of scholarship.

539 'The making of victorian England' by G Kitson Clark (Methuen, 1962), the printed version of the author's Ford Lectures at Oxford in 1960, outlines 'some particular factors, or possibly it would be best to call them forces, which called into existence a historic situation with special characteristics in England in the middle of the nineteenth century.' These factors include the dramatic rise in population, industry, the nobility and gentry, and the popular religious movements.

540 'A manual of British historians to AD 1600' *containing a chronological account of the early chroniclers and monkish writers their printed works and unpublished manuscripts* by W D Macray (1845) is confined to national histories, omitting all but two local chronicles. The historians are arranged in chronological order with an alphabetical index. A table of the years in which the histories conclude is a useful addition. A facsimile reprint edition was published by Anton van Bekhoven in Naarden in 1967.

541 'Manuscripts and men' was published to mark the centenary of the Royal Commission on Historical Manuscripts 1869-1969 and served as a catalogue of an exhibition of manuscripts, portraits and pictures held at the National Portrait Gallery June-August 1969. It also includes a valuable short history and explanation of the commission by Roger H Ellis; the commissioners and their principal officers 1869-1969; and an alphabetical list of the collections upon which the commission has reported.

542 'The march of America' is the name given to a facsimile reprint series of 100 significant titles on the theme of the expanding frontier of America, intended to stimulate and facilitate the writing and teaching of history in schools and colleges, issued by University Microfilms Library Services. Introductory notes at the beginning of each volume indicate its particular importance in the historical study of America. A lavish brochure to advertise the series contains a short essay, 'A continuing tradition,' by Peter C Welsh, itself an interesting and informative commentary on American historiography as evidenced by the books included. Titles (in chronological sequence of contents):

1 Cristoforo Colombo *Epistola de insulis nuper inventis* (1493).

And *The Columbus letter of 1493 ... a new translation into English* by Frank E Robbins, 1952.

2 Martin Waldseemuller *Cosmographiae introductio cum quibusdam geometriae ac astrono miae principiis ad aem rem necessariis. Insuper quattuor Americi Vespucii navigationes ...* (1507) and The cosmographiae introductio of Martin Waldseemuller ... translation and introduction by Joseph Fischer and Franz von Wieser, edited by Charles George Herbermann, 1907.

3 Sebastian Munster *A treatyse of the newe India ... translated out of Latin into Englishe* by Rycharde Eden (1553).

4 Pietro Martire D' Anghiera *The Decades of the new worlde or west India ... by Peter Martyr of Angleria and translated into Englysshe (from Latin) by Rycharde Eden* In Eden, Richarde, ed *The decades of the newe worlde of west India ...* 1555.

5 Richard Hakluyt *Divers voyages touching the discoverie of America, and the ilands adjacent unto the same ...* 1582.

6 Francisco Lopez de Gomara *The pleasant historie of the conquest of the Weast India, now called new Spayne ...* translated out of the Spanish by TN (1578).

7 Bernal Diaz Del Castillo *The true history of the conquest of Mexico ... written in the year 1568 ... translated from the original Spanish* by Maurice Keatinge, 1800.

8 Bartolome de Las Casas *The Spanish Colonie, or Briefe Chronicle of the Acts and gestes of the Spaniardes in the West Indies, called the newe Worlde ... translated into english* by MMS, 1583.

9 Alvar Nunez Cabeza de Vaca *Relation of Alvar Nunez Cabeca de Vaca* translated from the Spanish by Buckingham Smith, 1871.

10 Jacques Cartier *A Shorte and briefe narration of the two navigations and discoveries to the north weast partes called Newe Fraunce: first translated out of French into Italian by ... Gio: Bapt: Ramutius, and now turned into English by John Florio ...* 1580.

11 Sir Francis Drake *The world encompassed by Sir Francis Drake, being his next voyage to that to Nombre de Dois formerly imprinted ...* 1628.

12 Richard Hakluyt *Virginia richly valued, by the description of the maine land of Florida ... Written by a Portugall gentleman of Elvas ...* 1609.

13 George Parker Winship *The journey of Coronado, 1540-1542 ... as told by himself and his followers* 1922.

14 Richard Hakluyt *The Relation of David Ingram from The principall navigations, voyages and discoveries of the English nation ...* 1589.

15 Theodore Bry *A briefe and true report of the new found land of Virginia ... In the yeere 1585 ... At the speciall charge and direction of ... Sir Walter Raleigh ... This fore booke is made in English by Thomas Hariot* 1590.

16 John Brereton *A briefe and true relation of the discoverie of the north part of Virginia ... Made this present yeere 1602 ...* 1602.

17 James Rosier *A true relation of the most prosperous voyage made this present yeere 1605 ...* 1605.

18 John Smith *The Generall Historie of Virginia, New-England, and the Summer isles ... from 1584 to this present 1624* 1624.

19 Samuel Purchas *Henry Hudson's Voyages from Purchas his Pilgrimes ...* 1625. Part 3.

20 Samuel Champlain *Les voyages du sieur de Champlain Xaintongeois ...* 1613.

21 Mourt's relation *A relation or Journall of the beginning and proceedings of the English plantation setled at Plimoth in New England ...* 1622.

22 *A relation of Maryland; together, with a map of the countrey, the conditions of plantation, His Majesties Charter to the Lord Baltemore* translated into English, 1635.

23 John Mason *A brief history of the Pequot War; especially of the memorable taking of their fort at Mistick in Connecticut in 1637 ...* 1736.

24 Edward Bland *The discovery of the New Brittaine, Began August 27, AD 1650, by Edward Bland, Abraham Woode, Sackford Brewster, Elias Pennant ...* 1651.

25 John Lederer *The discoveries of John Lederer, in three several marches from Virginia to the west of Carolina ... collected and translated out of Latine from his discourse and writings, by Sir William Talbot* 1672.

26 Daniel Denton *A brief description of New-York: formerly called New-Netherlands* 1670.

27 Jasper Danckaerts *Journal of a voyage to New York, and a tour in several of the American colonies in 1679-80, by Jasper*

Dankers and Peter Sluyter Translated ... and edited by Henry C Murphy, 1867.

28 Jacques Marquette *Voyages du P Jacques Marquette, 1673-75, in The Jesuit relations and allied documents: Travels and explorations of the Jesuit missionaries in New France, 1610-1791* edited by Reuben Gold Thwaites, 1896-1901.

29 *King Philip's War Narratives: The present state of New-England, with respect to the India war. London, 1675. A continuation of the state of New-England; being a farther account of the Indian warr. London, 1676. A new and further narrative of the state of New-England being a continued account of the bloody Indian War. London, 1676. A true account of the most considerable occurrences that have happened in the warre between the English and the Indians in New-England. London, 1676. The war in New-England visibly ended 1677.*

30 Louis Hennepin *A description of Louisiana* Translated ... by John Gilmary Shea, 1880.

31 Henri Joutel *A journal of the last voyage perform'd by Monsr de La Sale, to the Gulph of Mexico* ... 1714.

32 Thomas Budd *Good order established in Pennsilvania and New-Jersey in America* ... 1685.

33 Arthur Fallows *'Journal'* from *Discoveries beyond the Appalachian Mountains in September, 1671* by David I Bushnell, Jr in *American Anthropologist* IX (1907).

34 John Williams *The redeemed captive returning to Zion* ... 6th ed 1795.

35 John Lawson *A new voyage to Carolina* ... 1709.

36 Pierre Francois Xavier de Charlevoix *Journal of a voyage to North-America* ... 1761.

37 William Stephens *A journal of the proceedings in Georgia, beginning October 20, 1737* ... 1742.

38 Miguel Venegas *A natural and civil history of California* ... London, 1759.

39 Israel Acrelius *A history of New Sweden* ... translated from the Swedish ... by William M. Reynolds, 1874.

40 William Coxe *Account of the Russian discoveries between Asia and America* ... 2d ed 1780.

41 John Bartram *Observations on the inhabitants, climate, soil* ... 1751.

42 George Washington *The journal of Major George Washington* ... 1754.

43 Alexander Henry *Travels and adventures in Canada and the Indian territories* ... 1809.

44 Robert Rogers *Journals of Major Robert Rogers* ... 1765.

45 William Smith *An historical account of the expedition against the Ohio Indians* ... 1765.

46 Thomas Morris *Journal of Captain Thomas Morris ... from Miscellanies in prose and verse* 1791.

47 John Rickman *Journal of Captain Cook's last voyage to the Pacific Ocean* ... 1781.

48 William Hayden English *Conquest of the country northwest of the River Ohio* 1896.

49 Francisco Palou *Relacion historica de la vida ... Junipero Serra* ... 1787.

50 John Filson *The discovery, settlement and present state of Kentucke* ... 1784.

51 Manasseh Cutler *An explanation of the map which delineates that part of the federal lands* ... 1787.

52 Sir Alexander MacKenzie *Voyages from Montreal, on the river St. Laurence* ... 1801.

53 Oliver M Spencer *Indian captivity* ... 1835.

54 Robert Breckinbridge McAfee *History of the late war in the western country* 1816.

55 Abraham Bishop *Georgia speculation unveiled, 1797-1798* 2 v.

56 Meriwether Lewis *History of the expedition under the command of Captains Lewis and Clark* ... by Paul Allen, 1814, 2 v.

57 Zebulon Montgomery Pike *An account of expeditions to the sources of the Mississippe* ... 1810.

58 Alexander Ross *Adventures of the first settlers on the Oregon or Columbia river* ... 1849.

59 John Bradbury *Travels in the interior of America, in the years 1809, 1810, and 1811* ... 1817.

60 Henry Marie Brackenridge *Views of Louisiana* ... 1814.

61 Zadok Cramer *The navigator* ... 8th edition, 1814.

62 Morris Birkbeck *Notes on a journey in America, from the coast of Virginia to the territory of Illinois* 4th edition, 1818.

63 Thomas Nuttall *A journal of travels into the Arkansa territory, during the year 1819* ... 1821.

64 John Stillman Wright *Letters from the West; or a caution to emigrants* ... 1819.

65 Edwin James *Account of an expedition from Pittsburgh to the Rocky mountains ... under the command of Major Stephen H. Long* ... 1822-1823.

66 Henry Rowe Schoolcraft *Narrative journal of travels through the north western regions of the United States ... in the year 1820* ... 1821.

67 James Ohio Pattie *The personal narrative of James O Pattie of Kentucky* ... edited by Timothy Flint, 1833.

68 Catherine Stewart *New homes in the west* 1843.

69 Zenas Leonard *Narrative of the adventures of Zenas Leonard* ... 1839.

70 *A visit to Texas: being the journal of a traveller* ... 1834.

71 Josiah Gregg *Commerce of the prairies: or, The Journal of a Santa Fe trader* ... 1844.

72 John B Wyeth *Oregon; or, A short history of a long journey from the Atlantic Ocean to the region of the Pacific by land* ... 1833.

73 D Griffiths, Jr *Two years' residence in the new settlements of Ohio* ... 1835.

74 William Nowlin *The bark covered house, or Back in the woods again* ... 1876.

75 Charles Fenno Hoffman *A winter in the West. By a New-Yorker* ... 1835.

76 Joseph Holt Ingraham *The South-west. By a Yankee* ... 1835, 2 v.

77 Woodburne Potter *The war in Florida ... By a late staff Officer* 1836.

78 George Wilkins Kendall *Narrative of an expedition across the great south western prairies, from Texas to Santa Fe* ... 1845.

79 John Charles Fremont *Report of the exploring expedition to the Rocky mountains in the year 1842, and to Oregon and north California in the years 1843-44* ... 1845.

80 James Leander Scott *A journal of a missionary tour through Pennsylvania, Ohio, Indiana* ... 1843.

81 William Oliver *Eight months in Illinois* ... 1843.

82 Overton Johnson *Route across the Rocky mountains, with a*

description of Oregon and California ... by Overton Johnson and Wm H Winter ... 1846.

83 Joel Palmer *Journal of travels over the Rocky mountains, to the mouth of the Columbia river* ... 1847.

84 Charles Fayette McGlashan *History of the Donner party, a tragedy of the Sierras* (1879).

85 Frank S Edwards *A campaign in New Mexico with Colonel Doniphan* ... 1847.

86 Edward Gould Buffum *Six months in the gold mines* ... 1850.

87 Lorenzo D Aldrich *A journal of the overland route to California and the gold mines* ... 1851.

88 Howard Stansbury *An expedition to the valley of the Great Salt Lake of Utah* ... 1852.

89 Alonzo Delano *Life on the plains and among the diggings* ... 1854.

90 William Lewis Manly *Death Valley in '49* ... 1894.

91 Mrs Miriam (Davis) Colt *Went to Kansas; being a thrilling account of an ill-fated expedition* ... 1862.

92 Horace Greeley *An overland journey, from New York to San Francisco, in the summer of 1859* ... 1860.

93 Frederick Whymper *Travel and adventure in the territory of Alaska* ... 1868.

94 Samuel Bowles *Across the continent: a summer's journey to the Rocky mountains, the Mormons, and the Pacific states* ... 1865.

95 Thomas Josiah Dimsdale *The vigilantes of Montana, or Popular justice in the Rocky mountains* ... 1866.

96 Joseph Geiting McCoy *Historic sketches of the cattle trade of the West and Southwest* ... 1874.

97 Grenville Mellen Dodge *How we built the Union Pacific railway, and other railway papers and addresses.*

98 Charles King *Campaigning with Crook and stores of Army life* ... 1890.

99 Theodore Roosevelt *Ranch life and the hunting-trail* ... 1899.

100 Frederick Jackson Turner The significance of the frontier in American history, in *Annual report of the American Historical Association for the year 1893* ... 1894.

A set of Library of Congress catalogue cards and an annotated *Bibliography* for *March of America* by A T Klyberg accompanied the collection. It will be apparent from the titles that few libraries would be able to acquire most of these books in any other form.

Unfortunately, however, the series is now virtually out of print as a collection although some individual titles are still available. Enquiries should be made to University Microfilms Ltd, St John's Road, Tylers Green, High Wycombe, Buckinghamshire.

543 'The maritime and colonial expansion of England under the stuarts (1603-1714)' by A D Innes (1931) is a study of the first phase of British imperial expansion. The early days of the East India Company, the beginnings of the New England settlements, and the birth of the old colonial system, are carefully examined.

544 Matthew of Paris (1200-1259), an English monk of St Albans, was a prolific historian, and deservedly ranks with the giants of English historical writing not only for his breadth of interests but also for his unrelenting opposition to the expansion of royal and papal intervention in the liberties and customs of church and state. His great work, the *Chronica Majora* (from the creation to 1259) is little more than an embellishment of Roger of Wendover's *Flores Historiarum* (*qv*) down to 1235 but from then onwards it becomes a completely independent work of great historical value since he was writing within a year or two of the events he was relating. He was assiduous in collecting and incorporating documents, many to be found in the *Chronica* are known only in that work. Many of them were later included in an appendix, the *Liber additamentorum*. The *Chronica Majora* were well named, so copiously did they overflow with all sorts of information, on art, architecture, heraldry, and natural history, and so extensive was his narration of European events (also of immense value) that Matthew was forced to compile an epitome: his *Historia Anglorum* consisted of extracts from the *Chronica* with the addition of new material chronicling events 1067-1253. Matthew was a staunch Englishman with all the native English prejudices against foreigners and heavy handed government, his chronicles which suffer from his intemperate language are nevertheless a vivid record of his times. The *Chronica Majora* appeared in the *Rolls series* in seven volumes (1872-1884) and *Historia Anglorum* (1863-1869) in three volumes edited by H R Luard and Sir Frederick Madden respectively. A full study, *Matthew Paris* by Richard Vaughan was published in the Cambridge Studies in Medieval Life and Thought series in 1958.

545 The Medieval Academy of America was founded in 1925 for the promotion of research and publication in all aspects of medieval civilisation. Its publishing activities include *Speculum*, a quarterly journal printing learned articles, book reviews, and a bibliography of editions and translations in progress.

546 'Medieval history in the tudor age' by May McKisack (OUP 1971) traces the 'activities of a number of sixteenth century Englishmen who were concerned to preserve the memory of their country's past.' John Leland, John Bale and Matthew Parker are singled out but other lesser-known antiquarians and collectors are not forgotten. There is a chapter on the general histories of Britain published during the period and the book ends with a study of the tudor local historians and topographers and the Elizabethan Society of Antiquaries.

547 'Men and their times' is a series intended 'by way of a biography of a great man to open up a significant historical theme' which was formerly known as the *Teach yourself histories* published by the English Universities Press (now taken over by the imprint of the parent company, Hodder and Stoughton). The editor of the series is A L Rowse who writes in his general introduction, 'My hope is, in the end, as the series fills out and completes itself, by a sufficient number of biographies to cover whole periods and subjects. ... To give you the history of the United States, for example, or the British Empire or France, *via* a number of biographies of their leading historical figures.' And further: 'I need hardly say that I am a strong believer in people with good academic standards writing once more for the general reading public, and of the public being given the best that the universities can provide. From this point of view this series is intended to bring the university into the homes of the people.' Titles so far published are conveniently grouped under the labels of Britain and the Commonwealth, Europe, America, Russia and the east, and Ancient history. Each book is written by an eminent authority and Dr Rowse himself contributes the introductory or 'key' volume *The use of history* first published in 1946 and heavily revised in 1963 which remains essential reading for all students of history. That Dr Rowse's hopes for the series have been fulfilled is not open to question, the series contains some masterly compact summaries although it would be invidious to single out particular titles. Herbert Butterfield's 'The teach yourself history library' (*History* XXXIII (189) October 1948: 193-202) is an interesting early view.

548 'Methuen's history of England' in eight volumes was originally intended to fill the gap when the standard works of the nineteenth-century historians were rendered obsolete by the flood of new knowledge resulting from the opening up of most European archives. Students and research workers were becoming very wary of rewriting history of a large scale mainly because they were reluctant to step outside their own special areas lest some obscure or newly discovered source prove them wrong. And so they confined themselves to writing specialized monographs or biographies, editing old texts or selections of letters. Consequently the general reading public, still anxious to read standard histories, discovered there were only school manuals or minutely argued special studies available. The Methuen volumes, edited by Sir Charles Oman, attempted to meet the demand by dividing English history into periods that were neither too long to be dealt with by a single competent expert, nor so short as to 'tempt the writer to indulge in that abundance of detail which repels the general reader.' Each volume is designed to provide something more than just an outline but, Sir Charles warned, 'they have little space for controversy or the discussion of sources.' The first volume appeared in 1904 and all of them were frequently revised and reprinted. Until the *Oxford history of England* began publication they were undoubtedly the most scholarly textbooks on the market and were a standard requirement for undergraduate courses. Titles: *England before the Norman conquest* by Sir Charles Oman; *England under the Normans and Angevins 1066-1272* by H W C Davis; *England in the later middle ages* by Kenneth Vickers; *England under the Tudors* by A D Innes; *England under the Stuarts* by G M Trevelyan; *England under the Hanoverians* by Sir Charles Robertson; *England since Waterloo* by Sir J A R Marriott; and *Modern England 1885-1945* by Sir J A R Marriott. They are now gradually being replaced by seven new volumes of which two have so far been published: *England in the later middle ages* by M H Keen and *England under the Tudors* by G R Elton. Other volumes in preparation are *From*

Roman Britain to Norman England; England under the Normans and Angevins; Stuart England; England under the Hanoverians; and England 1815-1914.

549 **'The middle ages and the renaissance'** is a catalogue issued jointly by the American and European divisions of the Kraus-Thomson Organisation containing lists of reprints of reference works, bibliographies, journals, etc, of importance to the study of medieval history. A section, Periodicals, sets, reference works, includes useful bibliographical and historical notes and is indexed by the second section: Books and monographs.

550 **'The middle ages in recent historical thought; selected topics'** by Bryce Lyon (1959) is no 23 in the AHA *Service center series.* It sensibly limits itself to a consideration of five subjects that most often find their way into textbooks. 'When did middle ages begin?' is included simply because marked differences of opinion exist. 'The meaning of manorialism' and a similar section of feudalism are listed because between them they dominate political and economic life up to the fourteenth century whilst 'The value of Magna carta' and 'Representative institutions' reflect the preoccupation of the western democracies with these themes. A select list of readings in the English language and notes on the text indicating detailed bibliographical references bring this pamphlet to an end.

551 **The Mitchell Library** was established in Sydney in 1907 by a private benefactor who donated over 60,000 manuscript, printed, and painted items of Australiana together with sufficient endowment funds to secure the library's future. He directed the library should be run on the same lines as the British Museum. The State Government of New South Wales recognised its special status and transferred more and more of its departmental records there for safe keeping. Today no serious history of Australia is possible without research in its unique collection of primary source material.

552 **'Modern Britain 1885-1955'** by Henry Pelling (1960) is the last volume in Nelson's *History of England* series. His method is to set the events of British political, social and cultural history against world events and to this end each of his chapters opens with foreign affairs, with domestic politics and legislation taking second place, and major social changes being considered last. Within the constrictions of space the author manages to summarise and comment on events in masterly fashion especially in the diplomatic sphere.

553 'Modern British history 1485-1939; a short bibliography' (1952) was published by The Historical Association in their *Helps for students of history* series with the object of suggesting the 'general line of reading which every student of the period ought to follow.' Although intended primarily for undergraduates it will also prove useful to teachers and scholarship candidates. Its emphasis is uncompromisingly placed on political and constitutional history. Admirable comments punctuate the lists of titles which are arranged in a chronological sequence. A section on original authorities adds a touch of professional scholarship.

554 'Modern England from the eighteenth century to the present' by R K Webb was first published in the United States by Dodd Mead and has been available in Great Britain from Allen and Unwin since 1969. It is a general political and social account based on the assumption that people in power are the principal stuff of history. An unusual feature is a number of appendices the author recommends should be read first: Kings and queens 1688-1968; titles, honours, and the peerage; the Church of England; and English courts. There is also a classified guide to further reading.

555 'Modern England 1885-1945; a history of my own times' by Sir J A R Marriott (4th ed, 1948) is the grandiloquent title of the last volume of Methuen's *History of England*, a sequel to the previous volume in the series *England since Waterloo* by the same author. It was first published in 1934 but three extra chapters were eventually added as new editions were called for. There is an interesting paragraph or two in the preface on the difficulties which confront the historian of modern times in compiling even a modest select bibliography.

556 'Modern historians and the study of history' by F M Powicke (1955), a volume of collected lectures and papers is divided into two distinct sections, the first is devoted to studies of particular historians, and the second is concerned with general aspects of the historian's work.

557 'Modern historians on British history, 1485-1945; a critical bibliography, 1945-1969' by G R Elton (1970) is a personal commentary by an eminent Cambridge historian on the writings of his contemporaries. Written in the belief that all pre-1945 publications in this area need to be reexamined not only because so much more material is now available but also because an increasing number of historians have introduced more precise methods of enquiry. Omits all articles subsequently incorporated in books, all local history and the history of British expansion overseas, but includes all reviews and articles from *English historical review* (*qv*).

558 'The modern researcher' by Jacques Barzun and Henry F Graff (New York, Harcourt Brace, rev ed 1970) is primarily aimed at 'anyone who is or will be engaged in research and report writing, regardless of his field of interest' but the fact that at the time of writing both authors were colleagues in the history department of Colombia University inevitably accords a historical bias to the precepts, questions and examples examined and quoted. The book is divided into three parts: 'First principles' is concerned with the mechanical aspects of research technique; Part II 'Research' reveals the intellectual challenge of historical objectivity, finding the facts, verifying them, investigating truth and causation; and, Part III 'Writing' examines how to effectively present and communicate knowledge.

559 'Monumenta Historica Britannica' or *Materials for a history of Britain from the earliest period to the end of the reign of Henry VII* by Henry Petrie, John Sharpe, and Thomas Duffus Hardy was published by The Record Commission in 1848. In the winter of 1818-1819 it was decided at meetings held at Spencer House attended by a number of noblemen and gentlemen interested in historical literature to recommend to the Record Commission (*qv*) that a National Collection of Material for the History of Britain be published at the public expense and that Henry Petrie, Keeper of His Majesty's Records in the Tower of London, should be requested to draw up a plan for collecting and publishing the historical muniments of the kingdom extending from the earliest notices of the island down to the death of Henry VII. Petrie agreed and drew up a detailed conspectus comparing unfavourably the British lack of a published historical collection such as the *Recueil des Historiens des Gaules et de la France*. He proposed that 'all the ancient evidences relating to Britain, whether printed or in manuscript, domestic or foreign, should be collected, the genuine separated from the spurious or interpolated, and original writers from abbreviators and transcribers, so that all information might be traced back as far as practicable to its original source, and all mere compilations rejected: that the text of each author should be taken from the best manuscripts extant, and that all variations should be placed in notes at the foot of each page: that no liberty, however slight, should be taken with, or abridgement made in, original matter: that whenever a writer, in copying a preceding one, had made any addition to, or alteration in, the work of the author from whom he was compiling, such additions or alterations should be given in notes at the foot of the text of the original writer: and that critical and explanatory notes should be added, together with complete indices and glossaries.' Material was to be collected from different sources and to include excerpts from Greek and Roman writers; inscriptions on marble or stone; general histories, chronicles or annals, histories of particular monasteries if intermixed in some degree with public affairs; lives of celebrated men and Saints; miracles of saints if illustrating manners and contemporary usages; letters; charters, papal bulls, and other diplomatic writings; the proceedings of councils and synods; laws; historical poems if contemporary or nearly so with their subject matter; miscellanea from other than strictly historical writers; coins and medals and seals. The government approved and Petrie started work in May 1823 as principal editor and as a subcommissioner of the public records. Shortly afterwards John Sharpe was appointed coeditor. Progress was slow and when Petrie died in 1842 the project was moribund for twelve years. Then Thomas Duffus Hardy resumed work and in 1848 the first volume down to the Norman conquest appeared. Basically it followed Petrie's plan: it contained a general introduction describing various works of a similar nature that had been published before and outlining the progress and scope of the present undertaking; then came Greek and Latin geographical, historical excerpts, inscriptions, coins, facsimiles of manuscripts and annotated lists of fifteen preNorman historians in a folio volume. It was intended to be the first of twenty to twenty five similar volumes but in the event no others appeared. Afterwards of course further prompting resulted in *The rolls series* (*qv*).

560 More, Sir Thomas (1478-1535) the author of *Utopia* also wrote a *History of King Richard III*. There are discrepancies between various English and Latin versions and there is some doubt whether it can be wholly attributed to More or whether it should be accredited to Archbishop Morton who played an important part in affairs 1483-1485. Certainly More relied on his patron's reminiscences. The *History* contrasts the virtues of Edward IV with the crimes of Richard III and has a heavy tudor bias and so must be used with caution. It was the first history which was not 'a mere collection of facts, but a deliberately designed and carefully finished whole.' Later tudor chroniclers had no hesitation in adapting it in their own works. Volume 2 of *The Complete works of St Thomas More* edited by Richard S Sylvester (Yale University Press, 1963) presents Rastell's 1557 English edition parallel with the Louvain Latin version of 1565, together with notes and commentary on the texts, authorship, dating, and sources of the *History*. Alison Hanham's *Richard III and his early historians 1483-1535* (OUP, 1976) puts forward the intriguing theory that More's work was written as a satirical drama.

561 'Muir's atlases' of which there are now four take their name from Ramsay Muir who first compiled them fifty years ago for use in the examination classes of schools and colleges. When first published they pioneered a trail in demonstrating how much more interesting and comprehensible history could be if studied in conjunction with a specially designed atlas. *Muir's atlas of ancient and classical history* spans nearly 2,000 years from the ancient cradles of civilisation to the eve of the barbarian invasions. The story is taken further in *Muir's historical atlas—medieval and modern* which includes ten maps of the world since 1926. A composite volume, *Muir's historical atlas—ancient, medieval and* *modern* adds fourteen maps from the classical atlas to the later volume to form a complete atlas of the world through the ages in ninety six pages of full colour maps. An odd anomaly is that it is cheaper to buy the two works separately rather than the composite volume which is not so complete. A condensed volume *Muir's new school historical atlas* traces world history from the Roman Empire to the second world war. Published by George Philip and Son Ltd, the atlases have gone through many revisions. The present editors are H Fullard and R F Treharne.

562 Namier, Sir Lewis (1888-1960): After *England in the age of the American revolution* was published in 1930 it was remarked that hitherto there had been three ways of writing history, Gibbon's, Carlyle's, and Macaulay's. Now there was a fourth way, Namier's. To appreciate the impact of this work and *The structure of politics at the accession of George III* it is essential to remember that eighteenth century political history was regarded as the same as nineteenth century political history except for the presence of parliamentary corruption and the absence of a reformed electoral system. Namier, by working on contemporary sources, especially the Duke of Newcastle's papers, and not relying like nineteenth century historians on Horace Walpole's memoirs, produced convincing evidence that George III did not deliberately attempt to subvert the constitution, that a party system on the modern pattern did not exist at the beginning of his reign, and that despite the deceptively similar political terminology there were fundamental differences between the eighteenth and the nineteenth century constitutions. Namier was one of the first to recognise the advantages to be derived from a group of scholars working together and in the closing years of his life he directed work on a massive *History of parliament* the first volume of which was published four years after his death. Not all historians agreed with his methods but at least one historiographer has suggested that future generations of historians may well describe our own times as the Age of Namier in historiography. His contribution to historical studies is well outlined by Henry R Winkler in his article 'Sir Lewis Namier' *Journal of modern history* XXXV (1) March 1963: 1-19. *Essays presented to Sir Lewis Namier* edited by Richard Pares and A J P Taylor (1956), most exceptionally for

234

English *festschriften*, did not include a bibliography of Namier's writings.

563 'Narrative and critical history of America' edited by Justin Winsor in eight volumes (1884-1889) was instigated in 1887 by the Massachusetts Historical Society who appointed an advisory committee to hold a watching brief. Winsor, corresponding secretary to the society and librarian of Harvard University, agreed to act as editor. From his long experience as a librarian Winsor was fully aware of the need for a fully documented history so that students and scholars alike might benefit from a close juxtaposition of historical narrative and its source materials. He was of the mind that a series of monographs by learned and able historical scholars each working in their own specialist fields offered the best possible approach for such a history and so it was planned on cooperative lines with a team of historians being assembled through the good offices of societies affiliated to the Massachusetts society. Winsor was under no illusions as to the difficulties of this type of history but was confident of his editorial ability to overcome them. He was also one of the first to insist on the relevance of geography in works of history and he was adamant that for American history in particular historians needed a thorough awareness of the state of geographical knowledge at the time of the discoverers and explorers. The work consists of long narrative chapters most of which are followed by a series of critical essays on the sources of information contributed by Winsor himself. European archives, libraries and museums were documented and henceforward no scholar could plead ignorance of the existence or whereabouts of source material. As a bibliographical record the work remains unsurpassed and hardly equalled even by the large scale Oxford or Cambridge histories and although some criticism has been levelled against the text on the grounds that it fails to achieve a balanced proportionate narrative, with four volumes devoted to the colonial and revolutionary period and only one for the sixty years from 1789 to 1850, there can be no doubt that it is a major contribution to American history. The work ends with an imaginative chronological conspectus ranging from Homer's geographical conclusions in the tenth century BC, right down to the year 1887. It is still in print now being published by AMS Press Inc, of New York. Volumes:

Aboriginal America; Spanish explorations and settlements in America from the fifteenth to the seventeenth century; English explorations and settlements in North America 1497-1689; French explorations and settlements in North America and those of the Portuguese, Dutch, and Swedes 1500-1700; The English and French in North America 1689-1763; The United States of North America (2 vols); and *The later history of British, Spanish and Portuguese America.*

564 National Historical Society of the United States 'seeks to expand and enrich knowledge of the American past and, through its programs and services, to bring its members a fuller appreciation and deeper understanding of the people and events that came together to create the great history that is our heritage.' Members are entitled to a subscription of *American history illustrated,* a bimonthly newsletter, and membership of the society's bookclub.

565 National Maritime Museum Library in the UK has grown into a collection exceeding 50,000 volumes since its inception in 1934. A short title catalogue in several volumes is in process of publication: *Volume one; voyages and travel* was published by HMSO in 1968. The major part of the catalogue is arranged geographically to which are added sections on collective voyages, circumnavigations, and general voyages. In each part entries relating to particular voyages are grouped together and are listed chronologically with each section being prefaced by a chronological table of voyages. Although described as a short title catalogue entries are annotated wherever necessary. A comprehensive subject index and an index of ships complete an unusual but extremely useful bibliographical work.

566 National Register of Archives was established as part of the Historical Manuscripts Commission in 1945. Its function is to record and index information on documentary source material for British history housed elsewhere than the Public Record Office or other official repositories. It also encourages owners of large archives to deposit them on permanent loan with approved repositories. Publications: a *Bulletin* largely inaugurated in response to requests from county committees anxious to know

236

how others were coping in reporting records to the register was issued erratically 1948-1967 when it ceased publication on the appearance of *Secretary's report* to the Historical Manuscripts Commission. Details of annual accessions to archive offices were published as *National register of archives list of accessions to Repositories* 1957-1971, and as *Accessions to repositories and reports added to the National Register of Archives* from 1972 onwards. The function of this annual list is to indicate as succinctly as possible whatever new source material has been acquired by British libraries and record offices by gift or deposit or purchase and which has become available to research workers. At present the policy is to list only material of national importance leaving that of local interest only to the reports of the individual institutions. *An index to lists of accessions to repositories from 1954-1958* was published in 1967. This is arranged in four parts: Personal names, Papers of families, estates etc, Subjects, and Place names. A full account of the circumstances leading up to the establishment of the register and of its objectives and work, by Felicity Ranger, appeared in the April 1969 issue of the *Journal of the Society of Archivists*.

567 'The nature of history' by Arthur Marwick (Macmillan, 1970) 'is aimed at the general reader and at the student who is just embarking upon the serious study of history,' and is written in the belief 'that, for the intelligent layman as well as the serious student, the value of any historical reading that he may do will be greatly enhanced if he first has a grasp of the nature and basic principles of historical study.' A short exposition of what true history is and what it is not precedes a historical survey of historiography. Then the study of history is compared with other disciplines, geography and the whole gamut of the social sciences, and lastly come chapters on the historian at work, a survey of the present state of historical studies, and a close look at some examples of problems in history. It is hard to imagine a more practical introduction to history for students of the Open University in which the author is professor of history.

568 'Neale, J E' (1890-   ) has played an increasingly influential part in elizabethan studies since his *Queen Elizabeth* was published in 1934. This was an immediate success, it was awarded the James Tait Black memorial prize, it was a Book Society choice, and it has been frequently reissued in various series, translations, and paperback editions since. But it was his trilogy on the elizabethan parliaments that won him widespread scholarly acclaim. *The elizabethan House of Commons* (1949) explains who the members were, their origins, the social class they belonged to, how they were elected, and investigates the house at work, its officials, its ceremonies and procedures, and even the style of speaking in the debates. This was followed by *Elizabeth I and her parliaments 1559-1581* (1953) in which the narrative is concentrated on the relations between crown and parliament in order to reveal the significance of the period in the constitutional development of England, and to correct the old illusion that the pretensions of the early stuart parliaments had no precedents in elizabethan times. *Elizabeth I and her parliaments 1584-1601* followed in 1957. The pattern is the same for both: each parliament is considered in turn first by an introductory chapter, then its major business, and completed by another on minor matters. The narrative was enriched by material from hitherto unused manuscript sources. *Essays in elizabethan history* (1958) comprises articles and reviews and lectures and is worth reading if only for 'The biographical approach to history,' a lecture to the Anglo-American Historical Conference 1950, and for 'Professor A F Pollard' contributed to the *English historical review* at Pollard's death. A list of Neale's historical writings compiled by Helen Miller appeared in *Elizabethan government and society essays presented to Sir John Neale* edited by S T Bindoff, J Hurstfield and C H Williams, published by the Athlone Press in 1971 to commemorate his seventieth birthday. This attained a more solid appearance than most *festschrift* volumes largely because it had a clear discernible theme: to present a balanced picture of the age from the economic experiments of the early period to the succession struggle at the end. Since his retirement Sir John has been supervising the 1558—1603 volume of *The history of parliament*. An appreciative essay by Harold Hulme, 'Elizabeth I and Her Parliaments: The Work of Sir John Neale', appeared in *Journal of modern history* XXX (3) September 1958: 236-240.

569 'Nennius' a Welsh monk, compiled the *Historia Brittonum*, a chaotic collection of historical and topographical information relating to Britain, between the years 796 and 830. It contains a description of Britain, a history of the Britons, a life of St Patrick, and what has excited most attention, a chapter on Arthur *'dux bellorum.'* Despite its many errors, its inconsistencies, and its frequent introduction of legends, the *Historia* provides a tantalising glimpse of early Anglo-Saxon history based on earlier sources now irretrievably lost.

570 'The new American nation series' (1954-   ) edited by Henry Steele Commager and Richard B Morris, published by Harper and Row of New York, is a comprehensive cooperative survey of the history of the United States from the time of discovery to the mid twentieth century, and replaces the original *American nation* series edited by Albert Bushnell Hart. The new series, seeking to apply a cautious reappraisal, employing new techniques of investigation in order to synthesize new interpretations, is intended for the general reader as well as the scholar. Each volume although complete in itself is designed to be accommodated in a planned, coordinated series that for the most part follows a chronological pattern with odd volumes devoted to cultural history, constitutional history, and foreign affairs. Extensive bibliographies arranged by chapter are included. At first twenty five titles were envisaged by the publishers but Professor Commager extended it to a planned forty five volumes. Later titles were published simultaneously in hard covers and as paperbacks. Volumes: *Founding the American colonies 1583-1660* (John E Pomfret); *The English people on the eve of colonisation 1603-1630* (Wallace Notestein); *The cultural life of the American colonies 1607-1763* (Louis B Wright); *The colonies in transition 1660-1713* (Wesley Frank Craven); *Spain in America* (Charles Gibson); *The rise of the west 1784-1830* (Francis S Philbrick); *The coming of the revolution 1763-1775* (Lawrence Henry Gipson); *The American revolution 1775-1783* (John Richard Alden); *The cultural life of the new nation 1776-1830* (Russel B Nye); *The growth of southern civilisation 1790-1860* (Clement Eaton); *The federalist era 1789-1801* (John C Miller); *The democratic republic 1801-1815* (Marshall Smelser); *The awakening of American nationalism 1815-1828* (George Dangerfield);

The Jacksonian era 1828-1848 (Glyndon G Van Deusen); *The far western frontier 1830-1869* (Ray A Billington); *The crusade against slavery 1830-1860* (Louis Filler); *The new Commonwealth 1877-1890* (John A Garraty); *Politics, reform and expansion 1890-1900* (Harold V Faulkner); *America's rise to world power 1898-1954* (Foster Rhea Dulles); *The Era of Theodore Roosevelt 1900-1912* (George E Mowry); *Woodrow Wilson and the progressive era 1910-1917* (Arthur S Link); *Republican ascendancy 1921-1933* (John D Hicks); *Franklin D Roosevelt and the new deal 1932-1940* (William E Leuchtenburg); and *The United States and World War II* (A Russell Buchanan).

571 'New Cambridge modern history' (14 vols, 1957-) replaces the *Cambridge modern history* (qv) from which it differs fundamentally in approach. The new work was planned 'not as a stepping stone to definitive history, nor as an abstract or a scale reduction of all our knowledge of the period, but as a coherent body of judgements true to the facts'. In the old volumes the authors of the various chapters were expected to conceal their individual convictions but, half a century later, historians were well aware that differences of opinion existed and no longer pretended their conclusions would pass unchallenged. The purpose of the *New modern* is to 'set out the ascertained results of research into the history of that 'civilisation' which, from the fifteenth century spread from its original European homes ... until it was more or less firmly planted in all parts of the world. The civilisation is to be treated in all its aspects, political, economic, social, cultural and religious. Whenever it is possible to combine these aspects, or some of them, in a single presentation, this will be the plan; but there will be no forced synthesis or artificial simplification.' In pursuit of this purpose the course of events is not described *in vacuo* but related to the general structure of society. One obvious difference between the *Cambridge modern* and the *New modern* is the complete absence in the new of the chapter bibliographies which were so useful a feature of the old. This is justified on the grounds that when the *Cambridge modern* was published there were comparatively few bibliographies of history available but this could obviously no longer be argued. In the meantime the editors promised to consider what kind of bibliography, if any, was required. (For the result of their deliberations *vide supra, A bibliography of modern history.*) Each self contained volume covers a chronological period but chronology is not allowed to be too restrictive, each subject is discussed at length and as a coherent whole. The authors and editors represent many schools of thought but achieve a remarkable uniformity of tone and style. Volumes: 1 *The renaissance, 1493-1520*; 2 *The reformation, 1520-1559*; 3 *The counter-reformation and price-revolution, 1559-1610*; 4 *The decline of Spain and the thirty year's war, 1610-1648/59*; 5 *The ascendancy of France 1648/59-1688*; 6 *The rise of Great Britain and Russia, 1688-1715/25*; 7 *The old regime, 1713-1763*; 8 *The American and French revolutions, 1763-1793*; 9 *War and peace in an age of upheaval, 1793-1830*; 10 *The zenith of European power, 1830/2-1870*; 11 *Material progress and world-wide problems, 1870-1898/1901*; 12 *The shifting balance of world forces, 1898-1945* is a revised edition of *The era of violence* (two thirds of the contents being new). Vol 13 *Companion to modern history* has not yet been published. Vol 14 *The new Cambridge modern history atlas* is discussed below.

572 **'New Cambridge modern history vol XIV atlas'** edited by H C Darby and Harold Fullard (1970). The cartographic staff of George Philip and Son Ltd, using the latest mapmaking techniques, cooperated with the CUP in producing this work intended primarily to complement *The New Cambridge modern history.* Coverage is almost evenly balanced between European and non European countries and the maps are grouped by area in chronological sequence. The subject index is arranged in similar fashion. Its admirable clarity and indisputable authority encourage its extensive use on school and university modern history courses.

573 **'A new history of Australia'** edited by F K Crowley (Heinemann, 1974) is a large scale cooperative history by academic historians in Australian universities. It is arranged into twelve chapters each representing consecutive periods and each written by a different author free to emphasise those aspects which seem to him to most truly reflect his particular period. Economic and social history find a place along with government and politics. There is an extensive bibliography arranged by chapter and intended as a working tool for students and teachers.

574 'New interpretations of American colonial history' by Louis B Wright (2nd ed, 1963) is the shortest of the AHA *Service center series*. It takes the form of a single continuous and very instructive review of the works of both British and American historians, principally of those published in the postwar period.

575 'New ways in history' was the name given to three special issues of *The times literary supplement* written by young British historians (7 April), United States and commonwealth historians (28 July) and European historians (8 September) in 1966. The close connection between history and sociology, the history of non European nations, contemporary history, and the use of quantitative methods and computers were among the topics aired.

576 'New Zealand' by Harold Miller published in Hutchinson's University Library in 1950 is a concise history divided into two sections: The period of race conflict 1814-1865 and Towards a socialist state 1865-1947. There is an annotated bibliography.

577 'The New Zealand journal of history' (1967-   ) is published by the University of Auckland with the help of subsidies from other NZ universities. Besides articles and book reviews it also contains a register of research theses recently completed and in progress.

578 'The nineteenth century; the contradictions of progress' edited by Asa Briggs (Thames and Hudson, 1970) belongs to *The great civilizations* series and 'sets out to place the century in perspective, examining continuities and discontinuities.' Each of the chapters, written by different hands, is deliberately planned to disregard the barriers sometimes erected between different kinds of history. Topics include the social revolution, the growth of national states, and the acquisition of overseas empires. The editor endeavours to draw the threads together in three chapters. Full advantage is taken of the wealth of illustrations offered by the nineteenth century development of the camera. There is a select bibliography.

579 'The nineteenth-century constitution 1815-1914; documents and commentary' edited and introduced by H J Hanham (CUP, 1969) extends the selection of documents printed in this series from 1485 to 1914. (Previous volumes: *Tudor constitution* by G R Elton; *Stuart constitution* by J P Kenyon; and *The 18th century constitution* by E Neville Williams.) This fourth volume is similar in pattern and arrangement to the others, the documents arranged under appropriate headings, are accompanied by authoritative introductions. There is a list of works cited and a classified table of documents.

580 'The Norman conquest' by H R Loyn, published in Hutchinson's University Library in 1965, is a compact interpretation of the period for the undergraduate. Equal emphasis is placed on Anglo-Saxon continuity and Norman innovation as the English and European backgrounds are sketched and the Norman settlement and government outlined. A bibliographical note provides a commentary on modern works for those needing to proceed further.

581 'North American Discovery circa 1000-1612' edited by David B Quinn (Harper, 1971) consists of a selection of documents illustrating the range and variety of European contacts with North America before the establishment of permanent colonies in the seventeenth century. In selecting the extracts an attempt is made to show how the east coast of North America gradually became known to the European maritime nations. Eight maps and an extensive bibliography contribute towards a most useful volume in the *Documentary history of the United States* series.

582 'Notes on British history' by William Edwards have rarely been out of print in the last four decades. Published in five volumes they were designed to supplement textbooks for scholars preparing for university scholarships and other public examinations. The sheer volume of factual information crammed into them, and the severe note form in which that information was presented, earned for them an enviable reputation as cram books. The compiler allowed himself one relaxing feature: after each main topic had been dissected with each salient point remarked and briefly annotated, there were appended three classes of references. 'A' references were standard histories and biographies to be found in every well-equipped library; 'B' references were passages of prose and poetry suitable for reading aloud in class;

and 'C' references were recommended historical novels. Titles: *Prehistoric times to Richard III 1485; Beginning of modern history 1485-1660; Restoration to Treaty of Versailles 1660-1783; Versailles to end of Queen Victoria's reign 1783-1901;* and *1900 to 1920.*

583 'On the writing of history' by Sir Charles Oman (1939) suggests ways in which those who wish to study history and especially to those who wish to write it should set about it. The author is fully committed to the principle that the writing of history is a matter for individuals and not, *pace* Lord Acton, for an editor and a postbag of contributors however eminent both might be. Contents include essays on the nature of history, on sources and evidence, and the testing of authorities.

584 'The Open University' markets an enterprising selection of paperback textbooks, tapes and films for use on its various courses. Four books of general interest prepared by Professor Arthur Marwick are *What history is and why it is important* which justifies the relevance of historical study and defines the historian's main concerns; *Primary sources* examining the basic raw material of history; *Basic problems of writing history* which ranges widely over the problem of communicating history; and *Common pitfalls in historical writing* which considers the more obvious problems encountered when writing history. A two part *Collection of nineteenth and twentieth century documents* bring together an interesting selection of primary documents for use on the third level 'War and society' course. Two cassette or open reel tapes also prepared by Marwick provide another guide to historical source material: *Handling primary sources* examines letters, speeches, folk-songs and novels, whilst *Assessing secondary sources* analyses extracts from radio programmes, books and journals in an attempt to warn students of possible snags in the use of this sort of material. Four 16 mm black and white sound films, each running twenty five minutes, introduce the study of history. *The necessity of history* shows how contemporary events are only comprehensible with a knowledge of history, that history is in fact the collective memory of society, and that it is vitally important that history should be studied scientifically and systematically. *Primary sources* is a disappointing film on the vast range of historical source material available; and *The historian at work* follows a professional historian's research in the writing of a book. *About Trevelyan* takes the form of a discussion between four academic historians about the merits and faults of the work of G M Trevelyan. All these are only examples of the full range of OU history texts, tapes and films; colleges and schools requiring more comprehensive details should write to The Marketing Division, The Open University, PO Box 81, Walton Hall, Milton Keynes, MK7 6AT, for two catalogues, *History* and *History and social and economic history catalogue supplement 1975.*

585 Ordericus Vitalis (1075-1142), an English born monk of St Evroul in Normandy, was asked by his abbot to write the monastery's history. His response was the *Historia Ecclesiastica* (1123-1141) in thirteen books which included a history of Normandy to the mid-tenth century, the reigns of the first three Norman kings of England, a résumé of English, Norman and French history 688-1087, prefaced by a life of Christ and a universal history from the creation. The story of Greece and Rome is omitted because its pagan nature had no place in a work designed to instruct and edify and remind readers of the transitory glory of earthly achievements. Although his vast, untidy narrative is exasperating in its disordered confusion—he worked haphazardly and concurrently on several books—the *Historia* is a well researched and documented source of English history 1082-1141 and is enlivened by some shrewd character assessments of many leading personages. Orderic enjoyed the benefit of an extensive library at St Evroul, he was able to consult many visitors to the abbey, and he himself travelled widely to gather material. His sources include William of Poitiers *Gesta Willelmi* the last books of which have survived only in Orderic's work. The *Historia* was not widely read in the medieval period, only two early manuscripts are extant and it was not widely referred to by later historians. In the light of his breadth of vision and concept of history as the testimony of God's will on earth this occasions no little surprise. *The Ecclesiastical History of Orderic Vitalis* edited by Marjorie Chibnall is in the process of publication in the *Oxford medieval texts* series.

586 Ordnance Survey publishes a number of very useful historical maps in addition to the more familiar one, six and twenty-five inch national grid series. *List of maps available: Ancient Britain* (ten miles to one inch) in two sheets, north and south, showing almost 1000 of the more important visible antiquities from the earliest times to 1066 AD; *Southern Britain in the ice age* (10m:1 inch) illustrating all sites belonging to the 500 years period before the Roman occupation south of a line drawn from Scarborough to the Isle of Man; *Roman Britain* (16m:1 inch) depicting Britain from 43-410 AD; *Britain in the dark ages* (16m:1 inch) for the time after the Roman evacuation down to King Alfred *ie*, 410-870; and *Monastic Britain* (10m:1 inch), north and south sheets, showing British monasticism in great detail from the Norman conquest to the dissolutions of 1539. Of these the iron age, Roman and monastic maps are also available, mounted and folded to informative booklets. There are also maps of *Hadrian's wall* (1m:2 inches) and facsimiles of the *Bodleian map of Great Britain (14th Century)* dated circa 1325-1350 and *Ancient map of Kent*, Philip Symonson's map of 1596. A leaflet with full descriptions, *Archaeological and historical maps*, may be obtained from Headquarters Ordnance Survey, Romsey Road, Southampton. *The historian's guide to ordnance survey maps* published for The Standing Conference for Local History by the National Council of Social Service in 1964 should also be consulted.

587 '**Original letters illustrative of English history**' *including numerous royal letters from autographs in the British Museum and one or two other collections* by Henry Ellis (3 vols 1824). A second and third series each of four volumes appeared in 1827 and 1846. The author, principal librarian of the British Museum, described the letters as supplements to our histories. In the first two volumes the letters printed started in the reign of Henry IV because not until then were letters written in English and not Latin or French but in the third volume they range from the early norman period to George III's time. Each letter is prefaced with an introductory note setting it in its historical context.

588 '**Original narratives of early American history**' (1906-1917) is the self explanatory general title given to a series of volumes edited by J Franklin Jameson and published by Scribners under the auspices of the American Historical Association who approved the venture in December 1902. The purpose of the series 'was to provide individual readers of history, and the libraries of schools and colleges, with a comprehensive and well-rounded collection of those classical narratives on which the early history of the United States is founded or of those narratives which … hold the most important place as sources of American history anterior to 1700.' This was to be a series consisting not of volumes of extracts but the republication of whole works or at least substantial parts of works that were otherwise virtually unobtainable. The texts in each case are of the earliest editions; each volume is the responsibility of a special editor who contributes an introduction setting out in brief the author's career, the value of the text as an original source, and its status in the literature of American history. The series was reprinted by Barnes and Noble in 1959. Volumes: *Narratives of early Virginia; Bradford's history of Plymouth Plantation; Winthrop's journal 'History of New England'* (2 vols); *Narratives of early Carolina; Narratives of early Maryland; Narratives of early Pennsylvania, West New Jersey and Delaware; Narratives of New Netherland; Early English and French voyages* (chiefly from Hakluyt); *Voyages of Samuel de Champlain; Spanish explorers in the Southern United States; Spanish exploration in the Southwest; Narratives of the insurrections; Narratives of the Indian wars; Johnson's wonder-working providence; Journal of Jasper Danckaerts; Narratives of the Northwest; Narratives of the witchcraft cases;* and *The Northmen, Colombus, and Cabot.*

589 **'The origins of the English civil war'** edited by Conrad Russell (1973) is one of Macmillan's *Problems in focus* series. Nine different contributors each write on key issues and the editor surveys the period and its historiography, concentrating on modern historians, in a long introduction. A table of events conveniently precedes the text; a critical bibliography supplements it; and references and notes support it.

590 **Otterbourne, Thomas** who lived in the reigns of Henry IV and Henry V was the author of a contemporary history, *Chronicon Regum Angliae* (1423?) which is of considerable value for Richard II's time onwards. Although relying to some extent on

Thomas of Walsingham he generally worked independently of other writers and he includes many facts unrecorded elsewhere.

591 'The Oxford companion to American history' (1966). 4700 articles (1835 of which are biographies) arranged in dictionary order summarise the lives, events and places of significance in the founding and growth of the United States. The copious use of cross references enable most entries to be kept brief, none exceeding 2000 words. A useful addition is the full text of the constitution of the United States including all the amendments.

592 'The Oxford companion to Canadian history and literature' (1967) by Norah Story is arranged in dictionary form and provides 'a single source in which anyone reading a Canadian book in English or French can find an explanation of references that would otherwise be obscure'. Historical entries include articles on political and constitutional issues, places, and many special subjects. Most major articles are complemented with extensive critical bibliographies. A *supplement* was published in 1973.

593 'Oxford history of England' (1934-1961) after many years of negotiations finally took shape and secured approval by the delegates of the Oxford University Press in 1929. At meetings in Oriel College in June and July it was proposed that this new standard history should have two characteristics distinguishing it from others: a special attention to geography, and a much greater stress on social and economic history as opposed to a full treatment of military matters. Another important decision was that each volume was to be written by a different author on the one man, one period system; the precedent of the Cambridge histories whereby chapters were handed out to different historians had not proved an entirely happy one. In December contributors were present at another meeting when it was agreed that each volume would stretch to 175,000 words which might be extended to 200,000 if circumstances warranted it, and that the proportion of social and economic history to political and constitutional should be approximately half and half. Each volume would include a chapter surveying the contemporary state of society but these chapters would be so arranged that they would not be contiguous, at the end of one volume and at the beginning of the next; authors concerned would settle this between themselves. It is interesting to note that at one time Winston Churchill was seriously considered as a prospective author for the last volume. Each volume concludes with an impressive annotated bibliography and whilst it is explicitly stated these are not put forward as exhaustive, it is clear that if they were printed together in a volume of their own a far from negligible general bibliography of English history would result. The *History* is complete in fifteen volumes, the general editor is Sir George Clark. Authors and titles: *Roman Britain and the English settlements* by R G Collingwood and J N L Myres (2nd ed, 1937); *Anglo-Saxon England* by Sir Frank Stenton (3rd ed, 1971); *From Domesday book to Magna carta* by Austin Poole (2nd ed, 1955); *The thirteenth century* by Sir Maurice Powicke (2nd ed, 1962); *The fourteenth century* by May McKisack (1959); *The fifteenth century* by E F Jacob (1961); *The earlier Tudors* by J D Mackie (1952); *The Reign of Elizabeth* by J B Black (2nd ed, 1959); *The early Stuarts* by Godfrey Davies (2nd ed, 1959); *The later Stuarts* by Sir George Clark (2nd ed, 1956); *The whig supremacy* by Basil Williams (2nd ed, 1962); *The reign of George III* by J Steven Watson (1960); *The age of reform* by Sir Llewellyn Woodward (2nd ed, 1962); *England 1870-1914* by R C K Ensor (1936); and *English history 1914-1945* by A J P Taylor (1965).

594 **'Oxford history of India'** by V A Smith was first published in 1919 and carried the story down to 1911; the current third edition (1958) is arranged in three parts: Ancient and hindu India, revised by Sir Mortimer Wheeler and A L Basham; India in the muslim period, revised by J B Harrison; and India in the British period extensively rewritten by Percival Spear who edits the volume. The whole is a compact compendium of solid merit. A general introductory chapter considers India as a cultural, political, and geographical entity and discusses the nature of the sources of Indian history, closing with a list of authorities. The chapters that follow also end with similar notes. Part III has been reprinted and published separately as *The oxford history of modern India 1740-1947* (1965) and treats the subject 'not as the story of the rise and decline of the British power, its successes and failures, but as the history of India during the period of British activity.'

595 'Oxford history of South Africa' (2 vols 1969-1971) was planned and written 'in the belief that the central theme of South African history is interaction between peoples of diverse origins, languages, technologies, ideologies and social systems, meeting on South African soil'. Leo Kuper's chapter 'African nationalism in South Africa' was judged to infringe South African law and was therefore deleted from the South African edition. A full bibliography listing manuscripts, government publications, books and articles, is found in each volume.

596 'Oxford history of the American people' (1965) by S E Morison is not a textbook 'but a history written especially for my fellow citizens to read and enjoy'. Consequently 'footnote references, bibliographies and other scholarly apparatus have been suppressed' although he does permit himself an index. The history is carried from pre-Colomban discovery to the Kennedy administration 1961-1963. A brief history of Canada enhances the work.

597 'Oxford in Asia historical reprints' is a series designed to make available to present day scholars and students specialised out of print books on South East Asia. The general editor is John Bastin.

598 'Oxford medieval texts' a series of parallel Latin-English texts, first began publication in 1949 under the imprint of Thomas Nelson but in 1965 responsibility for publication was transferred to the Oxford University Press. In many cases they have superseded the less accessible *Rolls series* volumes by virtue of their authoritative introductions, texts, and translations. Titles (with name of editor): *Chronica Jocelini de Brakelonda* (H J Butler); *Diaglogus de scaccario and Constitutio domus regis of Richard Fitzneale* (Charles Johnson); *Life of Ailred of Rievaulx* (F M Powicke); *Decreta Lanfranci* (David Knowles); *Annales Gandenses* (Hilda Johnstone); *Regularis concordia* (Thomas Symons); *Selected letters of Pope Innocent III concerning England (1198-1216)* (C R Cheney and W H Semple); *Gesta Stephani* (K R Potter); *The De Moneta of Nicholas Oresme* (Charles Johnson); *Historia Pontificalis of John of Salisbury* (Marjorie Chibnall); *Vita Edwardi Secundi of the so-called monk of Malmesbury* (N Denholm-Young); *Fourth book of the Chroni-*

cle of Fredager (J M Wallace-Hadrill); *Hugh the Chantor History of the Church of York 1066-1127* (Charles Johnson); *Vita Aedwardi Regis* (F Barlow); *The Life of St Anselm of Eadmer* (R W Southern); *The chronicles of Aethelward* (A Campbell); *Cronichon Richardi Divisensis de Tempore Regis Richardi Primi* (John T Appleby); *Gesta Francorum et aliorum Hierosolimitanorum* (Rosalind Hill); *Chronica Buriensis* (A Gransden); *Tractatus de legibus et consuetinibus regni Anglie qui Glanvilla vocatur* (G D G Hall in association with Selden Society); *Select documents concerning Anglo-Scottish relations 1174-1328* (E L G Stones); *De gestis concilii Basiliensi Commentariorum* (Denys Hay and W K Smith); *Bede's ecclesiastical history of the English people* (Bertram Colgrave and R A B Mynors); *William Worcestre Itineraries* (John Harvey); *Scripta Leonis, Rufini et Angeli Sociorum S Francisci* (Rosalind Brooke); *The ecclesiastical history of Orderic Vitalis* (Marjorie Chibnall); *The Carmen De Hastingae Proelio of Guy Bishop of Amiens* (Catherine Morton and Hope Muntz); *Libellus de Diversis Ordinibus et Professionibus Qui Sunt in Aecclesia* (G Constable and B Smith); *The Epistolae vagantes of Pope Gregory VII* (H E J Cowdrey); *Documents of the Baronial movement of reform and rebellion 1258-1267* (I J Sanders); and *Chronicle of the election of Hugh, Abbot of Bury St Edmunds* (R M Thomson). The General Editors are V H Galbraith, Sir Roger Mynors and C N L Brooke.

599 **'Oxford microfiche editions'** comprise special reissues of selected out of print books from the Oxford University Press back list. The first series concentrates on history and English literature; sixty historical works most of them specialised monographs, are available including Stubbs' *The Constitutional history of England in its origin and development*; F M Stenton's *The first century of English feudalism*; S Pargellis and D J Medley *Bibliography of British history 1714-1789*; V Harlow and F Madden *British colonial developments 1774-1834*; and W P Morrell *British colonial policy in the age of Peel and Russell*. Details of range of readers suitable etc, may be obtained from OUP, (CMP) Ely House, 37 Dover Street, London W1X 4AH.

600 **'Oxford paperbacks university series'** aims to provide authoritative introductions to most of the important branches of the humanities and sciences. It forms the modern day counterpart to the old established *Home university library* (*qv*) and most of the standard works in that series will gradually reappear in this new format. A steady stream of new titles is also envisaged.

601 'The pageant of America; a pictorial history of the United States' edited by Ralph Henry Gabriel published by the Yale University Press (1925-1929) consists of fifteen volumes, each dealing with a specific subject of American life. In all, over 12,000 illustrations, at least one and usually two or three per page, enliven the text. Notes on the pictures appear in every volume and in the last there is a bibliography 'prepared to meet the demands of the general reader who may wish to pursue further his studies in certain phases and periods of American history.'

602 'The Paladin history of England' (1974-   ) edited by Robert Blake and published by Hart-Davis MacGibbon is intended as a major history for the 1970s and beyond, attempting to convey to the general reader all the painstaking historical research over the last twenty years which has for the most part been confined to specialist journals. The series will not just present a standard chronological sequence of events but is designed to sift evidence as well as reciting facts. Three volumes have now appeared: Richard Sherman's *The crisis of imperialism 1865-1915* (1974); H P R Finberg's *The formation of England 550-1042* (1974); and C S L Davies' *Peace, print and protestantism* (1976). The first two are available in paperback. Other volumes planned are: *Pre-Roman and Roman Britain* (G D Barri Jones); *Conquests and conflicts 1042-1450* (John Prestwich); *Reformation and revolution 1558-1660* (Robert Ashton); *England's rise to power 1660-1760* (Stephen Baxter); *England transformed 1760-1865* (F B Smith); and *The decline of power 1915-1970* (Robert Blake).

603 Parkman, Francis (1823-1893). Perhaps the greatest historian yet produced by the United States. His main work consists of a history of the English—French struggle for the domination and possession of the North American continent and the large part played by the American Indians. His first book, *The Oregon trail* (1849) was the outcome of a journey to Wyoming to visit remote Indian tribes living beyond the Rockies. Next came *The* conspiracy of Pontiac and the Indian War after the conquest of Canada (1851) and there followed, despite serious health difficulties, seven more volumes to complete a history of almost heroic proportions: *Pioneers of France in the New World; The Jesuits in North America; La Salle and the discovery of the great west; The old regime in Canada; Count Frontenac and New France under Louis XIV; Montcalm and Wolfe;* and *A half-century of conflict.* A great believer in historians sharing in what they describe, 'the narrator', he said, 'must seek to imbue himself with the life and spirit of the time'; Parkman succeeded as no other historian before or since in reconciling the different needs of the general reader and the student. His style owed a lot to the imaginative writings of Fenimore Cooper and Sir Walter Scott but at the same time he was assiduous and thorough in his research. Basil Williams' 'The centenary of Francis Parkman 1823-1893' (*History* 8 (32) January 1924: 269-274) is an appreciative critique and includes a bibliographical note.

604 **'Past and present'** a journal published from Oxford three times a year since 1952, slightly left wing in bias, aims to include scholarly articles concerned primarily with the causes and effects of social, economic and cultural change designed for specialists and non specialists alike. As a possible forum for academic debate: X on Y on X's book or article, it has attracted many writers who regard the *English historical review* as too staid or perhaps too representative of the professional establishment. In 1974 a number of articles centred round a common theme were reprinted in book form as 'The past and present series' published by Routledge.

605 **'Pastmasters; some essays on American history'** edited by Marcus Cunliffe and Robin W Winks (Harper, 1969): We are informed that the historians appraised here 'are people who, either as teachers and inspirers of research or through the effect of their interpretations, or both, have had a noticeable impact on the very shape of American historical scholarship.' In addition all of them have been associated with a broad interpretation of the nature of the American historical experience. They include Francis Parkman, Henry Adams, Frederick Jackson Turner, Charles A Beard, Vernon Louis Parrington, Perry Miller, Samuel Flagg Bemis,

Daniel J Boorstin, Oscar Handlin, Richard Hofstadter, David M Potter, Arthur M Schlesinger Jnr, and C Vann Woodward. Extremely valuable bibliographies limited to books and scholarly journal articles to illustrate each historian's development are included in an appendix.

606 **'Pelican history of England'** in eight volumes, fully maintains Penguin Books' reputation for *multum in parvo* texts. Each volume in this series, planned as a guide to the development of English society, has been written by a specialist author: *Roman Britain* by Ian Richmond; *The beginnings of English society (From the Anglo-Saxon invasion)* by Dorothy Whitelocke; *English society in the early middle ages* by D M Stenton; *England in the late middle ages* by A R Myers; *Tudor England* by S T Bindoff; *England in the seventeenth-century* by Maurice Ashley; *England in the eighteenth-century* by J H Plumb; and *England in the nineteenth-century* (1815-1914) by David Thomson.

607 **'Penguin African library'** a series designed to explain what goes on behind the newspaper headlines and the embassy hand outs, seeks to present an authoritative picture of African nations and peoples. An early book in the series, *A short history of Africa* (1962) by Roland Oliver and J D Fage, who at the time were editors of the *Journal of African history* is a more than useful concise account of Africa from the earliest times to postwar nationalism and the pan-African movements. It is well sprinkled with maps and concludes with expert guidance to further readings.

608 **'Penguin atlas of medieval history'** by Colin McEvedy (1961) consists of thirty eight maps, covering Europe, North Africa, and the Middle East and spanning AD 362-1478, arranged in five sections each containing 5-6 maps showing the political state of a particular area at intervals and two others depicting the extent of Christendom and the development of the economy for each period. The maps in black, blue and white carry no geographical detail as the aim is to present a continuous flow of history but are accompanied by facing pages of text. There is also an introduction on the area covered, the limitations of maps for historical studies, and background notes on the fall of Rome, feudal society, and the nomads.

609 'The Penguin atlas of modern history (to 1815)' by Colin McEvedy (1973) has as its main aim the provision of a digest of a narrative of Europe's history and overseas expansion. Almost forty maps are supplemented by detailed commentaries.

610 'The Penguin atlas of world history' *Vol 1 From the beginning to the eve of the French revolution* (1974) is a translation of *dtv-Atlas zur Weltgeschichte* published ten years earlier in Germany. All maps are in colour, and for the most part, face a page of text giving a detailed chronology of the chief cultural, scientific, religious and political events of the period in question, although very occasionally more than one page of text is deemed advisable. The maps are models of clarity and are well served by conventional symbols and abbreviations. Vol II *From the French Revolution to the present* appeared in 1976.

611 'A people's history of England' by Alan Morton (Gollancz, 1938) 'sets out to give the reader a general idea of the main lines of the movement of our history ... Whatever value this book may have must lie ... in the interpretation than in the novelty of the facts it presents.' Although written with a strong left wing bias it shows signs of historical objectivity despite Morton's distrust of so called 'liberal historians.' Today it would be described as an 'alternative' history. A revised paperback edition was published by Lawrence and Wishart in 1966.

612 'Pergamon general historical atlas' (1970) makes no pretence to scholarship although it displays in attractive fashion boldly coloured maps arranged in two sequences. The first tells the story of the ancient civilizations in the Near East, followed by a series of European maps; the second depicts the history of the British Isles and the British Empire and Commonwealth.

613 'Periodicals in the Library and Resource Centre Commonwealth Institute London,' compiled by Sylvia Whitehouse, published in 1975, lists holdings both alphabetically by title and under alphabetical subject, form and area headings.

614 'Philips' atlas of modern history' prepared under the direction of the atlas subcommittee of the Historical Association covers the events of the last 200 years in such a way that the teaching of history and current affairs in examination classes can be closely linked. 'It relates present situations to the formative events of the past and illustrates the causal chain between them. Chronologically, it covers the eighteenth, nineteenth and twentieth centuries up to 1962; spatially, it spans the world, treating Africa, America, Asia and Australasia as integral parts of "one world" and not as mere historical appendages to Britain and Europe.' The maps fully conform to Philips' widely acknowledged high standards.

615 **'Philip's intermediate historical atlas for schools'** prepared under the direction of the Historical Association (twenty third ed, 1973) has developed from the *Junior history atlas* first published in 1921. Later editions have acknowledged that nowadays pupils are not expected to memorise as many facts as in the past and consequently this practical atlas for 12-15 year olds has been noticeably simplified. The time range is from 1500 BC to 1960 and the maps maintain the high standard associated with the firm of George Philip and Son.

616 **'The pioneer histories'** edited by V T Harlow and J A Williamson and published by Adam and Charles Black in the 1930s were broad surveys of the European migrations and settlements overseas designed to illustrate that peculiar expansion which has resulted in our complex world today. Although each volume covers one particular movement there is an obvious similarity between all volumes in the series. Titles: *The age of Drake* by James A Williamson; *England's quest of eastern trade* by Sir William Foster; *The European nations in the West Indies* by A P Newton; *The exploration of the Pacific* by J C Beaglehole; *The explorers of North America 1492-1806* by John Bartlett Brebner; *The gold rushes* by W P Morrell; *The great trek* by Eric Anderson Walker; *The Spanish conquistadores* by F A Kirkpatrick; *The Portuguese pioneers* by Edgar Prestage; and *The invasion of China by the western world* by E R Hughes. All are provided with at least four maps.

617 The Pipe Roll Society for the publication of The Great Rolls of the Exchequer, commonly called the pipe rolls, and other documents prior to the year AD 1200, was established in 1883. An annual series of publications commenced a year later, the first series of thirty eight volumes running 1884-1925 and a second series, forty volumes so far, from 1925-1966. In latter years the emphasis has been on 'other documents.' *An introduction to the study of the pipe rolls* appeared as volume three of the original series in 1884 intended for the use of beginners not familiar with the text, arrangement, form, or general nature of the early rolls. This contained a list of abbreviations commonly encountered, a brief explanation of the system of the exchequer, and a glossary of some of the technical terms used in the rolls. The first series and volumes 1-36 (1925-1962) of the second series are available from Kraus Reprints.

618 **'The place and purpose of history'** is the title of a paper originally prepared by the History Association's Higher Education Committee for discussion at the 1970 annual conference. It was considered to be of such use and value that it was reprinted as a leaflet in 1972. It seeks to defend the relevance of the study of history to modern society and education against those who would steer it towards the social sciences or limit it to the very recent past. Its thesis is a simple one: the whole range of historical studies is relevant to an understanding of the modern world. And, furthermore, history has made, and will continue to make, a significant contribution to contemporary education and culture, for it is more than an intellectual discipline, it is an everlasting source of pleasure. Copies of the leaflet are still obtainable from the Historical Association.

619 **'The Plantagenets'** by John Harvey (2nd ed, 1959) is now included in the *British monarchy* series published by Batsford. Perhaps more than other volumes in the series it concentrates on the lives of the monarchs. A useful survey of their Angevin antecedents serves as a prelude to the main body of the text. There is a short bibliographical note consisting of a list of the more important works consulted, notes on the text and illustrations, and a pedigree.

620 **Plumb, J H** (1911-   ), most readable of modern English historians, has made the late stuart, early hanoverian period very much his own. His major work is undoubtedly the political biography of Sir Robert Walpole, an attempt to reconstruct his character and politics as viewed by his contemporaries and to describe the nature of the institutions through which he worked. So far two out of the projected three volumes have appeared *The making of a statesman* (1956) and *The king's minister* (1967). Of equal significance in the historiography of the period is *The growth of political stability in England 1675-1725* (1967), a printed version of the 1966 Ford Lectures. *Historical perspectives: studies in English thought and society in honour of J H Plumb* edited by Neil McKendrick (Europa, 1974) contains a perceptive valedictory tribute and a select bibliography of his writings, both contributed by the editor.

621 '**The political History of England**' in twelve volumes edited by William Hunt and R L Poole (Longmans, 1905-1910) was conceived at a time when a mass of newly available source material had thrown new light upon almost every aspect of English history. The times seemed ripe for a new conspectus presenting in readable form for the general public the results of many years of delving into archives by professional historians. So numerous and varied were these new sources that it became imperative that the new history should enlist a team of writers and it was eventually decided that each volume should be written by a different hand, with the editors ensuring a similarity, if not a uniformity of treatment. Despite the limitation of theme implied by the general title, full account of all the various forces exercising an influence upon political events was taken, religion, social and economic development, intellectual progress. The scholarly value of the series (and it vied with Methuen's *History of England* (*qv*) for academic preeminence before the publication of the *Oxford history of England*) was considerably enhanced by an appendix to each volume presenting in lucid and competent fashion an account of the chief original and secondary authorities for the period in question. The latter, of course, have long since been superseded but the notes on the medieval chronicles for example still retain their usefulness to students. Titles: *From the earliest times to the Norman conquest* by Thomas Hodgekin; *From the Norman conquest to the death of John (1066-1216)* by George Burton Adams; *From the accession of Henry III to the death of Edward III (1216-1377)* by T F Tout; *From the accession of*

Richard II to the death of Richard III (1377-1485) by C Oman; From the accession of Henry VII to the death of Henry VIII (1485-1547) by H A L Fisher; From the accession of Edward VI to the death of Elizabeth (1547-1603) by A F Pollard; From the accession of James I to the restoration (1603-1660) by F C Montague; From the restoration to the death of William III (1660-1702) by Richard Lodge; From the accession of Anne to the death of George II (1702-1760) by I S Leadam; From the accession of George III to the close of Pitt's first administration (1760-1801) by William Hunt; From Addington's administration to the close of William IV's reign (1801-1837) by George Brodrick and J K Fotheringham and During the reign of Victoria (1837-1901) by Sidney Low and Lloyd Sanders.

622 'Political history: principles and practice' by G R Elton (Allen Lane, 1970) continues his reflections on the methods and purposes of political history first adumbrated in his Practice of history. The subject is defined, reasons for its fall from favour are discussed, and the material with which the political historian works is examined. Finally the continuing importance of narrative political history is reasserted.

623 'Politics and the nation 1450-1660; obedience, resistance and public order' by D M Loades (1974) is the first volume to appear in the Fontana library of English history. It is 'basically a political narrative; the story of the rise and fall of a system of government which may loosely be called the tudor monarchy.' The select bibliography is intended for students and others who need to investigate further and includes printed sources, contemporary published works, and general studies in monograph and article form.

624 Pollard, A F (1869-1948) was responsible for 500 entries in the Dictionary of national biography whilst assistant editor 1893-1901. In 1903 he was appointed to the new chair of constitutional history in University College London. Three years later he was instrumental in establishing the Historical Association and in 1916 he became editor of History when the association assumed responsibility for that journal. The Institute of Historical Research (1920) also owed much to his energy and influence. His own best known works are *Wolsey* (1929) and *Factors in modern history* (1907) the last chapter of which contains a vivid narrative of the early progress of historical studies in the University of London.

625 'Post-victorian Britain 1902-1951' by L C B Seaman (Methuen, 1966) is an unusual attempt to survey the whole period in one volume. The main themes of British history are set against the backcloth of world events which flow on, resisting all attempts to compartmentalise them in the chronological straitjacket which British historians habitually try to impose with pre 1914 events being tacked on to nineteenth century histories, the two world wars treated in isolation, the between-war period regarded as a separate entity, and the postwar years in some sort of limbo. The book is well illustrated, adequately adorned with maps, but containing only a perfunctory list of works consulted. A University Paperback edition was issued in 1970.

626 'Practical approaches to the new history; suggestions for the improvement of classroom method' edited by R Ben Jones (Hutchinson, 1973) is a volume of essays indicating lines along which a new history can develop based upon a framework of established skills and objectives and using wide-ranging resources and techniques. Topics discussed include an introduction to the new history; training students and teachers; what sort of history should be taught; different approaches to GCE courses; the provision, organisation and use of resources; and the place of history in integrated studies.

627 'The practice of history' by G R Elton (Methuen, 1967) assumes that the study and writing of history need no justification and suspects that a philosophic concern as to the nature of history does nothing but hinder its writing. 'Most books on history have been written by philosophers analysing historical thinking, by sociologists and historiographers analysing historians, and by the occasional historian concerned to justify his activity as a social utility. This contribution seeks to avoid the last, ignores the second, and cannot pretend to emulate the first.' Professor Elton gives close attention in turn to the purpose of history, to research; to the writing and to the teaching of history. Practising historians themselves no doubt discovered reading this book to be a salutary exercise.

628 'The present state of the history of England in the eighteenth century' a bibliographical article by W T Lamprade, published in the *Journal of modern history* IV (4) December 1932: 581-603, holds that the history of the period contained in current books 'was sketched in the nineteenth century and has been modified only in details by later scholars'. Few would have agreed to that even in 1932, least of all Namier, whose books are described as 'the best published so far,' but even he is charged with neglecting 'to make adequate use of the newspapers, periodicals, and pamphlets which the rival politicians and their lieutenants used in their struggles.' The article is especially valuable for its notices of contemporary historians of the eighteenth century.

629 'The prime ministers' edited by Herbert Van Thal is published in two volumes by Allen and Unwin. Vol I *From Sir Robert Walpole to Sir Robert Peel* (1974) opens with a chapter 'The office of prime minister' by G W Jones, and Vol II *Lord John Russell to Edward Heath* (1975) begins with Robert Blake on 'The prime minister 1835-1974.' The remainder of the text consists of essays contributed by various political historians on the character, actions, and achievements of each of Britain's forty seven premiers.

630 'Problems in American history' a series from John Wiley of New York soundly based on primary source material with many volumes including an authoritative bibliographical essay.

631 'Problems in focus' is a series published by Macmillan designed to make available to students important new work on significant historical problems and key periods they are confronted with on their courses. Each volume contains specially commissioned essays from appropriate scholars. An editorial introduction reviews the topic or period as a whole and each essay points out areas of recent work and differences of opinion besides indicating where further research is demanded. An annotated bibliography assists in further reading. Titles: (with their editors) *Britain after the glorious revolution 1689-1714* (Geoffrey Holmes); *Britain*

261

preeminent: studies of British world influence in the nineteenth century (C J Bartlett); *Popular movements 1830-1850* (J T Ward); *The hundred years war* (Kenneth Fowler); *The interregnum: the quest for settlement 1646-1660* (G E Aylmer); *The origins of the English civil war* (Conrad Russell); *The reign of James VI and I* (Alan G R Smith); *Industrial revolutions* (R M Hartwell); *The conservative leadership 1831-1937* (Donald Southgate).

632 'The progress of historical studies in Australia' a bibliographical article by Herbert Heaton, examines the beginnings of historical studies at Australian universities, the progress of historical publishing, and the accessibility of records. It appeared in *Journal of modern history* XV (4) December 1943: 303-310.

633 Public Record Office: the documents housed in the PRO belong to two distinct categories: 1) legal records of the king's court in all its ramifications dating from the conquest onwards, and 2) state papers, the records of government departments dating from the accession of Henry VIII in 1509. Until 1838 there was no central repository for these documents, each court or department preserving its own records but in that year there was passed an act 'for keeping safely the Public Records' *ie,* 'all rolls, records, writs, books, proceedings, decrees, bills, warrants, accounts, papers and documents whatsoever of a public nature belonging to Her Majesty, or now deposited in any of the offices or places of custody.' This was reinforced by an order in council in 1852 making it explicitly clear that departmental as well as court records were to be placed into the charge of the master of the rolls. By 1954 it was manifest that existing administrative arrangements were failing to cope with the enormous increase of documents accumulating in government departments and a Committee on Departmental Records, under the chairmanship of Sir James Grigg, was established to consider the problems relating to their proper preservation and care. A new Public Records Act 1958 reconstituted the PRO and responsibility for the custody of all public records devolved upon the Lord Chancellor. From time to time he has designated other institutions as repositories, the Commonwealth Office has care of the old India Office records, the National Maritime Museum assumes responsibility for certain categories of admiralty material, whilst the National Film Archive and the Imperial War Museum store cinematograph films. In January 1968 the majority of records became available for public scrutiny after thirty years (a relaxation of the old 'fifty years rule') although the Lord Chancellor has a discretionary power to shorten or lengthen this period. If documents contain personal information of a distressing or embarrassing nature, if they contain information obtained under a pledge of confidence, if they are confidential commercial correspondence, or are of an exceptionally sensitive nature affecting the security of the state, then the Lord Chancellor will restrict their use even after the thirty year period has elapsed. V H Galbraith's *An introduction to the use of the public records* (*qv*), first published in 1934 and still in print, is prescribed reading for all students unfamiliar with the use of original records and their provenance, and the official *Guide to the contents of the PRO* describes in detail the material to be deposited there. An extensive history of the public records may be found in *Libraries and the founder of libraries* (1835) by Edward Edwards, a name familiar to all professional librarians. *Publications:* The Public Record Office Act of 1838 empowered the Master of the Rolls to print catalogues and indexes of the records and in the course of the next fifty years a number were published as appendices to the *Deputy keeper's reports*. Calendars also made their appearance from 1856 onwards, continuing the work of the State Paper Commission. In 1890 a switch in emphasis heralded the development of six main types of publication: transcripts, *ie*, full texts; calendars, usually in the form of a precis, obviating the necessity of consulting the document itself; lists of certain classes of records; descriptive lists with brief abstracts; indexes to persons, places and subjects; and catalogues, calendars or lists of records of a similar nature, sometimes prepared for an *ad hoc* purpose. At the present time the policy is to continue to concentrate efforts on the records housed in the PRO. A complete list is included in *British national archives* (*qv*).

634 'Public Record Offices lists and indexes': Between 1892 and 1936 the PRO issued fifty five volumes of lists and indexes providing for historians finding aids to the massive archives of the great legal and administrative departments of the king's court in the medieval period and the departments of state which emerged under the tudors. By arrangement with HMSO, Kraus Reprints began to reissue these in 1964 incorporating amendments made in the unique reference copy in the PRO containing extensive updatings and additions. In addition a set of new volumes, known as the supplementary series, a continuation of the original series, were also published.

635 'Publications of the Royal Commission on Historical Manuscripts' *Government publications sectional list no 17* revised 1 January 1975 (HMSO). All publications sponsored by the commission whether still in print or not are listed here for the benefit of librarians and research workers. There is an alphabetical list of owners or place of origin of manuscript collections with cross references from short titles by which collections have come to be known and also a chronological summary of reports.

636 Purchas, Samuel (1577-1626) earned a lasting importance for his *Hakluytus Posthumus, or Purchas His Pilgrimes, contayning a History of the World in Sea Voyages and Lande Travells by Englishmen and others* (1625) based on a considerable quantity of material mainly on the English voyages to Virginia and to the Indies and on the various expeditions for a North West or North East passage to China amassed by Richard Hakluyt possibly for a third edition of his *magnum opus* which Purchas had somehow managed to acquire. Unfortunately Purchas was not content to publish an updating supplement to Hakluyt's work but persisted with a more grandiose project which would supersede rather than supplement Hakluyt. The work was poorly edited and lacks scholarly balance, many original sources were treated exiguously whilst other material already available in print was afforded badly needed space. The work is in four volumes which contain extracts from journals otherwise lost to us, a factor which has offset Purchas's historical defects. A full list of the principal voyages included may be consulted in the *National Maritime Museum catalogue of the Library; Volume one voyages and travel* pp 20-22.

637 The Raleigh Lecture on a historical subject is delivered annually to the British Academy and printed in the *Proceedings*; usually it is published subsequently as a separate pamphlet. It was endowed munificently by Viscount Wakefield to mark the tercentenary of Sir Walter Raleigh's death, 29 October 1918. A full list of the lectures may be found in K B Gupta's *Cumulated index to the proceedings of the British Academy* (1971).

638 Raleigh, Sir Walter earns his place in historiography for his *History of the world* written whilst he was imprisoned in the Tower of London. The work was never finished, it breaks off in the third century of the christian era, and Raleigh abandoned it after the death of his patron, Prince Henry. His plan seems to have followed that of the medieval chroniclers who thought nothing of prefacing a history of their own times with the story of the world from the creation onwards. The contemporary circumstances surrounding the publication of the first part of the *History* in 1614 are well recounted by C H Firth in an essay, 'Sir Walter Raleigh's History of the world,' collected in *Essays historical and literary* (1938). Macmillan Press publish selections from the work edited by C A Patrides.

639 Ralph de Diceto (1120/30-1202?), Dean of St Paul's, was the author of two historical works of importance: *Abbreviationes Chronicorum* (Epitome of chronicles) an ambitious compendium of world history from the creation down to the year 1148 supported by an impressive list of authorities; and *Imagines Historiarum* (Outlines of history) which took up the story at that date in the form of an abstract of earlier chronicles until 1183 when it expands and contains much original material, and thenceforward to 1202 is a contemporary account of the utmost value especially for the reign of Richard I. His offical position afforded him a vantage point close to government and he could count many influential figures in his circle of friends. The *Outlines*, written in annalistic form, record and comment upon mainly English affairs but items of significant European interest were also included. An intriguing development in method is to be found in the *Epitome* where Ralph introduced a list of signs by which readers could refer direct to passages in the text. The text, edited by Stubbs, was printed in the *Rolls series* in 1876.

640 Ralph of Coggeshall (fl. 1207) was the author of the *Chronicum Anglicanum* extending 1066-1223. Very little is recorded until the reign of John and for this period it is one of the most trustworthy sources as it is for the story of the Fourth Crusade. He is well informed and possessed a true historian's appreciation of accuracy. The text edited by Joseph Stevenson was printed in the *Rolls series* in 1875.

641 Rand McNally atlas of world history edited by R R Palmer has earned an enviable reputation since its publication in 1957. Its hallmarks are an exceptionally high standard of clarity and its arrangement for quick reference use. A second edition appeared in 1965. It should on no account be confused with the *Rand McNally historical atlas of the world* (1961), also edited by Palmer, which is only one fifth the size of the full volume.

642 'The readers' adviser' (Bowker 11e, 1968-1969) first appeared in 1921 as *The bookman's manual* compiled by Bessie Graham. It is designed to present a select annotated bibliography of the best books in print published in English in the United States. The work was divided into two volumes for this edition and 'History, government and politics' takes its place as chapter nine of Volume 2 *A layman's guide*. First comes a short introduction, then books on the writing of history, reference and important series, American history (subdivided by form, chronology, and topic), and continues with a number of area divisions. The vast majority of books listed and annotated are of recent publication: many pre-1964 titles contained in the tenth edition have been omitted although a good number of old works reprinted are included.

643 'Readers' guides' to *Medieval Britain, Tudor and stuart Britain, Hanoverian Britain,* and *Victorian Britain* are pamphlet checklists issued by the former County Libraries Group of the Library Association. Each containing roughly 300 titles listed under appropriate headings; they were intended to indicate to users of small, remote branch libraries in the UK the range of literature which could be obtained through the county library system.

644 'Readers guide to the commonwealth' (2nd ed, 1971), published by the National Book League with the Commonwealth Institute, constitutes an annotated reading list prepared for the Commonwealth Book Fair held at the institute 17th September—10th October 1971. All titles listed were in print when the fair took place. The arrangement is geographical and most items included are books either of a historical nature or relate to contemporary politics.

645 'Readings in African history' (1968) in three volumes *Africa from early times to 1800, Nineteenth century Africa,* and *Twentieth century Africa* edited by P J M McEwan, bring together definitive readings not generally available to students, either because of a lack of adequate library facilities or because they first appeared in obscure journals, perhaps in a language other than English. They are designed to enable students to undertake a closer examination of the major events and developments as recorded and summarised by recognised authorities. An added advantage of this method of imparting knowledge is that it allows a juxtaposition of conflicting views, thus forcing students to think out problems for themselves. All three volumes are arranged on a common geographical pattern: West Africa, North Africa, Egypt (which traditionally exerted a lasting influence), Ethiopia (a long history of independence), East Africa and Southern Africa. Within these sections items are arranged chronologically but a number of important and pervasive issues like the spread and influence of christianity and islam, partition, the rise of nationalism, are treated separately. Most emphasis is placed on the last 150 years and there is a distinct political bias in the extracts but economic, social and religious developments are not forgotten. The topics discussed frequently reflect examination requirements.

646 'The reappraisal of the American revolution in recent historical literature' by Jack P Greene (AHA Service Center Series no 68) published in 1967 complements and updates Edmund Morgan's pamphlet *The American revolution* (*qv*) published nine years earlier in the same series. Although the author is more concerned with postwar interpretations there is a thoughtful comparative resumé of the earlier conceptions, 'whig' and 'imperial,' of this significant period which understandably is of absorbing interest to most Americans. A select list of titles referred to in the text includes much specialist material from learned journals many of which are not easily accessible outside North America.

647 'Recent books on British history since about 1800' (*British book news* 296, April 1965: 241-246 and 297, May 1965: 309-313) is a critical guide intended for the serious student and discriminating adult general reader. Political and constitutional, labour, economic, social and religious, and nineteenth century Irish history are all included.

648 'Recent books on modern Indian history' by Malcolm Yapp (*British book news* August 1975: 525-530) updates earlier surveys published in the same journal January and February 1967. It is arranged by a general and four chronological periods 1500-1947. 'By far the greatest number of books in English on Indian history is now produced by Indian publishers. Many of these, however, bear traces of haste and inadequate preparation by their authors and low standards by the publishers. Consequently, very many of the best books are brought out by British and American publishers.'

649 'Recent British publications on commonwealth West African history' a crisp guide to general histories and works on the separate West African nations which were formerly British colonies, Nigeria, Ghana, Sierra Leone, and the Gambia, by M D Mckee was published in *British book news* November 1971: 855-862. The point is made that the division of West Africa into English and French speaking states is artificial and that a clear understanding of West African history cannot rest solely on British publications.

650 'Recent trends and new literature in Canadian history' by Robin W Winks (1959) is no 19 in the AHA Service Center Series. It is arranged in four sections: Early historiography; Changing interpretations; Prospects and problems; and Recent literature since 1939. Unlike others in the series it attempts to survey the writings relating to the entire history of a nation rather than to a more limited selection of period. Because of this three categories of material are omitted: literature on North America; local history, and (with a few exceptions) periodical articles. The readership is the high school teacher, *ie*, at a level somewhere between the general reader and the higher degree candidate.

651 'Recent writings on William III' by Stephen Baxter is a bibliographic article discussing the writings on the king and his surroundings published since the appearance of Sir Charles Firth's *A commentary on Macaulay's History of England* (1938). Foreign language material is included. Source: *Journal of modern history* 38 (3) September 1966: 256-266.

652 The Record Commission: In 1800 the House of Commons appointed a Select Committee to enquire into the state of the Public Records of Great Britain and to report to the house on their nature and condition and to recommend what needed to be done 'for the better arrangement, preservation, and more convenient use of the same.' Following their report, the commons presented an address to the crown representing 'that the public records of the kingdom were in many offices unarranged, undescribed, and unascertained; that many of them were exposed to erasure, alteration, and embezzlement, and were lodged in buildings incommodious and insecure; and that it would be beneficial to the public service that the records and papers contained in many of the principal offices and repositories should be methodized; and that certain of the more ancient and valuable amongst them should be printed; and humbly beseeching his majesty, that he would be graciously pleased to give such directions thereupon, as his majesty in his royal wisdom should think fit.' Accordingly in 19th July 1800 a commission was appointed to give effect to the measures recommended in the address, 'to make a diligent and particular inquiry into the several matters which our faithful commons have ... represented as fitting to be provided for by our royal authority.' These several matters included appropriate buildings, the provision of calendars and indexes, the transfer of documents, the establishment of an office, and the selection of original records and documents for publication. Further royal commissions were promulgated in 1806, 1817, 1821, 1825 and 1831. A detailed and at times confused history of the establishment of the Record Commission and other steps leading to the establishment of the Public Record Office is recounted in *An account of the most important public records of Great Britain and the publications of The Record Commissioners together with other miscellaneous, historical, and antiquarian* *information* by C P Cooper (2 vols 1835). A more convenient list of the publications is to be found in *British national archives* (*qv*).

653 'Record repositories in Great Britain' (5th ed, 1973), a publication of the Historical Manuscripts Commission, serves as a guide to students requiring to know where record material may be located. It lists therefore only those libraries and record offices where provision is made for regular public use. Entries are arranged geographically.

654 'The records of the Colonial and Dominions Offices' by R B Pugh is no 3 in the Public Record Office handbooks and was first published in 1964. There are three sections: the first describes the home government's arrangements for administering the various overseas territories it accumulated and which eventually evolved into the commonwealth; the second is a guide to the records themselves; and the third is an annotated list of all records in the PRO of this particular category drawn up alphabetically by geographical area. The author is at pains to point out that this is a guide to archives held at the PRO, and not a comprehensive guide to sources of American or imperial history available elsewhere in the United Kingdom.

655 'A reference guide to the literature of travel' by Edward Godfrey Cox was published in Seattle by the University of Washington Press in three volumes (1935-1949). The first two volumes list in chronological order works of foreign travels, voyages, and descriptions printed in Great Britain down to 1800 together with translations into English. *The old world* begins with collections, circumnavigations, and general works, before settling down to a geographical arrangement of Europe, Asia and Africa. *The new world* continues with North and South America, the South Seas, and Australia, with concluding chapters on geography, navigation, maps and atlases, naval and military expeditions, adventures, disasters and shipwrecks, fictitious voyages, and general reference works and bibliographies. The last chapter provides valuable details of individual works and general series which could not be mentioned in this present work. Entries are serially numbered and give full titles and whatever explanatory annotation deemed necessary. Volume III *Great Britain* provides an equally comprehensive guide to historical and topographical literature on the same pattern beginning with Leland. Chapter fourteen, History and chronicle, is especially valuable for its details of printed versions of the early medieval manuscript works. Evidence of research is everywhere apparent although there are some surprising *lacunae*, the *Monumenta Historica Britannica*, for example, receives no annotation whatsoever. A projected fourth volume on Ireland, which was also planned to include items missing from the other three, has not materialised. A library edition is in print from Greenwood Press Inc, of Westport, Connecticut.

656 'The reign of Elizabeth 1558-1603' by J B Black (2nd ed, 1959) in the *Oxford history of England* is substantially revised compared to the first edition published in 1936. This particular volume is of special interest for its method of presentation: a workable compromise has been successfully devised in order to obviate the disadvantages posed by the two usual methods of relating a detailed narrative over a lengthy period. A strict chronological order implies confusion since it is almost impossible to consider every essential topic at all adequately in this way; similarly, a topical arrangement has the effect of producing a book of disconnected essays. The author's solution is to arrange chapters in rough chronological sequence whilst the chapters themselves are limited to a treatment of one particular issue or question. In the middle, specialised studies are inserted without interfering too much with the march of events.

657 'The reign of George III in recent historiography' by Jean Hecht was included in *The bulletin of the New York Public Library* 70, May 1966: 279-304 and reprinted in *Changing views on British history* (*qv*). The essay is written in the full knowledge that 'no period of English history has been the subject of more intensive examination in recent years than the reign of George III.' Unfortunately, however, 'no really adequate attempt has yet been made to incorporate the vast accretions of this recent work into a general synthesis.' The multiplicity of books and articles discussed in this critique on all aspects of hanoverian history indicate what a daunting task a full scale synthesis would be.

658 'The reign of George III 1760-1815' by J Steven Watson (1960), the twelfth volume of the *Oxford history of England*, possesses especial value in that for the first time this critical and controversial period in English history is studied and summarised with the help of the considerable research devoted to it over the last four decades. One thing the author of this particular volume could be sure of, his analysis and interpretation would be scrutinized with more than usual care and interest.

659 'The reign of Henry VII from contemporary sources' compiled by A F Pollard, published in three volumes *Narrative extracts, Constitutional documents and social and economic history* and *Foreign relations, the church, Ireland*, was the first and most ambitious work in the University of London Historical Series. Publication was prompted by the difficulties experienced by students in laying their hands on original source material. Unfortunately they were long ago allowed to slip out of print although to some extent G R Elton's *The tudor constitution* replaces them.

660 'The reign of James VI and I' edited by Alan G R Smith, published in 1973, is included in Macmillan's *Problems in focus* series. A historical and historiographical summary of the reign is followed by eleven further chapters each by a different hand on various aspects of the years 1603-1625. Each chapter is supported by extensive notes and there is a detailed annotated bibliography and guides to further reading.

661 'Rerum Anglicarum Scriptorum veterum' compiled by William Fulman and published in 1684 directed the attention of scholars to the texts of medieval chronicles emanating from the lesser religious houses which proved so essential to the development of historical knowledge of the middle ages in England.

662 'Researching and writing in history; a practical handbook for students' by F N McCoy (University of California Press, 1974) analyses the stages involved in a research paper from the viewpoint of the time devoted to each, and in the order they should be undertaken over the typical twelve weeks' college or university term. 'It is written for the history student, whether graduate or undergraduate, or for any student who faces the task of writing a research paper that involves the use of historical tools and the historical method.' Full of sound, common sense advice but why is it that one can never imagine any student conscientiously following it?

663 'Restoration England 1660-1689' by William L Sachse (CUP, 1971) is one of the bibliographical handbooks compiled for the Conference on British Studies and is designed to provide as comprehensive a general bibliography of the period as can be contrived in the space available. Every item listed receives usually a one line summary and the arrangement follows that of the series as a whole, *ie*, bibliographies, catalogues, and general surveys preceding subject headings covering all conceivable aspects of history. It is intended primarily for advanced students and mature scholars.

664 'Retrospective index to theses of Great Britain and Ireland' (Clio Press 5 vols, 1975-1976) records over 40,000 theses accepted for higher degrees in twenty one British universities from the eighteenth century to 1950. Each volume is devoted to a major subject field with history taking its place in vol I *Social sciences and humanities* which indexes approximately 12,000 theses. Author, title, degree, university and year of award are given.

665 'Revolutions in the modern world' is a series of books published by Weidenfeld devoted to combining the results of research conducted by sociologists into the general phenomenon of revolutions and of historians who have examined many of them in great detail. Each volume will provide 'a coherent narrative of developments, an assessment of causes and meaning, and an analysis of the nature of a particular revolution ...' As yet only three volumes have appeared but many others are in preparation. W W Norton of New York is the American publisher.

666 Rhodes House Oxford, opened in 1929, the headquarters of the Rhodes Scholarships, also serves as a centre for the advanced study of imperial, African, and American history. The library is a department of the Bodleian Library and houses all post-1760 books on these subjects including all British publications received at the Bodleian under the copyright regulations. The American and Commonwealth governments and the United Nations supply a considerable number of their official publications. Other noteworthy collections include extensive runs of nineteenth century American, Canadian, and South African newspapers on microfilm; the Cecil Rhodes Papers and archives of the British South Africa Company; and many other manuscripts. Consequently the library has developed into a first rate research collection and there are also American and Commonwealth lending libraries. *Cecil Rhodes and Rhodes House* a pamphlet published by the Oxford University Press, gives a brief description of the scholarships and the building together with an outline of Rhodes' career. Louis B Frewer's *Rhodes House library its function and sources* is an offprint from the October 1956 issue of *The Bodleian Library record* and contains a summary of its collections.

667 '**Richard Hakluyt and his successors; a volume issued to commemorate the centenary of the Hakluyt Society** edited by Edward Lynam was published by the society in 1946 as number ninety four in their second series of publications. *Contents:* 'Richard Hakluyt' by J A Williamson; 'Samuel Purchas' by Sir William Foster; 'English collections of voyages and travels 1625-1846' by G R Crone and R A Skelton, a magisterial compendium; 'The Hakluyt Society 1846-1946 A retrospect' by Sir William Foster, a member of the society since 1893, Secretary 1893-1902 and President 1928-1945; and, 'The present and the future' by Edward Lynam. A prospectus of the society is also included.

668 '**Richard Hakluyt and the English voyages**' by George Bruner Parks edited with an introduction by J A Williamson (New York, Frederick Ungar, 2nd ed, 1961) was first published by the American Geographical Society in 1928. Its intention was threefold: to assemble a record of Hakluyt's life, to relate that life to the contemporary expansion of English voyages of trade and discovery, and to provide a literary study of Hakluyt's publications. But the author achieves more than this: in setting the scene and placing Hakluyt's career and writings in context he also provides an extensive survey of the geographical knowledge of renaissance

England. A valuable bibliography of Hakluyt's writings, manuscripts, letters, and printed works, together with lists of reprints of the *Voyages* from 1800 onwards, and of studies of Hakluyt since the seventeenth century, adds further distinction. It is available in the United Kingdom from Frank Cass and Co Ltd.

669 Robert of Torigni (1109-1185?), a Norman monk, was captivated by the deeds of Henry I and Henry II and the intricacies of the diplomatic history associated with Henry II's continental campaigns. His *Chronicle* is little more than a straight lift from others up to the year 1147 but from then onwards it is original and of considerable value especially for his detailed examination of Henry's war strategy.

670 Roger of Wendover (11?-1234) was the first of a renowned school of historians associated with the abbey of St Albans whose *Flores Historiarum* was a compilation of sources from the creation to 1202 at which date Ralph de Diceto's *Imagines Historiarum* closed. His account of John's reign and of the early years of Henry III is original and has the added value of being a contemporary narrative.

671 'The rolls series': *Rerum Brittanicarum Medii Aevi Scriptores* or *Chronicles and memorials of Great Britain and Ireland during the middle ages* published by the authority of Her Majesty's Treasury under the direction of the Master of the Rolls (1858-1896). It was on 25 July, 1822 that the House of Commons, mindful that the works of many of our ancient historians still remained in manuscript form, in some cases in a single copy only, presented an address to the crown suggesting 'that an uniform and convenient edition of the whole, published under His Majesty's royal sanction, would be an undertaking honourable to His Majesty's reign, and conducive to the advancement of historical and constitutional knowledge; that the House therefore humbly besought His Majesty, that He would be graciously pleased to give such directions as His Majesty ... might think fit, for the publication of a complete edition of the ancient historians of this realm.' Nothing, however, came of this and it was not until thirty-five years later when the Master of the Rolls submitted on 26 January, 1857 a proposal to the treasury for the publications of primary source materials for the history of Great Britain from the Roman invasions to the reign of Henry VIII that the project was further advanced. These materials should be selected by competent editors 'without reference to periodical or chronological arrangement, without mutilation or abridgment, preference being given, in the first instance, to such materials as were most scarce and valuable.' Each document was to be treated as if the editor were engaged upon an Editio Princeps, ie, the most correct text should be formed from an accurate collation of various extant manuscripts. To enhance this project still further the editor should introduce each volume by adding an account of the manuscripts, their age and peculiarities, and also a brief account of the life and times of the author, and any necessary notes explaining the chronology. No other notes apart from those elucidating the correctness of the text were to be allowed. On 9 February, the Lords of the Treasury opined that the Master of the Rolls' proposal 'was well calculated for the accomplishment of this important national object, in an effectual and satisfactory manner, within a reasonable time, and provided proper attention be paid to economy, in making the detailed arrangements without unnecessary expense.' They even suggested that each volume's preface should include 'a biographical account of the author, so far as authentic materials existed for that purpose, and an estimate of his historical credibility and value'. The first eleven volumes appeared the following year. For a review of the preliminary moves leading up to this great enterprise, the parts played by John Romilly, Thomas Duffus Hardy, and Joseph Stevenson in getting the project started, the various editorial mishaps, the inherent faults and the criticism levied against the Series, refer to Professor M D Knowles' presidential address to the Royal Historical Society printed in *Transactions of the R Hist Soc* 5th series, vol 11, 1961. *List of volumes:*

1 *The chronicle of England by John Capgrave* edited by F C Hingeston (1858).

2 *Chronicon Monasterii de Abingdon* (2 vols) edited by Joseph Stevenson (1858).

3 *Lives of Edward the Confessor I. La estoire de Seint Aedward le Rei; II. Vita Beati Edvardi Regis et Confessoris; III. Vita Aeduuardi Regis qui apud Westmonasterium requies edited by Henry Richard Luard (1858).*

4 *Monumenta Franciscana* (2 vols) edited by J S Brewer and Richard Howlett (1858, 1882).

5 *Fasciculi Zizaniorum Magistri Johannis Wyclif cum Tritieo* ascribed to Thomas Netter of Walden edited by W W Shirley (1858).

6 *The buik of the chroniclis of scotland or a metrical version of the history of Hector Boece by William Stewart* edited by W B Turnbull (1858).

7 *Johannis Capgrave Liber de Illustribus Henricis* edited by F C Hingeston (1858).

8 *Historia Monasterii S Augustini Cantuariensis by Thomas of Elmham* edited by Charles Hardwick (1858).

9 *Eulogium (Historiarum sive Temporis): Chronicon ab Orbe condito usque ad Annum Domíni 1366* (3 vols) edited by F S Haydon (1858-1863).

10 *Memorials of Henry VII* edited by James Gairdner (1858).

11 *Memorials of Henry V* edited by Charles A Cole (1858).

12 *Munimenta Gildhallae Londoniensis: Liber Albus, Liber Custumarum et Liber Horn, in archivis Gildhallae asservati* (3 vols in 4) edited by Henry Thomas Riley (1859-1862).

13 *Chronica Johannis de Oxenedes* edited by Sir Henry Ellis (1859).

14 *Political poems and songs relating to English history, from the accession of Edward III to the reign of Henry VIII* (2 vols) edited by Thomas Wright (1859-1861).

15 *Opus Tertium, Opus Minus etc of Roger Bacon* edited by J S Brewer (1859).

16 *Bartholomaei de Cotton, Monachi Norwicensis, Historia Anglicana 449-1298 Liber de Archiepiscopis et Episcopis Angliae* edited by Henry Richards Luard (1859).

17 *Brut Y Tywysogion or the chronicles of the Princes of Wales* edited by John Williams ap Ithel (1860).

18 *Royal and historical letters during the reign of Henry IV 1399-1404* edited by F C Hingeston (1860).

Note. Eight copies only were printed of Vol II 1405-1413 because of numerous minor errors in the text. It was issued as a photographic reprint *With amendments entered in calligraphy supplied by The Public Record Office* (1965).

19 *The repressor of over much blaming of the clergy by Reginald Pecock* (2 vols) edited by Churchill Babington (1860).

20 *Annales Cambriae* edited by John Williams ap Ithel (1860).

21 *Works of Giraldus Cambrensis* (8 vols) edited by J S Brewer, James F Dimock and George F Warner (1861-1891).

22 *Letters and papers illustrative of the wars of the English in France during the Reign of Henry VI, King of England* (2 vols in 3) edited by Joseph Stevenson (1861-1864).

23 *Anglo-Saxon chronicle, according to the several original authorities* (2 vols) edited and translated by Benjamin Thorpe (1861).

24 *Letters and papers illustrative of the reigns of Richard III and HenryVII* (2 vols) edited by James Gairdner (1861-1863).

25 *Letters of Bishop Grosseteste* edited by Henry Richards Luard (1861).

26 *Descriptive catalogue of manuscripts relating to the history of Great Britain and Ireland* (3 vols in 4) edited by Thomas Duffus Hardy (1862-1871).

27 *Royal and other historical letters illustrative of the reign of Henry III* (2 vols) edited by W W Shirley (1862-1866).

28 *Chronica Monasterii S Albani* (7 vols in 13) edited by Henry Thomas Riley (1863-1876). I. Thomas Walsingham Historia Anglicana 1272-1422. II. Willelmi Rishanger Chronica et Annales 1259-1307. III. Johannis de Trokelowe et Henrici de Blaneforde Chronica et Annales 1259-1406. IV. Gesta Abbatum Monasterii S Albani a Thoma Walsingham 793-1411. V. Johannis Amundesham Annales. VI. Registra Quorundam Abbatum Monasterii S. Albana, qui Saeculo Xvmo Floruere. VII. Ypodigma Neustriae a Thomas Walsingham.

29 *Chronicon Abbatiae Eveshamensis ... ad Annum 1418* edited by W D Macray (1863).

30 *Ricardi de Cirencestria Speculum Historiale de Gestis Regum Angliae 447-871, 872-1066* (2 vols) edited by John Mayor (1863-1869).

31 *Year Books of the reign of Edward I Years 20-21, 21-22, 30-31, 32-33 and 33-35 Edw I and 11-12 Edw III* edited by A J Horwood. *Years 12-13, 13-14, 14, 14-15 and 15 Edw III* edited and translated by Luke Owen Pike (1863-1891).

32 *Narratives of the expulsion of the English from Normandy, 1449-1450* edited by Joseph Stevenson (1863).

33 *Historia et Cartularium Monasterii S. Petri Gloucestriae* (3 vols) edited by W H Hart.

34 *Alexandri Neckam de Naturis Rerum* edited by Thomas Wright (1863).

35 *Leechdoms, Wortcunning, and Starcraft of Early England; being a collection of documents illustrating the history of science in this country before the Norman Conquest* (3 vols) edited by T Oswald Cockayne (1864-1866).

36 *Annales Monastici* (5 vols) edited by Henry Richards Luard (1864-1869).

37 *Magna vita S. Hugonis Episcopi Lincolniensis* edited by James F Dimock (1864).

38 *Chronicles and Memorials of the reign of Richard I* (2 vols) edited by William Stubbs (1864-1865).

39 *Recueil des chroniques et anchiennes istories de la Grant Bretaigne a present nomme Engleterre, par Jehan de Waurin* (5 vols) edited by Sir William Hardy and Edward Hardy (1884-1891).

40 *Collection of the chronicles and ancient histories of Great Britain, now called England, by John de Waurin* (3 vols) edited and translated by Sir William Hardy and Edward Hardy (1864-1891).

41 *Polychronicon Ranulphi Higden with Trevisa's Translation* (9 vols) edited by Churchill Babington and Joseph Rawson Lumby (1865-1886).

42 *Le Livere de Reis de Brittanie e Le Livere de Reis de Engleterre* edited by John Glover (1865).

43 *Chronica Monasterii de Melsa ab anno 1150 usque ad annum 1405* (3 vols) edited by E A Bond (1866-1868).

44 *Matthaei Parisiensis Historia Anglorum 1067-1253* (3 vols) edited by Sir Frederick Madden (1863-1869).

45 *Liber Monasterii de Hyda: a chronicle and chartulary of Hyde Abbey Winchester 455-1023* edited by Edward Edwards (1866).

46 *Chronicon Scotorum: a chronicle of Irish affairs, from the earliest times to 1135; and supplement containing events from 1141 to 1150* edited and translated by W M Hennessy (1866).

47 *Chronicle of Pierre de Langtoft in French verse from the earliest period to the death of Edward I* (2 vols) edited by Thomas Wright (1866-1868).

48 *The war of the Gaedhill with the Gaill, or The invasions of ireland by the Danes and other Norsemen* edited and translated by J A Todd (1867).

49 *Gesta Regis Henri Secundi Benedicti Abbatis. Chronicle of the reigns of Henry II and Richard I 1169-1192 known under the name of Benedict of Peterborough* (2 vols) edited by William Stubbs (1867).

50 *Munimenta Academica or Documents illustrative of academical life and studies at Oxford* (2 vols) edited by Henry Austey (1868).

51 *Chronica Magistri Rogeri de Houedene* (4 vols) edited by William Stubbs (1868).

52 *Willelmi Malmesbiriensis Monachi de Gestis Pontificum Anglorum Libri Quinque* edited by N E Hamilton (1870).

53 *Historic and municipal documents of Ireland, from the archives of the City of Dublin 1172-1320* edited by John Gilbert (1870).

54 *The annals of Loch Ce. A chronicle of Irish affairs, from 1041 to 1590* (2 vols) edited and translated by W H Hennessy (1871).

55 *Monumenta Juridica. The black book of the Admiralty* (4 vols) edited by Sir Travers Twiss (1871-1876).

56 *Memorials of the reign of Henry VI. Official correspondence of Thomas Bekynton, Secretary to Henry VI, and Bishop of Bath and Wells* (2 vols) edited by George Williams (1872).

57 *Matthaei Parisiensis, Monachi Sancti Albani, Chronica Majora* (7 vols) edited by Henry Richards Luard (1872-1884).

58 *Memoriale Fratris Walteri de Coventria—The historical collections of Walter of Coventry* (2 vols) edited by William Stubbs (1872-1873).

59 *Anglo-Latin satirical poets and epigrammatists of the twelfth century* (2 vols) edited by Thomas Wright (1872).

60 *Materials for a history of the reign of Henry VII from original documents preserved in the Public Record Office* (2 vols) edited by William Campbell (1873-1877).

61 *Historical papers and letters from the Northern registers* edited by James Raine (1873).

62 *Registrum Palatinum Dunelmense. The Register of Richard de Kellawe, Lord Palatine and Bishop of Durham 1311-1316* (4 vols) edited by Sir Thomas Duffus Hardy (1873-1878).

63 *Memorials of St Dunstan, Archbishop of Canterbury* edited by William Stubbs (1874).

64 *Chronicon Angliae, ab Anno Domini 1328 usque ad annum*

1388 auctore monacho quodam Sancti Albani edited by Edward Maunde Thompson (1874).

65 *Thomas Saga Erkibyskups A life of Archbishop Thomas Becket in Icelandic* (2 vols) edited and translated by M Eirikr Magnusson (1875-1884).

66 *Radulphi de Coggeshall Chronicon Anglicanum* edited by Joseph Stevenson (1875).

67 *Materials for the history of Thomas Becket Archbishop of Canterbury* (7 vols) edited by J G Robertson and J B Sheppard (1875-1885).

68 *Radulfi de Diceto Decani Lundoniensis Opera Historica. The Historical works of Master Ralph de Diceto, Dean of London* (2 vols) edited by William Stubbs (1876).

69 *Roll of the proceedings of the King's Council in ireland, for a portion of the 16th year of the reign of Richard II 1392-93* edited by James Graves (1877).

70 *Henrici de Bracton de Legibus et Consuetudinibus Angliae Libri Quinque in Varios Tractatus Distincti* (6 vols) edited by Sir Travers Twiss (1878-1883).

71 *The historians of the Church of York, and its archbishops* (3 vols) edited by James Raine (1879-1894).

72 *Registrum Malmesburiense. The Register of Malmesbury Abbey preserved in the Public Record Office* (2 vols) edited by J S Brewer and C T Martin (1879-1880).

73 *Historical works of Gervase of Canterbury* (2 vols) edited by William Stubbs (1879-1880).

74 *Henrici Archidiaconi Huntendunensis Historia Anglorum AD 55—AD 1154 in eight books* edited by Thomas Arnold (1879).

75 *The historical works of Symeon of Durham* (2 vols) edited by Thomas Arnold (1882-1885).

76 *Chronicle of the reigns of Edward I and Edward II* (2 vols) edited by William Stubbs (1882-1883).

77 *Registrum Epistolarum Fratris Johannis Peckham, Archiepiscopi Cantuariensis* (3 vols) edited by C T Martin (1882-1886).

78 *Register of S Osmund* (2 vols) edited by W H Rich Jones (1883-1884).

79 *Chartulary of the Abbey of Ramsey* (3 vols) edited by W H Hart (1884-1893).

80 *Chartularies of St Mary's Abbey Dublin with the register of*

its house at Dunbrody County of Wexford, and Annals of Ireland, 1162-1370 (2 vols) edited by J T Gilbert (1884-1885).

81 *Eadmeri Historia Novorum in Anglia, et Opuscula duo de Vita Sancti Anselmi et Quibusdam Miraculis Ejus* edited by Martin Rule (1884).

82 *Chronicles of the reigns of Stephen, Henry II and Richard I* (4 vols) edited by Richard Howlett (1884-1890).

83 *Chronicles of the Abbey of Ramsey* edited by W D Macray (1886).

84 *Chronica Rogeri de Wendover, sive Flores Historiarum* (3 vols) edited by H G Hewlett (1886-1889).

85 *The Letter Books of the Monastery of Christ Church, Canterbury* (3 vols) edited by J B Sheppard (1887-1889).

86 *The Metrical Chronicle of Robert of Gloucester* (2 vols) edited by W A Wright (1887).

87 *Chronicle of Robert of Brunne* (2 vols) edited by F J Furnivall (1887).

88 *Icelandic sagas and other historical documents relating to the settlements and descents of the Northmen on the British Isles* (4 vols) edited and translated by Gudbrand Vigfusson and Sir George Dasent (1887).

89 *The Tripartite life of St Patrick* (2 vols) edited by Whitley Stokes (1887).

90 *Willelmi Monachi Malmesbiriensis de Regum Gestis Anglorum, Libri V; et Historiae Novellae Libri III* (2 vols) edited by William Stubbs (1887-1889).

91 *Lestorie des Engles Solum Geffrai Gaimar* (2 vols) edited and translated by Sir Thomas Duffus Hardy and C T Martin (1888-1889).

92 *Chronicle of Henry Knighton* (2 vols) edited by Joseph Rawson Lumby (1889-1895).

93 *Chronicle of Adam Murimuth with the chronicle of Robert of Avesbury* edited by Edward Maunde Thompson (1889).

94 *Chartulary of the Abbey of St Thomas the Martyr, Dublin* edited by J T Gilbert (1889).

95 *Flores Historiarum* (3 vols) edited by Henry Richards Luard (1890).

96 *Memorials of St Edmunds Abbey* (3 vols) edited by Thomas Arnold (1890-1896).

97 *Charters and documents illustrating the history of the*

cathedral and city of Sarum 1100-1300 edited by W D Macray (1891).

98 *Memoranda de Parliamento 25 Edward I 1305* edited by F W Maitland (1893).

99 *The red book of the Exchequer* (3 vols) edited by Hubert Hall (1896).

In 1965 the whole series was issued in reprint form by Kraus Reprint Ltd.

672 'Roman Britain' by I A Richmond (Cape, 1963) originally published as a Penguin paperback in 1955 consists of outline chapters on military history, towns, the countryside, economics, and religion, each supplied with a bibliography containing journal articles for further investigation.

673 'Roman Britain' by R G Collingwood, in print continuously since it was first published in 1923, provides 'a general sketch of Roman Britain ignoring details of history and archaeology, and concentrating on the broadest and most characteristic features.' Aimed unreservedly at the general reader, it offers an uncluttered review of all aspects of Britain during the Roman occupation. For those who wish to investigate further there is a bibliography designed to refer to material supporting the general conclusions of the text.

674 'Roman Britain and early England 55 BC-AD 871' by Peter Hunter Blair (1963) is the first of Nelson's History of England and begins most intelligently by looking at the sources of information available to historians of this remote period. Deprived of the historian's customary type of raw material the author has recourse to archaeological discoveries and scholarship. The bibliography is presented in imaginative fashion and the reader who genuinely wants to continue his studies further will appreciate the guiding hints and directions supplied by the author.

675 'Roman Britain and the english settlements' by R G Collingwood and J N L Myres (2nd ed, 1937) is the opening volume of the *Oxford history of England*. It is not a collaboration but two independent studies. By far the greater portion relates to the Roman period in which Professor Collingwood presents Britain as a distinct and separate region upon which an alien military rule was imposed. In terms of time this Roman section is extended well into the sixth century at which point a comparatively short account of the Anglo-Saxon conquest of southern Britain is added. The bibliography is similarly divided: material for the earlier period is arranged under ancient writers, books of reference, inscriptions, general works on Roman Britain, archaeology and topography, county histories etc, periodicals, monographs on special sites, and special subjects, all designed as a general review of sources and not as a collection of text references; and for the later period under ancient texts, inscriptions and documents, bibliographies and reference works and periodicals, general works, archaeology and topography, place names, and the continental background.

676 **'The Roman occupation of Britain'** by Francis Haverfield (OUP, 1924) forms the printed version, revised by George MacDonald, of six Ford Lectures delivered in 1907. First comes a historiographical chapter 'The study of Roman Britain: a retrospect;' then follow 'The geography of Britain and the Roman conquest;' 'The permanent military occupation of Britain;' 'The civilisation of the province' and 'Roman Britain and Saxon England.' An appendix discusses the list of twenty eight cities of Britain mentioned first by Gildas and perpetuated by later writers. A biographical notice of the author and a chronologically arranged bibliography of his important writings is also included in the volume. Later scholars continue to acknowledge the importance of Haverfield's work.

677 **'A Romano-British bibliography (55 BC-AD 449)'** by Wilfrid Bonser (Blackwell, 1964) includes material published to the end of 1959. Three types of user are envisaged by the author who was himself librarian of the University of Birmingham for over twenty years: librarians who should be able to satisfy all enquiries on the period; the student and general reader; and research workers who may find the work useful for looking up references which have slipped the memory or to be sure of what has already been published on a particular topic. The bibliography is purely descriptive, the author offers no evaluation which he insists is the function of the user who must 'exercise his judgement, from the date of the work or his knowledge of its writer, as to what is valuable and reliable, also as to what is now obsolete, redundant, or prejudiced'. To arrange the 10,000 entries a whole enumerative classification is outlined in two parts: Part 1. Conspectus of history and culture is divided into general topics; History subdivided by period; Army fleet and defence; Social and economic; Religion; Geography; Archaeology; Numismatics; and art. Part 2. Sites (local history, records of excavations and finds) is divided by geographical area. Each entry gives author, title, an indication of its scope and an abbreviated citation if it is a periodical article. There is a list of periodicals and collective works abstracted. Four indexes, author, subject, personal names, and place names were published in a separate volume in order to facilitate reference to the bibliography proper.

678 **'The Romans in Britain; a selection of Latin texts'** edited with a commentary by R W Moore was first published by Methuen in 1938 and was last revised in 1954. It provides a collection of passages from a number of Roman writers, including Caesar, Tacitus, Suetonius, and Ammianus, and also two British writers, Bede and Gildas, concerning Britain. The extracts are preceded by an outline history of Roman Britain, an account of the writers extracted, a note on the archaeological evidence, and a list of recommended books. There is also a detailed commentary on the text.

679 **'The rough and the smooth'** is the title of a review article on the writing of Australian history by Donald Horne which appeared in *TLS* 9 April 1976. The rough, *ie*, a general emphasis on democracy and the Australian labour movement, and the smooth—the long craving for respectability—are seen as rival themes.

680 **The Round Table Movement,** largely the creation of Lord Milner, developed out of the Closer Union Society which in the first decade of this centuury was urging the South African colonies to unite into a single dominion. It was organized in the Spring and Summer of 1909 and formally established in September with financial support from the Rhodes Trust. Another prominent founder member was Lionel Curtis who based a lifelong campaign for the organic union of the Empire on the assumption that it ought to be invested with visible collective power sufficient to prevent the outbreak of a world war. His main consideration was a healthy fear of Germany. Since then, of course, the fervid imperialism has vanished but the movement still exists as a study group and continues to publish *The round table* a quarterly review of commonwealth affairs, which was first published in 1910 to revive and promote the idea of a federal council of empire. Today it is a cooperative enterprise conducted by members living in different parts of the commonwealth and is intended to act as a comparative review of commonwealth politics freed from the bias of local party issues. In addition it endeavours to provide an impartial treatment of outstanding international problems affecting the commonwealth. Each national committee is responsible for all articles on the politics of their own country and it is hoped that this will ensure the journal will reflect current opinion and at the same time present a survey of contemporary problems. A separate *Index of twenty-five years 1910-1935* covering Volumes I-XXV, numbers 1 to 100 was published by Macmillan in 1936. A subject index is arranged under mainly geographical sub-headings and this is followed by an alphabetical names index. Back issues 1910-1954 are available in microform from University Microfilms, St John's Road, Tylers Green, High Wycombe, Bucks. *The round table movement and imperial union* by John E Kendle, based on meticulous research, published by the University of Toronto Press in 1975, is an exhaustive study especially of the London group.

681 The Royal Commonwealth Society whose aim it is, in the words of their supplemental charter dated 13 October 1964, 'to promote within our United Kingdom and overseas the increase and spread of knowledge respecting the peoples and countries of the commonwealth,' was founded as The Colonial Society at a meeting called by public advertisement in June 1868, and attended by public figures who had been showing an active interest in colonial affairs. It became the Royal Colonial Society in 1869 but changed to The Royal Colonial Institute following representations from the Royal College of Surgeons who feared the initials might cause confusion. It became The Royal Empire Society in 1928 and assumed its present name in 1958. A full account of the origins, aims, activities and history of the society may be found in *The* *history of the Royal Commonwealth Society 1868-1968* by Trevor Reese (OUP, 1968) which is designed to relate the development of the society to that of the empire and commonwealth itself. The author describes it as 'an essay on the evolution of the empire and commonwealth as reflected in the activities of the voluntary society founded … to foster imperial sentiment and promote the empire's interests.' It is based ·largely on the society's records, proceedings and minutes. There are a number of appendices printing the declared objectives of the Royal Colonial Institute and the Royal Commonwealth Society and lists of presidents, chairmen, secretaries, and librarians, and also a list of works cited. *The library*: as early as the inaugural meeting the need for a library and reading room had been recognised and by 1873 a sizeable collection of books and journals had accumulated following an appeal to colonial governors to donate suitable material. Now, of course, the library is acknowledged as one of the foremost collections in the world and its catalogues have acquired the status of indispensable bibliographies. Following two earlier and very much thinner catalogues the *Catalogue of the library of the Royal Colonial Institute* compiled by J B Boosé was issued in 1896. This was arranged under fourteen headings beginning with collections of voyages, continuing with area headings, and finishing with forms of material like transactions of societies, handbooks, and parliamentary publications. *The first supplementary catalogue of the library of the Royal Colonial Institute* again compiled by Boosé, appeared in 1901 to be used in conjunction with the earlier edition and including the library's accessions down to 1900. To give some idea of the rapid growth of the library the 1896 catalogue comprised 700 pages, and the supplement 1000 plus of closely printed entries. And neither included an author index. By the 1920s the library housed over 200,000 books and a new subject catalogue was put in hand with the financial support of the Carnegie United Kingdom Trust and other foundations. *The subject catalogue of the Royal Empire Society formerly Royal Colonial Institute* compiled by Evans Lewin was published in four volumes 1930-1937. It is arranged on a geographical basis, each country being divided by alphabetical subject headings under which entries were listed chronologically. An author index including, whenever judged necessary, the dates of birth and death of each author, important positions held, and any other details to indicate his reputation and authority is appended to each volume. Its value as a bibliography was enhanced by the inclusion of articles appearing in the principal reviews and journals, papers read before learned societies, and analytical entries for miscellaneous volumes of papers and essays. Full catalogue: 1 *The British Empire generally, and Africa* (1930); 2 *The Commonwealth of Australia, The Dominion of New Zealand, The South Pacific, general voyages and travels, and Arctic and Antarctic Regions* (1931); 3 *The Dominion of Canada and its provinces, The Dominion of Newfoundland, The West Indies, and Colonial America* (1932); and 4 *The Mediterranean Colonies, The Middle East, Indian Empire, Burma, Ceylon, British Malaya, East Indian Islands, and The Far East* (1937). A biography catalogue of the library of the Royal Commonwealth Society compiled by Donald H Simpson (1961) lists books added up to the autumn of 1960 and includes material on those born in or actively connected with countries of the commonwealth who have been of some significance in imperial and commonwealth affairs. There are two main divisions: Individual biographies listed in alphabetical order of biographee containing dates of birth and death; and collective biography and country indexes. An index of authors completes the search tools. The catalogue also includes a memoir of Evans Lewin, librarian to the society 1910-1946. *Publications:* The Society's journal *United empire* started in 1910 and continued until 1958 when it altered its title to *Journal of the Royal Commonwealth Society* changing again in 1961 to *Commonwealth journal.* A series of bibliographies, mostly either area studies or select lists of recent accessions to the library, many compiled by Evans Lewin, appeared 1915-1946. There is also an infrequent imperial studies series comprising specialised monographs.

682 'The Royal Historical Society' after a precarious beginning in 1868 and a twelve year period of controversy and recrimination, became established on a sound basis in the early 1880s. Gradually it attracted the support of influential historians at the universities, and its standing as a professional society was signalled by a royal charter of incorporation in 1889. Its growing reputation and professionalism was confirmed seven years later when the Camden Society, a publishing society concerned with the editing of historical texts, initiated discussions for a merger. About this time it looked as if the Society would become involved in encouraging historical teaching in schools but this came to nothing as did a later plan to establish a School of Advanced Historical Studies, projects which were left to the Historical Association and the Institute of Historical Research to foster. A long period of gentle stagnation came to an end when the Society was revitalized in the 1930s: a substantial publishing programme, guides and handbooks, bibliographies and other aids to research, was set in motion, and the library, enriched by valuable donations, at last became worthy of the name. In the late sixties the library and offices accepted the hospitality of University College, London and today the society can justifiably claim to be 'the principal organization representing English historical scholarship' and its future seems assured. A short history *The Royal Historical Society 1868-1968* was published to mark its centenary. Besides the *Bibliography of British history* (qv) and *Writings on British history* (qv) publications include *Transactions of the Royal Historical Society* (1871-   ), the printing of papers read to the society; the *Camden series* (1897-   ); and a number of guides and handbooks. A detailed list of all RHS publications and their contents with exact page references appeared in *A centenary guide to the publications of the Royal Historical Society 1868-1968 and of the former Camden Society 1838-1897* (1968).

683 Rushworth, John (1612-1690) the author of *Historical collections of private passages of state, weighty matters in law, remarkable proceedings in five parliaments* (8 vols 1659-1701), was close to the centre of public affairs for many years. In his preface he could claim 'I did personally attend and observe all occurrences of moment during that interval in the star-chamber, court of honour, and exchequer chambers, when all the judges of England met there upon extraordinary cases, when great causes were heard before the King and Council ... I began early to take in characters, speeches and passages at conferences in parliament, and from the king's own mouth, when he spake to both the houses; and have been upon the stage continually, and an eye and ear-witness of the greatest transactions; imployed as an agent in, and intrusted with the affairs of weightiest concernment.' Although there is so much more source material available now, the *Historical collections* still remains of value especially for the civil war period. Originally the work was planned to start with the parliament which met on 3 November, 1640 but like a good many historians since Rushworth found himself going further and further back, and eventually he started at 1618 to bring his fully documented history (which was intended 'to consider indifferently how we came to fall out among ourselves, and so to learn the true causes, the rises and growths of our late miseries') down to 1648. Despite his further claim that the work was a bare narrative of fact, digested in order of time, and that he had not interpolated his own opinions, the royalists vehemently attacked it on the grounds of bias, distortion, and error.

684 **'Rymer's Foedera'** - *Conventiones, Literae, et cujuscunque generis Acta Publica inter Reges Angliae, et alios quosvis Imperatores, Reges, Pontifices, Principes, vel Communitates ab ineunte saeculo duodecimo, viz ab anno 1101, ad nostra usque tempora, habita aut tractata; ex autographis, infra secretiores Archivorum Regiorum thesaurarias, per multa saecula reconditis fideliter exscripta in lucem missa de mandato Reginae accurante Thoma Rhymer ejusdem Serenissimae Reginae Historiographo.* Enjoying the powerful support of men of influence at court, Lord Somers and Charles Montague (later Lord Halifax) among them, and spurred on by the knowledge that similar collections had been successfully published on the continent, plans to compile an authoritative collection of all the transactions England had ever entered into with foreign powers had come close to fruition by the year 1693. Although the duties of the historiographer royal were vague and ill defined he seemed the obvious choice to supervise matters should such a work go ahead at the public expense. The post was currently held by Thomas Rymer (1641-1713) and on 26 August 1693 he was directed by a royal warrant 'to transcribe and publish all the leagues, treaties, alliances, capitulations, and confederacies, which have at any time been made between the Crown of England and any other kingdoms, provinces, and states, as a work highly conducing to our service and the honour of this our realm.' So that he might tackle this task expeditiously he was empowered 'to have free liberty and access ... to search into the records in our Tower of London, in the rolls, in the augmentation office, our exchequer, the journals of both houses of parliament, or any other place where records are kept ... and the same to transcribe: And that he also have access ... to our library at St James's and our paper office.' Rymer lost no time in reducing the scheme to manageable proportions by deciding to start from the year 1101 and to restrict his collection to originals preserved in the royal archives and such supplementary material as could be found in the Cottonian, Lambeth, and Bodleian libraries. Faced with all sorts of difficulties including the reluctance of keepers of the records notwithstanding the royal warrant to allow him reasonable facilities, and not least to government parsimony, Rymer toiled for ten years before the first volume was ready for publication and another ten before the project was near to completion. By 1713 fifteen volumes of documents ranging 1101-1586 had been published and had met with a generally favourable reception although it was accepted that there were some faults. At times Rymer had collected his texts from printed sources and not from the original records, errors had crept in, his dating was by no means infallible. Yet his vast labours had resulted in an outstanding contribution to the nation's history and it was acknowledged as such. After Rymer's death in December 1713 two more volumes appeared (1715 and 1717), the last being inefficiently compiled by Robert Sanderson, Rymer's assistant, who included much material of purely domestic interest. These seventeen volumes constitute the first edition. Rymer had also collected and bound fifty nine volumes of manuscripts which eventually found their way to the British Museum (Additional Mss 4573-4630 and 18911). Jacob Tonson was later authorised to reprint these and added (perhaps at his own expense) three other volumes also under Sanderson's direction which included documents down to 1654. In 1806 the record commission appointed Dr Adam Clarke as editor of a new edition which was to continue the work down to the Revolution or perhaps even to the accession of George I but by 1830 work had proceeded only to 1383 and the project was abandoned. For a biography of Thomas Rymer, the circumstances surrounding the original plans, the personalities involved, and for a critical history of the various editions, and for a synopsis of their contents, recourse should be made to *Syllabus (in English) of the documents England and other kingdoms contained in the collection known as Rymer's Foedera* by Thomas Duffus Hardy, Deputy Keeper of the Public Records, published under the direction of the Master of the Rolls

(3 vols 1869-1885). A convenient assessment of Rymer may be found in *English scholars* by David C Douglas (*qv*).

685 'The Saxon and Norman kings' by Christopher Brooke was published in their *British monarchy* series by Batsford in 1963. It investigates the concept of kingship as it was understood and practised by the Germanic peoples who conquered Britain in the early medieval period. The author's method is to pose a series of problems, and endeavour to solve them by depicting how modern research has interpreted what fragmentary source material still remains. Although intended for the general reader the scholarly apparatus is not lacking: a bibliographical note arranged by chapters fulfils the dual function of acting as a guide for further reading and also as an indication of the evidence on which the text is based. There are also four clearly arranged genealogical tables.

686 'Scholarly collection of American history' consisting of 2813 titles dealing with all aspects of America's past, its politics, literature, and society, is published in microfiche form by Microcards Edition in recognition of the bicentennial in 1976. The collection is divided into eight sections: American revolution (histories, biographies, source material, archives and the *Journal of the continental congress*); The civil war; Political history; American statesmen of the eighteenth century (the writings of James Madison, Alexander Hamilton, Thomas Jefferson, George Washington and Benjamin Franklin); American statesmen of the nineteenth century; American literature nineteenth century (the works of Thoreau, Fenimore Cooper, Washington Irving, Emerson, Poe and Whitman amongst others); American racial and ethnic groups; and American history general. Each of these can be ordered separately. There is an author-and-subject index to the entire collection. Details from Microcards Edition, Denver Technological Center, 5500 South Valentia Way, Englewood, Colorado 80110, USA.

687 School of Oriental and African Studies was opened in 1917 as a constituent college of the University of London and is now a world renowned graduate school providing a wealth of postgraduate courses and regularly arranging international study conferences. The Library has expanded its nucleus collections of oriental books from the London Institution, the University Library, and the libraries of King's and University colleges, and now houses in the region of 350,000 books. It is recognised as the national lending library of oriental and African studies. In 1969 the School published a substantial *Library guide* which includes general information on the history and scope of the library, its catalogues, and detailed notes on the various divisions together with a list of the main bibliographical and reference works shelved in each. The library catalogue was reproduced in book form by G K Hall and Co, in 1964.

688 **'Scriptores Rerum Anglicarum'** was the name given to a projected *National historians of the middle ages* on the model of the *Receuil des historiens des Gaules et de la France*. At the close of the eighteenth century John Pinkerton had called attention to the neglected state of English records in a series of letters to the *Gentleman's magazine*. Edward Gibbon was attracted to the idea and wrote an elegant and powerful address expressing the hope his life might be extended twenty years so that he might see its completion. But on the very day a joint prospectus from Pinkerton and himself was to have appeared Gibbon died and the project was abandoned.

689 **Seeley, Sir Robert** (1834-1895) is remembered especially for *The expansion of England* (1883) and *The growth of British policy an historical essay* (2 vols, 1895). The former undoubtedly caught public attention: comprising two courses of lectures at Cambridge, where he was Regius Professor of Modern History, this outlined with sturdy vigour the great rivalry between Britain and France which held the world stage 1688-1815. No previous historian had placed such stress as Seeley on the widespread colonial and imperial aspects of this national struggle. The book appeared at an opportune moment and perhaps contributed more than any other history to the marked change in the feelings of metropolitan Britain to the fledgling colonies. It is certainly not recommended reading for latter day internationalists. *The growth of British policy* was originally designed to examine in detail the period covered in the *Expansion* but Seeley found himself researching further and further back to the reign of Elizabeth I. The theme of

293

the work is the lasting influence exerted by the elizabethan religious settlement on Britain's subsequent relations with the continental maritime powers. The Seeley History Library commemorates his name in Cambridge. A modern assessment is Peter Burroughs' 'John Robert Seeley and British imperial history,' *Journal of imperial and commonwealth history* 1 (2) January 1973: 191-211.

690 The Selden Society was founded in 1887 largely due to the efforts of F W Maitland to encourage the study and advance the knowledge of the history of English law. An annual series of publications now runs to ninety one volumes most of which contain an English translation of the original Latin or French reports of court proceedings. Since each volume carries an explanatory introduction a substantial body of research material is accumulating as the series continues. In 1965 a supplementary series was started consisting of relevant works whose nature and size render them unsuitable for the main series. So far only four have appeared but others are in active preparation. *A general guide to the society's publications, a detailed and indexed summary of the contents of the introductions volumes 1-79* by A K R Kiralfy and Gareth H Jones was published by Quaritch in 1960. All volumes are kept in print so that new members, personal or institutional, may obtain them if required. These of course present very specialised information but of direct relevance to the advanced study of medieval English history.

691 'A select bibliography of the history of the United States' compiled by Allan Nevins (Historical Association pamphlet no 121) appeared in 1942 and is still a useful introductory guide.

692 'A select bibliography of the teaching of history in the United Kingdom' by John Fines (1969) is published by the Historical Association as one of their *Helps for students of history* series. It is primarily intended for teachers in schools although a good deal of material relating to university teaching has also been included. Entries refer mainly to twentieth century English books and journal articles and are arranged alphabetically with the index acting as a subject guide. Addenda are published at regular intervals in *Teaching history*.

693 'Select documents for Queen Anne's reign' down to the union with Scotland 1702-1707 edited by G M Trevelyan (CUP, 1929) are arranged as follows: Foreign treaties of alliance, home politics, Gibraltar, Blenheim and Ramillies, the Marlborough papers, and Scotland and the union. The documents were specifically selected for use by undergraduates studying Queen Anne's reign as a special subject in the historical tripos.

694 'Select documents in Australian history 1788-1850' (Angus and Robertson 1950) selected and edited by C M H Clark, was followed five years later by Vol 2 1851-1900. They are intended for students on undergraduate courses reading Australian history and not for specialists or the general reader. An attempt is made to select those documents that contain the evidence for the different interpretations of Australian historians and they are almost entirely from printed sources—statutes, government gazetteers, parliamentary papers and debates, newspapers and periodicals, pamphlets etc—because these are more easily followed up by students. Arrangement is by topic: Vol 1 British background, first settlements, transportation, immigration, land policy, squatters, constitutional history and social and economic conditions; Vol 2 gold, economic, political and social history. Notes on sources and an efficient index confirm their usefulness.

695 'Select documents of English constitutional history 1307-1485' edited by S B Chrimes and A L Brown (Black, 1961) is confined to documents of major historical importance illustrating constitutional developments in the reigns of Edward II and Richard III when fundamental changes were taking place. Editorial matter is kept to an absolute minimum in order to include as many documents as possible but there are brief notes on the sources of the texts and specialised bibliographical references where desirable.

696 'Select documents on British colonial policy 1830-1860' edited by Kenneth Bell and W P Morrell (OUP, 1928) brings together material from many diverse sources—official despatches, private letters, evidence submitted to parliamentary committees, reports of commissioners, proclamations and acts of parliament—classified under six major subject headings: self government, colonialisation, transportation, commercial policy, slavery, and native and frontier policy.

697 'Select documents on the history of India and Pakistan' are published by OUP in four volumes. These extensive collections of documents illustrating the political, military and administrative, social and economic, and constitutional history of the two peoples were compiled by a group of British, Indian, Pakistani, and Sri Lankan historians working under the direction of C H Philips at the School of Oriental and African Studies. Copious use is made of the voluminous state papers of the Indian and home governments and also of the numerous collections of papers in the hands of British families connected with India. Together they provide a valuable *corpus* of source material for the study of the history of the subcontinent. Titles: *Early India; The era of muslim rule; India under the East India Company;* and *The evolution of India and Pakistan 1858-1947.*

698 'Select statutes and other constitutional documents illustrative of the reigns of Elizabeth and James I' edited by G W Prothero, was first published in 1894 and has now gone out of print, but it is included here because so many authoritative texts still refer to it. An introduction surveys the whole period with particular attention to the monarchy; the relationship of church and state; parliament; the council, ministry and starchamber; the army and navy; and the royal prerogative. Then follow the documents classified under appropriate headings: statutes, parliamentary proceedings, unparliamentary taxation, the judicature, the military system, political writings, and ecclesiastical affairs. At the time of publication the work was designed to complement Stubb's *Select charters* and Gardiner's *Constitutional documents of the puritan revolution.*

699 'Select statutes cases and documents' *to illustrate English constitutional history 1660-1832 with additional matter on Irish and Canadian documents (1840-1931)* edited by Sir Charles Grant Robertson has undergone frequent revisions and reprintings since it was first published in 1904. It was designed to complement Stubb's, Prothero's and Gardiner's selections of documents for students of the modern period of constitutional history and is arranged in three sections: Statutes and documents, 'the most

296

important legislative enactments between 1660 and 1832;' Cases in constitutional law each prefaced by a brief introduction explaining its significance; and an appendix consisting of the texts of various articles and impeachments of the lords and commons, together with some important Irish and imperial legislation of the nineteenth and twentieth centuries.

700 'Selected readings on great issues in American history 1620-1968' contains 269 extracts from *The annals of America* (*qv*) divided into nine chronological sections and four sections on foreign policy, urban problems, technology, and the arts, and is designed as a basic text for American studies in history, economics, government, civics, or literature. There are three indexes: author, subject and name.

701 'Selected speeches and documents on British colonial policy 1763-1917' edited by Arthur Berriedale Keith was first published in two volumes in the *Worlds classics* series in 1918 and subsequently reprinted complete in one volume. First the growth of responsible self government in the old 'white' dominions is outlined; secondly, their relations with foreign powers is indicated; and, lastly, there is a section with the Unity of Empire as its theme. This concept has, of course, been overtaken by events but the historical value of the speeches and documents remains. A further selection *Speeches and documents on the British dominions 1918-1931* was published in 1932. The extracts included mark the new stature of the dominions before this was explicitly acknowledged by the statute of Westminster in 1931, being concerned with the Imperial War Cabinet and the peace treaties; the Imperial and Washington Conferences 1921-1930: the establishment of the Irish Free State and the enactment of its constitution; relations between the dominions; the Westminster statute itself, and defence and foreign policies. Both volumes were reprinted with paper covers in the 1960s. In turn they were supplemented by *Imperial constitutional documents 1765-1965* by Frederick Madden (1967).

702 'Shepherd's historical atlas' (9th ed, 1966) is now printed by offset lithography because the original plates were unfortunately destroyed, which means that the clarity of delineation which characterised the earlier editions has been irretrievably lost, some of the finer wording of the maps and legends can in all fairness only be described as indistinct. Nevertheless, the atlas, ranging in time from Ancient Egypt to Europe in the 1960s, otherwise fully lives up to its reputation as being the most complete one-volume historical atlas on the market. A gazetteer index uses simple map references to locate places easily and precisely.

703 **'A short history of Australia'** by Manning Clark (Heinemann, 1964) is based on material collected by the author when researching for his *Selected documents in Australian history* and his more detailed history of Australia now in progress and is probably intended for those readers who might reasonably be of the opinion these latter books tell them more about Australian history than they need to know. It consists of a straightforward chronological narrative concluding with a note on the sources.

704 **'A short history of British colonial policy'** by Hugh Edward Egerton first published in 1897 was last revised by A P Newton in an eleventh edition issued in 1945. This longevity is a sure indication of its reputation as an authoritative account of the commercial factors, philosophies of government, and sense of imperial destiny that influenced British policy from the days of the early attempts at colonization in the sixteenth century onwards. A list of important dates bearing upon colonial policy and an annotated bibliography are included.

705 **'A short history of British expansion'** by James A Williamson was first published by Macmillan in 1922 as one volume but it was rewritten and enlarged into two volumes in 1930 and has seen many revisions and corrections since then. The work summarises not only colonization and the administration of overseas territories but also the impulses which led up to the foundation of empire—trade, economic forces, and the religious and political causes of emigration from Britain. *The old colonial empire* is divided into four parts: Overseas commerce in the middle ages, a period when foreign trade was limited to the seas and shores of Europe; The tudor experiments in oceanic enterprise, commerce, politics and hostilities abroad; The foundation of the mercantile empire, organised colonization in the stuart period; and The zenith and fall of the mercantile empire through overseas wars and the American revolution. *The modern empire and commonwealth* is in two parts: The foundation of the British commonwealth, exploration and the expansion of trade, the founding and development of the old dominions, the extension of British control over India, and the scramble for Africa; and The growth of commonwealth and Empire, the story of the rise and fall of imperialism and the transformation of empire into commonwealth through the vicissitudes of two world wars. Each volume is well furnished with maps and the sections on authorities which end both volumes point the way to detailed further reading. The latest reprintings contain a concluding passage by George Southgate bringing the story down to 1945.

706 'The short Oxford history of the modern world' is a series intended to be of practical value to students and teachers engaged in meeting examination syllabuses and is specifically designed to take account of the most important, recent historical work. The series is tripartite: there are four volumes on European history in which the British Isles are treated as part of the general European society; there are another four volumes confined to English history; and a third, larger group covers African, Asian, and Latin American history. Their essential unity stems from the 'modern world' aspect referred to in the designation which is defined for each volume as the era when the fundamental institutions of modern European society first influenced that particular area. The general editor J M Roberts hopes each volume will be acknowledged as scholarly in its standards and imaginative in its presentation. Titles published so far include *The crisis of parliaments 1509-1660* by Conrad Russell (1971), *Empire to welfare state 1900-1967* by T O Lloyd (1970). They are also available in paper covers.

707 The Society of Archivists was founded as the Society of Local Archivists in 1947 changing its name eight years later. It acts as the professional body for archivists in this country and has played an important part in improving archive services and professional studies in the United Kingdom. *The journal of the Society of Archives* is published twice yearly in April and November.

299

708 'Some contemporary accounts of the great civil war' a bibliographical essay by C V Wedgwood, was included in *The transactions of the Royal Society of Literature* new series XXVI 1953: 73-88. Clarendon's work is singled out but that of Thomas May and Denzil Holles also receives special attention.

709 'Some modern historians of Britain; essays in honour of R L Schuyler' edited by Herman Ausubel, J Bartlet Brebner, and Erling M Hunt, published to mark his election to the presidency of the American Historical Association, presents twenty two studies of historians of Britain, both English and American. *List of essays:* John Lingard, Henry Hallam, Thomas Carlyle, J A Froude, Sir Henry Maine, Goldwin Smith, S R Gardiner, Sir Leslie Stephen, W E H Lecky, Lord Morley, Sir G O Trevelyan, G B Adams, Sir Charles H Firth, C M Andrews, Elie Halevy, Sir William Holdsworth, George Louis Beer, A P Newton, Sir Winston Churchill, R H Tawney, Sir Lewis Namier and Eileen Power.

710 'Some recent writings on twentieth century Britain' by Henry R Brinkler was first published in *Journal of modern history* XXXII, March 1960: 32-47, and subsequently collected in *Changing views on British history* (*qv*). It surveys in magisterial fashion all aspects of contemporary and near contemporary history, noting that the researcher into constitutional and economic questions enjoys ✦the advantage that his basic source material is largely public but for the student of diplomatic and military history the archives are closed. Since this was written, of course, the period embargoed has been relaxed from fifty to thirty years. Generally speaking, however, the historian faces a daunting mountain of books, journals, and official papers. This survey will supply a much needed preliminary guide.

711 'A source book of Canadian history; selected documents and personal papers' (Toronto, Longmans, 1951), addressed to high school and university students, incorporates a selection from various kinds of source material—state papers, letters, diaries, travellers' accounts, legislative debates, proceedings, periodicals, memoirs—which may be difficult to locate or which may not have been published previously. The sources have been chosen with three ends in mind: to convey the complexity of historical sources, to indicate the breadth and drama that characterize the Canadian scene, and to examine a number of problems in considerable detail. They are grouped under ten headings: The discoverers; The French in Canada; The conquest and its problems; British North America to 1849; Problems of union after 1849; Confederation; Transportation and nationalism; Political parties and the party system; and Some recent views of the 'Canadian question'. Incredibly there is no index.

712 'Sources and literature of English history from the earliest times to about 1485' by Charles Gross (2nd ed, 1915) contains a systematic survey of printed materials relating to the political, constitutional, legal, social and economic history of England, Wales and Ireland. The greatest emphasis is placed on sections dealing with primary sources. Coverage of books, pamphlets, collective essays, journals, and society transactions does not pretend to be exhaustive but an effort was genuinely made to include all material likely to be of value to students. Many titles are accompanied by brief notes explaining contents of the book and perhaps also estimating its true worth. Long the only bibliography available it was supplemented by the series *Bibliography of British history* (qv).

713 'Sources in British political history 1900-1951' compiled for the British Library of Political and Economic Science by Chris Cook is a four volume work reporting the results of a survey of twentieth century British political archives planned at a meeting of archivists, historians, and librarians held at Nuffield College, Oxford, in October 1967. Volume 1 *A guide to the archives of selected organisations and societies* (Macmillan Press, 1975) lists the archives of political parties, trade unions, and other organisations involved in politics, arranged alphabetically under the last known name of the organisation. Each entry gives a short summary of the history and aims of the organisation, a survey of its records still extant, and notes on their location and accessibility. When convenient some organisations are grouped together under a single subject heading. Volume 2 *A guide to the private papers of selected public servants* (1975) is concerned with the papers of 1500 senior public servants, diplomats, civil servants, colonial administrators, and senior officers in the armed services.

In this case entries consist of biographical details and a brief description of the extent and nature, and whereabouts of the papers. Volumes 3 and 4 will list the papers of MP's and writers, publicists, religious and trade union leaders whose political influence rested on personal and intellectual abilities rather than by virtue of their office.

714 'Sources of Australian history' selected and edited by M Clark was published as a double volume in the *Worlds classic* series in 1957. The extracts, from formal reports, parliamentary papers, newspapers, poems and ballads, are designed to illustrate the history of European civilisation in Australia up to 1919. Each of the six chronological sections begins with a page or two of explanatory comment. The editor disclaims all pretence to scholarship but students of Australian history will find it of great use.

715 'Sources of English constitutional history; a selection of documents from AD 600 to the present' edited and translated by Carl Stephenson and Frederick George Marcham was originally published by Harpers in three volumes in 1937. It was reissued unabridged in a two volume paperback edition in 1972. Apart from those documents that were absolutely essential, the choice of those to be included rested very largely on experience in the classroom with a pronounced bias in favour of those containing direct information on the organs of government. All documents are arranged in chronological sections with some attempt at a classified sequence. Each section is headed by an introduction designed to act as a brief guide to the principal sources of that period and to the most important historical literature. There are extensive bibliographies which have been updated in the later edition.

716 'The sources of history' studies in the uses of historical evidence, published simultaneously in hardback and paperback by Hodder and Stoughton, consists of a series of books devised to serve as a guide to primary source materials of either a distinct historical period or a significant historical theme. The uses and limitations of such sources are discussed and fruitful directions of further research indicated. Many titles are planned, the general editor is G R Elton, Professor English Constitutional History, Cambridge.

717 **'Sources of information in the social sciences; a guide to the literature'** by Carl M White (American Library Association 2nd ed, 1973) singles out the basic reference and monographic works judged to be the most crucial for understanding the content and organisation of the various disciplines which constitute the social sciences. History, in the opinion of the compiler, is to be regarded as one of these disciplines, and in the arrangement of subjects which follow the general section on social science literature, history is placed first 'because of the role it has played in understanding the human condition.' The history section itself is divided into two main parts: basic works on the discipline, an annotated bibliography designed to introduce the major fields of European and American history in chronological order; and guides to the literature—basic and general guides; reviews of the literature; abstracts and summaries; bibliographies of bibliographies; current and retrospective bibliographies (general and by period and geographical area); biography and genealogy; dissertations; directories and biographical information; dictionaries; encyclopaedias and encyclopaedic sets; handbooks; yearbooks; original sources; atlases, maps, and pictorial works; sources of scholarly contributions; journals; monograph series; organisations; and sources of current information. The work is especially useful for items too specialised to find entry into C M Winchell's *Guide to reference books* or A J Walford's *Guide to reference material.*

718 **'The south in American history'** by Otis A Singletary (AHA Service Center Series no 3) published in 1957 is a concise summary of recent developments in this area of study with the emphasis on literature written since 1945 which either includes new material or makes a significant contribution to existing historical schools of thought. Both text and bibliography are divided into five sections: south history and historiography; the antebellum south; civil war and reconstruction; the new south; and the negro and the south.

719 **Speed, John** (1552-1629), best known as a tudor cartographer, published his most famous collection of maps *Theatre of* *the empire of Great Britaine* in 1611. It was accompanied by *The historie of Great Britaine under the conquests of the Romans, Saxons, Danes and Normans ... With the successions, lives, acts, and issues of the English monarchs from Julius Caesar ... to King James,* the two works being paginated continuously. Comments from contemporary and later writers have varied: some have praised its comprehensive nature, asserting that Speed deserves to be regarded as the first true English historian as opposed to chronicler; others have claimed he perpetuated old blunders; whilst still others have inferred that he lifted material uncritically from earlier authors. Whoever is right, Speed will be chiefly remembered for his maps of the English counties.

720 **'The spirit of English history'** by A L Rowse first published in 1943 when Great Britain was deeply engaged in a world war understandably now reads a shade too self congratulatory but it would be wrong to dismiss the worth of this little book. The author professes to have had two aims in mind: to make the story of the English people intelligible and to include everything that is really essential. Nobody could seriously dispute that he clearly achieves these two aims and the book is still a sound choice for initial reading by the intelligent sixth former or undergraduate before embarking upon a restricted specialised course of study in English history.

721 **'Steinberg's dictionary of British history'** (2nd ed, 1970) is a revised edition of S H Steinberg's *A new dictionary of British history* (1963) which itself replaced *A dictionary of British history* (1937) by J A Brendon. Entries include political, constitutional, administrative, legal, ecclesiastical and economic events but exclude literature, music, the arts and architecture, science and all biographical material. Covers all countries which are or were in the commonwealth for as long as the British connection lasted. Commendable commonsense has been brought to play in the choice of headings which are those that 'come most readily to mind when looking for information even if they are not strictly accurate'. A generous sprinkling of cross references ensures this arrangement succeeds.

722 'The story of New Zealand' by W H Oliver (Faber, 1960) is 'an essay designed to give an overall picture of origins and development' not an attempt at a standard history. Notwithstanding this disclaimer it provides a useful summary of the dominion's history from the impact of the early colonists on the Maoris to the dilemmas of the mid-twentieth century. There is a helpful critical bibliography.

723 **Stow, John** (1525-1605) was an assiduous collector of manuscripts, several early chronicles are known only through his transcripts, and he was the first English historian to make systematic use of the public records. In 1564 'seeing the confused order of our late English chronicles, and the ignorant handling of ancient affairs,' he devoted himself to searching for famous antiquities. A year later he published his *Summarie of Englyshe Chronicles conteyning the true accompt of yeres, wherein every Kyng of this Realme ... began theyr reigne, howe long they reigned: and what notable thynges hath bene doone durynge theyr Reygnes.* He is generally regarded as one of the most accurate of tudor chroniclers and he fully lived up to his own maxim: 'In history the chief thing that is to be desired is truth.' His *Annales of England* (1592) had no pretence to literary style being no more than an exact chronological narrative.

724 'The strange death of liberal England' by George Dangerfield was first published in 1935. Its theme was the growing decay of the liberal society established in England towards the end of the nineteenth century. The author limited himself to the years 1906-1914 and argued that even at the heights of its electoral triumph when a cabinet of all the talents was assembled, it was being undermined by a combination of forces outside its control: the tory rebellion over Ulster, the rise of organised labour and the suffragette movement. After being out of print for many years when those few public libraries still possessing a copy saw it in continuous demand it was reprinted by MacGibbon and Kee in their Fitzroy Editions, 1966.

725 'The stuart constitution 1603-1688; documents and commentary' edited and introduced by J P Kenyon (CUP, 1966) is intended to provide an easily accessible selection of documents for the period. To a certain extent it replaces J R Tanner's *Constitutional documents of the reign of James I* and S R Gardiner's *Constitutional documents of the puritan revolution*. The documents are divided into four sections: The ancient constitution 1603-1640; The era of experiment 1640-1660; The restored constitution; and, Government, which deals with some problems of both central and local government manifest throughout the period. There is a list of books and articles referred to in the author's commentaries which introduce each section.

726 'The Stuarts; a study in English kingship' by J P Kenyon was first published by B T Batsford in 1958 and now forms one of their British Monarchy series. The successive stuart monarchs so occupied the limelight centre stage that the author has little difficulty in narrating the history of the period around them. Suggestions for further reading and a genealogical table are appended.

727 Stubbs, William (1825-1901), a towering figure in English medieval historical studies, was the author of two works which are still regarded as important secondary authorities, besides adding to his reputation with a series of brilliant introductions to the Rolls series (*qv*). The first *Select charters and other illustrations of English constitutional history to the reign of Edward I* (1870), a model for all other similar volumes, began with an introductory outline and then presented the most significant source material for medieval history—laws and charters, treaties, chronicles etc, etc, and is virtually a volume of annotated authorities for his *magnum opus, The constitutional history of England in its origin and development* (OUP, 3 vols, 1874-1878). Containing next to nothing on economic matters, military or diplomatic affairs, this is in essence a legal, administrative and constitutional history of England from the Romans to the conclusion of the fifteenth century civil wars. He alternates chapters of narrative and analysis to present a grand, ambitious investigation into English institutions. Since publication the volume spanning the Anglo-Saxon and Danish period has encountered some criticism but the next, covering the Normans and early Plantagenets, is the recognised starting point for research. In 1863, six years after Lord Romilly, Master of the Rolls, secured a treasury grant for the publication of critical editions of the primary authorities for English history to the end of the middle ages, Stubbs was appointed editor and for the next twenty five years his palaeographical skill and unsurpassed learning heralded a new landmark in historiography in his erudite introductions to nearly twenty volumes in the series. These were collected in *Historical introductions to the Rolls series by William Stubbs* edited by Arthur Hassall (1902). Notwithstanding the change of emphasis in medieval studies this century Stubbs' principal works continue to be universally admired for their exact scholarship and monumental learning although *Studies and notes supplementary to Stubbs' Constitutional history down to the great charter* by Charles Petit-Dutaillis (3 vols, 1908-1929) reproves him for being too engrossed with detailed research to spare time to pause and revise his work. In Dutaillis' view Stubbs was too much under the influence of the liberal German historians of the nineteenth century who discerned the beginnings of human dignity and freedom in primitive medieval institutions. Helen Cam, however, in her article 'Stubbs seventy years after' (*Cambridge historical journal* IX (2) 1948: 129-147) concludes that despite his faults of omission and commission 'a vital and magnificent achievement remains.'

728 'The taste for Tudors since 1940' by Lacey Baldwin Smith first appeared in *Studies in the renaissance* VII September 1960: 167-183 and was afterwards included in *Changing views on British history (qv)*. The historiography of the early Tudors is seen as in a period of reconstruction: the standard interpretations of the 'new monarchy,' the reformation, and the economic problems are in process of being reassessed and only the ever popular field of tudor biography remains constant in approach and method.

729 'Taswell-Langmead's English constitutional history; from the Teutonic conquest to the present time' eleventh edition by Theodore F T Plucknett (Sweet and Maxwell, 1960) has long been regarded as the standard work since it was first published in 1875. It was intended primarily as a textbook for university and Inns of Court students and planned to use general political history as a stepping stone to constitutional history and thereby facilitating the transition from school to university studies. The complete texts of the sources of what written constitution the United Kingdom possesses, Magna carta, the Petition of right, the Bill of rights, and the Act of settlement are presented.

730 'The teach yourself encyclopaedia of dates and events' (1968) is a quick reference book providing a chronological record of man's achievements. Each page is divided into four columns outlining historical events in politics, literature, the arts, and science and technology. The index includes entries on people, places and events.

731 'Teaching history' (1969-   ) is published twice a year by the Historical Association 'in the hope that it may encourage teachers of history to be adventurous in devising new ways of tackling the exciting possibilities of the past'. Contents include notes and articles on individual courses, types of material available, book lists, examination requirements, comment on BBC programmes, book reviews, and reports and news of courses, conferences and meetings.

732 '1066 and all that' *a memorable history of England, comprising all the parts you can remember, including 103 Good Things, 5 Bad Kings and 2 Genuine Dates* by W C Sellar and R J Yeatman (1930) is the textbook to end all textbooks. Whether aged eight or eighty, if you have not yet read this splendid concoction of outrageous puns, ingenious half truths, iniquitous spoofs and compulsive test papers, you must read it at once; if you have, you will not need urging to read it again.

733 'Texts and calendars; an analytical guide to serial publications' by E L C Mullins (Royal Historical Society, 1958) is the first instalment of a new catalogue of the Society's library but as it includes those few printed texts and calendars relating to English and Welsh history issued in general collections or in series by a public body or private society before the end of March 1957 it may validly be considered a bibliography and as such it was published as no 7 in the society's series of guidebooks and handbooks. The contents are arranged under four headings: Official bodies, National societies, English local and Welsh societies, with an addenda section. Analytical notes indicate which documents each published volume contains.

734 Thames and Hudson, the publishing firm which takes its name from the two rivers upon which the cities of London and New York stand is very active in the field of history. The costly *Great civilization* series, *The age of expansion* (Hugh Trevor-Roper); *The age of the renaissance* (Denys Hay); *American civilization* (Daniel Boorstin); *The birth of western civilization: Greece and Rome* (Michael Grant); *The dark ages* (David Talbot Rice); *The dawn of civilization* (Stuart Piggott); *The eighteenth century* (Alfred Cobban); *The flowering of the middle ages* (Joan Evans); *The nineteenth century* (Asa Briggs); and *The twentieth century* (Alan Bullock); combine modern scholarship with extravagant illustration in impressive presentations. There is a 'Library of American studies' dealing with different aspects of the history and culture of the Americas. 'The library of European civilizations' is an illustrated series concentrating on ideas and cultural developments as opposed to political events in European history, and the 'Library of medieval civilization' examines the main themes of medieval history.

735 'These states united; atlas of American history' is in full colour and is published by Longmans for use in schools especially in America's bicentenary year. Maps range from the early voyages to America's expansion and involvement in foreign affairs in the twentieth century.

736 'They were there; a guide to firsthand literature for use in teaching American History' by Richard C Brown (AHA Service Center Series no 45) published in 1962 is written in the conviction that teachers and students of American history should become much more aware of the vast corpus of firsthand literature—letters, diaries, autobiographies, travellers' accounts—now becoming increasingly available. A word of caution is sounded to the effect that although such material can bring history to life it is by no means a total substitute for an objective record of events. Unlike most other pamphlets in this series it does not take the form of a bibliographical essay, it is simply an annotated list arranged in two parts, general collections and individual accounts.

737 'The thirteenth century 1216-1307' by Sir Maurice Powicke (2nd ed, 1962), the fourth volume of the *Oxford history of*

England, takes full advantage of the research devoted to this period published during the last fifty years. Of all the Oxford volumes this is the one that takes least cognizance of the intent to relegate military affairs to the background in favour of social and economic matters. This is not to say these make no appearance at all but internal strife and foreign wars inevitably hold the author's attention. The bibliography is partly designed to act as a commentary on those matters that have either been overlooked entirely or received but a cursory treatment in the text.

738 **'The tides of history'** is the English title of a world history in seven volumes by Jacques Pirenne originally published as *Les grands courants de l'histoire universelle* tracing the actions of great men whose religious, moral, philosophic, or scientific ideals created humanity out of the human masses. Only two volumes have so far been translated: Vol I *From the beginnings to Islam* (1962) and Vol II *From the expansion of islam to the treaties of Westphalia* (1963) and it may well be that we shall not see the remaining volumes in English. The publishers are George Allen and Unwin in the UK, and E P Dutton of New York.

739 **'The timetables of history'** *a chronology of world events from 5000 BC to the present day* (1975) is a translation of Werner Stein's *Kulturfahrplan* first published in 1946. Each double spread in this substantial volume is divided into seven vertical columns: History and politics; Literature, theatre; Religion, philosophy, learning; Visual arts; Music: Science, technology, growth: and Daily life. The reader is thereby at ease to scan across the double page noting the events of any one particular year. Paul Jennings remarked in *The sunday times* that 'if you want to get to the finals of "Mastermind" this is required reading.' He could be right.

740 **Tout, Thomas Frederick** (1855-1929) was the complete academic historian who transformed the history faculty at Manchester after his appointment to the chair of medieval and modern history at the Victoria University in 1890. At first his writing was standard and conscientious rather than inspired, he contributed in the region of 200 articles to the *Dictionary of national biography,* he was active in the compilation of Low and Pulling's *Dictionary of English history,* he put together a school

310

textbook or two, and published a volume in Longman's *Political history of England* which attracted favourable comment not only for his text but for his notes on the original sources. Comparatively late in life, however, his publications took on a more significant aspect: *The place of the reign of Edward II in English history* (1914), an expanded version of the Ford Lectures at Oxford, investigated in detail the machinery of government, the struggle for power between the crown and the baronage, and the development of new institutions and responsibilities out of the king's household. This was a prelude to his *magnum opus, Chapters in the administrative history of medieval England* (6 vols 1920-1933) with special reference to The wardrobe, The chamber, and The small seals, which Tout intended should complement Stubb's work on the medieval origins of parliament. In Tout's view the preoccupation with parliament had overshadowed the importance of the great administrative departments of the king's household. This work of massive learning fully displayed Tout's mastery in handling complex and obscure material. His achievements were felicitously recognised by the publication of *Essays in medieval history presented to Thomas Frederick Tout* edited by A G Little and F M Powicke (1925) presented by his colleagues, pupils, and friends on the occasion of his seventieth birthday to mark his work as teacher, scholar and counsellor whilst professor at Manchester. This includes a list of his published writings.

741 Toynbee, Arnold (1889-1975) bestrides twentieth century historiography like a veritable Colossus. At a time when most contemporary historians were content to publish their modest books at a decent interval he occupied himself over a forty year period with a truly monumental work *A study of history* (3 vols 1934, 3 vols 1939, 4 vols 1954) and for much of that time was simultaneously at work on the annual *Survey of international affairs* published by the Royal Institute of International Affairs of which he was for many years director. For the starting point of his grand design Toynbee was content with nothing short of a study of civilization itself; he in fact distinguished twenty one civilizations in mankind's continuing progress, including seven that were still extant, in which he perceived a regular rhythm of rise and fall, progress and decline, growth and decay. Towards the end he prophesied a new world order based on religion, or rather on a synthesis of all true religions. Naturally enough such a huge conspectus encountered criticism, acrimony even. British historical studies were concentrating more and more on less and less; there was no easy or convenient corner where Toynbee could be lodged. In such an ambitious project there was inevitably much upon which specialists could leap but his breadth of vision and rich insight into mankind's historic dilemmas ensure him of an honoured place in modern scholarship. To his original ten volumes he added an eleventh *Historical atlas and gazetteer* and in 1961 a twelfth *Reconsiderations*, in which he replied to his critics. Although immensely readable in parts *A study of history* is not an easy work to embark upon. D C Somervell edited an abridgement of the first six volumes in 1964 and of the remaining four in 1957; Toynbee himself produced an illustrated abridgement in 1972. A cooperative appraisal *The intent of Toynbee's histories*, edited by E T Gargan was published in 1961.

742 Trevelyan, G M (1876-1962). Fittingly it was this great nephew of Lord Macaulay who rebelled against the narrow scientific view of history prevalent in the nineteenth century. In his celebrated essay *Clio, a muse*, he adumbrated three distinct stages in the process of writing history: the scientific, by which he meant the collecting and sifting of facts; the imaginative or interpretative phase; and the literary function, the practical aspect of the historian's craft. His professional reputation depends largely on *England under Queen Anne*, 3 vols (1930-1934) and his Garibaldi trilogy (1907-1911). To the general history reading public he is best known for his *History of England* (1926) and his *English social history* (1944). Social history he defined as 'the history of a people with the politics left out' and thousands of readers confirmed they relished such histories. Many professional historians, however, refrained from adding their voices from the praise lavished on Trevelyan and regarded his popular works with much reserve.

743 Trevelyan, Sir George Otto (1838-1938) is chiefly remembered as a historian for the biography of his uncle *Life and letters of Lord Macaulay* (2 vols 1876) and more especially for his six volume *The American revolution* (1899-1914), a history in the grand manner written with literary artistry, which made a great impact in the United States because of its open sympathy with the colonists against the mismanagement of Lord North's administration. It was reissued in 1965 in a condensed one volume edition shorn of much of the military detail to be found in the original work but retaining all that Trevelyan wrote on politics, manners, and ideas, considered to be his most enduring contribution, edited by Richard Morris, Professor of History at Colombia University.

744 Trevet, Nicholas (1258-1334): his most noted writings were the *Annales Sex Regum Angliae*, a record of the reigns of Stephen to Edward I. The passages on Henry III and Edward are enriched by anecdotes. The text was included in the English Historical Society publications.

745 'The tudor age' by James A Williamson (3rd ed, 1964), the fourth volume of Longman's *History of England*, avowedly reflects the personal interests of the author who openly confesses his predilection for mercantile and maritime affairs as opposed to the endless religious arguments. He justifies his personal bias by observing that at heart the English people at this time were suffering from a reaction against the excesses of the previous reigns which was to last until the emergence of the Puritans in the next. Nevertheless there is a balanced judgement of the times threaded round the theme of a restoration of order and of a strengthening of the central administration as the opening phase in the growth of modern England.

746 'Tudor and stuart Britain 1471-1714' by Roger Lockyer (Longmans 1964) synthesizes the outstanding work done on this period since the war and attempts to show the directions in which recent interpretation seems to be moving. The bibliography is designed to provide a guide for the reader who wishes to follow up specific topics and consists of the more important books and journal articles published in the previous twenty years.

747 'The tudor constitution; documents and commentary' edited and introduced by G R Elton (CUP, 1962), first intended as a revision of J R Tanner's *Tudor constitutional documents* has in

313

fact replaced it. Generally it follows the pattern of the earlier work, the documents are arranged by topics (the crown, council, the courts, parliament and the church) each introduced by extensive commentaries which the author designed as far as possible to act as bibliographic guides. A full list of books referred to in the commentaries, arranged alphabetically by author appears at the end. Not all the documents in Tanner's work are included here in order to accommodate Elton's own more varied and wider choice of extracts from acts of parliament, cases in the great courts, proceedings of the privy council etc. There is a convenient classified table of documents and a glossary of technical and archaic terms.

748 'Tudor constitutional documents AD 1485-1603' by J R Tanner (CUP, 1922) includes extracts from statutes, court records, and many other different types of documents linked together by a full commentary. The foundations of the tudor monarchy, the successive church settlements, the various administrative courts, parliament, and local government, are all brought into a close historical perspective. It has largely been replaced by G R Elton's *The tudor constitution* (1962).

749 'Tudor dynastic problems 1460-1571' by Mortimer Levine (1973) is included in Allen and Unwin's *Historical problems studies and documents* series, and analyses the constant tudor preoccupation with the succession to the throne. The various pretenders, their influence on events, are closely examined in the introductory chapters which precede the thirty five extracts from crucial documents and records relating to this question ranging from a statute of Edward III's reign of 1351 to the Treason Act of 1571.

750 'Tudor England' by S T Bindoff has achieved minor classic status since it appeared in the *Pelican history of England* in 1950. The author steps with a light but sure step over the well trodden ground, and within the restricted limits of space available in this modest sized volume, manages to squeeze in perceptive and stimulating comments on all aspects of English life and society. An extensive list of suggestions for further reading completes what

314

is essentially a scholarly work intended for the educated general reader.

751 'Tudor England 1485-1603' by Mortimer Levine (CUP, 1968) was compiled for the Conference on British Studies and is designed to provide a convenient guide to works relating to its period for mature scholars and advanced students. Annotation of the briefest kind is reserved for those items whose title is not self explanatory and is intended to reflect the progress of tudor studies in recent years. Entries are arranged in the fashion made familiar by this useful series: divisions for bibliographies, catalogues and general surveys followed by lists under standard topical headings.

752 'The Tudors' by Christopher Morris published by Batsford in their *British monarchy* series in 1955 consists of essays on the personalities of the five tudor monarchs and their impact on English history. A select bibliography offers guidance to the general reader who wishes to continue a course of reading. Authorities are listed by chapter and a genealogical tree of the more prominent persons in the tudor story is also appended.

753 **Turner, Frederick Jackson** (1861-1932) owes his preeminence in American historiography to his hypothesis, first expounded in a paper presented at the American Historical Association's meeting in Chicago 1893, that 'Up to our own day American history has been in a large degree the history of the colonization of the great west. The existence of an area of free land, its continuous recession, and the advance of American settlement westward, explain American development.' At one time his phrase 'the significance of the frontier' threatened to expunge all other hypotheses and interpretations of American history; his premise that the individualism of the pioneers, the men of the frontier, had indelibly stamped their ideals of American political thought had many attractions for his fellow citizens, they were masters of their own destiny. *The rise of the new west 1819-1828* (1906), a volume in the *American nations* series, postulated the theory that these years were of the utmost significance because it was then that Americans finally divorced themselves from the entanglements and traditions of the old world and advanced surely along the western trails towards a rugged and inalienable democracy.

315

754 'Twentieth-century Britain' by Alfred F Havighurst (Harper, 2nd ed, 1966) is a balanced survey intended for the general reader and the student rather than for the scholar and is probably the best overall introduction to the period so far published. The central focus is political although other factors are not ignored as the century unfolds. The select bibliography indicates some of the printed material used by the author in preparing the work and provides a starting point to further enquiry.

755 'The United States since 1945' by Dewey W Grantham (1968) is no 71 of the AHA Service Center Series. In the postwar period the United States, like most other countries, has experienced a traumatic change, 'old distinctions between what is history and what is present and future become increasingly blurred.' The author tackles his formidable task of surveying the general trends of American life and commenting on recent interpretations with remarkable aplomb. An extensive list of references is of particular value to British students and librarians since many of the titles cited were published this side of the Atlantic.

756 'Universal history for our times' by Niels Steensgaard discusses the underlying assumptions of the *History of mankind* published by Unesco and the *New Cambridge modern history*, and the present situation and possibilities for the study of universal history. Source: *Journal of modern history* 45 (3) September 1973: 72-82.

757 University Microfilms, a Xerox company, is active in the American history field. *United States history a catalog of demand reprints*, divided into two sections, general US history and local history, lists upwards of 2900 titles all of which are out of print from the original publishers but which can be obtained on demand either as bound xerographic or as microfilm reprints. An ambitious 1975 project is described in a catalogue/brochure, *Western Americana*, the title of a collection of 1000 books and government documents of the eighteenth, nineteenth and early twentieth centuries, including much primary source material, arranged under twenty two subject headings. *The march of America* series is described under a separate heading (*vide supra*). UK and other non American enquiries should be addressed to St

John's Road, Tylers Green, High Wycombe, Bucks. All continental American enquiries to Xerox University Microfilm, Books and Collections Customer Services, 300 North Zeeb Road, Ann Arbor, Michigan 48106.

758 'University of London intermediate source books of history' published by Longmans Green from 1918 onwards were early in the field of supplying printed original source texts which has been a prominent feature of the publishing of history since the second world war. Introduced by A F Pollard they were specifically designed to offset the difficulties experienced by students sitting the intermediate course and examination in history in the University of London but their practical use far outdistanced this narrow objective. A library of original materials for English history from the Roman occupation to the outbreak of the first world war in 1914 was of obvious value to countless others and it is surprising that the series has been allowed to slip out of print. The pattern of arrangement was standard: a note on original authorities or sources and then a series of extracts classified under appropriate headings in each volume. Titles: *England before the Norman conquest* by R W Chambers (with a foreword on Roman Britain by M Cary); *England under Henry III 1216-1272* by Margaret Hennings; *Illustrations of Chaucer's England* by Dorothy Hughes; *England under the lancastrians 1399-1460* by Jesse Flemming; *England under the yorkists 1460-1485* by Isobel Thornley; *England under the early tudors 1485-1529* by C H Williams; *England under the restoration* by Thora Stone.

759 'The University of Michigan history of the modern world' edited by Allan Nevins and Howard M Ehrmann consists of fifteen volumes designed to provide undergraduates and purposeful general readers with a historical background to modern world events. Titles: *The United States to 1865* by Michael Kraus; *The United States since 1865* by Foster Rhea Dulles; *Canada* by John B Brebner; *Latin America* by J Fred Rippy; *Great Britain to 1688* by Maurice Ashley (1961); *Great Britain since 1688* by K B Smellie (1962); *France* by Albert Guerard; *Germany* by Marshall Dill; *Italy* by Dennis Mack Smith; *Russia and the Soviet Union* by Warren B Walsh; *The near east* by Nathaniel Peffer; *The Southwest Pacific* by C Hartley Grattan; *Africa* by Ronald Robinson. Most titles were published in revised and enlarged editions 1968-1972.

760 'The use of history' by A L Rowse, first published in 1946 and heavily revised in 1962, is the introductory or 'key' volume to what was formerly the *Teach yourself histories* and what is now known as the *Men and their times* series (*qv*) of which the author is general editor. 'The whole intention of this book is practical and didactic. It is designed as a statement of the case for the study of history, a discussion of its uses and pleasures, and as a manual of instruction on how to approach the subject.' It would be difficult to conceive of a better introduction for the serious general reader, or for the university student for that matter. Dr Rowse succeeds both in conveying his own illimitable enjoyment of history and in avoiding the condescension that sometimes mars the popular writings of academic historians.

761 'The use of medieval chronicles' by John Taylor (1966), published by the Historical Association in their *Helps for students* series is in fact indispensable for all students embarking upon courses in medieval history. In the form of a continuous essay it discusses some of the principal documents, where they were written, what type of history they represent, their value to present-day historians; problems of dating, authenticity, provenance, the censoring by copyists, and modern editing. Two appendices, 'Standards of editing in the chronicles' and a short bibliography of printed texts complete a truly valuable introductory guide.

762 Vergil, Polydore, an Italian humanist and naturalised Englishman, was commanded in 1508 by Henry VII to write a history of England. The consequent *Anglica Historica*, first published in 1534 relating events down to 1509, and extended in a third edition to 1555, contains little that cannot be found elsewhere but is nevertheless of value for the reigns of Henry VII and Henry VIII not least for its influence on later historians like Edward Hall and Holinshed. Its prime importance in historiography is that it marks the end of the medieval stage of the chronicles. Vergil used virtually the same methods as modern historians, using his sources, weaving them into a readable and consecutive narrative. Although originally published in Latin its

318

speedy translation into English indicates the rising importance of the vernacular even in works of scholarship.

763 'The Victoria history of the counties of England' founded in 1899, aims to narrate the history of the English counties in a uniform and systematic way. From the start it was a cooperative effort in which historians of repute and authority were assigned tasks by a general editor. Each set of county volumes consists of 'general' and 'topographical' volumes: general volumes include those subjects it was deemed advisable to treat on a county wide basis, prehistory, ecclesiastical and economic history, and a translation of the appropriate sections from the Domesday book. The topographical volumes describe individually each city, town, and village within the county. At first it was thought that the *History* would be completed in 160 volumes within six years but if this was seriously considered possible disillusions must have been mercifully swift. The project encountered and survived many buffetings of fate and has been administered by the Institute of Historical Research since 1933. A history of the tortuous beginnings and the subsequent complexities is outlined in the *General introduction* volume edited by R B Pugh published in 1970 to mark the 150th volume published. This also contains a Bibliographical excursus; a list of all the volumes that appeared before the end of 1970 together with the names of their editors, year of publication; and lists of the contents of each volume augmented with indexes of authors and titles of articles. Many previously out of print volumes are available in photographic facsimile editions from William Dawson's. It is difficult to overestimate the part played by the *VCH*, as it is usually called, in the expansion of local studies which has occurred in recent years. Admittedly some of the earlier volumes may appear a little antiquated in content and method but its value to the professional historian and to lecturers engaged in adult education courses in local history, and the promotion of local studies in general, cannot seriously be doubted.

764 Victorian (modern history) Book Club is one of the book clubs grouped together round Readers Union now owned by David and Charles of Newton Abbot. 'The club publishes a most exciting range of vivid and lively books on every aspect of this dramatic era.'

765 'Victorian England 1837-1901' by Josef L Altholz (CUP, 1970) is one of the Conference on British Studies Bibliographical Handbooks designed to serve as a basic, convenient guide to materials on the period for advanced students and professional scholars. Confined to a size inviting frequent consultation it does not pretend to be exhaustive but it includes the most important books and articles, each with a brief annotation, arranged in the customary manner of the series, first under bibliographies, catalogues and handbooks and then under subject headings. The compiler emphasises the trend in historical studies away from religious and constitutional history towards social and economic aspects.

766 'The vision of history in early Britain' *from Gildas to Geoffrey of Monmouth* by Robert W Hanning (Colombia University Press, 1966) seeks to explore four prominent early medieval histories, Gildas' *De excidio et conquestu Britanniae*, Bede's *Historia ecclesiastica*, Nennius' *Historia Brittonum*, and Geoffrey of Monmouth's *Historia regum Britanniae*, all of which record the successful Anglo-Saxon invasions of the fifth and sixth centuries, in order to formulate a tentative analysis of the historical vision as it appeared to these native historians.

767 Walsingham, Thomas, the last of the St Alban's school of chroniclers, is noted in particular for his *Historia Anglicana* recording the years 1272-1422 which in its earlier portions is of no especial merit being a regurgitation of older writers. But for the period 1377-1422 (the reigns of Richard II, Henry IV and Henry V) it includes material not found elsewhere and is of great value for its account of the French wars. The text was edited for the *Rolls series* by H T Riley who included it in *Chronica Monasterii S Albani* in 1863.

768 'Websters guide to American history' a *chronological, geographical and biographical survey and compendium* (Springfield, Mass, Meriam, 1971). Of the three parts the first two are markedly superior to the third. The chronology is printed in parallel columns, on the left events are described year by year, and on the right quotations from appropriate primary documents exhibit a spark of imagination. The maps approach excellence, colour is used discreetly and some old maps are reproduced. Some rather pedestrian biographies of 1035 notable Americans complete a useful one volume reference work designed to make information on America's past readily available whenever required.

769 Wedgwood, C V (1910-   ) has written widely on seventeenth century English and European history. Her first book *Strafford* (1935), a surprisingly mature work of political biography outlining the influence he exercised on events in the last twelve years of his life was replaced in 1961 by *Thomas Wentworth first Earl of Strafford: a revaluation*, a dramatic reappraisal in the light of recent research and made possible by important new material in the form of the Strafford papers deposited in Sheffield City Libraries. Miss Wedgwood's major work, however, is *The great rebellion* of which so far only two volumes have been published, *The king's peace 1637-1641* (1955) and *The king's war 1641-1647* (1958), well written narratives based on an extensive knowledge of the sources. A fortuitous offspring of her research, *The trial of Charles I* (1964), retitled as *A coffin for King Charles* in the United States, is not part of the larger work.

770 Wells, H G (1866-1946) ventured temerariously into the field of history because of his conviction that the people of the world were conditioned by nationalist histories into a blind patriotism which he judged to be the foremost cause of the first world war. At first he proposed in a pamphlet *History is one* (1919), that a research committee should organize the writing and publishing of a general history of mankind whose theme would be how necessary it was if civilization was to continue that some form of world federation must come into being. It was soon clear that conventional authoritative historians were incapable of writing a broad but compact historical synthesis of the sort he had in mind and after much heart searching he decided to embark on the project himself. Working from the *Encyclopaedia Britannica* he planned his history to be a story of developing communication and increasing interdependence. His preliminary typescript was submitted to Gilbert Murray, Ernest Barker and Philip Guedalla

321

for their comments. First published in weekly parts the *Outline of history*, subtitled 'A plain history of life and mankind', appeared in 1920 and, much to his astonishment, its bold imaginative generalisations immediately earned him a huge runaway popular success. Even academic opinion admitted that despite some sweeping conclusions that were open to challenge he had produced an enduring work. A more generalized account, *A short history of the world*, intended for the busy general reader followed two years later.

771 Wharton, Henry (1664-1695) was the author of *Anglia Sacra* (2 vols, 1691) designed primarily as a reliable edition of ancient ecclesiastical histories, and as a corollary, a history of the sees of England together with the lives of their bishops. In the pursuit of the first of these aims Wharton provided what is in effect a union catalogue of English chronicles, an indication of their provenance, scope, and present whereabouts, so that for the first time a comparative study became possible.

772 'What is history?' by E H Carr (Macmillan, 1961) is the text of the G M Trevelyan lectures in the University of Cambridge January-March 1961. The author's own short answer is: 'it is a continuous process of interaction between the historian and his facts, an unending dialogue between the present and the past.' But it would be unwise for the serious student of history to leave it at that. Mr Carr's lectures on Society and the individual, History science and morality, Causation in history, History as progress, and The widening horizon are required reading. It is available as a Penguin paperback.

773 'The whig supremacy 1714-1760' by Basil Williams was first published in 1939 as one of the fifteen volumes of the *Oxford history of England*; a second edition revised by C H Stuart appeared in 1962. In the meantime, much scholarship and research was concentrated on the period as a result of Namier's pioneering work on the nature and structure of English politics in the eighteenth century. This research inevitably brought about a considerable change of emphasis especially on the composition of parties and parliament. Mr Stuart succeeded in incorporating its findings into the text and a corresponding addition to the bibliography ensures that students of the period are not misled.

774 **'Who killed the British empire?'** *an inquest* by George Woodcock (Cape, 1974) traces the decline and fall of the last of the European empires to 1930, the year when Gandhi was invited to the Viceregal residence for informal talks, when Weihaiwei was handed back to China in response to pressure from Japan and the United States, and when a conference of British and dominion representatives drafted a series of resolutions that were embodied a year later in the statute of Westminster. The book is divided into four parts: the first delineates the Empire at its furthermost territorial limits; then comes the story of the demand for and the achievement of self government in the 'old' dominions; the granting of independence to India and Pakistan takes up the third part; and lastly the final retreats are accounted for.

775 **'Who's who in history'** (Oxford, Blackwell's, 6 vols, 1960-   ) confesses it adds little to the sum total of organised historical knowledge but claims that each volume is a portrait of the age which will instruct, entertain, and satisfy the needs of those who are compelled to read history and those who read history for choice. Entries of generous size are arranged chronologically by date of subject's death and are sometimes grouped in the later volumes by subject, thus necessitating rigorously prepared indexes. Volumes: 1 *British Isles 55 BC-1485* (1960); 2 *England 1485-1603* (1964); 3 *England 1603-1714* (1965); 4 *England 1714-1789* (1969); 5 *England 1789-1837* (1974). A sixth volume is in preparation.

776 **William of Malmesbury** (1090/96-1143?) was the first writer of English history since Bede to whom we might safely accord the term 'professional historian'; he was the author of a number of historical works and he was moreover deeply interested in the art of writing history. He also anticipated the tudor antiquarians in recognising the value of topography and ancient monuments as witnesses of the historical record. He acknowledged Bede as his master and regarded himself as trying to emulate Bede's style, not satisfied with a mere chronicle, preferring a consciously well written, philosophic account of the most significant events. His political histories *Gesta Regum Anglorum* (*Deeds of the English* *kings*) which come to an end in the year 1120, a very popular work if we judge by the number of surviving manuscripts, and *Historica novella* (*Recent history*) which continues his narrative down to 1142, testify that he could switch successfully from a literary and well constructed historical account to the more pressing and urgent style of contemporary history without losing his detachment and objectivity. He is also renowned for his ecclesiastical histories: *Gesta Pontificum Anglorum* (*Deeds of the English bishops*), a commemoration of the Anglo-Saxon saints, and *De Antiquitate Glastoniensis Ecclesiae*, a treatise attempting to support the claims of Glastonbury Abbey to be of very ancient (British) foundation. William's methods of compiling his histories, collating texts, assiduously researching in monastic archives, the interviewing of eye-witnesses, the conscientious attempts to distinguish between fact and hearsay, preserving his detachment and regard for historical truth (except where the records of Malmesbury and Glastonbury Abbeys are concerned) earn him the well-deserved respect of later historians. The full text in Latin and English edited by K R Potter is available in the *Oxford medieval texts* series.

777 William of Newburgh (1135-1198?) bears a startling resemblance to a modern historian. His *Historia Rerum Anglicarum* (History of English affairs) starts with the conquest but the first three reigns are treated summarily and it is really his story of the latter half of the twelfth century that displays to a remarkable extent his desire not only to record events but to draw conclusions and to offer critical assessments of men and their measures. His shrewd historical acumen is best evidenced by his swift conclusion, based on internal evidence, that Geoffrey of Monmouth's account of King Arthur was pure fiction.

778 William of Poitiers was a chaplain to William I and Archdeacon of Lisieux whose biography of the King *Gesta Willelmi Ducis Normannorum et Regis Anglorum* (*Deeds of William, Duke of the Normans and King of the English*) provides much first hand information of the Norman conquest. As a member of court he had access to official documents but unfortunately his considerable talents as a historian were blemished by his self acknowledged omissions and his distortions of incon-

324

venient facts in the interests of the greater glory of the king and, more specifically, to authenticate his legitimate claim to the English throne. To this extent his account must be considered unreliable and his opinions viewed with suspicion although in many non-controversial areas his obvious knowledge shines through.

779 **'William the Conqueror; the Norman impact upon England'** (Eyre and Spottiswode, 1964) by David C Douglas is the first of the *English monarchs* series of which the author is general editor. Professor Douglas' main object is to show how an obscure province of Gaul was able to overthrow an ancient kingdom largely through the energy of one man, whilst his aim is to reconcile English and French scholarship, old and new, and to rescue William from the prejudices of successive historians from the sixteenth to the nineteenth century. In the belief that this can only be achieved by a close scrutiny of contemporary records he painstakingly cites his sources in full both in his footnotes and in his select bibliography which includes chronicles and narratives, documents, and records.

780 **Williamson, J A** (1886-1964). *The ocean in English history*, the title he gave his Ford Lectures, delivered in the summer of 1940 and published the following year, represents Williamson's lifelong interest in the history of British expansion overseas. The index should be consulted for titles described in detail.

781 **'A world history'** by William H McNeill (OUP, 1967) is divided into three parts: I Emergence and definition of the major Eurasian civilizations to 500 BC; II Equilibrium among the civilizations 500 BC-AD 1500; III The dominance of the west. An immensely valuable bibliographical essay follows each part. Described as a personal vision of the whole history of mankind, Professor McNeill achieves a solid coherence by relating his vision to the concept of cultural interaction of contiguous civilizations and thus constructs a true historical perspective in the place of a mere synthesis of compartmentalized national or area chronological histories.

782 'The world's history; a survey of man's record' edited by H F Helmolt with an introductory essay by James Bryce is an English adaptation published 1901-1907 of an original German text offering a comprehensive account of all mankind, the peoples who have played little part in history as well as those nations commonly regarded as the most important. It is a large scale cooperative history in eight volumes which seeks to obtain the best of both worlds by approaching its huge task from two directions, the strictly geographical and a consideration of the economic forces which have exerted powerful influences on groups and communities. Today it is almost forgotten but it serves to remind us of the rather solemn German historians of the turn of the century. Volumes: *Prehistory-America and the Pacific Ocean; Oceania, Eastern Asia and the Indian Ocean; Western Asia Africa; The Mediterranean nations; South Eastern and Eastern Europe; Central and Northern Europe; Western Europe to 1800;* and *Western Europe The Atlantic Ocean.*

783 'Writings on American history' a bibliography of books and articles on United States history (1902-   ) is an annual publication which has experienced many vicissitudes. For many years it was issued as part of the *Annual report* of the American Historical Association. Over the years there have also been changes in its scope, at various times items on Canadian and Latin American history have been included. Entries are arranged in a classified sequence with an author, title, subject index. For libraries deciding to acquire back runs the best method now would appear to subscribe to the joint publishing programme of the American Historical Association and the Kraus-Thomson Organisation. At the moment this comprises a reprint of *Writings on American history 1902-1948*, including a general index 1902-1940, but excluding 1904/1905 and 1941-1947 which were never published; *Writings on American history 1962-1973: A subject bibliography of articles* in four volumes based on the 'Recently published articles' features of the *American historical review*; and a new series of annual volumes 1973-1974 onwards also based on the material listed in the *AHR* using a new system of sixty chronological, geographical, and subject headings devised to classify entries from about 350 scholarly journals. The original *Writings* series will cease publication with the 1961 volume. It is a matter of some rejoicing that the lengthy gap between the year covered and date of publication has been bridged with the appearance of the 1962-1973 cumulative volumes.

784 'Writings on Australian history 1968-72' is a critical survey by D H Simpson of a productive period in Australian historical writing especially by Australian academics. It is arranged under broad subject headings: General history, Discovery and exploration, Special periods of history, Government and politics, Economics and communications, Social history, Religion and education, and Literature and art. Including one or two books outside the specified time limits and new editions of earlier works, it was published in *British book news* February 1973: 75-78.

785 'Writings on British history' *a bibliography of books and articles on the history of Great Britain from about 400 AD to 1914 ... with an appendix containing a select list of publications ... on British history since 1914*, compiled for the Royal Historical Society, and planned as an exhaustive record of the annual output of writings on British history in all languages, no matter where published, began publication in 1937 with the 1934 volume. Since then the project has been carried forward to 1951 and backwards to 1901 with the Institute of Historical Research assuming responsibility in 1965. Each volume is arranged in two parts: General works which contains the auxiliary sciences, bibliography, historiography, British history in general, and English local history listed alphabetically by county; and Period histories subdivided into the six conventional chronological periods: Preconquest, medieval, tudor, stuart, eighteenth, and nineteenth centuries. There are 4000-5000 entries to each volume, those recording books include notes indicating reviews in a dozen specified leading periodicals. Volumes: *1901-1933, Auxiliary sciences and general works, The middle ages 450-1485, The tudor and stuart periods 1485-1714, The eighteenth century 1714-1815* (2 parts) and *1815-1914 and appendix* (2 parts); *1934-1939* in annual volumes; *1940-1945* in 2 volumes; *1946-1948* (1973); *1949-1951* (1975) and *1952-1954* (1975), the last two differ in that the main sections now cover to 1939 and the appendix continues from that date. A eulogistic notice of the work plus a review of the arguments for and against exhaustive or selective bibliographies appears in 'Notes and news', *History* XLI Feb-Oct 1956: 361-363.

786 'Writings on Oliver Cromwell since 1929' by Paul H Hardacre first saw the light of day in the pages of the *Journal of modern history* XXXIII March 1961: 1-14 and was later included in *Changing views on British history*. It contains a description of the major narrative histories of the times, a topical treatment of the protectorate, the bibliography of Cromwell's career is examined stage by stage, and there is a concluding section on recent biographical studies.

787 Wykes, Thomas (1222-?) a canon of Osney Abbey whose chronicle from the conquest down to 1289 is of unique interest because of its royalist bias in its description of the wars of the barons.

Index

References are to entry numbers

Abbreviationes Chronicorum Ralph de Diceto 639

About Trevelyan 584

Abraham Lincoln Herbert Agar 536

Abraham Lincoln and the union Nathaniel Stevenson 167

Abrams, Richard: *Issues of the populist and progressive eras* 229

Accessions to repositories 566

An account of the most important public records of Great Britain C P Cooper 652

Adams, James Truslow: *Album of American history* 20; *Atlas of American history* 59; *Provincial society 1690-1763* 444

'Administrative history' F M Powicke 433

Adventures of Oregon Constance Lindsay Skinner 167

African travels and narratives series 160

Agar, Herbert: *Abraham Lincoln* 536

Age of absolutism Maurice Ashley 465

Age of big business Burton J Hendrick 167

Age of chivalry Sir Arthur Bryant 127

The age of Drake J A Williamson 11

Age of elegance Sir Arthur Bryant 127

Age of expansion Marcus Cuncliffe 465

Age of improvement Asa Briggs 14

Age of invention Holland Thompson 167

Age of Jackson Robert Remini 229

Age of revolution John Roberts 465

Agrarian crusade Solon Buck 167

Aids for teachers (Historical Association) 413

Alden, John Richard: *American revolution* 570

Alexander, Gerard: *Guide to atlases* 364

Alexandri Neckam de naturis rerum 671

Altholz, Josef F: *Victorian England* 765

Altschul, Michael: *Anglo-Norman England* 43

America in mid-passage C A Beard 72

'American character' H S Commager 433

American Historical Association newsletter 29

American revolution John Richard Alden 570

American revolution Richard B Morris 229

The American revolution Sir Otto Trevelyan 743

American spirit in education Edwin Slosson 167

American spirit in literature Bliss Perry 167

America's rise to world power Foster Rhea Dulles 507

Ancient Britain map 586

The Ancient world Luigi Pareti 458

Andrews, C M: *Colonial folkways* 167; *Colonial period of American history* 177; *Fathers of New England* 167

Anglia Sacra Henry Wharton 771

Anglica Historica Polydore Vergil 762

Annales Cambriae 671

Annales Canadiennes d'histoire 154

Annales monastici 671

Annales of England John Stow 723

Annales rerum Anglicarum et Hibernicarum regnante Elizabetha William Camden 100

Annales sex regum Angliae Nicholas Trevet 295 744

Anti-slavery crusade Jesse Macy 167

'Antiquarian thought in the sixteenth and seventeenth centuries' Stuart Piggott 294

Appreciations in history (Historical Association) 413

Arberry, A J: *The library of the India Office* 483

Archaeological and historical maps 586

Armies of labor Samuel P Orth 167

Ashantee and the Gold Coast John Beecham 176

Ashley, Maurice: *Age of absolutism* 465; *Churchill as historian* 171; *England in the seventeenth century* 273; *Great Britain to 1688* 759; 'King James and the revolution of 1688' 510; *King John* 511

Aspinall, A and E A Smith: eds *English historical documents 1783-1832* 290

Atlantic provinces W S MacNutt 151

Austrialia del Espiritu Sancto 379

Awakening of American nationalism George Dangerfield 507

Aylmer, G E: *Interregnum* 492

Bacon, Roger: *Opera* 671

Bagley, J J: *Documentary history of England* 228; *Historical interpretations* 420

Barlow, Frank: *Edward the Confessor* 245; *Feudal kingdom of England* 324

Barlow, Roger: *A briefe summe of geographie* 379

Barnes, Harry Elmer: *History of historical writing* 455

Barraclough, Geoffrey: *An introduction to contemporary history* 494; 'Larger view of history' 433

Barrow, G W B: editor Documents of medieval history 233; *Feudal Britain* 322

Barzun, Jacques and Henry F Graff: *The modern researcher* 558

Bases of plantation society Aubrey Land 229

Basic problems of writing history Arthur Marwick 584

Baxter, Stephen: *Recent writings on William III* 651

Beaglehole, J C: *Discovery of New Zealand* 224; *Exploration of the Pacific* 312; *Life of Captain James Cook* 379

Beales, Derek: *From Castlereagh to Gladstone* 340

The Beards basic history of the United States 72

The Beards new basic history of the United States 72

Becker, Carl: *Eve of the revolution* 167

Beecham, John: *Ashantee and the Gold Coast* 176

Beginnings of new France Marcel Trudel 151

Bekynton, Thomas: *Memorials of the reign of Henry VI* 671

Bell, H E: *Maitland* 533

Bell, Kenneth and W P Morrell: *Select documents on British colonial policy 1830-1860* 696

Bellot, H H: *American history and historians* 34

Beloff, Max: *Britain's liberal empire* 481; *Debate on the American revolution* 123; *Imperial sunset* 481

Bennett, C V: *White Kennett* 183

Bennett, George: *Concept of empire: Burke to Attlee* 184

Benzoni, Girolamo: *History of the new world* 379

Berwick, Keith: *Federal age 1789-1829* 319

Bettey, J H: *English historical documents 1906-1939* 291

A bibliographical guide to colonialism in sub-Saharan Africa 178

A bibliographical guide to the history of the British Empire 1748-1776 Lawrence Henry Gipson 110

Bibliographie internationale des travaux historiques publiés dans les volumes de Mélanges 321

Bibliography of Canadiana F M Stanton and Marie Tremaine 155

Billington, Ray Allen: *Far western frontier* 570; *Historian's contribution to Anglo-American misunderstanding* 408

Bindoff, S T: *Tudor England* 750

A biography catalogue of the library of the Royal Commonwealth Society Donald H Simpson 681

Birley, Robert: *Speeches and documents in American history* 232

Black, Eugene C: *British politics in the nineteenth century* 124

Black, J B: *The reign of Elizabeth* 656; *The art of history* 56

330

Black book of the admiralty 671

Blain, Jean: New France 1702-1743 151

Blair, Peter Hunter: Introduction to Anglo-Saxon England 493; Roman Britain and early England 674

Blake, Robert: editor Paladin history of England 602

Blows, R P: History at the universities and the polytechnics 440

Bodleian map of Great Britain 586

Boehm, H: Historical periodicals an annotated world list 424

Bolton, Herbert: Spanish border lands 167

Bombay in the days of Queen Anne 379

Bond, Maurice: Guide to the records of parliament 375

Bonser, Wilfrid: An Anglo-Saxon and Celtic bibliography 45; A Romano-British bibliography 677

The book of Francisco Rodrigues 379

Book of the knowledge of all the kingdoms ... 379

The bookman's manual Bessie Graham 642

Boorstin, Daniel J: American civilisation 24; An American primer 39

Boose, J B: Catalogue of the library of the Royal Colonial Institute 681; First supplementary catalogue of the library of the Royal Colonial Institute 681

Boss and the machine Samuel P Orth 167

Bowle, John: Concise encyclopaedia of world history 185; English experience 288; Imperial achievement 479

Brebner, J B: Canada 759; The explorers of North America 313

Brendon, J A: A dictionary of British history 216 721

Brewer, J S and J Gairdner and R H Brodie: Calendar of letters and papers, foreign and domestic, Henry VIII 134

A briefe summe of geographie Roger Barlow 379

Briggs, Asa: Age of improvement 14; Nineteenth century 578; Annual register 1758-1958 52

Brinkler, Henry R: Some recent writings on twentieth-century Britain 710

Britain and Europe: Pitt to Churchill James Joll 123

Britain in the dark ages map 586

Britain's liberal empire Max Beloff 481

Britannica Romana John Horsley 473

British constitutional history since 1932 R L Schuyler and C C Weston 54

British India Michael Edwardes 247

British politics and the American revolution Bernard Donoughue 266

Brogan, D W: Era of Franklin D Roosevelt 167

Brooke, Christopher: From Alfred to Henry III 339; The Saxon and Norman Kings 120 685

Brooke, John: The Chatham administration 266

Brown, R Craig and G R Cook: Canada 1891-1921 151

Brown, Richard C: They were there 736

Browning, Andrew: ed English historical documents 1660-1714 290

Brut y Tywysogion 671

Buchanan, A Russell: United States and world war two 570

Buck, Solon: Agrarian crusade 167

Buik of the chroniclis of Scotland 671

Bulletin of the International Committee for Historical Sciences 488

Bullock, Alan and Maurice Shock: Liberal tradition 123

Bullough, Geoffrey: Narrative and dramatic sources of Shakespeare 471

Bultmann, William A: Early hanoverian England 240

Burchell, R A: Westward expansion 1763-1890 31

Burke, Robert E: Domestic issues since 1945 229

Burns, Sir Alan: History of the British West Indies 463

Burpee, L J: Historical atlas of Canada 415

Burroughs, Peter: 'John Robert Seeley' 685

Burton, Hester: 'The writing of historical novels' 423

Butler, Sir James: History of England 454

Butterfield, Herbert: 'The teach yourself history library' 547

Cabot voyages and Bristol discovery under Henry VII 379

Calcott, Maria: *Little Arthur's history of England* 526

Cam, Helen: *England before Elizabeth* 263; *Historical novels* 423; *Selected historical essays of F W Maitland* 533; 'Stubbs seventy years after' 727

Camden, William: *Annales rerum Anglicarum et Hibernicarum regnante Elizabetha* 100; *Britannia* 100

Cambridge Historical Journal 421

Campbell, A E: *USA in world affairs* 31

Canada John B Brebner 759

Canada 1891-1921 R Craig Brown and G R Cook 151

Canada 1874-1896 P B Waite 151

Canada 1939-1967 D G Creighton 151

Canada 1922-1939 Roger Graham 151

Canada under Louis XIV W J Eccles 151

The Canadian dominion Oscar D Skelton 167

Canadian Historical Association booklets 152

The Canarian 379

Cappon, Lester J: 'Antecedents of the Rolls Series' 53

Captain Philip Carteret's voyage round the world 379

Captains of the civil war William Wood 167

Careless, J M S: *Canada* 150; *Union of the Canadas* 151

Carmen de Hastingae Proelio 598

Caron, P and Jaryc: *World list of historical periodicals* 424

Carr, E H: *What is history* 772

Carter, Harvey L: *The far west in American history* 317

Catalogue of the library of the Royal Colonial Institute J B Boose 681

Cattell, Jacques: *Directory of American scholars: history* 225

Cecil Rhodes and Rhodes House 666

Challenge of socialism Henry Pelling 123

Chambers, R W: *England before the Norman conquest* 758; *Thomas More* 74

Champlain, Samuel: *Narrative of a voyage to the West Indies and Mexico* 379

Champlain, Samuel: *Works* 164

Channing, Edward: *History of the United States* 464

Chapters in the administrative history of medieval England T F Tout 740

Charles I David Watson 511

Charles II Christopher Falkus 511

Charlton, Kenneth: *Recent historical fiction for secondary school children* 423

Charters and documents illustrating the history of the cathedral and city of Sarum 671

Chartulary of the Abbey of Ramsey 671

Chatham J H Plumb 536

The Chatham administration John Brooke 266

Cheney, C R: *Handbook of dates for students of English history* 387

Children and literature Virginia Haviland 423

Chrimes, S B: *English constitutional history* 286; *Henry VII* 399; *Introduction to the administrative history of medieval England* 495

Chrimes, S B and A L Brown: *Select documents of English constitutional history* 695

Chrimes, S B and I A Roots: *English constitutional history* 287

Christie, I R: *British history since 1760* 119; *Crisis of empire* 202; *The end of North's ministry* 266

Chronica Gervase of Canterbury 346

Chronica Roger of Howden 671

Chronica Roger of Wendover 295 671

Chronica Buriensis 598

Chronica Jocelini de Brakelonda 598

Chronica Johannis de Oxonedes 671

Chronica Majora Matthew of Paris 544 671

Chronica monasterii de Melsa 671

Chronica monasterii S Albani 671

Chronicle Adam Murimuth 295 671

Chronicle Henry Knighton 671

Chronicle Robert of Torigni 669

Chronicle at large Richard Grafton 352

Chronicle of England John Capgrave 156 671

Chronicle of Fredager 598

Chronicle of Pierre de Langtoft 671

Chronicle of Robert of Brunne 671
Chronicle of the reigns of Edward I and Edward II 671
Chronicles Jean Froissart 338
Chronicles and memorials of the reign of Richard I 671
Chronicles of Aethelward 598
Chronicles of the reigns of Stephen, Henry II and Richard I 671
Chronicon Adam of Usk 2
Chronicon Abbatiae Eveshamensis 671
Chronicon Angliae 1328-1388 671
Chronicon ex chronicis Florence of Worcester 295
Chronicon monasterii de Abingdon 671
Chronicon regum Angliae Thomas Otterbourne 590
Chronicque de la traison et mort de Richart Deux 295
Chronicum Anglicanum Ralph of Coggeshall 640 671
Chronology of the expanding world Neville Williams 170
Chronology of the medieval world R L Storey 170
Churchill as historian Maurice Ashley 171
The civil war James Shenton 229
Clark, C M H: 'Hancock's Australia and Australian historiography' 384; History of Australia 446; Select documents in Australian history 694; Short history of Australia 703; Sources of Australian history 714
Clark, G Kitson: The critical historian 205; Guide for research students working on historical subjects 362; Making of victorian England 331 539
Clark, G Kitson and G R Elton: Guide to research facilities in the universities of Great Britain and Ireland 369
Clark, Sir George: The Later stuarts 519; English history 296
Clarke, John: George III 511
The Cleveland era Henry Jones Ford 167
Clio, a muse G M Trevelyan 742
Clive, John: 'British history 1870-1914 reconsidered' 116
Cobban, Alfred: Debate on the French revolution 123; The eighteenth century 248

Coben, Stanley: World war reform and reaction 229
Codex diplomaticus aevi Saxonici 295
A coffin for King Charles C V Wedgwood 769
Cole, Arthur Charles: Irrepressible conflict 444
Collection of the chronicles and ancient histories of Great Britain John de Waurin 671
Collingwood, R G: Roman Britain 673
Collingwood, R G and J N L Myres: Roman Britain and the English settlements 675
Colonial folkways C M Andrews 167
Colonies in transition Wesley Frank Craven 570
Colonising expeditions to the West Indies and Guiana 379
Colonization of Australia 1829-42 R C Mills 176
The coming of the revolution 1763-1775 Lawrence Henry Gipson 570
Coming of the white men 1492-1848 Herbert Priestley 444
Commager, H S: 'American character' 433; Documents of American history 232; Defeat of the confederacy 54; Fifty basic civil war documents 54
Commager, H S and Richard B Morris: eds New American nations series 570
The commentaries of the great Afonso Dalboquerque 379
Commodore Byron's journal of his circumnavigation 379
Common pitfalls in historical writing Arthur Marwick 584
Commonwealth: a basic annotated bibliography Christiane Keane 182
Commonwealth Journal 681
Completion of independence John Allen Krout and Dixon Ryan Fox 444
Concise dictionary of American history 215
A concise dictionary of American biography 214
Confederation and constitution Forrest Macdonald 229
Conquest of New France George M Wrong 167
The conservative tradition R J White 123

333

Conspiracy of Pontiac Francis Parkman 603

Constitutio domus regis of Richard Fitzneale 598

Constitutional history of England from the accession of Henry VII to the death of George II Henry Hallam 383

Constitutional history of England in its origins and development William Stubbs 727

Cook, C and J Stevenson: Longmans' atlas of modern Britain 529

Cook, Chris: Guide to the archives of selected organisations and societies 713; Guide to the private papers of selected public servants 713; Sources in British political history 1900-1951 713

Cook, Chris and Brendan Keith: British historical facts 1830-1900 113

Cooper, C P: An account of the most important public records of Great Britain 652

Corwin, Edward S: John Marshall and the constitution 167

Cotton kingdom William E Dodd 167

Coulter, Edith M and Melanie Gerstenfeld: Historical bibliographies 418

Coulton, C G: Five centuries of religion 147

Count Frontenac and New France under Louis XIV Francis Parkman 603

Countries around the Bay of Bengal 379

Cowie, Leonard W: Hanoverian England 390

Cox, Edward Godfrey: Reference guide to the literature of travel 655

Craig, Gerald M: Upper Canada 151

Crane, Robert I: History of India 457

Craven, Wesley Frank: Colonies in transition 570; 'Historical Study of the British Empire' 431

Creasy, Sir Edward: Fifteen decisive battles of the world 325

Creighton, D G: Canada 1939-1967 151

The critical years W L Morton 151

Cronichon Richardi Divisensis 295 598

Cronne, H A: 'Edward Augustus Freeman' 337; 'Study and use of charters by English scholars in the seventeenth century' 294

Cross, Colin: Fall of the British Empire 316

Crowley, F K: A new history of Australia 573

Crusade against slavery Louis Filler 570

Crusaders of new France William Bennett Munroe 167

Cultural life of the American colonies Louis B Wright 570

Cultural life of the new nation Russel B Nye 570

Cumming, William P and Hugh F Rankin: The fate of a nation 318

Cumpston, I M: Growth of the British Commonwealth 361

Cumulated Fiction Index 423

Cuncliffe, Marcus: Age of expansion 465; Pastmasters 605

Cunningham, Noble: Early republic 1789-1828 229

Current research in British studies by American and Canadian scholars Anthony Forbes and Marion Johnson 189

Curtin, Philip D: African history 7; 'British Empire and commonwealth in recent historiography' 109

Dangerfield, George: Awakening of American nationalism 570; Strange death of liberal England 724

Darby, H C and Harold Fullard: New Cambridge modern history atlas 572

Davidson, Basil: Africa 4; African past 8

Davidson, J W: 'Problems of Pacific history' 508

Davies, Alun: editor documents of modern history series (Arnold) 234

Davies, Godfrey: The early stuarts 242; Stuart period 1603-1714 79

Davies, John: History of the Tahitian mission 379

Davies, E Jefferies and E G R Taylor: Guide to periodicals and bibliographies dealing with geography, archaeology and history 366

Davis, H W C: Age of Grey and Peel 13; England under the Normans and Angevins 279

Dawson, Robert MacGregor: The development of dominion status 211

334

Dawson, William and Sons 55 128 176 208 413 438 763

Day of the confederacy Nathaniel Stevenson 167

De Antiquitate Glastoniensis Ecclesiae William of Malmesbury 776

De gestis pontificum Anglorum William of Malmesbury 671 776

De gestis regum Angliae Walter of Heminburgh 295

De legibus et consuetudinibus Henry of Bracton 671

De moneta of Nicholas Oresme 598

De rebus gestis Aelfredi Asser 57

De regum gestis Anglorum William of Malmesbury 671 776

Debate on the American revoltuon Max Beloff 123

Debate on the French revolution Alfred Cobban 123

Decisive battles of the western world Major General J F C Fuller 325

Decline and fall of the Roman Empire Edward Gibbon 349

Decreta Lanfranci 598

Defeat of the confederacy H S Commager 54

Democratic republic Marshall Smelser 570

Descriptive catalogue of the works of the Camden Society John Gough Nichols 147

Dialogus de scaccario 598

The diary of A J Mounteney Jephson 379

The diary of Richard Cocks 379

The diary of William Hedges 379

Dickens, A G: ed documents of modern history series (Arnold) 234

Dictionnaire biographique du Canada 217

Directory of American scholars: history Jacques Cattell 225

The discoveries of the world Antonio Galvao 379

Discovery and conquest of Terra Florida 379

Discovery of America D B Quinn 229

The discovery of Guiana 379

The discovery of Tahiti 379

Divers voyages Richard Hakluyt 380

Divers voyages touching the discovery of America 379

The diversity of history 130

Dobson, R B: Peasant's revolt of 1381 443

Documents in the history of slavery Stanley Elkins and Gerald Mullin 229

Documents of modern history (Arnold) 15 227 234 361

Documents of the movement of reform and rebellion 1258-1267 598

Dodd, William E: Cotton kingdom 167

Domesday book and after F W Maitland 533

Domestic issues since 1945 Robert E Burke 229

Donoughue, Bernard: British politics and the American revolution 266

Douglas, David C: ed English historical documents 1042-1189 290; ed English monarchs series 299; English scholars 301 394; William the Conqueror 299 779

Dulles, Foster Rhea: America's rise to world power 570; United States since 1865 759

Dutch and English on the Hudson Maud Wilder Goodwin 167

Dutch and quaker traditions in America Milton Klein 229

Earle, Peter: Henry V 511; James II 511

Early chartists Dorothy Thompson 443

Early Dutch and English voyages to Spitzbergen in the seventeenth century 379

Early republic 1789-1828 Noble Cunningham 229

Early voyages and northern approaches Tryggvi Oleson 151

Early voyages to terra Australis 379

East and West Indian mirror Joris van Speilbergen 379

Eaton, Clement: Growth of southern civilization 570

Eccles, W J: Canada under Louis XIV 151

Ecclesiastical history of Orderic Vitalis 585 598

An economic interpretation of the constitution of the United States C A Beard 72

Edwards. J R: *British history 1815-1939* 115

Edwards, William: *Notes on British history* 582

Egerton, Hugh Edward: *Short history of British colonial policy* 704

Eighteenth century Stanley Pargellis and D J Medley 79

Elizabeth I and her parliaments J E Neale 568

Elizabethan House of Commons J E Neale 568

Elizabethan renaissance A L Rowse 251

Elizabethan sea dogs William Wood 167

Elkins, Stanley and Gerald Mullin: *Documents in the history of slavery* 229

Ellis, Henry: *Original letters illustrative of English history* 587

Elton, G R: *England 1200-1640* 276; *England under the tudors* 281; 'Fifty years of tudor studies at London University' 433; ed Fontana library of English history 330; ed Historical problems studies and documents 425; *Modern historians on British history* 557; *Policy and police* 254; *Political history* 622; *Practice of history* 627; ed sources of history 716; *Studies in tudor and stuart politics and government* 254; *Tudor constitution* 747; *Tudor revolution in government* 254

Elton, Lord: *Imperial commonwealth* 480

The embassy of Sir Thomas Roe to the court of the Great Mogul 379

Emergence of modern America Allan Nevins 444

Encyclopaedia Britannica Educational Corporation 50 700

End of North's ministry Ian Christie 266

England before the Norman conquest R W Chambers 758

England of Elizabeth A L Rowse 251

England under Henry III Margaret Hennings 758

England under the early tudors C H Williams 758

England under the lancastrians Jesse Fleming 758

England under the restoration Thora Stone 758

England under the tudors and stuarts Keith Feiling 320

England under the yorkists Isobel Thornley 758

English nunneries Eileen Power 147

English people on the eve of colonization Wallace Notestein 570

English privateering voyages to the West Indies 379

English radical tradition S Maccoby 123

English seamen in the sixteenth century J A Froude 343

English social history G M Trevelyan 742

English voyages to the Caribbean 379

English voyages to the Spanish Main 379

Ensor, R C K: *England 1870-1914* 265

Era of Franklin D Roosevelt D W Brogan 167

Era of Theodore Roosevelt George Mowry 570

Esmeraldo de Situ Orbis Duarte Pacheco Pereira 379

Essays in Elizabethan history J E Neale 568

Essays in medieval history presented to T F Tout 740

L'estorie des Engles Solum Geoffrey Gaimar 671

Eulogium (historiarum sive temporis): 671

European bibliographical center 23

Europeans in West Africa 379

Evans, Joan: *Flowering of the middle ages* 329

Evans, Lloyd: *Contemporary sources and opinions in modern British history* 201

Eve of the revolution Carl Becker 167

L'Evolution de l'humanite series 448

Expansion of elizabethan England A L Rowse 251

Expansion of England Sir Robert Seeley 689

Expeditions into the valley of the Amazons 379

Fabric of freedom Esmond Wright 537

Factors in modern history A F Pollard 624

336

Fage, J D: *Atlas of African history* 58; *Cambridge history of Africa* 141; *Introduction to history of West Africa* 497

Falkus, Christopher: *Charles II* 511

Far west in the twentieth century Earl Pomeroy 229

Far western frontier Ray Billington 570

Farrand, Max: *Fathers of the constitution* 167

Fasciculi Zizaniorum magistri Johaniss Wyclif ... 671

Fathers of new England C M Andrews 167

Fathers of the constitution Max Farrand 167

Faulkner, Harold V: *From Versailles to the new deal* 167; *Politics reform and expansion* 570; *Quest for social justice* 444

Federalist era John C Miller 570

The fifth letter of Herman Cortes 379

Fifty basic civil war documents H S Commager 54

'Fifty years of tudor studies at London University,' G R Elton 433

Fight for a free sea Ralph D Paine 167

Filler, Louis: *Crusade against slavery* 570

Finberg, H P R: *Formation of England* 332

Fines, John: *History* 437; *History student's guide to the library* 467; *Select bibliography of the teaching of history in the United Kingdom* 692

First Americans Thomas Wertenbaker 444

First century of English feudalism F M Stenton 599

First four Georges J H Plumb 120

First supplementary catalogue of the library of the Royal Colonial Institute J B Boose 681

The first voyage round the world by Magellan 379

Firth, C H: *Commentary on Macaulay's history of England* 530; 'Development of the study of seventeenth century history' 212; *Essays historical and literary* 638

Fish, Carl Russell: *Path of empire* 167; *Rise of the common man* 444

Fisher, D J V: *Anglo-Saxon age* 44

Fisher, Sydney G: *The quaker colonies* 167

Fite, Gilbert: *The west 1830-1890* 229

Five centuries of religion C G Coulton 147

Fleming, Walter Lynwood: *Sequel of Appomattox* 167

Flemming, Jesse: *England under the lancastrians* 758

Flint, John: *Books on the British Empire and commonwealth* 76 90; *Perspectives of empire* 353

Flores historiarum Roger of Wendover 670 671

Forbes, Anthony H and Marion Johnson: *Current research in British studies by American and Canadian scholars* 189

Ford, Henry Jones: *The Cleveland era* 167; *Washington and his colleagues* 167

Ford lectures 8 331 509 539 620 676 740 780

Formative years 1607-1743 Clarence Ver Steeg 537

The forty-niners Stewart Edward White 167

Foster, Sir William: *England's quest of eastern trade* 283

Foundations of modern history series (Arnold) 202 255 334

Foundations of the modern world 1330-1775 Louis Gottschalk 458

Founding the American colonies John E Pomfret 570

Foxcroft, H C: *A supplement to Burnet's history of my own times* 129

Francis Mortoft: His book 379

Franklin D Roosevelt and the new deal William E Leuchtenberg 570

Freeman-Grenville, G S P: *Chronology of African history* 169

The French revolution Thomas Carlyle 158

French tradition in America Y F Zoltvany 229

Frere, Sheppard: *Britannia* 99

Frewer, L B: *Bibliography of historical writings ...* 84 486; *Rhodes House Library* 666

From Versailles to the new deal Harold V Faulkner 167

Fryde, E B: *Historical studies of the English parliament* 430

Fulford, Roger: *Hanover to Windsor* 120 389

Fullard, Harold: ed Muir's atlases 561; *New Cambridge modern history atlas* 572

Fuller, J F C: *The decisive battles of the western world* 325

Fulman, William: *Rerum Anglicarum Scriptorum veterum* 661

Fur trade and the north west E E Rich 151

Furber, Elizabeth: *Changing views on British history* 165

Further English voyages to Spanish America 379

Gabriel, Ralph Henry: ed *Pageant of America* 601

Gaimar, Geoffrey: *Lestorie des Engles Solum* 671

Galbraith, V H: *Introduction to the study of history* 500; *Introduction to the use of the public records* 501 633; ed Oxford medieval texts 598

Gale, Thomas: *Historiae Anglicanae Scriptores Quinque* 405

Galvao, Antonio: *The discoveries of the world* 379

Gann, L H and Peter Duignan: *Colonialism in Africa* 178

Gardiner, S R: *Constitutional documents of the puritan revolution* 192

Gardiner, S R and J B Mullinger: *Introduction to the study of English history* 498

Gargan, E T: *The intent of Toynbee's histories* 741

Garraty, John: *New commonwealth* 570; *Transformation of American society* 229

Gash, Norman: *Age of Peel* 15

The geography of Hudson's Bay 379

George Peard's journal of the voyage of HMS Blossom to the Pacific 379

George III John Clarke 511

George III, Lord North, and the people Herbert Butterfield 130

Gesta Henrici Quinti Angliae Regis Thomas Elmham 253 295

Gesta pontificum Anglorum William of Malmesbury 671 776

Gesta regis Henri Secundi Benedicti Abbatis 671

Gesta regum Gervase of Canterbury 346

Gesta Regum Anglorum William of Malmesbury 295 671 776

Gesta Stephani 295 598

Gesta Willelmi ducis Normannorum et regis Anglorum William of Poitiers 778

Gibson, Charles: *Spain in America* 570; *Spanish tradition in America* 229

Gilbert, Martin: *American history atlas* 35; *British history atlas* 114

Gipson, Lawrence Henry: *The British Empire before the American revolution* 110; *The coming of the revolution 1763-1775* 570

Giuseppi, M S: *Guide to the manuscripts preserved in the Public Record Office* 372

Glorious sahibs Michael Edwardes 247

Gohdes, Clarence: *Bibliographical guide to the study of the literature of the USA* 77

Gooch, G P: *History and historians in the nineteenth century* 439

Goodwin, Maud Wilder: *Dutch and English on the Hudson* 167

Gottschalk, Louis: *Foundations of the modern world 1330-1775* 458

Graham, Bessie: *Bookman's manual* 642

Graham, Gerald S: *Canada* 149; *Concise history of Canada* 187; *Concise history of the British Empire* 188; *Great Britain in the Indian Ocean* 353

Graham, Roger: *Canada 1922-1939* 151

Gransden, Antonia: *Historical writing in England 550-1307* 434

Grant, A J: *English historians* 289

Grantham, Dewey W: *United States since 1945* 755

Graves, Edgar B: *Bibliography of English history to 1485* 81

Great Britain and the American colonies Jack P Greene 229

Great Britain since 1688 K B Smellie 759

Great Britain to 1688 Maurice Ashley 759

Great civilisation series 12 17 24 207 248 329 578 734

Great crusade Preston W Slosson 444

The great medieval civilisations Gaston Wier 458

The great rebellion C V Wedgwood 769

Green, V H H: The hanoverians 391; The later plantagenets 518

Greene, Evarts: Revolutionary generation 1763-1790 444

Greene, Jack P: Great Britain and the American colonies 229; Reappraisal of the American revolution in recent historical literature 646

Greenwood, Gordon: Australia: a social and political history 61

Grenville, J A S: The major international treaties 1914-1973 534

Griffiths, Sir Percival: Empire into commonwealth 256

Gross, Charles: Sources and literature of English history 81 712

Growth of British policy Sir Robert Seeley 689

Growth of political stability in England J H Plumb 620

Growth of southern civilization Clement Eaton 570

Guide to historical literature 30

Guide to historical periodicals in the English language J K Kirby 424

A guide to manuscripts relating to the history of the British Empire 1748-1776 Lawrence Henry Gipson 110

Guide to periodicals and bibliographies dealing with geography archaeology and history 366

Guide to the archives of selected organisations and societies Chris Cook 713

Guide to the contents of the PRO 633

A Guide to the India Office Library S C Sutton 483

Guide to the manuscript materials for the history of the United States to 1783 in the British Museum C M Andrews 41

Guide to the materials for American history to 1783 in the Public Record Office of Great Britain C M Andrews 41

Guide to the private papers of selected public servants Chris Cook 713

Guide to the reports of the Royal Commission on Historical Manuscripts 422

Guide to the reports on collections of manuscripts of private families corporations and institutions in Great Britain and Ireland 422

Guide to the study and reading of American history 392

Gupta, K Balasundara: Cumulative index to the proceedings of the British Academy 101 637

Hadrian's wall map 586

Hakluytus posthumus Samuel Purchas 636

Hale, J R: Evolution of British historiography 310

A half-century of conflict Francis Parkman 603

Hall, H Duncan: Commonwealth 180

Hall, Hubert: List and index of the publications of the Royal Historical Society 524

Hallett, Robin: Records of the African Association 6

Hancock, W K: 'Official history' 433

Hanham, Alison: Richard III and his early historians 560

Hanham, H J: The nineteenth century constitution 579; Zenith of empire 1851-1914 79

Hanning, Robert W: Vision of history ✦ in early Britain 766

Harbottle, Thomas Benfield: Dictionary of historical allusions 219

Harcup, Sara E: Historical archaeological and kindred societies in the British Isles 412

Hardacre, Paul H: 'Writings on Oliver Cromwell since 1929' 786

Hardy, Thomas Duffy: Descriptive catalogue of materials relating to the history of Great Britain 210; Syllabus ... Rymer's Foedera 684

Harlow, Vincent: Founding of the second British Empire 335

Harlow, Vincent and Frederick Madden: British colonial developments 1774-1834 105 599

Hart, Albert Bushnell: ed American history told by contemporaries 37; ed American nation series 38

Harvey, John: *The plantagenets* 120 619

Hastings, Margaret: 'High history or hack history' 402

Haverfield, Francis: *The Roman occupation of Britain* 473 676

Havighurst, Alfred F: *Twentieth century Britain* 754

Haviland, Virginia: *Children and literature* 423

Hawkes, Jacquetta: *Prehistory and the beginnings of civilization* 458

The Hawkins' voyages 379

Hay, Denys: ed *Age of the renaissance* 17; 'The historical periodical: some problems' 424

Hazelhurst, Cameron and Christine Woodland: *Guide to the papers of British cabinet ministers 1900-1951* 374

Heaton, Herbert: 'The progress of historical studies in Australia' 632

Hecht, Jean: 'Reign of George III in recent historiography' 657

Helm, P J: *England under the yorkists and tudors* 282

Helmolt, H F: ed *The worlds history* 782

Helps for students of history series (Historical Association) 241 287 489 553

Hendrick, Burton J: *Age of big business* 167

Hennings, Margaret: *England under Henry III* 758

Henry Hudson the navigator 379

Henry VIII Robert Lacey 511

Henry V Peter Earle 511

Hepworth, Philip: *How to find out in history* 474

Hewitt, A R: *Guide to resources for commonwealth studies ...* 370

Hicks, John D: *Republican ascendancy* 570

High noon of empire Michael Edwards 247

Hill, Christopher: *The century of revolution* 162

Hinton, R W K: 'History yesterday' 470

Hispanic nations of the new world William R Shepherd 167

Historia Anglicana Thomas of Walsingham 671 767

Historia Anglorum Henry of Huntingdon 396 671

Historia Anglorum Matthew of Paris 544 671

Historia Brittonum Nennius 295 569 766

Historia ecclesiastica gentis Anglorum Bede 73 766

Historia ecclesiastica Orderic Vitalis 585

Historia et cartularium monasterii S Petri Gloucestriae 671

Historia monasterii S Augustini Cantuariensis Thomas of Elmham 671

Historia novorum in Anglia Eadmer 237 671

Historia pontificalis of John of Salisbury 598

Historia regum Britanniae Geoffrey of Monmouth 345 766

Historia rerum Anglicarum William of Newburgh 295 777

Historian's guide to Ordnance Survey Maps 586

The historians of the church of York 671

Historica novella William of Malmesbury 776

'The Historical Association,' W F Medlicott 433

Historical collections ... John Rushworth 683

Historical collections of Walter of Coventry 671

Historical introductions to the Rolls Series William Stubbs 727

Historical novels for use in schools 423

Historical papers from the northern registers 671

Historical periodicals an annotated world list of historical and related serial publications 424

Historical periodicals—lists 424

Historical studies Australia and New Zealand 429

Historical works of Gervase of Canterbury 671

Historical works of Symeon of Durham 671

Historie of Great Britaine ... John Speed 719

The historie of travaile into Virginia Britannia 379

'History and literature', C V Wedgwood 433

History and politics of colonialism, 1870-1914, 1914-1960 178

'History in fiction', Mary Renault 423

History is one H G Wells 770

History of England Keith Feiling 320

History of England G M Trevelyan 742

History of England from the accession of James I to the outbreak of the civil war S R Gardiner 344

History of England from the fall of Wolsey to the defeat of the Spanish Armada J A Froude 343

History of England from the first invasion by the Romans to the revolution of 1688 John Lingard 523

History of England from the invasion of Julius Caesar to the revolution in 1688 David Hume 173 476

History of England in the eighteenth century W E H Lecky 521

History of English law F W Maitland 533

History of Friedrich II of Prussia, called Frederick the Great Thomas Carlyle 158

History of King Richard III Sir Thomas More 560

History of my own times Gilbert Burnet 129

'The history of parliament', Frank Stenton 433

The history of the Bermudas or Summer Islands 379

History of the colonies of the British Empire R M Martin 176

History of the commonwealth and protectorate S R Gardiner 344

History of the English people in the nineteenth century Elie Halevy 381

A history of the English-speaking peoples Winston Churchill 171

History of the great civil war S R Gardiner 344

History of the new world Girolamo Benzoni 379

History of the Norman conquest E A Freeman 173 323

History of the rebellion and civil wars in England Earl of Clarendon 172

History of the Royal Commonwealth Society Trevor Reese 681

History of the Tahititian mission John Davies 379

History of the tory party Keith Feiling 320

History of the United States George Bancroft 65

History of the United States from 1801-1817 Henry Adams 3

History of the world Sir Walter Raleigh 368

History of twenty five years Spencer Walpole 450

History research for university degrees in the United Kingdom Phyllis M Jacobs 427

Hodgkin, R H: History of the Anglo-Saxons 462

Holmes, Geoffrey: Britain after the glorious revolution 93

Holmes, Geoffrey and W A Speck: The divided society 227

Holmes, George: Later middle ages 516

Holt, J C: Magna carta 531

Holt, W Stull: Historical profession in the United States 426

Home university library 286

Horn, D B and Mary Ransome: eds English historical documents 1714-1783 290

Horne, Donald: 'The rough and the smooth' 679

Hough, Emerson: Passing of the frontier 167

Howland, Harold: Theodore Roosevelt and his times 167

Hughes, Dorothy: Illustrations of Chaucer's England 758

Hugins, Walter: Reform impulse 1828-1847 229

Hulbert, Archer B: Paths of inland commerce 617

Hudson's Bay series, Champlain Society 164

Hulme, Harold: 'Elizabeth I and her parliaments: the work of Sir John Neale' 568

Humphreys, R A: Royal Society 1868-1968 148

Hunt, William and R L Poole: eds Longmans political history of England 621

Huntington, Ellsworth: Red man's continent 167

341

Hutchinsons university library series 107 149 263 478 576 580

Huxley, Julian: *Unesco: its purpose and its philosophy* 458

The idea of history R G Collingwood 174

Illustrations of Chaucer's England Dorothy Hughes 758

Illustrium majoris Britanniae scriptorum John Bale 64

Imagines historiarum Ralph de Diceto 639

Imperial constitutional documents Frederick Madden 701

India in the fifteenth century 379

Influence of sea-power upon history 1660-1783 A T Mahan 532

Innes, A D: *Maritime and colonial expansion of England under the stuarts* 543

Intellectual origins of the English revolution Christopher Hill 403

The intent of Toynbee's histories E T Gargan 741

'The interaction of history and biography', J F Plumb 433

Irrepressible conflict Arthur Charles Cole 444

Issues of the populist and progressive eras Richard Abrams 229

Jacksonian era Glyndon G Van Deusen 570

Jacob, E F: *The fifteenth century* 326

Jacobs, Phyllis M: *History research for university degrees in the United Kingdom* 427

James II Peter Earle 511

Jameson, J Franklin: 'The American Historical Association' 29; 'The Anglo-American conference of professors' 42; 'History of historical writing in America' 456; ed *Original narratives of early American history* 588

The Jamestown voyages under the first charter 379

Janeway, Elliott: *Struggle for survival* 167

Jefferson and his colleagues Allen Johnson 167

Jennings, Sir Ivor: *The British Commonwealth of Nations* 107

Jensen, Merrill: *American colonial documents to 1776* 25

The Jesuits in North America Francis Parkman 603

John Jourdain's journal of a voyage to the East Indies 379

John Marshall and the constitution Edward S Corwin 167

Johnson, Allen: editor Chronicles of America series 167; *Jefferson and his colleagues* 167

Johnston, Mary: *Pioneers of the old south* 167

Joliffe, J E A: *Constitutional history of medieval England* 197

Joll, James: *Britain and Europe: Pitt to Churchill* 123

Jones, I Deane: *English revolution* 300

Jones, Michael Wyn: *Cartoon history of Britain* 159

Jones, R Ben: *Practical approaches to the new history* 626

The journal and letters of Captain Charles Bishop ... 379

Journal of American studies 103

Journal of British studies 189

The journal of Christopher Colombus 379

Journal of William Lockerby in Fiji 379

Journal of world history 458

The journals and letters of Sir Alexander Mackenzie 379

Journals of Captain Cook on his voyages of discovery 379

Junior fiction index 423

Keane, Christiane: *Commonwealth a basic annotated bibliography* 182

Keen, M H: *England in the late middle ages* 270

Keir, D L: *Constitutional history of modern Britain* 198

Keith, A B: *Constitution of England from Queen Victoria to George VI* 190; *Selected speeches and documents on British colonial policy* 701

Kellaway, William: *Bibliography of historical works ...* 83

Kendle, John Edward: *Colonial and imperial conferences 1887-1911* 175;

The round table movement and imperial union 680

Kendrick, T D: *British antiquity* 102

Kenyon, Sir Frederic: *The British Academy: the first fifty years* 101

Kenyon, J P: *The stuart constitution* 725; *The stuarts* 120 726

Kerr, D G: *Historical atlas of Canada* 415

King John Maurice Ashley 511

The king's minister J H Plumb 620

The king's peace C V Wedgwood 769

The king's war C V Wedgwood 769

Kingsford, C L: *English historical literature in the fifteenth century* 292

Kiralfy, A K R and Gareth H Jones: *A general guide to the (Selden) Society's publications* 690

Kirby, D P: *The making of early England* 538

Kirby, J K: *Guide to historical periodicals in the English language* 424

Klein, Milton: *Dutch and quaker traditions in America* 229

Knaplund, Paul: *Britain Commonwealth and Empire* 95; *British Empire 1815-1939* 111

Knighton, Henry: *Chronicle* 671

Knowles, David: *Great historical enterprises* 357

Koenig, W J and S L Mayer: *European manuscript sources of the American revolution* 306

Koht, Halvdan: *Origin and beginning of the International Committee of Historical Sciences* 487

Kraus, Michael: *United States to 1865* 759

Kraus Reprints 356 421 513 549 617 634 671 783

Krout, John Allen and Dixon Ryan Fox: *Completion of independence* 444

Kuehl, Warren F: *Dissertations in history* 225

La Salle and the discovery of the great west Francis Parkman 603

La Wanda and John Cox: *Reconstruction, the new south and the negro* 229

Lacey, Robert: *Henry VIII* 511

Lamprade, W T: 'Present state of the history of England in the eighteenth century' 628

Lancaster, Joan C: Bibliography of historical works ... 83; 'India Office Records' 484

Land, Aubrey: *Bases of plantation society* 229

Langer, William: *Encyclopaedia of world history* 260

Langlois C V and C Seignobos: *Introduction to the study of history* 499

Lapsley, Gaillard: 'Mr. Joliffe's construction of early constitutional history' 197

'The larger view of history', Geoffrey Barraclough 433

The last voyage of Drake and Hawkins 379

Last years of British India Michael Edwardes 247

Lectures on modern history Lord Acton 1

Lectures on the French revolution Lord Acton 1

Leechdome, wortcunning, and starcraft of early England ... 671

Legendary history of Britain J S P Tatlock 345

Leland, Waldo G: 'The Anglo-American conference of historians' 42

Letter books of the monastery of Christ Church Canterbury 671

Letters and papers illustrative of the reigns of Richard III and Henry VII 671

Letters and papers illustrative of the wars of the English in France during the reign of Henry VI 671

The letters of Amerigo Vespucci 379

Letters of Bishop Grosseteste 671

Leuchtenberg, William E: *Franklin D Roosevelt and the new deal* 570; *The new deal* 229

Levine, Mortimer: *Tudor dynastic problems* 749; *Tudor England* 751

Lewin, Evan: *Best books on the British Empire* 76 90; *Subject catalogue of the Royal Empire Society* 681

Liber de illustribus Henricis John Capgrave 156 671

Liber monasterii de Hyda 671

Liber querulus de excidio et conquestu Britanniae Gildas 295 350 766

Liberal tradition Alan Bullock and Maurice Shook 123

Library of American studies series 734

Library of European civilizations series 734

Library of medieval civilization series 734

The library of the India Office A J Arberry 483

Life and letters of Lord Macaulay Sir Otto Trevelyan 743

Life of Ailred of Rievaulx 598

Life of Anselm of Eadmer 598

The Life of Captain James Cook J C Beaglehole 379

Life of Neville Chamberlain Keith Feiling 320

'Limitation of historical knowledge', Arnold Toynbee 437

Linguarum veterum septentrionalium thesaurus grammatico-criticus et archaeologicus George Hickes 400

Link, Arthur: Woodrow Wilson and the progressive era 570

Lives of Edward the Confessor 671

Le livre de Reis de Brittainie 671

Lloyd, T O: Empire to welfare state 257

Loades, D M: Politics and the nation 1450-1660 623

Lockyer, Roger: Tudor and stuart Britain 746

Longmans history of England 451

Longmans political history of England 621

Lord, Clifford and Elizabeth Lord: Historical atlas of the United States 416

Lord Randolph Churchill Winston Churchill 171

Low, Sydney and F S Pulling: Dictionary of English history 218

Lower Canada Fernand Oullet 151

Loyn, H R: The Norman conquest 580

Lucas, C P: Historical geography of the British colonies 419

Lynam, Edward: Richard Hakluyt and his successors 667

Lyon, Bryce: A constitutional and legal history of medieval England 191; From Hengist and Horsa to Edward of Caernarvon 342; Middle ages in recent historical thought 550

McClymount, W G: Exploration of New Zealand 311

Maccoby, S: English radical tradition 123

McCoy, F C: Researching and writing in history 662

McDonald, Gregory D: 'American history' 33

Macdonald, Forrest: Confederation and constitution 229

McEvedy, Colin: Atlas of world history 60; Penguin atlas of medieval history 608; Penguin atlas of modern history 609

McEwan, P J M: Readings in African history 645

McGarry, Daniel D and Sarah Harriman White: World historical fiction guide 423

Mckee, M D: Recent British publications on Commonwealth West African history 649

McKendrick, Neil: Historical perspectives 620

Mackie, J D: The earlier tudors 238

McKisack, May: The fourteenth century 336; Medieval history in the tudor age 546

McNaught, Kenneth: History of Canada 447

McNeill, William H: A world history 781

MacNutt, W S: Atlantic provinces 151

Macray, W D: Manual of British historians 540

Macy, Jesse: Anti-slavery crusade 167

Madden, Frederick: Imperial constitutional documents 701

Madox, Thomas: Formulare anglicanum 333

Magellan's Strait 379

Magna vita S Hugonis Episcopi Lincolniensis 671

Makers of the realm Sir Arthur Bryant 127

The making of a statesman J H Plumb 620

Man in the making Sir Arthur Bryant 127

Man on his past Herbert Butterfield 1 130

Mandeville's travels 379

Mansergh, Nicholas: The commonwealth 179; *Constitutional relations between Britain and India* 199; *Documents and speeches on British Commonwealth affairs* 231; *Documents and speeches on commonwealth affairs* 231

Marlborough: his life and times Winston Churchill 171

Marriott, Sir J A R: *England since Waterloo* 275; *Modern England 1885-1945* 555

Marsh, Henry: *Dark age Britain* 206

Marshall, Dorothy: *Eighteenth century England* 250; *Victoria* 511

Martin, R M: *History of the colonies of the British Empire* 176

Marwick, Arthur: *Basic problems of writing history* 584; *Common pitfalls in historical writing* 584; *Nature of history* 567; *Primary sources* 584; *What history is* 584

Masters of capital John Moody 167

Materials for a history of the reign of Henry VII from original documents preserved in the PRO 671

Materials for the history of Thomas Becket 671

Mathews, Noel: *Materials for West African history in the archives of the United Kingdom* 377

Matthew, David: *James I* 502

Medieval foundation Sir Arthur Bryant 127

Medlicott, W N: *Contemporary England* 200; 'Historical Association' 433; ed Longmans history of England 451

Memoranda de parliamento 25 Edward I 1305 671

Memorials of Henry V 671

Memorials of Henry VII 671

Memorials of St Dunstan 671

Memorials of St Edmund's Abbey 671

Memorials of the reign of Henry VI Thomas Bekynton 671

Metrical chronicle of Robert of Gloucester 671

Microcards edition: *Scholarly collection of American history* 686

Middlemas, Keith: *Edward VII* 511

Miller, Harold: *New Zealand* 576

Miller, Helen and Aubrey Newman:

Early modern British history 1485-1760 241

Miller, J D B: 'Hancock, Mansergh, and commonwealth surveys' 384

Miller, John C: *The federalist era* 570

Milne, A T: *Centenary guide to the publications of the Royal Historical Society* 524 682

Mills, R C: *Colonization of Australia 1829-42* 176

Missions to the Niger 379

Mr secretary Cecil Conyers Read 74

Modern history abstracts 411

Monastic Britain map 586

Monasticon Anglicanum Sir William Dugdale 236

Montcalm and Wolfe Francis Parkman 603

Monumenta Franciscana 671

Monumenta historica Britannica Ethelweard 303

Monumenta juridica 671

Moody, John: *Masters of capital* 167

Moore, R W: *The Romans in Britain* 678

Moorehead, Alan: *The fatal impact* 71

Morgan, Edmund S: *American revolution* 40

Morgan, William Thomas: *Bibliography of British history (1700-1715)* 80

Morison, S E: *Oxford history of the American people* 596; *The european discovery of America* 305

Morrell, W P: *British colonial policy in the age of Peel and Russell* 106 599; *British colonial policy in the midvictorian age* 106; *Britain in the Pacific Islands* 97; *British overseas expansion and the history of the commonwealth* 122; *The gold rushes* 616

Morris, Christopher: *The tudors* 120 752

Morris, James: *Heaven's command* 395; *Pax Britannica* 395

Morris, John: *Age of Arthur* 9

Morris, Richard B: *American revolution* 229; *Basic documents in American history* 67; *Basic documents on the confederation and constitution* 69; *Documents in American history* 54; editor *Documentary history of the United States* 229

Morris, Richard B and Graham W Irwin: *Encyclopaedia of the modern world* 259

Morton, Alan: *A people's history of England* 611

Morton, Louis: *United States and world war two* 229

Morton W L: *The critical years* 151

Mowat, C L: *Britain between the wars* 94; *British history since 1926* 118

Mowry, George: *Era of Theodore Roosevelt* 570; *Urban nation* 537

Mullins, E L G: *Guide to the historical and archaeological publications of societies ...* 373; *Texts and calendars* 733

Munimenta academica 671

Munimenta Gildhallae Londoniensis 671

Munroe, William Bennett: *Crusaders of new France* 167

Murimuth, Adam: *Chronicle* 295 671

Myers, A R: *England in the late middle ages* 268; ed *English historical documents 1327-1485* 290

Namier, Sir Lewis: *England in the age of the American revolution* 266

Narrative of a voyage to the West Indies and Mexico Samuel Champlain 379

Narratives of the expulsion of the English from Normandy 671

Narratives of voyages towards the north-west 379

Nationalising of business Ida M Tarbell 444

Neatby, Hilda: *Quebec* 151

Nelson's history of England 452

Nevins, Allan: editor *Chronicles of America* series 167; *Emergence of modern America* 444; *New deal and world affairs* 167; *Select bibliography of the history of the United States* 691; *United States in a chaotic world* 167; ed *University of Michigan history of the modern world* 759

New commonwealth John Garraty 570

New deal William E Leuchtenberg 229

The New deal and world affairs Allan Nevins 167

A new dictionary of British history S H Steinberg 721

New France 1744-1760 G F S Stanley 151

New France 1702-1743 Jean Blain 151

New light on Drake 379

New light on the discovery of Australia 379

New nation 1800-1845 Charles M Wiltse 537

The new south Holland Thompson 167

A new voyage and description of the Isthmus of America 379

Newe chronycles of Englande and of Fraunce Robert Fabyan 315

Newton, A P: *European nations in the West Indies* 307; *Hundred years of the British Empire* 477

Nicholl, Allardyce and Josephine: *Holinshed's chronicles as used in Shakespeare's plays* 471

Nichols, John Gough: *Descriptive catalogue of the works of the Camden Society* 147

Nichols, Roy F: *Stakes of power* 537

Noble, David W: *Historians against history* 406

The north 1914-1967 Morris Zaslow 151

Notestein, Wallace: *English people on the eve of colonization* 570

Nye, Russel B: *Cultural life of the new nation* 570

The, observations of Sir Richard Hawkins 379

Ocean in English history J A Williamson 780

'Official history', W K Hancock 433

Ogg, David: *England in the reign of Charles II* 272; *England in the reigns of James II and William III* 272

Ogg, Frederic Austin: *The old north west* 167; *Reign of Andrew Jackson* 167

The old merchant marine Ralph D Paine 167

The old north west Frederic Austin Ogg 167

The old regime in Canada Francis Parkman 603

Oleson, Tryggvi: *Early voyages and northern approaches* 151

Oliver Cromwell's letters and speeches Thomas Carlyle 158

Oliver, Roland and J D Fage: *A short history of Africa* 607

Oliver, W H: *Story of New Zealand* 722

Oman, Sir Charles: *England before the Norman conquest* 264; *On the writing of history* 583

Ontario series Champlain Society 164

Opening of the Canadian north Morris Zaslow 151

Opening of the west Jack M Sosin 229

Opera Roger Bacon 671

Opera historica Ralph de Diceto 671

The Oregon trail Francis Parkman 603

The original writings and correspondence of the two Richard Hakluyts 379

Orth, Samuel P: *Armies of labour* 167; *The boss and the machine* 167; *Our foreigners* 167

Oullet, Fernand: *Lower Canada* 151

Our foreigners Samuel P Orth 167

Outline of history H G Wells 770

Paine, Ralph D: *Fight for a free sea* 167; *The old merchant marine* 167

Palmer, A W: *A dictionary of modern history 1789-1945* 220

Papers of Thomas Bowrey 379

Pareti, Luigi: *The ancient world* 458

Pares, Richard: *King George III and the politicians* 331 509

Pares, Richard and A J P Taylor: *Essays presented to Sir Lewis Namier* 562

Pargellis, Stanley and D J Medley: *Eighteenth century* 79 599

Parker, John: *Books to build an empire* 91

Parks, George Bruner: *Richard Hakluyt and the English voyages* 668

Parry, Clive and Charity Hopkins: *An index of British treaties* 482

Passing of the frontier Emerson Hough 167

Path of empire Carl Russell Fish 167

Paths of inland commerce Archer B Hulbert 167

Peacock, Reginald: *The repressor of over much blaming of the clergy* 671

Peasant's revolt of 1381 R B Dobson 443

Peckham, Johannis: *Registrum epistolarum* 671

Pelling, Henry: *Challenge of socialism* 123; *Modern Britain* 552

Perman, Dagmar Horna: *Bibliography and the historian* 78

Perry, Bliss: *American spirit in literature* 167

Perspectives of empire John Flint 353

Peter Floris his voyage to the West Indies 379

Petit-Dutaillis, Charles: *Studies and notes supplementary to Stubbs constitutional history* 727

Petrie, Henry: *Monumenta historica Britannica* 559

Philbrick, Francis S: *The rise of the west 1784-1830* 570

Philips junior history atlas 615

Pickthorn, Kenneth: *Early tudor government* 243

Piggott, Stuart: 'Antiquarian thought in the sixteenth and seventeenth centuries' 294

Pike, Douglas: editor *Australian dictionary of biography* 62

Pioneers of France in the new world Francis Parkman 603

Pioneers of the old south Mary Johnston 167

Pioneers of the old south west Constance Lindsay Skinner 167

Pirenne, Jacques: *Tides of history* 738

Place of the reign of Edward II in English history T F Tout 740

The plantagenets John Harvey 120

Plassey Michael Edwardes 247

Plucknett, T F T: ed *Taswell-Langmead's English constitutional history* 729

Plumb, J H: *Chatham* 536; *England in the eighteenth century* 267; *First four Georges* 120 328; *G M Trevelyan* 280; *Growth of political stability* 620; 'Interaction of history and biography' 433; *Kings minister* 620; *Making of a statesman* 620; *Men and places* 280

Pole, J R: *Revolution in America* 433; *Slavery, race and civil war in America* 31

Policy and police G R Elton 254

Political poems and songs relating to English history 671

'Politics and historical research in the

347

early seventeenth century', Philip Styles 294

Politics reform and expansion Harold V Faulkner 570

Pollard, A F: *History of England* 453; *Reign of Henry VII from contemporary sources* 659

Polychronicon Ranulph Higden 401 671

Pomeroy, Earl: *Far west in the twentieth century* 229

Pomfret, John E: *Founding the American colonies* 570

Poole, Austin: *From Domesday book to Magna carta* 341

Poole, R L: *Chronicles and annals* 166

Porter, H C: *Puritanism in tudor England* 443

Poulton, Helen J: *The historian's handbook* 408

Power, Eileen: *English nunneries* 147; *Wool trade in English medieval history* 331

Powicke, Sir Maurice: 'Administrative history' 433; *Handbook of British chronology* 386; *Modern historians and the study of history* 556; *The thirteenth century* 737; 'Value of sixteenth and seventeenth scholarship to modern historical research' 294

Pratt, Fletcher: *War for the world* 5

Prehistory and the beginnings of civilization Jacquetta Hawkes and Sir Leonard Woolley 458

Priestley, Herbert: *Coming of the white men 1492-1848* 444

Principall navigations Richard Hakluyt 380

Problems in focus series (Macmillan) 93 492 631 660

Proceedings of the association for promoting the discovery of the interior parts of Africa 176

Protestant island Sir Arthur Bryant 127

Prothero, G W: 'Historical societies in Great Britain' 428; *Select statutes and other constitutional documents* 698

Prouty, Roger M: *England and Wales 1820-1870 in recent historiography* 262

Provincial society 1690-1763 James Truslow Adams 444

'Public records in the sixteenth and seventeenth centuries', R B Wernham 294

Publications of the Champlain Society 164

Pugh, R B: *General introduction to the Victoria History of the counties of England* 763; *Records of the Colonial and Dominions Offices* 654

Purchas his pilgrimes Samuel Purchas 636

Puritan tradition in America Alden T Vaughan 229

Puritanism and revolution Christopher Hill 403

Puritanisam in tudor England H C Porter 443

The quaker colonies Sydney G Fisher 167

Quebec Hilda Neatby 151

Queen Elizabeth J E Neale 74 568

Queen Elizabeth Milton Waldman 536

The quest and occupation of Tahiti 379

Quest for social justice Harold V Faulkner 444

Quinn, David Beers: *Discovery of America* 229; *England and the discovery of America 1481-1620* 261; ed *Hakluyt handbook* 378; *North American discovery* 581

Read, Conyers: *Mr secretary Cecil* 74; *Tudor period 1485-1603* 79

Readers' guide to hanoverian Britain 643

Readers' guide to medieval Britain 643

Readers' guide to tudor and stuart Britain 643

Readers' guide to victorian Britain 643

Recent historical fiction for secondary school children Kenneth Charlton 423

Reconsiderations Arnold Toynbee 741

Reconstruction, the new south, and the negro La Wanda and John Cox 229

Recueil des chroniques et anchiennes istories de la Grant Bretaigne 671

Red book of the exchequer 671

Red man's continent Ellsworth Huntington 167

The Red Sea and adjacent countries at

the close of the seventeenth century 379

Red year Michael Edwardes 247

Reese, Trevor: *History of the Royal Commonwealth Society* 681

Reeves, William: *Long white cloud* 528

Reform impulse 1828-1847 Walter Huggins 229

A Regiment for the sea ... 379

Register of Malmesbury Abbey preserved in the PRO 671

Register of S Osmund 671

Registrum epistolarum Johannis Peckham 671

Registrum Palatinum Dunelmense 671

Regularis concordia 598

Reign of Andrew Jackson Frederic Austin Ogg 167

Remini, Robert: *Age of Jackson* 229

Renault, Mary: 'History in fiction' 423

The repressor of over much blaming of the clergy Reginald Peacock 671

Republican ascendancy John D Hicks 570

Rerum Britannicarum Medii Aevi Scriptores 671

The review of historical publications relating to Canada 153

Revolution in America J R Pole 443

Revolutionary generation 1763-1790 Evarts Greene 444

Reynolds, E E and N H Brasher: *Britain in the twentieth century* 98

Rhodesian history 161

Ricardi de Cirencestria speculum historiale de gestis regum Angliae 671

Rice, David Talbot: *Dark ages* 207

Rich, E E: *Fur trade and the north west* 151

Richard III and his early historians Alison Hanham 560

Richman, Irving: *Spanish conquerors* 167

Richmond, Admiral Sir Herbert: *Statesmen and sea power* 331

Richmond, Ian: *Roman Britain* 672

Rise of American civilization C A Beard 72

Rise of British Guiana 379

Rise of the city Arthur M Schlesinger 444

Rise of the common man Carl Russell Fish 444

Rise of the new west F J Turner 753

The rise of the west, 1784-1830 Francis S Philbrick 570

Roanoke voyages 379

Robert Harcourt's voyage to Guiana 379

Robert of Brunne: *Chronicle* 671

Robert of Gloucester: *Metrical chronicle* 671

Roberts, John: *Age of revolution* 465

Robertson, Sir Charles Grant: *England under the hanoverians* 278; *Select statutes cases and documents* 699

Robinson, Ronald and John Gallagher: *Africa and the victorians* 5

Roger of Howden: *Chronica* 671

Roger of Wendover: *Chronica* 671

Roman Britain map 586

Roots, Ivan: *The great rebellion* 358

Roper, Hugh Trevor: *Age of expansion* 12

Ross, Charles: *Edward IV* 246

Rothwell, Harry: ed *English historical documents 1189-1327* 290

Round, J H: *Feudal England* 323

The round table 680

The round table movement and imperial union J T Kendle 680

Rowse, A L: *Use of history* 547 760; *Elizabethan renaissance* 251; *England of Elizabeth* 251; *Expansion of elizabethan England* 251; *Spirit of English history* 720

Royal and historical letters during the reign of Henry IV 671

Royal and other historical letters illustrative of the reign of Henry III 671

Royal Commission on Historical Manuscripts 422

Russell, Conrad: *Crisis of parliaments* 204; *Origins of the English civil war* 589

Sachse, William L: *Restoration England* 663

Sainsbury, Keith: *International history 1939-1970* 489

Saviour of the navy Sir Arthur Bryant 127

Sawyer, P H: *Age of the Vikings* 18; *Anglo-Saxon charters* 46; ed *International medieval bibliography* 491

Saxon and Norman kings Christopher Brooke 120

Scarisbrook, J J: *Henry VIII* 397

Schlesinger, Arthur M: editor History of American life series 444; *Rise of the city* 444

Schlesinger, Arthur M junr: *History of American presidential elections* 445

Schuyler, R L and C C Weston: *British constitutional history since 1832* 54

Schuyler, R L and C C Weston: *Cardinal documents in British history* 54 157

School library fiction 423

Seaman, L C B: *Post victorian Britain* 625

Search for order Robert H Wiebe 537

A season in hell Michael Edwardes 247

The second tory party Keith Feiling 320

The second world war Winston Churchill 171

Select charters ... of English constitutional history William Stubbs 727

Select documents concerning Anglo-Scottish relations 1174-1328 598

Select letters of Christopher Colombus 379

Selected letters of Pope Innocent III concerning England 598

Selections from the Smuts papers Sir Keith Hancock 384

Sellar, W C and R J Yeatman: *1066 and all that* 732

Sequel of Appomattox Walter Lynwood Fleming 167

Service Center for teachers of history 7 10 40 317 319 355 426 457 550 646 718 736 755

Seymour, Charles: *Woodrow Wilson and the world war* 167

Shannon, Richard: *Crisis of imperialism* 203

Sharp, Andrew: *Discovery of Australia* 223

Shaw, W A: *Bibliography of the historical works of Dr Stubbs, Dr S R Gardiner ... Lord Acton* 86

Shenton, James: *The civil war* 229

Shepherd, William R: *Hispanic nations of the new world* 167

Shera, Jesse H: *Historians books and libraries* 407

Sherman, Richard: *The crisis of imperialism* 203

A short history of Africa Roland Oliver and J D Fage 607

A short history of the English people J R Green 360

A short history of the world H G Wells 770

Simpson, Donald H: *A biography catalogue of the library of the Royal Commonwealth Society* 681; 'Writings on Australian history' 784

Sinclair, Keith: *History of New Zealand* 459

Singletary, Otis A: *South in American history* 718

Sir Francis Drake J A Williamson 536

Sir Francis Drake his voyage 379

Skelton, Oscar D: *The Canadian dominion* 167

Sketch of Europe in the middle ages Henry Hallam 383

Skinner, Constance Lindsay: *Adventures of Oregon* 167; *Pioneers of the old south west* 167

Slosson, Edwin: *American spirit in education* 167

Slosson, Preston W: *Great crusade* 444

Smalley, Beryl: *Historians in the middle ages* 410 '

Smellie, K B: *Great Britain since 1688* 759

Smelser, Marshall: *The democratic republic* 570

Smith, Alan G R: *The reign of James VI and I* 660

Smith, Lacey Baldwin: 'The taste for tudors since 1940' 728

Smith, V A: *Oxford history of India* 594

Smollett, Tobias: *History of England* 476

Society and puritanism in pre-revolutionary England Christopher Hill 403

Somerville, Robert: *Handbook of record publications* 388

Somner, William: *Dictionarum Saxonico-Latino-Anglicum* 213

Sosin, Jack M: *Opening of the west* 229

Southern Britain in the ice age map 586

Spain in America Charles Gibson 570

Spanish border lands Herbert Bolton 167

Spanish conquerors Irving Richman 167

Spanish tradition in America Charles Gibson 229

Speculum 545

Speeches and documents in American History Robert Birley 232

Speilbergen, Joris van: East and West Indian mirror 379

Sphere library history of England 452

Stakes of power Roy F Nicholls 537

Stanley, G F S: New France 1744-1760 151

Stanton, F M: and Marie Tremaine: Bibliography of Canadiana 155

Statesmen and sea power Admiral Sir Herbert Richmond 331

Steensgaard, Niels: 'Universal history for our times' 458 756

Steinberg, S H: A new dictionary of British history 721; Historical tables 432

Stenton, D M: English society in the early middle ages 302

Stenton, Sir Frank: Anglo-Saxon England 49; First century of English feudalism 599; 'History of parliament' 433

Stephens, Lester D: Historiography: bibliography 435

Stephenson, Carl and F G Marcham: Sources of English constitutional history 715

Stevenson, Nathaniel: Abraham Lincoln and the union 167; Day of the confederacy 167; Texas and the Mexican war 167

Stone, Thora: England under the restoration 758

Storey, R L: Chronology of the medieval world 170

Story, Norah: Oxford companion to Canadian history and literature 592

The story of England Sir Arthur Bryant 127

Strafford C V Wedgwood 769

The strange adventures of Andrew Battell of Leigh in Essex 379

Stickland, Agnes: Lives of the queens of England 527

The structure of politics at the accession of George III Lewis Namier 562

Struggle for survival Elliott Janeway 167

Stuart period 1603-1714 Godfrey Davies (Mary Frear Keeler) 79

The stuarts J P Kenyon 120

Studies in tudor and stuart politics and government G R Elton 254

'Study and use of charters by English scholars in the seventeenth century', H A Cronne 294

A study of history Arnold Toynbee 741

Styles, Philip: 'Politics and historical research in the early seventeenth century' 294

Summaries of Engliyshe chronicles John Stow 723

Survey of British Commonwealth affairs Sir Keith Hancock 384

Survey of international affairs 741

Sutton, S C: A guide to the India Office Library 483

Talman, James J: Basic documents in Canadian history 68

Tanner, J R: English constitutional conflicts of the seventeenth century 285; Tudor constitutional documents 747 748; Constitutional documents of the reign of James I 193 725

Tarbell, Ida M: Nationalising of business 444

Tatlock, J S P: Legendary history of Britain 345

Taylor, A J P: English history 1914-1945 298

Taylor, John: The universal chronicle of Ranulph Higden 401; Use of medieval chronicles 761

Teach yourself histories 547

'The teach yourself history library,' Herbert Butterfield 547

Teaching of history (Historical Association) 413

Tedder, Henry: 'The forthcoming bibliography of modern British history' 79

Texas and the Mexican war Nathaniel Stevenson 167

Theodore Roosevelt and his times Harold Howland 167

Thomas More R W Chambers 74

Thomas Wentworth first Earl of Strafford C V Wedgwood 769

Thompson, Dorothy: Early chartists 443

Thompson, Holland: *Age of invention* 167; *The new south* 167

Thomson, David: *England in the nineteenth century* 271; *England in the twentieth century* 274

Thomson, Mark A: *Constitutional history of England 1642 to 1801* 194

The three voyages of Sir Martin Frobisher 379

The three voyages of William Barents to the Arctic regions 379

Thornley, Isobel: *England under the yorkists* 758

Tractatus de globis 379

Tractatus de legibus et consuetinibus regni Anglie qui Glanvilla vocatur 598

Transformation of American society John Garraty 229

Travels of John Sanderson in the Levant 379

The travels of Peter Mundy 379

Treharne, R F: *Bibliography of historical atlases* 82; *Constitutional history of England* 194; ed Muir's atlases 561

Trevelyan, G M: *British history in the nineteenth century* 117; *Clio: a muse* 742; *England under Queen Anne* 277 742; *England under the stuarts* 280; *English social history* 742; *History of England* 742; *Select documents from Queen Anne's reign* 693

Trevor-Roper, H R: *Essays in British history* 320

The trial of Charles I C V Wedgwood 769

The troublesome voyage of Captain Edward Fenton 379

Trudel, Marcel: *Beginnings of new France* 151

A true description of three voyages by the north-east 379

Tudor period 1485-1603 Conyers Read 79

Tudor revolution in government G R Elton 254

The tudors Christopher Morris 120

Turnbull, Clive: *Concise history of Australia* 186

The twentieth century Caroline Ware 458

Twentieth century abstracts 411

Unesco: its purpose and its philosophy Julian Huxley 458

Union of the Canadas J M S Careless 151

Union of the two noble and illustre famelies of Lancastre and Yorke Edward Hall 382

United empire 681

United States and world war two A Russell Buchanan 570

United States and world war two Louis Morton 229

United States history a catalog of demand reprints 757

United States in a chaotic world Allan Nevins 167

United States since 1865 Foster Rhea Dulles 759

United States to 1865 Michael Kraus 759

'Universal history for our times', Niels Steensgaard 458

University microfilms: *The march of America* 542

Upper Canada Gerald M Craig 151

Upton, Eleanor Stuart: *Guides to sources of English history ... in reports of Royal Commission on Historical Manuscripts* 371

Urban nation George E Mowry 537

'Value of sixteenth and seventeenth century scholarship to modern historical research', F M Powicke 294

Van Deusen, Glyndon G: *Jacksonian era* 570

Van Thal, Herbert: *The prime ministers* 629

Vaughan, Alden T: *Puritan tradition in America* 229

Vaughan, Richard: *Matthew of Paris* 544

Ver Steeg, Clarence: *Formative years 1607—1763* 537

Vickers, K H: *England in the late middle ages* 269

Victoria Dorothy Marshall 511

Vile, M J C: *The presidency* 31

Vita Aedwardi regis 598

Vita Edwardi secundi of the so-called monk of Malmesbury 598

The voyage of Captain John Saris to Japan 379

The voyage of Nicholas Downton to the East Indies 379

The voyage of Robert Dudley to the West Indies and Guiana 379

The voyage of Sir Henry Middleton to Bantam and the Maluco Islands 379

The voyage of Sir Henry Middleton to the Moluccas 379

The voyage of the Endeavour 379

Voyage of the Resolution and Adventure 379

Voyage of the Resolution and the Discovery 379

Voyage of Thomas Best to the East Indies 379

The voyages and colonising enterprises of Sir Humphrey Gilbert 379

The voyages and works of John Davis the navigator 379

The voyages of Captain Luke Foxe ... 379

Voyages of Colombus 379

The voyages of Sir James Lancaster to the East Indies 379

The voyages of William Baffin 379

Waite, P B: Canada 1874-1896 151

Walcott, Robert: 'The later stuarts 1660-1714' 520

Waldman, Milton: Queen Elizabeth 536

Walford, A J: Guide to reference material 368

Walker, E A: The British Empire 108; The great trek 359; History of South Africa 461; History of southern Africa 461

Walpole, Spencer: History of England 450; History of twenty five years 450

Walter of Coventry: Historical collections 671

War for the world Fletcher Pratt 167

Ward, A W and G P Gooch: Cambridge history of British foreign policy 142

Ward, John M: Empire in the Antipodes 255

Ware, Caroline: The twentieth century 458

Warner, William: Albion's England 19

Warren, W L: Henry II 398

Washburn, Wilcomb: Age of discovery 10

Washington and his colleagues Henry Jones Ford 167

Washington and his comrades in arms George M Wrong 167

Watson, David: Charles I 511

Watson, J Steven: Reign of George III 658

Watt, D C: History of the world in the twentieth century 466

Waurin, John de: Collection of the chronicles and ancient histories of Great Britain 671

Webb, R K: Modern England 554

Wedgwood, C V: Edward Gibbon 349; 'History and literature' 433; 'Some contemporary accounts of the great civil war' 708

Wedgwood, Josiah: History of parliament 460

Wernham, R B: Public records in the sixteenth and seventeenth centuries 294

Wertenbaker, Thomas: First Americans 444

The west 1830-1890 Gilbert Fite 229

West Indian studies series 160

West americana 757

What history is and why it is important Arthur Marwick 584

Wheeler, Sir Mortimer: The British Academy 101

Whig interpretation of history Herbert Butterfield 130

White, Carl M: Sources of information in the social sciences 717

White Kennett C V Bennett 183

White, R J: The conservative tradition 123

White, Stewart Edward: The forty-niners 167

Whitehouse, Sylvia: Periodicals in the library and resource centre Commonwealth Institute London 613

Whitelocke, Dorothy: Anglo-Saxon chronicle 47; Beginnings of English society 75; ed English historical documents 500-1042 290

Wiebe, Robert H: Search for order 537

Wiener, Joel H: Great Britain: foreign policy and the span of empire 354

Wier, Gaston: The great medieval civilisations 458

Wilkinson, B: Constitutional history of

England 1216-1399 196; Constitutional history of England in the fifteenth century 195; Later middle ages in England 517

William Worcestre itineraries 598

Williams, Basil: 'Centenary of Francis Parkman' 603; Whig supremacy 773

Williams, C H: England under the early tudors 758; ed English historical documents 1485-1558 290

Williams, G A: ed History in depth series 443

Williams, Gwyneth: Guide to illustrative material for use in teaching history 365

Williams, Neville: Chronology of the expanding world 170; Chronology of the modern world 170; The eighteenth century constitution 249

Williamson, J A: The age of Drake; Tudor age 745; Short history of British expansion 705; Short history of England; Sir Francis Drake 536

Wills, A J: Introduction to the history of Central Africa 496

Wiltse, Charles M: New nation 1800-1845 537

Winchell, Constance M: Guide to reference books 367

Winkler, Henry R: Great Britain in the twentieth century 355; 'Sir Lewis Namier' 562

Winks, Robin W: Recent trends and new literature in Canadian history 650

Winsor, Justin: Narrative and critical history of America 563

Wolsey A F Pollard 624

Wood, G A: A guide for students of New Zealand history 363

Wood, William: Captains of the civil war 167; Elizabethan sea dogs 167

Woodcock, George: Who killed the British Empire? 774

Woodrow Wilson and the progressive era Arthur Link 570

Woodrow Wilson and the world war Charles Seymour 167

Woodward, Sir Llewellyn: The age of reform 16; British historians 112

Wool trade in English medieval history Eileen Power 331

Works of Giraldus Cambrensis 671

The world crisis Winston Churchill 171

The world encompassed by Sir Francis Drake 379

World historical fiction guide 423

World list of historical periodicals and bibliographies P Caron 424

The world turned upside down Christopher Hill 403

World war reform and reaction Stanley Coben 229

Wright, Esmond: Fabric of freedom 537

Wright, Louis B: Cultural life of the American colonies 570; The elizabethan's America 252; New interpretations of American colonial history 574

Wright, Louis B and Elaine W Fowler: English colonisation of North America 284

Wrong, George M: Conquest of new France 167; Washington and his comrades in arms 167

Yapp, Malcolm: 'Recent books on modern Indian history' 648

Year books on the reign of Edward I 671

Years of endurance Sir Arthur Bryant 127

Years of peril Sir Arthur Bryant 127

Years of victory Sir Arthur Bryant 127

Young, G M and W D Handcock: eds English historical documents 1833-1874 290

Zagorin, Perez: 'English history 1558-1640' 297

Zaslow, Morris: The north 1914-1967 151; Opening of the Canadian north 151

Zoltvany, Y F: French tradition in America 229

100983